RETRIEVAL & RENEWAL

Ressourcement

IN CATHOLIC THOUGHT

The middle years of the twentieth century marked a particularly intens time of crisis and change in European society. During this period (1930-1950), a broad intellectual and spiritual movement arose within the European Catholic community, largely in response to the secularism that lay at the core of the crisis. The movement drew inspiration from earlier theologians and philosophers such as Möhler, Newman, Gardeil, Rousselot, and Blondel, as well as from men of letters like Charles Péguy and Paul Claudel.

The group of academic theologians included in the movement extended into Belgium and Germany, in the work of men like Emile Mersch, Dom Odo Casel, Romano Guardini, and Karl Adam. But above all, the theological activity during this period centered in France. Led principally by the Jesuits at Fourvière and the Dominicans at Le Saulchoir, the French revival included many of the greatest names in twentieth-century Catholic thought: Henri de Lubac, Jean Daniélou, Yves Congar, Marie-Dominique Chenu, Louis Bouyer, and, in association, Hans Urs von Balthasar.

It is not true — as subsequent folklore has it — that those theologians represented any sort of self-conscious "school": indeed, the differences among them, for example, between Fourvière and Le Saulchoir, were important. At the same time, most of them were united in the double conviction that theology had to speak to the present situation, and that the condition for doing so faithfully lay in a recovery of the Church's past. In other words, they saw clearly that the first step in what later came to be known as *aggiornamento* had to be *ressourcement* — a rediscovery of the riches of the whole of the Church's two-thousand-year tradition. According to de Lubac, for example, all of his own works as well as the entire *Sources chrétiennes* collection are based on the presupposition that "the renewal of Christian vitality is linked at least partially to a renewed exploration of the periods and of the works where the Christian tradition is expressed with particular intensity."

In sum, for the *ressourcement* theologians theology involved a "return to the sources" of Christian faith, for the purpose of drawing out the meaning and significance of these sources for the critical questions of our time. What these theologians sought was a spiritual and intellectual communion with Christianity in its most vital moments as transmitted to us in its classic texts, a communion that would nourish, invigorate, and rejuvenate twentieth-century Catholicism.

The *ressourcement* movement bore great fruit in the documents of the Second Vatican Council and deeply influenced the work of Pope John Paul II.

The present series is rooted in this renewal of theology. The series thus understands *ressourcement* as revitalization: a return to the sources, for the purpose of developing a theology that will truly meet the challenges of our time. Some of the features of the series, then, are a return to classical (patristic-medieval) sources and a dialogue with contemporary Western culture, particularly in terms of problems associated with the Enlightenment, modernity, and liberalism.

The series publishes out-of-print or as yet untranslated studies by earlier authors associated with the *ressourcement* movement. The series also publishes works by contemporary authors sharing in the aim and spirit of this earlier movement. This will include any works in theology, philosophy, history, literature, and the arts that give renewed expression to Catholic sensibility.

The editor of the Ressourcement series, David L. Schindler, is Gagnon Professor of Fundamental Theology and dean at the John Paul II Institute in Washington, D.C., and editor of the North American edition of *Communio: International Catholic Review,* a federation of journals in thirteen countries founded in Europe in 1972 by Hans Urs von Balthasar, Jean Daniélou, Henri de Lubac, Joseph Ratzinger, and others.

VOLUMES PUBLISHED

Mysterium Paschale
Hans Urs von Balthasar

Joseph Ratzinger in Communio, Volume 1: The Unity of the Church
Pope Benedict XVI

Joseph Ratzinger in Communio, Volume 2: Anthropology and Culture
Pope Benedict XVI

The Heroic Face of Innocence: Three Stories
Georges Bernanos

Maurice Blondel: A Philosophical Life
Oliva Blanchette

The Letter on Apologetics and History and Dogma
Maurice Blondel

Prayer: The Mission of the Church
Jean Daniélou

On Pilgrimage
Dorothy Day

We, the Ordinary People of the Streets
Madeleine Delbrêl

The Discovery of God
Henri de Lubac

Medieval Exegesis, Volumes 1-3: The Four Senses of Scripture
Henri de Lubac

Opening Up the Scriptures:
Joseph Ratzinger and the Foundations of Biblical Interpretation
José Granados, Carlos Granados Jr., and Luis Sánchez-Navarro, eds.

Letters from Lake Como:
Explorations in Technology and the Human Race
Romano Guardini

The Epiphany of Love:
Toward a Theological Understanding of Christian Action
Livio Melina

Divine Likeness: Toward a Trinitarian Anthropology of the Family
Marc Cardinal Ouellet

The Portal of the Mystery of Hope
Charles Péguy

Analogia Entis: Metaphysics: Original Structure and Universal Rhythm
Erich Przywara

In the Beginning:
A Catholic Understanding of the Story of Creation and the Fall
Joseph Cardinal Ratzinger

In the Fire of the Burning Bush:
An Initiation to the Spiritual Life
Marko Ivan Rupnik

The Catholicity of Reason
D. C. Schindler

Love Alone Is Credible:
Hans Urs von Balthasar as Interpreter
of the Catholic Tradition, volume 1
David L. Schindler, ed.

Hans Urs von Balthasar: A Theological Style
Angelo Scola

The Nuptial Mystery
Angelo Scola

The Catholicity of Reason

D. C. Schindler

William B. Eerdmans Publishing Company
Grand Rapids, Michigan / Cambridge, U.K.

Published 2013 by
Wm. B. Eerdmans Publishing Co.
2140 Oak Industrial Drive N.E., Grand Rapids, Michigan 49505 /
P.O. Box 163, Cambridge CB3 9PU U.K.

Printed in the United States of America

19 18 17 16 15 14 7 6 5 4 3 2

Library of Congress Cataloging-in-Publication Data

Schindler, D. C.
The Catholicity of reason / D.C. Schindler.
pages cm
Includes bibliographical references and index.
ISBN 978-0-8028-6933-3 (pbk.: alk. paper)
1. Catholic Church — Europe — History — 20th century.
2. Catholic Church — History of doctrines. I. Title.

BX1490.S36 2013
230′.2 — dc23

2013006753

www.eerdmans.com

Contents

Preface

In his 2006 "Regensburg Address," Benedict XVI concluded his critique of the form that reason has tended to take in modernity with a charge: "The West has long been endangered by [an] aversion to the questions which underlie its rationality, and can only suffer great harm thereby. The courage to engage the whole breadth of reason, and not the denial of its grandeur — this is the programme with which a theology grounded in Biblical faith enters into the debates of our time." We might add that it is also, and perhaps even more directly, the program for philosophy. Benedict's charge might at first appear to come from some other world, unfamiliar with our own: the response to the rational domination of nature in science and technology that acknowledges no boundaries, on the one hand, and the violence of absolutist claims, on the other, would seem to require above all a restraining of reason. And so do a great many contemporary thinkers believe. But the present book seeks to defend the idea that a recovery of "the whole breadth" of reason is the only adequate response to the problems of modernity. We aim to show in the following pages from diverse perspectives and in a variety of contexts that the attempt artificially to "set limits" to reason and relativize or attenuate its claims inevitably entails "totalizing" self-imposition. It is not the grandeur of reason but its impoverishment that leads to oppressive rationalism and the arbitrary irrationalism inseparable from it.

The book begins with a programmatic introduction in chapter one, which aims to sketch the parameters of a "catholic" — that is, a comprehensive or nonexclusive — sense of reason and to argue that only a robust reason can be genuinely humble, open to mystery and abiding "otherness." This introduction is followed by nine essays, grouped thematically under three headings.

The three chapters in part one reflect on aspects of the nature of truth and knowledge from the vantage of a radically open and so "dramatic" conception of reason. Chapter two, "Surprised by Truth," addresses the problem of fundamental theology — namely, how we can affirm the rationality of revelation without reducing it to a function of reason? — and considers in the light of this problem the implications of basic philosophical positions. Chapter three argues for the primacy of beauty in a catholic notion of reason, showing that beauty invites reason into the drama that takes place under the sign of the good, before the final unveiling of truth. So conceived, truth proves to be a genuine disclosure in which transparency and mystery coincide, and exhibits an analogical form that remains open even in its completion. The coincidence between truth and mystery forms the backdrop for chapter four, "Does Love Trump Reason?" which explores the problems generated by an unnuanced Thomistic understanding of the relation between the intellect and will, and argues for the priority of intellect only within the absoluteness of love.

Part two investigates the understanding of being necessary for a catholic notion of reason by reflecting on the nature of causality. Chapter five, "The Iconoclasm of the Intellect in Early Modernity," shows how the displacement of the traditional Platonic view of *goodness* as cause by *power* in early modernity sets the imagination outside the act of knowledge. "Historical Intelligibility," chapter six, considers the significance of an Aristotelian conception of substance, and the "interweave of causes" it represents, for the intelligibility of being; it then engages the challenge to this intelligibility that arises with the introduction of the importance of history in modernity. The chapter contends that the only alternative to a reductive temporalizing of being that dissolves meaning is a metaphysics of creation that includes history without surrendering substance. Chapter seven presents the unity of Plato and Aristotle in Dionysius' notion of causality as a response to Heidegger's fundamental critique of causality in Western thought. This chapter defends the classic notion of causality, transformed within the Christian notion of creation as superabundant gift, and shows how this notion ultimately implies a convertibility of knowledge and wonder. It thus connects part two with the coincidence of truth and mystery argued for in part one.

The final three chapters that comprise part three explore the question of philosophy's access to God and the implications of God's self-revelation in history for philosophy. Chapter eight counters Heidegger's critique of "ontotheology," which has its paradigm in the philosophy of Hegel, by offering in turn a critique of Heidegger based on Hegel's *Lectures on the Philoso-*

phy of Religion. The chapter contends that Christian postmodern thinking runs into the problems Hegel indicates if it concedes the terms of Heidegger's critique of ontotheology, and proposes instead a recovery of metaphysics with a catholic notion of reason. Chapter nine, then, aims to show how this approach differs from a traditional recovery of metaphysics in the face of postmodern critiques of reason by considering the achievements and shortcomings of a recent defense of Thomistic natural theology. Finally, the concluding chapter proposes in a schematic way a new model for the relationship between philosophy and theology that a genuinely catholic view of reason offers.

Not only is a catholic sense of reason open from within to the theological order, it also bears a positive relationship to what may be called the "perennial philosophy." Thus, in contrast to the different strains of suspicion in modernity and postmodernity, a catholic approach to reason affirms its roots in the Western tradition. Accordingly, the chapters of this book carry out their inquiry in dialogue with some basic representatives of that tradition, Plato, Aristotle, Augustine, Dionysius, and Aquinas, as well as with those thinkers in modernity who most profoundly (though of course critically) appropriate classical thought, namely, Hegel and Heidegger. But the figure who appears most frequently as an authoritative voice in these pages is Hans Urs von Balthasar. Though he is not known in the first place for his contributions to philosophy, he represents one of the most genuinely catholic thinkers in our age, and thus has opened up a field for philosophical reflection that will bear good fruit for years to come. This book is dedicated to the members of the secular institute that Balthasar founded with Adrienne von Speyr, the Community of St. John.

I would like to thank the people who read drafts of these essays at various stages and offered suggestions and comments: Michael Hanby, Nicholas Healy, Adrian Walker, my father, Kevin Hughes, Peter Kwasniewski, Chad Engelland, an anonymous reviewer at the *American Catholic Philosophical Quarterly*, and Joshua Nunziato. I would also like to express my gratitude to Stratford Caldecott and Mary Taylor for their insight and enthusiasm, and above all to Cardinal Francis Stafford for his ongoing interest and support. As always, I am deeply grateful to my wife, Jeanne, without whom this book could not have been written.

Acknowledgments

All but chapters 1, 7, and 10 are revisions of essays that originally appeared in the following places. The author gratefully acknowledges the permission to reprint the material.

Chapter 2: "Surprised by Truth: The Drama of Reason in Fundamental Theology," in *La missione teologica di Hans Urs von Balthasar: Atti del simposio internazaionale di Teologia in occasione del centesimo anniversario della nascita di Hans Urs von Balthasar, Lugano 2-4 marzo 2005*, ed. A.-M. Jerumanis and A. Tambolini (Lugano: Eupress FTL, 2005), pp. 131-50.

Chapter 3: "Beauty and the Analogy of Truth: On the Order of the Transcendentals in Hans Urs von Balthasar's *Trilogy*," *American Catholic Philosophical Quarterly* 85, no. 2 (Spring 2011): 296-321.

Chapter 4: "Toward a Non-Possessive Concept of Knowledge: On the Relation Between Reason and Love in Aquinas and Balthasar," *Modern Theology* 22, no. 4 (October 2006): 577-607.

Chapter 5: "Truth and the Christian Imagination: The Reformation of Causality and the Iconoclasm of the Spirit," *Communio* 33 (Winter 2006): 521-39.

Chapter 6: "Historical Intelligibility: On Creation and Causality," *Anthropotes* 26, no. 1 (2010): 15-44.

Chapter 8: "'*Wie kommt der Mensch in die Theologie?*' Hegel, Heidegger, and the Stakes of Ontotheology," *Revista Española de Teología* 65 (October-December 2005): 437-65.

Chapter 9: "Discovering the Given: On Reason and God," *Nova et Vetera* 10, no. 2 (Spring 2012): 563-604.

Abbreviations

BQ	Heidegger, *Basic Questions of Philosophy: Selected "Problems" of "Logic"*
BW	Heidegger, *Basic Writings*
De ver.	Aquinas, *De veritate*
DN	Dionysius, *Divine Names*
E	Balthasar, *Epilogue*
GL1-7	Balthasar, *The Glory of the Lord*, vols. 1-7
ID	Heidegger, *Identity and Difference*
In caus.	Aquinas, *In librum de causis exposition*
In metaph.	Aquinas, *In duodecim libros Metaphysicorum Aristotelis exposition*
In sent.	Aquinas, *Scriptum super libros Sententiarum magistri Petri Lombardi episcopi Parisiensis*
In symb. apost.	Aquinas, *Collationes super Credo in Deum*
PR	Hegel, *Lectures on the Philosophy of Religion*
SCG	Aquinas, *Summa Contra Gentiles*
ST	Aquinas, *Summa Theologiae*
TD1-5	Balthasar, *Theo-Drama*, vols. 1-5
TL1-3	Balthasar, *Theo-Logic*, vols. 1-3

Introduction

1 Reason as Catholic

Reason is essentially catholic — καθ' ὅλον, "according to the whole" — in four senses: in terms of its principles, (1) it is defined by its relation to being as a whole, and (2) it involves the whole person in its specific operation; and in terms of its exercise, (3) it always grasps the (whole as) universal, on the one hand, and (4) the (whole as) concrete, composite being or individual thing in each particular act, on the other hand, even if it thematizes only one or the other in any given instance. There are, evidently, certain tensions between these dimensions, most obviously between the latter two, but to affirm the catholicity of reason, which is to say, to affirm reason in its fullest and most proper sense, is to affirm all four dimensions at once. In this initial chapter, we intend first of all in a general way to trace out the features of a catholic sense of reason, which is the notion of reason that is presupposed in all of the chapters that follow, and indeed which they serve to elaborate in one direction or another. Second, through a reflection on a basic theme in Plato's philosophy, we will propose an argument that only an affirmation of the catholicity of reason preserves genuine humility, so that the typical strategies for avoiding the "excesses" of reason that one finds in modern and postmodern thought, to the extent that they impoverish reason or attempt to impose artificial limits on its use, inevitably undermine their own aims. Our thesis is that catholicity — "wholeness" — is not "totalizing," but is rather the only adequate resistance to it.

We preface our reflections with an observation: the notion of a whole is inescapably paradoxical. On the one hand, to be a whole is to be complete, and, to that extent, self-sufficient.[1] A whole, in this relative respect, is

1. "Self-sufficient," here, does not mean "autonomous" in the modern sense that op-

"closed," and does not require reference beyond itself for its being or its meaning. On the other hand, however, as Hegel pointed out in a different context, one cannot define a limit unless one is already beyond it.[2] Indeed, a limit cannot *exist* except within the context of what exceeds it. This is, of course, what represents the great enigma of cosmology: Is the universe a limited whole? If so, what lies on the other side of its borders such that it makes sense to speak of a border? What, in other words, does the whole of the cosmos lie *in?* This greater "context" would have to be part of the *whole* of the cosmos, but in recognizing this we are faced with the same question once again, namely, whether this context has a limit, and so on. Now, this cosmological paradox is simply a basic instance of what we might call a metaphysical truth: every whole simultaneously includes and excludes what lies beyond it. While the paradox presents itself in any instance of a limit, it comes especially to the fore whenever we talk specifically about a *whole,* which implies comprehensiveness and so the inclusion of everything that is in any way relevant. It is this paradox that lies behind the analogical character of being, and why there is no "getting beyond" the *analogia entis.* But even to call analogy ultimate is another instance of the same paradox: being is everything . . . and *more.* We must keep this paradox in mind at every stage of our discussion.

Wholly Ecstatic

It is best to think of the four dimensions of the catholicity of reason as a pair of inseparable, but irreducible, polarities: on the one hand, there is a polar relation between subject (whole soul) and object (being as a whole), and, on

---

poses itself to heteronomy. Instead, "self" is meant in the more concrete, and indeed "naïve," sense of taking for granted any other and all others that are included in the constitution of the self as a complete self.

2. Hegel criticizes Kant's setting limits to reason in his critical philosophy thus: "It is the supreme inconsistency to admit . . . cognition *cannot* go any further, this is the *natural,* absolute *limitation* of human knowing. Natural things are limited, and they are just natural things inasmuch as they *know nothing* of their universal *limitation,* inasmuch as their determinacy is a limitation only *for us,* not *for them.* Something is only known, or even felt, to be a limitation, or a defect, if one is at the same time *beyond* it." *Enzyklopedia* (1830), §60 *Anmerkung.* Cf. Hegel's observation in the *Philosophy of Spirit:* "The very fact that we know a limitation is evidence that we are beyond it, evidence of our freedom from limitation" (§386, *Zusatz*).

the other, there is a polarity, in any given concrete whole, between the subsisting individual and the universal. We will consider each of these polarities in turn. The point in each case is not to offer a complete presentation of the issue and justification for it, but, once again, simply to sketch the parameters of the notion of reason presupposed by the chapters in this book.

1. According to Aquinas, being *(ens)* is the "first concept to fall into the imagination of the intellect."[3] No matter what we know, we know, whether consciously or not, specifically *as* being, taken at this point in the widest possible sense, which means that every instance of knowledge is a further specification, in some respect, of this "foundational" act. But the nature of this foundational act, this initial grasp of being, can be and has been variously interpreted. Precisely because of its primordial character, the way one interprets it will have endless reverberations; one might say that the quality of all of one's thinking is most basically determined here. We propose that an adequate interpretation of this foundational act must exhibit two features: on the one hand, one must affirm a genuine grasp of being as a whole, but, on the other hand, it must be a grasp that does not simply anticipate any particular act of knowledge, any further specification.

Let us consider a few possible interpretations and their implications. One might, first of all, take the being that one knows before all else as a general concept, which can "fit" everything that is to come precisely because it anticipates nothing at all: it is universal because it is purely formal and so essentially void of determinate content. In this sense, being is most basic because it is the most *minimally* determined concept there is,[4] nothing more than the purely formal positing of existence. Now, what speaks in favor of this interpretation is that it at least apparently preserves the significance of *(a posteriori)* experience by minimizing the significance of what is *a priori*. But this approach turns out to undermine itself: if what is most basic is a merely logical form, if being qua being is, in other words, nothing more than an "entity of reason," one will eventually be led to a Kantian dualism that posits reality as something precisely external and indeed inaccessible to the

3. "Primum enim quod cadit in imaginatione intellectus, est ens, sine quo nihil potest apprehendi ab intellectu." Aquinas, *In sent.* 8.3. Cf. *De ver.* 1.1: "Illud autem quod primo intellectus concipit quasi notissimum, et in quod conceptiones omnes resolvit, est ens." Aquinas is drawing here, through Avicenna (*Metaphysics* 1.2.1), on an old philosophical tradition that begins with Parmenides. B3; cf. B8, line 34: "Thinking and the thought that it is are the same." Plato, too, strictly links intellect and being. *Republic* V, 476e-477b.

4. Hegel, *Science of Logic,* trans. A. V. Miller (Atlantic Highlands, NJ: Humanities Press International, 1969), p. 82.

mind *(das Ding an sich)*. We have in this case the situation that Robert Sokolowski has memorably described as the "egocentric predicament," a characteristically modern problem entailed by the conception of consciousness essentially as a self-enclosed sphere or bubble.[5] This conception constantly generates the problem of finding a "bridge" from consciousness to the world outside. The problem results from a conception of reason that sets the terms in such a way that no resolution is possible in principle. Descartes is a paradigm here, but the problem haunts modern empiricism as much as modern rationalism.[6]

Heidegger has famously criticized the Cartesian conception as subordinating being to consciousness in a privileging of "theory," and his insights on this score have found echoes in postmodern criticisms of the elevation of "Erlebnis" as the criterion of truth in phenomenology.[7] To simplify a notion that develops in significant ways over the course of his thinking, we may characterize Heidegger's alternative proposal as man's "standing out" into the truth of being;[8] what is most essential in the human essence is our openness to (or better: *in*) the openness *(Lichtung)* of being. This profound understanding of reason has the crucial advantage of affirming being as something ever-greater than man, while at the same time attributing to man a privileged relation to being. On the other hand, however, because this being, as *Lichtung*, is wholly indeterminate and without content, because it gives itself only by "hiding," there seems to be nothing in the end to prevent the "a priority" of this openness to being from devolving into a simple reflection of man's essence back onto itself.[9] It is no wonder, then, that some of the most knowledgeable readers of Heidegger are able to make the case that what seems to be a kind of radical prioritizing of being in Heidegger's later

5. Robert Sokolowski, *Introduction to Phenomenology* (Cambridge: Cambridge University Press, 2000), pp. 9-11.

6. On this, see Robert Spaemann, "Wirklichkeit als Anthropomorphismus," in *Grundvollzüge der Person*, ed. H.-G. Nissing (München: Institut zur Förderung der Glaubenslehre, 2008), pp. 13-35. Spaemann often refers in his writings to Hume's observation that "we never advance one step beyond ourselves" (see, for example, "Wirklichkeit," p. 26).

7. See, for example, Jean-Luc Marion, *Reduction and Givenness: Investigations of Husserl, Heidegger, and Phenomenology*, trans. Thomas A. Carlson (Evanston, IL: Northwestern University Press, 1998), pp. 49-56.

8. Martin Heidegger, "Letter on Humanism," in *Basic Writings* (New York: Harper & Row, 1977), p. 206.

9. See our discussion in chapter eight, "On the Problem of the Problem of Ontotheology," below.

thought is in fact another version of man as "thrown projection," which one finds articulated already in *Being and Time.*[10]

As a contrast to the indeterminacy of openness at the start of all thinking, Jacques Maritain notoriously proposed what he calls the "intuition of being." It is notorious because, for some, it has seemed a kind of "mystical" experience that can be only inappropriately posited at the foundation of *reason,* and because, for others, it appears to take too much for granted at the outset of philosophy: it assumes that we have a grasp of the whole specifically in the form of a concept or idea, a concept that contains within itself all the other concepts — not only the most basic, the transcendentals, but in fact all concepts in general[11] — insofar as they resolve back into being. The being one intuits, here, has always already been grasped in the context of everyday experience, but the possibility of metaphysics begins with a "separation" of being from everything else that one then perceives in an *immediate* way. Like Schelling in the nineteenth century, Maritain insists that this is an *intellectual* intuition, an eidetic insight into being, which has a universal scope, rather than a *sense* experience, as the word "intuition" more typically designates in modern philosophy. But just as Hegel complained that the notion of an intellectual intuition presents the "Absolute" too immediately, like a "shot from a pistol,"[12] so too one might suggest that the intuition of being anticipates too much. Is this intuition simply a clarification of what we already grasped in the first moment of consciousness, so that all further experience adds ultimately nothing of significance to our understanding of reality? Do we, to the extent that we are in possession of reason, already stand in possession of everything, so that we suffer what Nietzsche referred to as the greatest of all poverties, namely, the absolute wealth that is therefore permanently unable to receive?

Both Heidegger and Maritain affirm a dimension that is evidently indispensable, and at the same time they appear — at least as we have presented them here in an oversimplified form — to present the matter in pre-

10. See Thomas Sheehan, "Geschichtlichkeit/Ereignis/Kehre," *Existentia* 11, nos. 3-4 (2001): 241-51; Laurence Paul Hemming, "Reading Heidegger's Turn," in *Heidegger's Atheism: Rejection of a Theological Voice* (South Bend, IN: University of Notre Dame Press, 2002), pp. 75-102.

11. Jacques Maritain, *Preface to Metaphysics: Seven Lectures on Being* (New York: Sheed & Ward, 1939), p. 55.

12. Hegel, "Preface" to *The Phenomenology of Spirit,* trans. A. V. Miller (Oxford: Oxford University Press, 1977), p. 16: "least of all will [genuine science] be like the rapturous enthusiasm which, like a shot from a pistol, begins straight away with absolute knowledge, and makes short work of other standpoints by declaring that it takes no notice of them."

cisely opposed ways. For Heidegger, being is greater than man; because it exceeds him, man ek-sists, he stands out into being. We might say that reason in this sense is most fundamentally characterized as "inserted *into* being." For Maritain, by contrast, reason definitely *grasps* being; man has a concept of what is greatest at the very start of (properly metaphysical) thinking, as the most appropriate context in which everything is thought in its foundations. Being is thus *given* to man, or more specifically: being is "inserted into reason." What we wish to propose here is that a fully adequate — a "catholic" — conception of reason has to include both of these apparently opposed dimensions at one and the same time. The conception of reason that is presupposed by the various chapters in the present book is therefore the following: reason is "structurally" ecstatic; it is the very nature of reason to be always already out beyond itself, and both aspects of this paradoxical statement have to be affirmed. On the one hand, reason *transcends* itself and, on the other hand, *reason* transcends itself. There is an "out beyond" in every act of reason, but this is precisely what constitutes it as reason, so that in transcending itself it can be said to be doing nothing more than catching up with its own essence. Both are true: reason is in being, and being is in reason. Gustav Siewerth expresses the point well:

> [R]eason is not a power that man sets into motion by his own effort. It is instead being as being that enables reason to come to itself and to attain truth. If man believes he is able to come to think "by his own effort," it is only because he has this empowerment and illumination, this primal harmony [*Ureinklang*] of the spirit, always already behind him. It is not he who "grasps" being; rather, all of his grasping and perception occurs only insofar as the power of being, from which he and things emerged, has appropriated him to himself and, in the same event, to being.[13]

There is a similarity between this formulation of reason and the understanding of consciousness as intentional that defines phenomenology, insofar as both reject a concept of consciousness as a sort of "thing" juxtaposed to the other things of the world. But there are fundamental differences between what we are proposing here and the notion of consciousness in phenomenology: first, although it rejects a simple "inside" and "outside" dichotomy, phenomenology nevertheless tends to present intentionality as ra-

13. Gustav Siewerth, *Metaphysik der Kindheit* (Einsiedeln: Johannes Verlag, 1957), pp. 51-52.

diating outward, so to speak, from an ego, whether the latter be conceived empirically, or, more appropriately, transcendentally. We are suggesting, by contrast, that reason is not a sphere with a center. If it is appropriate at all to use a geometric shape as a model in this context, we would do better to say that consciousness is an ellipse with two centers: reason does not (merely) reside "in" the soul, or intellect, as one of its powers or faculties, but belongs as much to the world, to being, as it does to a knowing subject (though this does not mean it does so in simply symmetrical ways). One way of formulating this point with respect to phenomenology is to say that the ecstasis of reason in and with the other precedes and makes possible the intentionality of consciousness; it is not itself an intentional act of consciousness. Ecstasis, or self-transcendence, is not something that reason achieves as a kind of crowning act at the end of all of its labors, as one finds, for example, in Schelling; instead, reason is ecstatic from the beginning, and the achievement is, rather, a gradual reception of, a taking in, of reason by the soul.

Another difference between this proposal and the intentionality offered by phenomenology lies in the specifically *catholic* character of reason, by which we mean, in this particular context, that reason is always *of* the whole. On the one hand, reason has already grasped the whole of being in some respect "before" it has grasped any particular being, and it has grasped the whole of any particular being in some respect before it grasps any one of its parts. We will return to elaborate this claim further on, but for the moment the point is that reason has a certain intimacy with reality, or rather *is* a certain intimacy with reality: to understand is to read the interior of things *(intelligere = legere ab intus).* Phenomenology tends to begin with what is most immediately given, and then to build up partial intentionalities into a whole. This is connected with a certain embarrassment regarding the distinction between being and appearance, insofar as the distinction seems to recall the dualism between the phenomenon and the noumenon in Kantian thought. But what we are proposing here avoids the dualism without any compromise of the distinction between being "for us" and being "in itself," since it affirms that reason is always already out beyond itself — and so in and with the other — from the beginning. As natively ecstatic, reason always exceeds explicit consciousness. It thus preserves the difference between the appearance of reality for us and the way it is "in itself," independently of us, not by placing the "*Ding an sich*" outside of reason, but rather by placing it *inside* of reason, which is nevertheless *outside of itself.* These two dimensions can be genuinely opposed to each other even within the unity of reason, because, as ec-static, reason can stand over-against itself.

Once we grasp this, which is admittedly quite paradoxical, but nevertheless unavoidable, we can see how it can be possible to say that reason *is* reason only as already having grasped the "whole" of being, without falling into the "intuitionism" we criticized above. Being is, as Aquinas said, the first notion to fall into the intellect. It is not a "mere" concept, i.e., an abstract thought somehow extrinsic to being, nor is it a *part* or some aspect of being. Instead, it is being's self-communication, so to speak; it is being's *giving* itself, its wholeness, to be known. But in this being known, being does not disappear into the concept. It remains transcendent to reason precisely in its immanence within, and this coincidence is nothing other than the "flip side," as it were, of reason's ecstatic character. In this sense, then, we can say that there is a "direct" intuition of being, but that this intuition is not something we have circumscribed within ourselves; it is rather a kind of grasp that remains in some sense always out beyond us. Gabriel Marcel describes the matter in just these terms, correcting what he takes to be a note of "possessiveness" in Maritain: "intuition in an existential philosophy such as this [Marcel's own] is not something that lies at our disposal, something we have, but rather is a source, in itself inaccessible, from which we set out to think. It is what I have called a blinded intuition [*intuition aveuglée*]; moreover, it is also a 'forefeeling' or premonition."[14] Further: "This intuition cannot be brought into the light of day, for the simple reason that it is not, in fact, possessed."[15] Marcel connects this notion with a certain interpretation of Platonic recollection, which we will discuss below. But our proposal differs from Marcel's by insisting that this source cannot be "inaccessible" simply, nor can the intuition, as an act of reason, be "blinded." It is, rather, a lucidity of a particular sort. And if it is precisely *reason* that is thus put ahead of itself, we ought not to call it a fore-*feeling*, except in a metaphorical sense.[16] The ecstatic quality of reason is thus both a true grasp — because it is a reception of being, which gives itself — and yet at the same time this reception has specifically a "nonpossessive" form.

14. Gabriel Marcel, "Author's Preface to the English Edition," in *Metaphysical Journal*, trans. Bernard Wall (Chicago: Regnery, 1952), p. x.

15. Gabriel Marcel, *Position et Approches du mystère ontologique* (Paris: Desclée de Brouwer, 1933), p. 8, n. 1, cited in Maritain, *Preface to Metaphysics*, p. 59, n. 1.

16. Maritain makes the same criticism of Marcel: *Preface to Metaphysics*, pp. 59-60, n. 1. As he explains, it cannot *but* be a specifically intellectual intuition insofar as it represents the "summit . . . of intellectuality" and belongs in some sense to every act of knowing. The resistance to its intellectual character, he claims, can only be due to an "idealist" interpretation of intelligence.

To summarize so far, reason is essentially catholic in the sense that it is always already with the whole, or of the whole. But wholeness, properly understood, is self-transcending precisely as a whole. Being is not a "fixed" concept, but a "super-determined" whole; it is always itself and more, which is to say that it is analogical. And reason, which is defined in its essence as a reception of being, is likewise inescapably analogical.

Now, Maritain had described the intuition of being as an act of intellect, and, indeed, apparently as one without the mediation of the will. This conception corresponds to the pure passivity of the act as he characterizes it: it is a "taking in" of being.[17] But we are suggesting that the one-sidedness of this view (its noncatholicity, as it were) is not unrelated to the criticisms that have been made of it, namely, that it prematurely anticipates everything to come, insofar as all other concepts are in some sense already contained within what is immediately given in the concept of being. This problem is avoided if we recognize that the "grasp" of being does not happen simply "inside" of the intellect, but that reason "has" being in a more basic way outside of itself. But this means that the fundamental act of reason cannot simply be a passive taking in; instead, it is, so to speak, a "going out to meet" being. And because it occurs thus "outside the soul," or perhaps better, inside the soul that is, qua reason, outside of itself, the act will necessarily include the "other-directedness" that we associate with appetite or the will. Indeed, if it includes both the intellect and will, which are, we might say, the two relatively opposed "poles" of the soul, it is because it is a "movement," not of one aspect or another, but of the *center* of the soul beyond itself: in other words, it is an act of the whole soul.

To say that reason is "of the whole," this time in the subjective sense of the genitive, is to conceive reason, not as one of the faculties of the soul which itself is one "part" of the rational animal that coexists somehow with the body. Instead, what we have here is a sort of retrieval of a classic Neoplatonic notion, namely, that being, life, and thought are analogous "intensifications" of a single reality rather than three separate principles.[18] Thus, the rationality that belongs to personhood is what makes personhood, according to Aquinas, the "most perfect" mode of being.[19] What this means in the

17. "But the intellect and its act are fulfilled by existence affirmed or denied by a judgement, by existence attained — as it is lived or *possessed* by a subject — within the mind, within the mind's intellectual act." Maritain, *Preface to Metaphysics*, p. 21.

18. As *analogical*, they are — it must be noted — irreducible to one another within their continuity. While this point is more ambiguous, admittedly, in ancient Neoplatonism, we affirm it as a Christian transformation of the tradition.

19. Aquinas, *ST* 1.29.3.

present context is that reason is not "super-added" to being, but just *is* being, precisely insofar as being is already "out beyond itself." In other words, the "rational soul" is the paradigm of the analogy of being. To say that human beings "have reason" is to say that we share in a privileged way in being's being more than itself, and, in so doing, bring to light what is true about all being, expressed in relatively distant ways according to the *regula analogiae*. When we know something different from ourselves we are therefore in ontological communion in some genuine way with that other. It follows, then, that we can affirm the phenomenological insight that the ego itself is already, so to speak, a manifestation of being, understood not as *phenomenon* here, but as a kind of *focal* point, a concentration of reality simply.

Hans Urs von Balthasar speaks of the soul's most fundamental relation to the world as an "affirmation and joy in being," which he says "lie at a much deeper level than the *delectatio* which naturally accompanies all the individual spiritual acts which are ordered to their proper object and which proceed from the storehouse of that primal and original consonance."[20] It is both an affirmation and a delight because it is just as much an intellectual act as it is an act of the appetite and will. If he goes on to refer to it specifically as a "feeling," he does not mean this in the sense of sentiment, a spiritual act that lies "below" intellect and will, but rather as "the heart of human wholeness, where all man's faculties *(potentiae)* appear rooted in the unity of his *forma substantialis*."[21] The term "feeling" connotes actual contact and thus expresses the intimacy that this act necessarily involves. In other words, to say it is the unity of the soul wherein the faculties are rooted does not mean it is an "interior" act that then must proceed outward to the "external" world. Instead, this internal point is an essentially ecstatic one. Specifically, Balthasar goes on to call this fundamental act a "consent," and appeals to Aquinas to elaborate the significance of the term. According to Aquinas, consent is primarily associated with the appetitive power, the act of which is "a kind of inclination to the thing itself," and in this respect it — as a "feeling-with" *(con-sentire)* rather than merely a "feeling-toward" *(ad-sentire)* — is more intimate than the assent ascribed to the intellect, considered in itself, insofar as the intellect so considered does not require the actual presence of its object.

At the same time, however, consent is not "mere" feeling, but, as Aquinas puts it, "belongs in the higher reason, but in that sense in which reason

20. Balthasar, *GL1*, p. 244.

21. Balthasar, *GL1*, pp. 242-43.

includes the will."[22] It is thus a particular kind of *knowledge* that is acquired in this intimacy. Thus, in a word, this fundamental act is an act of the whole soul in which reason "grasps" its object — namely, being as such, which means in a certain respect the *whole* of being — in an intimacy whereby it is out beyond itself in and with this whole.[23] Any particular act of reason, any particular instance of knowledge, occurs, then, inside of this context, which is presupposed as its "condition of possibility," and so the character and form of each of these acts will necessarily bear some trace of the context in which they occur. What significance it has will be elaborated in part below, and then more substantially over the course of the other chapters in the present book.

But it is crucial to avoid a possible misunderstanding here: if we call this fundamental act a "condition of possibility" for each "subsequent" individual act of reason, this does *not* imply that it is an *"a priori"* structure, i.e., that it precedes all experience, and so for that reason stands as a feature of the immanent structure of consciousness prior to its "connection" with the world. Although it may seem similar in some respect, this fundamental act is not a "horizon," as the term is typically understood in phenomenology or hermeneutics. Rather, we must never lose sight of an essential paradox: while the fundamental act does indeed precede all individual experiences as a condition of possibility, and so is in that particular respect *"a priori,"* it is given by being (or more precisely: it is being's giving itself), and so is not (exactly) an immanent structure of consciousness. Instead, *it is an "immanent" structure of consciousness only as already outside of itself — with being.* The *actuality* of being precedes in some respect all possibility, even the possibility determined by logic, the inner necessities of reason.

Now, the insistence that reason becomes luminous only "inside" the light of being, as *actually* given rather than as an *a priori* structure, leads us to the second polarity that is part of the catholicity of reason, namely, the poles of the universal and the subsisting individual to which reason relates in each of its particular acts. If we speak of reason's grasp of the whole of being as *preceding* the particular acts, this cannot be interpreted in a *temporal* sense. To interpret the matter thus would in fact eventually bring us back to some version of an immediate vision of being in separation from all else,

22. Aquinas, *ST* 1-2.15.4.

23. As we suggested above, one might fruitfully compare what we are proposing here to Heidegger's notion of being-in-the-world, which has the structure of an ecstasis of being and therefore of consciousness. The difference, though, is that we wish to affirm a reciprocal intimacy, so to speak: the mind stands out into being, which gives itself into the mind.

which we criticized in Maritain's notion of the intuition of being. Rather, because it depends on being as actual, which means being as *given*, it also depends precisely on the *way* in which being is given. And being is not given as *actualized* — *esse* is not an *ens* — but always only as the *actuality* of some being or other. The consent to being as a whole occurs only in the actual encounter with particular beings, even as it remains the context in which that encounter is possible. If this seems like a contradiction, namely, that a condition of possibility appears in this case to depend on and so follow upon what it makes possible, this is simply yet another iteration of the same paradox that we have been discussing from the beginning: reason is always already out beyond itself, which means it is always in the process of catching up with itself.

2. Let us now turn to the catholic character of reason in its particular acts. According to the classical tradition, the objects of reason are universal, while the objects of the senses (and one may include the order of the will in this context) are particulars: one sees and feels *this* table, but one knows it as this *table*. Within the contemporary epistemological climate of nominalism and positivism, it is typical to think of things as unique individuals, which are then referred to categories that exist "in the mind," which are related to existing things at best as generalizations produced by inevitably fallible induction. Concepts are taken to be "abstractions," in opposition to particulars, which stand as the "concrete." But in the classical tradition,[24] which we affirm here, existing things are never mere particulars; rather, an existing thing is always "τόδε τί," a "this such."[25] What is grasped by the intellect as a universal *belongs to* the concrete thing in its wholeness, so that the universal concept is not something separate from and extrinsic to the individual thing. The universal concept, in other words, just *is* the individual thing according to the mode of existence it possesses in being received into the intellect.[26] It

24. To be sure, the "classical tradition" is quite broad, and includes irreducibly different views of this matter. Our purpose here is not to judge among them, but simply to indicate the view that we are adopting in the present book.

25. Aristotle, *Metaphysics* VII.3.1029a28.

26. It might seem that this point marks a fork in the road at which Plato and Aristotle — or, in the scholastic debate, realism and moderate realism — part ways: Plato affirms that the universal is the really existing reality, whereas Aristotle insists that universals do not exist in reality but only in the mind that knows reality (though there is a *fundamentum in re* of the universals). But we are suggesting that both positions are true, in different respects. For an elaboration of this suggestion, see "What's the Difference? On the Metaphysics of Participation in Plato, Plotinus, and Aquinas," *Nova et Vetera* 5, no. 3 (2007): 583-618.

is not something *other* than the thing, but is the thing as being "more than itself" in reason, which is always the *thing*'s being more than itself. Aristotle recognized that there is an irreducible duality in οὐσίαι, which came to be described as a distinction between primary substance (*this* such) and secondary substance (this *such*). While we cannot develop the point here, we may at least observe that this duality has an ontological basis in the nature of the form that constitutes substance: the form is able to gather parts into a concrete whole only insofar as it transcends those parts, but if it transcends the physical parts, it transcends the physical thing — i.e., the thing as located in time and space — as a whole, which means it belongs in some sense as much to the species as it does to the individual members of the species.[27] In this sense, it is *one and the same thing* that makes a thing a concrete whole and makes it intelligible, i.e., graspable qua universal, even while this "one thing" exhibits an irreducible duality of aspects. We will come back to this in a moment.

We proposed above that reason is always out beyond itself in and with the whole, and that it is so only as involving the soul as a whole. This description bears on the present point in two respects: it means that reason includes the activity of the senses, as that which is "beyond" reason, and it means that reason grasps whatever it grasps in each of its particular acts always from the perspective of the whole. Let us reflect on each of these in turn.

First, while it is true that the objects of reason (insofar as we take reason in isolation) are universals, it is also true that reason *exceeds itself.* One dimension of this ecstatic character of reason is its embodied state in human beings. What would seem to be a certain violence to reason in the strict sense of the term (that which is contrary to nature) — as we see, for example, in Kant, for whom reason is essentially autonomous and the life of the body is heteronomy precisely *as* the life of the body — comes to reveal itself as a positive contribution to reason when viewed in terms of catholicity. There is something in sense experience that can never be translated adequately into concepts, not only what may happen to be absolutely unique in any particular experience, but even what may be repeatable, but only in the form of other particular experiences. For example, we have the "qualia" or what was called in early modern thought the "secondary qualities" of things: the softness of cotton, the "greenness" of green, not to mention the startling beauty

27. On this, see Jonathan Lear, *Aristotle: The Desire to Understand* (Cambridge: Cambridge University Press, 1988), p. 274.

of a particular melody. These may be experienced, not simply as opaque sense data, so to speak, but precisely as *disclosive*, as meaningful, as having a significance that lies beyond the moment in which they occur. In this case, we are relating sense experience with reason.

But the crucial question is: *How* precisely are we doing so? It is not uncommon in contemporary thinkers, because of a heightened sense of the significance of individuality and the unique to seek to correct the classical notion that knowledge is always of universals by insisting that reason is in fact also *capax individualis.* But this effort needs to be cautioned: as we pointed out above, the connection between reason and universality is not due to some premodern bias, but rather concerns in the first place the transcendent nature of reason. We cannot deny this nature without far-reaching consequences. A more fruitful approach would seem to be to affirm that the content of sense experience, and the individuality associated with it, is in fact "outside" of reason — but at the same time to insist that reason is always also outside of itself. In this sense, we can say that sense experience is not *foreign* to reason; it is included in reason precisely insofar as reason is conceived analogically, so that its inclusion within reason does not at all compromise its irreducible difference from reason. By the same token, sense experience may also be interpreted itself by analogy to reason — an approach that would cast a certain light on the "confused" insights of Alexander Baumgarten as he gave birth to the new study of "aesthetics" in philosophy.[28] In a word, reason is indeed ordered in a certain respect to the concrete individual, in all of its uniqueness, because reason is always out beyond itself, and because each of its acts acts within the fundamental act, which belongs, not to intellect in isolation, but to the whole soul in all of its dimensions as it exists concretely, which means in an ecstatic relation to the whole of being.

Second, because of the ecstatic character of the fundamental act, reason always comes at its particular object in some respect "from above." To explain this, it is helpful to appeal to Michael Polanyi's notion of the "tacit dimension" of reason.[29] According to Polanyi, in every single one of its acts, reason always "knows more than it can tell," which of course is simply an-

28. According to Alexander Baumgarten (*Aesthetica*, 1750), the founder of modern aesthetics, there is an analogy between the perception of the senses and that of reason. The former grasps "confused" ideas of perfection, under the aspect of beauty, while the latter grasps clear and distinct ideas under the aspect of truth. The point was to justify the aesthetic realm of sense experience as a sphere of its own, but of course one would have to provide a more directly positive ground for the distinctive truth of this sphere.

29. Michael Polanyi, *The Tacit Dimension* (London: Routledge, 1966).

other way of saying that reason is always out beyond itself. For Polanyi, reason knows more than it can say because the explicit grasp of a particular object always takes place within a broader context, of which one is always implicitly aware coincidently with the cognition: an object stands out against a background, and one grasps the contextualizing background peripherally as one grasps the object. Polanyi thus explains the importance of what he calls "indwelling," which is similar to what Balthasar had described under the term "consent," namely, a kind of intimacy, a direct contact, with a being as the proper context within which one grasps any aspect of that being. If the mind does not in fact "indwell" the whole that is at issue, none of the particulars that constitute that whole will be understood properly. Note that in both cases, what is at issue is not a purely theoretical projection of a horizon, such as one finds in certain interpretations of hermeneutics, nor is it, on the other hand, a "pre-theoretical" or "pre-conceptual" grasp that will come to stand as a basis for conceptual constructions. Rather, it is an indwelling specifically of the mind; it is reason's taking up residence, so to speak, in a place beyond the mind, and specifically doing so in terms of what Polanyi has elsewhere elaborated as personal involvement.[30] The "tacit"-ness of the tacit dimension, in other words, is not a subconscious feeling or intuition, but instead it is consciousness's self-transcendence in being.

Because of the *actuality* of this involvement, because, that is, what we have here is not (merely) an *a priori* structure, experience is necessary. Polanyi gives the example, in another context, of the training of doctors to make diagnoses: in many cases, one cannot simply collect a list of symptoms and infer the essential cause; instead, one has to see them all together in the configuration that constitutes a particular illness or affliction. The reality one is seeking to identify is precisely a whole that cannot be identified with any parts, or even with the simple sum of those parts. Instead, it is a wholeness, which as such must be "indwelt," precisely as one attends focally to the various parts. For this reason, it is *essentially* something about which one must say, "I'll know it when I see it," and which one can be trained to see only by being guided through repeated experience by someone who has already learned to identify it.[31] What Polanyi describes here must be said analogously about every single act of intelligence without exception, insofar as

30. Michael Polanyi, *Personal Knowledge: Towards a Post-Critical Philosophy* (Chicago: University of Chicago Press, 1962).

31. Michael Polanyi, "Faith and Reason," *The Journal of Religion* 41, no. 4 (1961): 237-47; here, 239-40.

every act grasps an intelligibility only always as a whole that transcends its constitutive parts. Even the grasp of a part is an attention to it as a whole in itself, and thus as a transcendent unity. The less transcendent the unity is, the more "elemental" the understanding will be, and thus the more adequately one will be able to bring what one can say to coincidence with what one knows, though without breaking the analogy we have posited. On the other hand, however, just as elements usually do not exist in themselves but rather as parts of larger wholes, we cannot in fact understand them except in terms of their actual contexts, and so on up the line: the intelligibility of every part depends on its more encompassing whole.

This "opening up" brings us to a further point, implied by Polanyi but not made thematic by him: ultimately, the grasp of any particular thing, not simply as a whole but more specifically as a being, i.e., in its "in-itself-ness," requires an "indwelling" in being as such, that is, an awareness of reality in its most fundamental sense (with "awareness" here meaning the fundamental consent to/with being). Being as such, of course, is not some "thing" existing in itself, over-against other individual things. On the other hand, it is not simply identical with all that actually exists, so that it becomes meaningless to speak of "being as such." Instead, being transcends each being and all beings together, not by subsisting somewhere else, but by being present precisely "as a whole" *tacitly* in everything that is. We thus do not need to journey to some place apart in order to discover being; it is in fact always already given to us. The discovery of being is a distinctive way of grasping the particular beings that one has already encountered. Indeed, our suggestion is that reason is already, from the beginning, in and with being, and that this is precisely what characterizes it as reason.

Concretely speaking, it means that we do not "begin" our reasoning from a position outside of things, and gradually by degrees make our way toward them. Instead, conceived ecstatically, reason is already, from the beginning, at the destination of this path: it begins its activity already from within the beings it encounters, and, indeed, as profoundly intimate with beings as it is possible to be. As Aquinas famously observes, being is what is innermost *(magis intimum)* in things,[32] and it is just this that first falls into the intellect when we know anything at all. In this regard, the phenomenon of empathy is not an "extreme" achievement of an otherwise self-preoccupied being, but is rather simply a recapitulation at the level of feeling (and in this respect *can* be a particular achievement) of the natural "structure" of spirit simply.

32. Aquinas, *ST* 1.8.1.

Now, it may seem that we have in the end backed into the "intuitionism" we criticized at the beginning of this chapter, whereby reason finds itself in possession of the whole from the outset, and therefore incapable of making any discoveries in the strict sense. In this case, we would already "have" whatever particular being we might encounter, and indeed have it in the most intimate way possible. But such an interpretation would represent a misunderstanding of what we mean by speaking of reason as "ecstatic." The objection permits a helpful clarification in this regard. Aquinas insists, rightly, that human knowing has a real dependence on sense experience, which is to say that our minds have a genuine receptivity to the "world outside," as it were. At the same time, he does not — contrary to common interpretations — conceive the soul as a "blank slate" upon which experience is recorded. This image, appropriate more for modern empiricism than for a classical epistemology such as that of Aquinas, cannot think of universals as anything but inductive generalizations — as Locke, for example, clearly does. But Aquinas recognizes that properly intellectual understanding has an essential quality that cannot be derived from sense experience as such, namely, the universality of intelligible species. The reason it cannot be so derived is that intelligibility represents a kind of wholeness, an "all-at-onceness," a perfection or actuality, that cannot be "worked up to" one step at a time, through successive additions. Potency can be reduced to act *only by actuality,* and never by the force, as it were, of its own potency. This is the logic behind the classical axiom that the perfect must ultimately necessarily precede the imperfect. The potency of the soul with respect to *sensible* objects is reduced to actuality by the sensible thing itself, which is why one can sense something only if it is actually present. But the intellect truly "grasps" its object; it takes the object in some sense into itself, so that the actuality of knowledge does not depend on the actual presence of the thing known. It therefore follows that to the extent that intelligible species exist *at all,* i.e., if there is such a thing as intelligence, then reason must always "already" grasp its object in order to be able to learn it: knowledge is not possible unless it is anteriorly actual.

This, of course, is (again!) a paradox. It is the mystery that lies behind Plato's notion of recollection, which we will discuss in a moment. Aquinas, for his part, rejects Platonic recollection,[33] and appeals instead to the Aristotelian notion of the so-called "agent intellect":[34] our mind is in potency with

33. Aquinas, *ST* 1.84.3.

34. Aquinas, *ST* 1.84.4 and 6; 1.88.1.

respect to its proper objects, but is able to reduce this potency to act by virtue of the agent intellect, which is already *perfect,* already actualized, already "one in act" with its proper objects. But how exactly are we to understand this? What exactly is the relationship between the agent and the patient intellect? This is an extraordinarily difficult question. It is easy, perhaps, to dismiss the Arabic Neoplatonist idea of a "separate" agent intellect as unnecessarily mystical, and, more incisively, as simply deferring the problem of the actual understanding "achieved" by the individual soul. This interpretation at least has the advantage of clearly acknowledging the *potency* that belongs to our soul. Aquinas affirms an individual agent intellect, which is one of the "powers" of the rational soul.[35] It is common to imagine the individual agent intellect as "shining the light of intelligibility" onto the objects it happens to encounter, in a way that enables the abstraction of the species. But this picture is problematic, because it avoids the "separateness" of the agent intellect only by "potentializing" it: now, the agent intellect is in potency with respect to its object. What, then, reduces *its* potency to act? The only way out of the dilemma, it seems, that would affirm *both* the possibility of learning *and* the integrity of what is learned, is to say that reason is always out beyond itself. It is *actual,* but this actuality is not something it (yet) possesses *in* itself — or, more adequately, the actuality is *in* reason only as *outside itself.* It is an ecstatic, a nonpossessive, perfection. Such a conception allows for the gradualness of our learning, the priority of sense experience to understanding *quoad nos,*[36] and at the same time the fact that reason, in approaching what truly *is,* is catching up with itself. The image that we proposed above, namely, that of reason starting already *from within* the being that it seeks to know, thus needs to be qualified in order to do justice to the entirety of the event of knowledge: reason starts at one and the same time from inside being and from outside being, and its "work" is to make the connection, which is thus — as we will elaborate in chapter nine — a genuine discovery of what has already been given.

Let us draw some of the foregoing threads together. Reason begins in and with the whole in each of its acts. The "whole" of each thing that is known is irreducibly twofold: on the one hand, it is the "quiddity" of the thing, a universal intelligibility, which includes the particular thing as one of its instances; there is, in one respect, nothing in a particular tree qua tree that is not "contained" in the universal form. On the other hand, the whole is

35. Aquinas, *ST* 1.79.4 and 5.

36. Cf. Aquinas, *ST* 1.85.3.

the concretely subsisting being, which in turn "contains" the universal form as one aspect of its own being. Each sense of wholeness thus "includes" the other in itself, but in a nonreductive way, i.e., in a sense that does not eliminate the ultimately irreducible difference. To describe reason as catholic in this particular context is to say that it embraces the unity-in-difference of these two modes of wholeness: it is always already in and with both from the beginning. This means that the "abstraction" of one from the other — whether it be the universal from the individual or the individual from the universal — is not a separating out, but rather a focusing of the attention on one aspect or the other, but *always within a prior grasp of the inclusive whole*, i.e., of both together. Thus, we attend to the uniqueness of the individual always in some sense from the perspective of the whole that is always already grasped: we say, "What a unique *person!*" because uniqueness *simpliciter* is meaningless. And, conversely (but *not* in a symmetrical way), we grasp the universal "in itself," not as a separate "thing" but always only with its analogical "distribution," so to speak, among particulars. As Aquinas puts it, the intelligible species, in the end, is not *what* is known, but that by which we know,[37] and so even when we thematize the universal for its own sake it is never without some anterior awareness of the concrete whole, or wholes, from which it is abstracted.

Moreover, a grasp of the *whole* whole, of the unity of the two senses of wholeness, is possible only if there is a grasp of *being* as such, which, understood analogically, transcends the difference between universals and particulars. But, to grasp being precisely as analogical means not to subsume it under a univocal concept — the intellectual intuition of being — but rather *to be* with and in it as it opens unceasingly beyond itself in ever-new beings. To the analogy of being corresponds an essentially ec-static conception of reason. And this means, as we have seen, that reason is in fact the whole soul, the substance of the rational animal, out beyond itself in and with the world. The *whole* absolutely considered — the catholicity of reason, which is the nonreductive convergence of all four senses of the whole — is then the foundation of, the anterior context for, every single act of consciousness, no matter how apparently insignificant. Reason always, in every single act, grasps *being*, even if it is "being qua *x*." We come to know any particular being, and indeed any part of any particular being, always only in relative abstraction from, and so in some basic way in the light of, the prior illumination of the whole of wholes.

37. Aquinas, *ST* 1.85.2.

Ignorance and Presumption

Insisting on the catholicity of reason might seem out of tune with the ethos of the postmodern age, which has reacted for many good reasons against the presumptuousness of reason that characterizes certain dominant strands of the Enlightenment precisely by cultivating an apparently more self-aware "weak thinking" (*pensiero debole:* Vattimo). The emphasis on wholeness evokes the "totality" that Levinas associated with the oppressiveness of what we might call the "heterophobia" of closed systems, to which he opposed the "idea" of the infinite that can alone give a certain priority to the Other.[38] One of the first and most decisive forms of this self-restriction of reason is no doubt Kant's determination to set limits to reason "in order to make room for *faith*."[39] Such a determination seems eminently reasonable: the remedy for presumption is modesty, and modesty would seem to be best ensured by restricting reason's scope, which would cause it to respect what lies beyond it as genuinely "beyond." But our argument is that setting limits to reason in this way in fact makes modesty impossible, and that the only way to avoid a closed system is vigilantly to *insist* on "totality." The problem with Hegel, for example, who is typically presented as the very peak of Western rational presumption, is not that he claimed too much for reason, but too little: his system closed in on itself the moment he allowed reason to lose sight of the whole. We will elaborate this argument by reflecting, in a somewhat speculative way, on the nature of Socratic ignorance.

The most obvious way to interpret Socrates' well-known refrain, "I know that I don't know," is as a confession of radical skepticism: the fact that there is no determinate object to the verb in the relative clause apparently implies universality; what Socrates claims not to know is literally without bounds, which is to say that Socrates is affirming that he knows in fact nothing, not one thing, at all. But of course the claim itself refutes this inference, since it claims at least *one thing* that Socrates *does* know, even if this one thing is only that the claim to knowledge extends no further. This reading would seem to be the most radical self-limitation of reason that is logically possible, insofar as it admits under reason's certain grasp only the most minimal content that is required to avoid self-contradiction. So our first question is: How minimal in fact is this content?

38. Emmanuel Levinas, *Totality and Infinity,* trans. Alphonso Lingis (Pittsburgh: Duquesne University Press, 1969), pp. 35-40, 48-52.

39. Immanuel Kant, *The Critique of Pure Reason,* Bxxx (Kemp Smith translation, p. 29).

To determine this, we must ask first, What is implied by saying specifically that one *knows* that one doesn't know, as opposed to saying, with some uncertainty, I *think* or *suppose* or *believe* that I don't know? The question immediately presents a paradox, which in fact turns out to be unavoidable. As Socrates makes clear in a different context,[40] to be sure that one does not know, one actually needs to know a great deal: it is not enough to say indeterminately *that* one does not know, but one needs to have insight precisely into *what* one does not know. Let us take the classic example of justice. How would I determine whether or not I know what justice is? To begin, I would have to fish around in my soul, as it were, to locate whatever impressions or opinions I might have about justice. Already here, though, *before* I take this first step, I need to have some idea of what my opinion might be, an idea that guides my search. As Socrates points out in the *Meno*,[41] the search, obviously, cannot be "random": there is a difference between the act of formulating my opinion about justice and simply uttering whatever words happen to be in my head at the moment, even if the resultant content turns out to be indistinguishable. But the next moment is the decisive one: in order to determine whether the opinion, once formulated, is true, I of course need to know what justice in truth *is*. By the same token, to see that my opinion falls short of the reality, I need to see through the opinion to the reality itself. And note, there is a difference between having some vague sense that one's notion falls short and being able to say, with complete certainty, indeed, with what Socrates calls "knowledge," that it falls short. If even the former case requires some grasp of the reality, the latter requires a sure insight into its truth. There might seem to be a tension, if not a contradiction, between Socratic ignorance and the Platonic idea of learning as recollection, which implies that the soul is already in possession of the truth, and one might be tempted to resolve this tension by separating the skeptic Socrates from the dogmatist Plato, but in fact these two ideas are simply two different ways of articulating the very same point. We said above that knowing that one doesn't know requires knowing a great deal. In fact, the universality of the claims requires that one know everything, that one have a solid insight into the whole. Socratic ignorance represents no

40. In the *Charmides*, a dialogue that inquires into the nature of σωφροσύνη (moderation or self-restraint), which is arguably the virtue at issue in the present chapter, Socrates shows that, if this virtue is only a knowledge *that* one knows and does not know, and not more precisely a knowledge of *what* one knows and does not know (which he later admits to be quite paradoxical), it is essentially useless; see 170a-172c.

41. Plato, *Meno* 80e.

minimalist epistemology; rather, it is a claim "than which nothing greater can be thought," as we will see in a moment.

Before we turn to that issue, let us first ask whether, in light of the comprehensive content that turns out to lie, admittedly somewhat hidden, in Socrates' knowing that he does not know, the more typical claim of ignorance is more modest than the Socratic variety. In other words, is it less presumptuous simply to say I *think* that I don't know, but I could be wrong? Or perhaps to admit that I know some things, in a delimited area, but to make no claim one way or the other about anything that lies outside of that area? What connects these statements is the assumption that a suspension of judgment is a gesture of modesty, though that suspension has a different scope in the two cases. In the first, the scope is universal: one expresses a general reluctance to claim truth, "absolute knowledge," in any particular instance. But note: this stance implies that the question of whether or not one's ideas, in one case or another, are *true* in fact is, for all intents and purposes, irrelevant. The phrase "all intents and purposes" is particularly appropriate here because the stance willy-nilly absolutizes pragmatism. But there is an outrageous presumption in this: if pursuing the question of truth requires one to venture, as it were, beyond one's thinking to reality, dismissing this question means resolving *not* to venture beyond one's own thinking *as* one's own, which is to say that one keeps oneself away from the world and in one's own head — which is to say, further, that one absolutizes one's own ego over and against God, reality, others, whatever it may be, all of which is equally irrelevant to that ego. What reason does one have for dismissing the question of truth and suspending one's judgment? While it could turn out in a particular case or another that suspending judgment is prudent, there can *in fact* be no reason at all for a universal suspension of judgment, insofar as accepting a reason as true requires suspending this suspension. It follows that this suspension is strictly groundless; it is a wholly arbitrary *a priori,* which claims preemptively that no statement will ever have a claim on one's judgment without obliging oneself to listen to and consider any given statement. It may be that one opinion or another that one happens to hold is in fact true, but the suspension of judgment neutralizes its significance for me qua truth, again for no reason. I thus absolve myself of all responsibility: if I make no claim on truth, then truth never has a claim on me.

The second alternative above, namely, that I claim knowledge about things in a delimited area, but make no judgment one way or the other regarding anything outside the limits, is at least apparently less presumptuous than the first, ironically because it does indeed admit that some of its knowledge is true. The difficulty is in fact twofold. On the one hand, as we observed at the outset of this chapter, one can set limits in the proper place only if one is already beyond those limits, which means that to the extent that self-limitation is strictly *a priori,* and not the fruit of an encounter with what lies outside of oneself, the limitation is an act of presumption: one is acting as if one knows what one does not in fact know. On the other hand, and perhaps more profoundly, to allow oneself judgment on one side of a boundary and at the same time to suspend judgment on the other side is to claim — again, in an *a priori* way, which is to say without any sufficient reason — that what lies on the other side does not in any significant sense bear on my understanding of the matter or matters lying on *this* side. But of course to make this claim without investigation and justification is presumptuous.

It does not in the least do to insist, "But I am *limiting* my claims only to this particular aspect!" because this begs the very question being raised here. Plato describes the tendency of experts in a particular craft to presume expertise about the whole.[42] If we penetrate below the surface, however, we see that this is not a (mere) moral critique about the way some people happen to act. Instead, there is a logical necessity here: to claim expertise about a part *is already* — and precisely insofar as it is a claim of expertise concerning the part — to presume regarding the meaning of the whole. The ignorant presumption can be very obvious, or it may be subtle. For example, one might isolate economics from politics as a closed system in itself, which is evidently misleading insofar as the "agents" of economic transactions are living members of communities whose choices inevitably reflect in a significant way the nature and structure of those communities. Perhaps less obviously, but with analogous implications, one might also separate politics from philosophical anthropology, anthropology from metaphysics, or metaphysics from theology. The problem will be there whenever one isolates a part from the whole in a way that excludes the relevance of the meaning of the whole to the meaning of the part, which is to say that one fails to approach the part *as* a part, i.e., as *related* to what is greater than it, and so one (presumptuously) makes it an absolute in itself. To avoid this presumption, one might first seek to attenuate one's insistence on knowledge within the delimited sphere in light of one's ignorance of the larger whole, which would seem to acknowledge at least in principle the significance of that whole. But in fact this is a retreat into what we showed above to be the greatest possible presumption, namely, the universal sus-

42. Plato, *Apology* 22d-e.

pension of judgment. The only way to avoid the dilemma is in fact to achieve actual knowledge about the whole.

To make this argument more concrete, let us consider the general status of scientific reasoning in the present age. Modern science was born precisely as a result of the kind of self-limitation of reason that we have been discussing. Galileo was revolutionary for criticizing what he took to be the presumption of classical philosophy to see into the "essences" of things. He thus proposed, instead, to "bracket out," as it were, the metaphysical question of "what" things are, and to attend only to the mathematically formulizable laws that govern their locomotion, laws that reveal themselves only to controlled experiment. The "conceit" of modern science, as generally understood, is this: we can learn a lot about the world, or at least about how the world works, if we abstract one feature of reality — i.e., quantifiable change — which we rationally master as far as we are able, and we leave the "big questions" concerning meaning, ethical implications, and so forth, to the philosophers and theologians. Now, the precise relationship between science, philosophy, and theology is of course a vast one, and we are not claiming to do it justice here (and, note, we are able thus to limit ourselves because we *know* it is a vast question!), but we wish only to observe the following: there has been a concern, from the very beginning of this sort of thinking, that this position, in spite of its explicit modesty, tends to *encroach* upon the "big questions" and in fact to impose certain answers to those questions. What we wish to propose, in the light of the discussion above, is that this encroachment is inevitable because it is "built into" the logic of epistemological modesty.

Along the lines we have been arguing, to say that one is attending *only* to the quantifiable aspect of change and that one is setting aside the philosophical question about the essence of a thing, or in other words to isolate this particular part from the whole, entails three claims: first, that the larger question about the nature of a thing does not bear on its movements in a way that might require a grasp of that nature properly to detect;[43] second,

43. The question, in other words, is whether motion is *meaningful*, that is, whether it ought to be in the first place interpreted as an activity of a *subject*, a "this such," and so analyzed in terms of act and potency, in which case motion would be recognized as an analogous concept, or whether it is most properly understood in abstraction, and so univocally, as simply quantifiable change of location in time, a notion that can then be applied indifferently to the various cases. While there may seem to be little at stake at the crudest level of reality, the question becomes decisive at higher levels — and will already have been decided in fact in the rudimentary case. On all this, see Simon Oliver, *Philosophy, God and Motion* (London: Routledge, 2005).

that this movement is not and indeed cannot be transformed in subtle but significant ways according to the context; and, third, that what is "bracketed out" is *extrinsic* to what one is studying, in abstraction, so that the *whole* at issue represents a mere addition of "all the rest" to the part that had been isolated. Note that one cannot isolate the part in this absolute way without making a judgment, willy-nilly, about the *nature* of the whole of which it is a part — and indeed to do so in spite of one's professed ignorance. The isolation and the presumptuous judgment are one and the same act. Let us take an example, which is admittedly extreme but thereby serves to make the point in big letters. Richard Dawkins "modestly" confesses ignorance regarding the nature of consciousness, and sets this question aside in order to restrict himself to what one could call the mechanics of brain activity.[44] In doing so, he presumes from the outset, and so without reason or argumentation, that consciousness qua consciousness has nothing to do with what goes on in the brain. This strictly baseless assumption excludes from the outset the possibility consciousness might be an integral whole that includes the brain in its mechanical dimension even as it transcends it. Instead, because it requires conceiving consciousness as external to the mechanics of brain activity, Dawkins's starting assumption leaves only two alternatives: either consciousness is a product of the mechanics or it is a "ghost in the machine," i.e., some kind of "supernatural" entity one may or may not privately believe in, independently of one's scientific thinking.[45] The methodological practice of setting aside the question of the nature of consciousness is willy-nilly a

44. Richard Dawkins, *The Selfish Gene*, 30th anniversary ed. (Oxford: Oxford University Press, 2006), p. 50: "Each one of us knows, from the evidence of our own introspection, that, at least in one modern survival machine [Dawkins's term for 'organism'], this purposiveness has evolved the property we call 'consciousness.' I am not philosopher enough to discuss what this means, but fortunately it does not matter for our present purposes because it is easy to talk about machines that behave *as if* motivated by a purpose, and to leave open the question whether they actually are conscious." What he does not at all leave open is the question, *What* is consciousness? His "from below" method determines this in advance, and of course this is in the end the much more decisive question.

45. Regarding the reduction of consciousness to a function of the brain's activity, it is worth mentioning that Dawkins himself takes this position, but does so apparently without feeling any obligation to reckon, for example, with Husserl's conclusive refutation of psychologism at the turn of the twentieth century. The presumption is that a philosophical insight such as this has no relevance for a scientific study of brain activity. But, clearly, if logic is an activity of the brain at some level, and has a necessary structure and laws proper to it that can be made evident, the onus would fall to the scientist to recognize this at least to the extent that it is not positively excluded by the assumptions governing his research.

positive claim about the nature of consciousness; because it makes this claim without acknowledging it and accepting responsibility for it, the practice is *inherently presumptuous*, regardless of the moral character of the scientist or his explicit intentions in adopting the methodology.

Of course, an adequate treatment of everything implied here would require a much lengthier discussion that would elaborate responses for the many evident objections one could make. But our intention in the present context is simply to recognize a recurring pattern. A common response to what we are describing is to make a distinction between *science*, the systematic study of empirical facts, and *"scientism,"* which is the confusion of science with philosophy, the assumption that the part one studies under specific conditions gives an adequate understanding of the whole. In other words, science limits itself to the study of matter in motion; scientism says that matter in motion "is all there is." As long as scientists stick to the "how," it is said, and do not presume to answer the question "why," then science poses in principle no threat to philosophy or religion. But we wish to suggest, by contrast, that the only way finally to avoid scientific reductionism is to recover within science a more self-conscious sense that one is not studying only a part, but rather the whole, even if it is in a particular respect. In other words, the problem is not that certain scientists fail to adhere to the modesty that defines the scientific project; the problem lies in the modesty itself. Scientific reasoning will have humility only to the extent that it understands itself (once again) as a philosophy. In more technical language, we might say that reason is always inevitably "of being." Scientific reasoning, to be truly a mode of reasoning, would thus be of being, but in a particular respect: being qua that which changes in a quantifiable manner (or however one might need to specify in the particular context). If it "pretends" to be only the study of quantifiable motion qua quantifiable motion, it in fact *identifies* being with this particular respect, which is to say that it makes its object an unconditional absolute in itself, and so indifferent to anything outside of itself. The moment reason admits that it is philosophical, which means acknowledges it is a particular way of accounting for the whole, it then opens up from within to dialogue with the other accounts of the whole, because it is now *responsible to* that whole; it becomes "vulnerable" to the truth of the whole in a way that its self-proclaimed "modesty" precisely *protected* it from ever being. Ironically, the more one insists on modesty in science, the more "impenetrable" one makes it, i.e., the more one makes it an absolute in itself and so unable to be integrated into a larger whole. To set any absolute limit not only keeps reason from exceeding a boundary, it necessarily also keeps anything else from getting in.

But — to return to the general argument — if knowledge is necessary to be able to know that one does not know something, then doesn't the very requirement eliminate the possibility? In other words, would it not follow that to *know* that I don't know something is no longer to be in ignorance of it? Is Socratic ignorance simply a contradiction? One must respond that the contradiction would be inevitable if we took for granted a univocal sense of reason. But the analogical or ecstatic conception of reason that we have described as its catholic character allows the paradox to stand without contradiction. In this case, there is room *within* reason itself for the difference between possession and nonpossession. We might say, in fact, that the distance between the two expresses what Plato, more metaphorically, described as a "forgetting" in his notion of learning as recollection: the point in both cases is that an understanding of the matter at issue both *is* in the soul and *is not* in the soul in some sense at the very same time. Such a thing is possible, once again, only if reason is "structurally" out beyond itself. This interpretation allows us a different interpretation of the common failure in the Platonic dialogues to come to an adequate definition of an idea from the usual reading. Typically, the failure is taken to demonstrate the "skeptical" moment in Plato's (or more specifically Socrates')[46] thought, by which is meant that Socrates recognizes that the goal of knowledge that he presents is in fact impossible. According to this perspective, what Plato is offering, in these early dialogues at least, is not a search for knowledge; instead, he is encouraging his audience to give thought to these things, that is, to exercise reason rather than to satisfy it. But of course a purely instrumental notion of reason, which this interpretation, taken radically, implies, is altogether foreign to Plato, and in any event as we have seen a deep sense of one's failure to know something requires . . . knowledge of it. The alternative interpretation that arises from our consideration of the paradoxical character of Socratic ignorance is that one fails to formulate an adequate definition, not because the reality one seeks is ultimately inaccessible, but rather for the opposite reason,

46. The period in Platonic scholarship in which the dialogues are divided according to presumed times of composition into "early," "middle," and "late," under the assumption that these correspond to significant moments in Plato's intellectual development, has essentially come to an end. See John Cooper, "Introduction" to Plato's *Complete Works* (Indianapolis: Hackett, 1997), pp. xii-xviii. There is no clear evidence supporting this approach to Plato, which has always rested on a particular interpretation of Plato's philosophy. Even the scant evidence that Cooper admits for a grouping of "late" dialogues can quite persuasively be challenged. See Jacob Howland, "Re-Reading Plato: The Problem of Platonic Chronology," *Phoenix* 45 (1991): 189-214.

namely, that one is "too close" to it. In other words, reason, as always already out beyond itself, enjoys an immediate contact, an intimacy with reality, which eludes definition precisely because definition entails a kind of abstraction that indicates a departure from that intimacy. In the famous *Seventh Letter,* Plato describes the stages of reason's progress in relation to the being of things, a journey that culminates, significantly, *not* in knowledge, but beyond it in the being itself of things.[47] This is perhaps not as different as it might seem from Aquinas's statement that the concept is not the object of knowledge, but that by which we know. If, to use Plato's terminology, knowledge represents the reality insofar as it exists in my intellect, then the distinction between knowledge and being, insofar as being is not in Plato's description a noumenon outside of reason but where reason ultimately comes to rest, implies simply that reason is ecstatic. If knowledge is being in reason, then the distinction means that reason ultimately lies outside of itself in being. The failure to reach a definition in the dialogues would in this case be the dramatic opening of one's mind to this distinction. The goal, more precisely, is not to eliminate the distinction but instead to pass from ignorance of the distinction — which expresses itself as presumption — to knowledge of the distinction. We can make progress toward knowledge only because in some sense we have always already been at the end; or, as Socrates puts it, all learning is recollection.

We are now in a position to see why knowing that one doesn't know is not a skeptical self-limitation of reason *a priori,* but is rather the most comprehensive — most catholic — conception of reason possible. It might seem at first that one would be claiming *more* for reason to say that it knows that it knows, to say, in other words, that reason is (or can be) in full possession of the truth. But in fact this collapses reason back into itself. As we mentioned at the beginning of this section, Hegel is no doubt the best example of this apparently extreme claim for reason — better, for example, even than Descartes with his project of a universal *mathēsis,* insofar as Descartes assumed consciousness as a sort of sphere outside the world whereas Hegel affirmed *Geist* as a kind of self-transcendence inclusive of the world — and he illustrates the problem that arises when reason prematurely limits itself. For Hegel, "an out-and-out Other simply does not exist for spirit,"[48] by which he

47. Plato, *Seventh Letter* 343c. For a fuller discussion of this point, see *Plato's Critique of Impure Reason* (Washington, DC: Catholic University of America Press, 2008), pp. 228-40.

48. Hegel, *Philosophy of Mind,* trans. A. V. Miller (Oxford: Clarendon, 1971), p. 1 (§377 *Zusatz*). Translation slightly modified.

means that, no matter how transcendent its object, reason can grasp that object ultimately without leaving itself. Spirit is perfect self-relation, which can be, as it were, "at home" *(bei sich)* no matter where it is. But in this conception of reason, Hegel rejects the possibility of reason being "more." In other words, he rejects *a priori* the possibility of reason being genuinely more than itself, being capable of leaving its home, so to speak, and entering the home of another. Hegel does not claim too much for reason, in this regard, but too little: he limits reason specifically to itself, which means that it can relate to its object *as* reason only to the extent that the object enters into it; the object must come to reason's terms, but reason is incapable of coming to terms with the object. In a word, Hegel's conception of reason is less than catholic, and *it is precisely this failing of the whole,* which he himself says is the truth of truth,[49] *that makes Hegelian reason "totalizing."*

With this last point, we have reached our conclusion. A great deal of postmodern thought is driven by a kind of nostalgia for "epistemic humility," which in its best sense means a respect for the deep mystery of things. This nostalgia becomes urgent to the point of desperation as the sense for mystery grows weaker, to the point that the human spirit feels compelled in the end simply to fabricate its own mysteries, to play ever more hysterically with its own fictions.[50] The phenomenon gives rise to the suspicion that there is a deep pathology at work here, that the response to the problem is itself a function of the problem, which thus causes it to worsen rather than improve: far from bringing any peace, it only generates a greater need, so that one is prompted to answer with an even more intensified version of the same, and so on. Can one in fact make the claim, without embarrassment, that reason's embrace of a radical modesty in the birth of modern science, for example, ushered in a reverence for the mystery of the natural world and respect for its integrity that the world had never before seen? Our argument has been that there is in fact nothing more presumptuous than reason's

49. Hegel, "Preface" to *The Phenomenology of Spirit,* pp. 1-45, esp. 11.

50. Nietzsche gives poignant expression to just this in an early, unpublished notebook: "I call myself the last philosopher, because I am the last man. No one speaks with me but I myself, and my voice comes to me as the voice of one dying. Let me converse with you for just one more hour, beloved voice, with you, the last breath of all human happiness. With you I can deceive myself that my solitude is gone and lie myself back into multiplicity and love. For my heart refuses to believe that love is dead. It cannot bear the shudder of the loneliest solitude and compels me to speak to myself as if I were two." Friedrich Nietzsche, *Nachlaß 1869-1874,* vol. 7 of the collected works, ed. Giorgio Colli and Mazzino Montinari (Berlin: De Gruyter, 1999), pp. 460-61.

"modest" self-limitation. We will flesh out this argument in a variety of directions over the course of this book. What we are proposing here, and what is presupposed by all of the chapters to follow, is that reason is essentially catholic, and that it is only by recognizing this and being faithful to it that we will be able to recover the sense of mystery, the loss of which has been justly mourned in much postmodern thinking. We will recover humility only if we recover at the same time a robust sense of truth, and of the reason that grasps it. To say that reason is catholic is to say, not that it encompasses the whole in itself, but that it grasps the whole only in being called constantly beyond itself to what remains ever greater. Catholicity means that reason is responsible *to* the whole, and cannot absolve itself of this responsibility through protests of modesty. Only one who is open to the whole as such is vulnerable to the claims of truth.

PART ONE

Truth and Knowledge

2 Surprised by Truth: The Drama of Reason in Fundamental Theology

What can it mean to say that Christianity is true? This seemingly simple question contains a profound theoretical difficulty. We would be unable to affirm the truth of Christianity unless it made a claim on the assent of human reason, but such a claim is possible only if it in turn resonates in some respect within reason's own intrinsic necessities. To ask the question concerning the truth of Christianity plunges us immediately into a problem that lies at the center of fundamental theology, the discipline that inquires into the possibility of theology.[1] As a *logos,* a rational discourse, about God, theology is in some sense a human activity. But what distinguishes theology from philosophy, which possesses its own discourse about God, is that theology has its ultimate foundation not in reason's own exigencies, nor in natural evidences, but in that which properly speaking comes from *beyond* reason's horizon, and indeed in some sense from beyond the world itself: namely, in revelation.[2] Is rational discourse about God, then, possible? Indeed, is there in principle such a thing as a reasonable theologian?

If we admit this apparently unlikely possibility, we would seem to run the risk of reducing revelation to its universally accessible "sense" (are not the truths of reason necessarily universal?), thus depriving it precisely of its revealed character, forfeiting any genuine difference between faith and rea-

1. The two central themes of fundamental theology are revelation and its credibility. *Dictionary of Fundamental Theology,* ed. R. Latourelle and R. Fisichella (New York: Crossroad, 1994), pp. 326-27.

2. "The truth Revelation allows us to know is neither the mature fruit nor the highest reach of the reflections of human reason." *Fides et ratio,* 15 (translation, slightly modified, from *Restoring Faith in Reason,* ed. Laurence Paul Hemming and Susan Frank Parsons [London: SCM Press, 2002], p. 29).

son, theology and philosophy. But if we reject such a reduction and insist on revelation's transcendence with respect to reason, we would seem to condemn theology to the realm of the esoteric and irrational. With characteristic pithiness, Blondel expresses the difficulty that confronts fundamental theology in his *Letter on Apologetics* (1896): "If one insists on the conformity of dogmas with the requirements of human thought, one runs the risk of seeing in them nothing but a human doctrine of the most excellent kind; if one lays it down at the outset that it surpasses human reason and even disconcerts human nature, then one abandons the chosen ground and the field of rational investigation."[3] As revealed, the truth of Christianity cannot have been deduced or otherwise rationally inferred from the nature of man or the world. In other words, it arrives from beyond reason. However, it is just this transcendent and gratuitous character that would seem necessarily to deprive it of any binding force. If it is "imposed" simply from above, it carries with it no rational obligation; it would resemble in this respect another nation's customs or laws: curious, perhaps even daunting, but nevertheless not having any claim on me.

In order to avoid these two horns of the dilemma, we will have to find some way of affirming the discontinuity of revelation with respect to reason *as well as* a certain continuity. We wish to propose in the present chapter that the only way to fulfill both requirements is with a dramatic notion of truth.[4] We will draw this notion most basically from principles propounded by the Swiss theologian Hans Urs von Balthasar.[5] Our contention is that a genuinely catholic sense of reason will necessarily be dramatic in the sense that we describe below, because only such a conception of reason meets the criteria we presented in chapter one: namely, being at once comprehensive and open to what lies beyond itself.

Before we begin this discussion, it is worth noting that the problem of

3. Maurice Blondel, *The Letter on Apologetics & History and Dogma*, trans. Alexander Dru and Illtyd Trethowan (Grand Rapids: Eerdmans, 1994), p. 138.

4. To be sure, it is not necessary for a theory of knowledge to be *explicitly* dramatic in order to do justice to the problem of fundamental theology, but it must nonetheless affirm the simultaneity of continuity and discontinuity in some fashion. For another approach that articulates a notion of knowledge with a view to the problem of the appropriation of revelation, see R. Fisichella, "Oportet philosophari in theologia (III)," *Gregorianum* 76, no. 4 (1995): 701-28; here, 701-15.

5. For a more comprehensive presentation of a "dramatic" notion of truth based on the thought of Balthasar, see D. C. Schindler, *Hans Urs von Balthasar and the Dramatic Structure of Truth: A Philosophical Investigation* (New York: Fordham University Press, 2004).

fundamental theology we are addressing holds significance not only for endeavors in apologetics, but for theology in general, and perhaps even more for philosophy. It may seem to be too late to raise the question of the possibility of rational discourse about God's self-revelation: if theology is actual, after all, it must be possible. Nevertheless, we ought to see that the character of theology will be determined to some extent by the view of reason operative within it. If the "revelational" dimension of Christianity remains simply extrinsic to reason, theology will not possess the capacity to see Christianity as an organic *whole*, but will tend instead to reduce it positivistically to some aspect, for example, to a collection of propositions of faith. It will be unable to penetrate *into* dogma or reflectively appropriate it but will inevitably collapse into mere history, fideism, biblical positivism, moralism, or a program of social justice and political action. The sole task that a well-known Australian fundamental theologian accords to reason in theology is that of "clarifying concepts" and "providing criteria for verifying the specific claims that are made."[6] To be genuinely *contemplative*, theology must be what Balthasar has called a "seeking theology," and this requires taking reason's needs as in some sense its own.[7]

But, of course, to do so raises the question of the nature of the reason whose needs it takes on. Here we have to address the proper aspiration of philosophy. It seems obvious that the question of the relationship between reason and revelation would lie altogether outside the competency and therefore the concern of philosophy. Indeed, we would expect philosophy to plead that it has not yet finished with the question concerning the possibility of knowing the *world*, much less the question of knowing what lies *beyond*

6. See Gerald O'Collins, S.J., *Retrieving Fundamental Theology: The Three Styles of Contemporary Theology* (New York: Paulist, 1993), p. 39. One might suggest that, in giving philosophy the task of establishing the criteria of verification in this particular sense, O'Collins accords reason both too much and too little. On the one hand, such a task implies a rather empiricist or positivist — i.e., impoverished — view of reason; on the other hand, to allow such a notion of reason the authority over revelation to provide the measure for this latter clearly undermines the divine character of revelation from the outset. *Fides et ratio*, by contrast, envisions reason's role in theology not as an extrinsic logical instrument, but as a contemplative faculty ordered to being and united *intrinsically* to faith. Cf. *Fides et ratio*, 97.

7. R. Fisichella observes that, because of the transcendence of revelation, the work of understanding is in principle *never* finished. "Oportet philosophari in theologia (I)," *Gregorianum* 76, no. 2 (1995): 221-62; here, 222. The essay in which Balthasar most extensively develops the contemplative dimension that philosophy contributes to theology is "Philosophy, Christianity, Monasticism," in *Explorations in Theology*, vol. 2: *Spouse of the Word* (San Francisco: Ignatius Press, 1991), pp. 333-72.

the natural order, and that it does not in fact expect to resolve even the more modest question anytime soon. But we ought to note that these two questions are not unrelated: there is a certain analogy between reason's capacity to know the world, which as its "other" lies in some sense beyond reason itself, and its capacity to have access to what transcends it altogether. Moreover, if reason were capable of grasping the altogether transcendent, this would represent its highest act. If the possibility of this act were excluded *a priori* and as a matter of principle from philosophy's scope, it would undermine the impulse that all the great thinkers have recognized as reason's defining feature: an eros ordered to the ultimate, the original, and the comprehensive. What Nietzsche says about love applies to this eros as well: if limits are set to its aspirations from the outset, it inevitably suffers an internal collapse.[8] According to Socrates,[9] there is in fact nothing more fundamentally destructive to philosophical reason than this *a priori* limitation of its possibility, as we argued in the last chapter. When reason accepts such limits at the outset, it devolves into a meager and, consequentially for some, a contemptible instrument, which tests formal consistency in thinking but can never lay hold of what *is.*

As we have initially presented it, this problem arises within fundamental theology because of a notion of reason that is defined by its immanent necessities: in Kierkegaard's words, "All thought breathes in immanence."[10] Postmodern thinkers have identified such a notion of reason as the dominant one in modern philosophy, if not in the Western tradition more generally.[11]

8. See the aphorisms on love in Friedrich Nietzsche, *Anthologien: Vom vornehmen Menschen, Vergeblichkeit,* and *Von Gut und Böse* (Freiburg: Johannes Verlag, 2000), pp. 90-91. The aphorisms in this three-part anthology were selected and arranged by Balthasar.

9. Plato, *Meno* 86b-c.

10. Søren Kierkegaard, "Of the Difference Between a Genius and an Apostle," in *The Present Age* (New York: Harper & Row, 1962), p. 91. In this essay, Kierkegaard addresses precisely the same concern we are addressing in the present chapter, but he ends with what we might call a nondramatic paradox in the relation between reason and revelation: namely, pure discontinuity. Such a conclusion is necessary once one defines reason, as Kierkegaard does, in its natural operation wholly in terms of immanence.

11. See, e.g., Emmanuel Levinas's description of "Narcissism, or the Primacy of the Same," in his essay "Philosophy and the Idea of the Infinite," in *To the Other: An Introduction to the Philosophy of Emmanuel Levinas,* by Adriaan Peperzak (West Lafayette, IN: Purdue University Press, 1993), pp. 94-105. Here, he judges correctly that, given such a notion of reason, "The essence of truth will then not be in the heteronomous relationship with an unknown God, but in the already-known which has to be uncovered or freely invented in oneself, and in which everything known is comprised. It is fundamentally opposed to a God that reveals" (p. 96).

The limits of the present context make it impossible to explore the provenance of this notion in any detail. Nevertheless, in order to illuminate the significance of the dramatic notion of truth that one can draw from Balthasar's thought, it is first necessary, in the first part of the chapter, briefly to outline the basic contours of certain pivotal epistemologies, with a view to their tendency toward "immanence." I hasten to point out that I am not investigating these epistemologies for their own sake, but simply as a way of focusing the problem we are addressing, and thus I do not claim to be offering the best possible interpretation of these thinkers. In fact, I will be overlooking fruitful ambiguities and creative possibilities, and highlighting instead the more straightforward implications of basic affirmations in their philosophies. After laying out, in the second part of the chapter, the principles of a dramatic conception of truth in Balthasar's thought, I will suggest in the third and final section how this conception provides a response to the problem at the basis of fundamental theology, and so presents an essential feature of a catholic notion of reason.

Immanence and Reason's Other

Plato brings us directly into the heart of the matter. In the *Meno,* Socrates articulates the quandary that has come to be known as Meno's paradox. We discussed an aspect of this paradox in the previous chapter; here, we will focus the paradox in relation to the problem of fundamental theology. When he asks whether it is possible, in fact, to learn anything at all, the question amounts to whether it is possible to introduce something essentially *new* into the soul. In other words, can reason be genuinely taken by surprise? Is it capable of receiving anything other than what it always already anticipates, can it welcome anything but an expected guest? Socrates' answer is negative; learning is impossible, he says: one cannot find what one is not looking for, and one cannot look for something unless one already "possesses" it, that is, already knows what it is.[12] The most fundamental things, thus, cannot be received by the soul as something other than itself, but must be presupposed as part of the soul's reality; to use Plato's language, they cannot be discovered, but only recollected. In this case, as we have seen, reason can have access to what transcends it only if it is already built into reason, which means only if it does not in fact transcend reason.

12. Plato, *Meno* 80e.

What seems like mere sophistry turns out to present a truly formidable difficulty, which has been repeatedly confirmed by other major thinkers in history. We see it, for example, both in the Aristotelian/Thomistic and in the Kantian notions of the cognitive faculty of the soul. Aristotle, at first glance, seems to avoid the problem with his more empirical epistemology. In fact, he addresses the Meno paradox directly in the *Prior Analytics* (2.21) and the *Posterior Analytics* (1.1), and implicitly also in the *Metaphysics* (1.9). But in these texts, he affirms only that *particulars* (τά καθ' ἕκαστον) can be learned, and that they can be learned only on the basis of a universal (καθόλον) which is *already* known. Indeed, he also ultimately affirms that particulars, in any event, cannot be *known* as such. If we press the inquiry and ask after the origin of knowledge of universals, we eventually discover that Aristotle ends up affirming the same principle as Plato, however much the terms may have changed. As we discussed in chapter one, knowledge, according to Aristotle, is an actualization of the soul. Every actualization presupposes not only a general potentiality for knowledge, but a specific potential *for* this particular actuality.[13] But to be so disposed, of course, presupposes the actuality itself. Thus, act is prior to potency. The soul cannot take into itself, in other words, anything that it does not already have "space" for, a prior disposition for. To be sure, such a predetermined potentiality has room for an infinite variety of particulars, but it lacks the capacity to be taken by surprise in a fundamental way. If reason were able to know something, it would after all *already* have the capacity for it, and the capacity is derivative of the completed act. An object for the soul that was in some sense "discontinuous" with the soul's potentialities would simply make no sense for Aristotle. Any apparent surprise turns out to be nothing more than an unfolding of the soul's already latent potential. Whatever the human soul knows is necessarily humanly knowable.

We arrive at a similar conclusion if we take our bearings from the essential definition of truth that Aquinas offers in his *De veritate,* namely, truth as *adequatio intellectus et rei.*[14] Although Aquinas affirms that the act of knowledge — in the speculative rather than the practical order — takes its measure not from the soul but from the object known, nevertheless, insofar as the *adequatio* is a joining of two terms, the object's measure must be accommodated by the soul, and is therefore to that extent determined by the soul's intrinsic capacities: "Now the fulfillment of every motion or operation," Aquinas says, "lies in its end. The motion of the cognitive power, how-

13. See *De Anima* 2.2 (414a26-28), 3.4 (429a10-18), 3.5 (18-25).
14. Aquinas, *De ver.* 1.1.

ever, is terminated in the soul. For the known must be in the knower according to the mode of the knower."[15] *Adequatio* means correspondence, and a truth that does not "fit" the intellect, i.e., is not compatible with its own constitutive structure, cannot strictly speaking be said to be true.

One might argue that we ought not to view the intellect's structural capacities as constituted prior to and independently of the soul's most proper object, i.e., being itself, in which case the problem of measuring truth by the soul's immanent capacities need never arise. We will return to this promising possibility in a moment, but we ought to recognize the difficulty it still leaves in place, namely, the fact that revelation, though not lying *outside* of being, is nevertheless qua supernatural not deducible from the structure of *ens* or even of *esse creatum*. If we insist that it is not created being but rather *Ipsum Esse* that is the first thing to "fall" into the natural intellect, and thus forms its most proper object, we resolve the problem of the soul's capacity to understand revelation only at the cost of its gratuity.[16] Either way, there is no surprise.[17]

One of the things a more patient eye discerns in these classical epistemologies is a certain open "undecidedness" at the deepest level of the question of reason's relation to its objects. Plato hesitates to insist on any definitive account about the precise "mechanics" of recollection, for example; Aristotle seems to distinguish the intellect that always already knows all its

15. Aquinas, *De ver.* 1.2.

16. Moreover, to affirm that we have direct knowledge of God as the foundation for all other knowledge of the world, as this claim implies, would be the problem of ontologism: "Hence it must be said that God is not the first object of our knowledge" (*ST* 1.88.3).

17. Indeed, Aquinas clearly affirms the mind's natural desire to know the ultimate cause of things, and insists that this desire cannot be in vain (*ST* 1.12.1). At the same time, however, Aquinas is equally clear that "in our present life," the mind "has a natural aptitude for material objects," which aptitude the understanding of the Divine Essence necessarily exceeds (*ST* 1.86.2ad1). Still more, he insists that, even in the eschaton, the human intellect cannot reach God by its natural powers (*ST* 1.12.4ad5). Aquinas thus affirms that grace — in this case, "created light" — is necessary to bring the intellect beyond its natural powers. (On this, see Gilson's discussion of the disjunction between the intellect's "proper" or "natural object" and its "adequate object" in *The Spirit of Medieval Philosophy* [New York: Charles Scribner's Sons, 1940], pp. 248ff.) While all of this is true, it does not yet resolve the problem, but simply defers it: Does reason have the capacity to be so raised, without becoming something simply other than it is? This elevation can fulfill natural reason only if the power it adds is in fact proportionate in some way to the natural order of the intelligence, but it must at the same time exceed that order. I propose that the insight we will draw from Balthasar below, namely, that reason is "constitutionally dramatic," provides a way of affirming both necessities.

objects from the individual soul, but does not specify the relationship any further; and Aquinas locates the ultimate and defining adequation of truth, and thus the ultimate measure of both being and in turn the human soul's knowledge of it, in the mind of God and therefore infinitely above the natural powers of the soul. With the new philosophical spirit of the Enlightenment, however, whatever fruitful ambiguities may have lain in these epistemologies get mercilessly cleared away.

Descartes lays down the fundamental principle: ideas are true precisely to the extent that they can be derived from reason itself.[18] Kant differentiates this principle through an encounter with Humean empiricism into one of history's most sophisticated and comprehensive philosophies. But regarding the question of revelation, Kant's integration of empiricism does not bring him in any significant sense beyond Descartes. Critical philosophy exhaustively determines the subject's conditions of possibility *prior to* any encounter with what lies outside of the subject. Where the soul — as πῶς πάντα — had once been the place of the forms, it now becomes a Procrustean bed. On the one hand, only that which can be received within the understanding's *a priori* conditions is intelligible. On the other hand, what lies beyond these conditions simply cannot be received. For Kant, the mind is constitutionally lonely.

We see this loneliness specifically in two ways: first of all, everything that is ordered in one's experience, which means everything accessible to the soul's perceptive and cognitive powers, is exhaustively the product of the soul's spontaneous formal and categorial activity; what comes from outside the soul is nothing but the matter to receive this activity — in other words, the "world" is not ultimately what one understands but is rather the mere occasion for understanding.[19] Second, even this incidental contribution from outside the subject disappears at the supersensible level. The soul can "encounter" only what is physical; beyond the physical is nothing but the

18. The clarity and distinctness of ideas that Descartes takes to be the criteria of their truth derive from the immediacy with which they are related to the pure thought of the ego. See part IV of the *Discourse on the Method of Rightly Conducting the Reason,* in *The Philosophical Works of Descartes,* trans. Elizabeth Haldane and G. R. T. Ross, vol. 1 (Cambridge: Cambridge University Press, 1973), pp. 100-106; here, 102, and the second and third meditations in *Meditations on First Philosophy,* pp. 149-71.

19. However provocative this statement may seem at first, it is simply another way of articulating the basic Kantian thesis that the noumena, things in themselves, *cannot be* the proper object of knowledge, and that the formal aspect of the phenomena, which is what constitutes their intelligibility, derives *simply* from the subject's spontaneous activity.

pure spontaneity of reason. Indeed, the experience of the sublime — which is the moment in Kant's philosophy wherein the supersensible seems to impose itself most insistently — is, strictly speaking, not an experience at all, insofar as experience entails a moment of receptivity. As Kant remarks in the Third Critique, *because* the sublime is infinite, it cannot be encountered anywhere in the world, and turns out to be reason's "encounter" with itself.[20] We are reminded of Hölderlin's shock in stirring from a dream in which he believed he was encountering the glory of Nature herself face to face, but woke up alone: "es ist, als fühlt' ich ihn, den Geist der Welt, wie eines Freundes warme Hand, aber ich erwache und meine, ich habe meine eignen Finger gehalten."[21]

What looks like the in-breaking of the radically Other is in fact the moment of the purest introspection. For Kant, reason by its very definition *cannot* be moved by its other. The infinite, which would seem to challenge the soul's *a priori* conditions of possibility, in the end reinforces them all the more decisively, albeit at a different level. It is therefore no surprise that Kant explicitly affirms the impossibility of genuine supernatural revelation: "It sounds questionable," he says in *Religion within the Limits of Reason Alone,* "but it is in no way reprehensible to say that everyone makes his own God."[22] He makes this claim because we would not be able to recognize the revealed God as God unless he corresponded to our *a priori* notion of what it means to be God. Revelation can be true only if it reveals to us *what we already know.* Here we meet Meno's paradox again, though perhaps in a more ruthless form. For Kant, "revealed" religion has value only insofar as it aids in the understanding of natural religion, which is religion determined by reason's *a priori* and thus immanent horizon.

Now, although Kant represents an extreme form of the rationalism

20. "[T]rue sublimity must be sought only in the mind of the judging person, not in the natural object the judging of which prompts this mental attunement" (Kant, *Critique of Judgment,* trans. Werner Pluhar [Indianapolis: Hackett, 1987], p. 113 [Ak. 256]).

21. "It is as if I were touching the very spirit of the world, like a friend's warm hand, but I awoke and realized that I was only clutching my own finger." Friedrich Hölderlin, *Hyperion,* vol. 1, bk. 1, in *Sämtliche Werke und Briefe,* vol. 1 (Darmstadt: Wissenschaftliche Buchgesellschaft, 1998), p. 618.

22. Kant, *Religion within the Limits of Reason Alone,* trans. Theodore M. Greene and Hoyt H. Hudson (New York: Harper & Row, 1960), p. 157. It is interesting to note that Fichte's first, and anonymous, publication, the *Attempt at a Critique of All Revelation* (1792), which reduces God's will to reason's own moral law and allows a "sensuous" revelation only in relation to those whose corrupt nature keeps them from following that law, was initially thought to be written by Kant, and was in any event fully endorsed by him.

that necessarily excludes the possibility of an intelligible revelation, I hope this brief account shows that he in fact simply brings to clear expression a problem left unresolved in many more classical epistemologies, at least as they are conventionally interpreted, because it is, when all is said and done, simply an extraordinarily difficult philosophical question: How, indeed, can reason have a capacity for what lies beyond its capacity? It should equally be apparent that this question in fact concerns not merely a particular use of reason — i.e., the way reason functions in fundamental theology — but the very nature of reason, and therefore reason in all of its functions, in every single one of its acts: if reason is capable of understanding revelation without destroying its revelational character, it can only be because it is capable in principle of being beyond itself, and this capacity would have implications for all of its activities. We sketched this conception of reason in the previous chapter. The question of reason in fundamental theology turns out to be a paradigm for the more global question that Rousselot once referred to simply as "the problem of knowledge": "whether and how a being can be conscious of that which is not itself."[23] If this is true, we can see why Balthasar's approach to truth in view of the specifically theological question would also have exciting implications for philosophy in general. Let us now turn to look at this approach directly.

A Dramatic Conception

To sketch the basic contours of Balthasar's proposal, we will consider only two governing principles, the mother's smile and the identity of freedom and form in the *Gestalt,* and then see why these principles entail what we might call a "dramatic" structure of truth.

A common response in twentieth-century thought to what is referred to as the Cartesian problem — namely, the difficulty of accounting for the mind's capacity to make contact with the world, which is its "other" — is to dissolve the problem by affirming that consciousness itself is nothing but the world as manifest to me. In other words, the self is always already in contact with the world, and develops its own immanent structures from first to last only from within this contact. If this is indeed the case, the problem of the soul's transcending itself to its other finds a solution even before it arises. We

23. Pierre Rousselot, *The Problem of Love in the Middle Ages: A Historical Contribution,* trans. Alan Vincelette (Milwaukee: Marquette University Press, 2001), p. 76.

find versions of this response, for example, in both Thomism and phenomenology.[24] While in these philosophies, the intention is primarily to preserve (more or less successfully) an epistemological realism, for Balthasar — and indeed for the question of fundamental theology we are considering — the aim goes deeper: namely, to preserve an abiding *otherness* in the completed act of knowledge even within the soul's union with its object. It is possible to argue that this deeper aim is ultimately necessary even for a consistent realism. However that may be, while Balthasar agrees with this typical way of approaching the problem in principle, he roots the soul's contact with the world in a more fundamental "contact," one that gives everything else a particular coloring: namely, the mother's smile. As deceptively simple as it seems, this principle is arguably the foundation of Balthasar's epistemology, and fits essentially with the primacy of beauty that we will discuss in the following chapter.

"The little child awakens to self-consciousness through being addressed by the love of his mother," Balthasar writes in the first sentence of his essay, "Movement Toward God."[25] The personal gesture that the mother addresses to the child is what gives rise to his capacity to respond in kind. The view of consciousness implied in this exchange differs fundamentally from Kant's insofar as it affirms that the soul's conditions of possibility are not fixed prior to and thus independent of the (receptive) encounter with what is other than consciousness, but instead *occurs* in the encounter. The conditions of possibility arise, as it were, not wholly from below, but as a gift from above, which, precisely *because* of its generosity, creates the space for the "from below" capacity to receive it.[26] In other words, because the mother's smile is a gesture of love that "welcomes" the other, her child, it does not impose itself as an opaque and indeed violent demand, but as an enabling invitation:

24. See, e.g., Robert Sokolowski, *Introduction to Phenomenology* (Cambridge: Cambridge University Press, 2000), pp. 8-16; cf. Josef Pieper, *Wahrheit der Dinge* (München: Kösel-Verlag, 1947), pp. 70-71.

25. Hans Urs von Balthasar, "Movement Toward God," in *Explorations in Theology*, vol. 3: *Creator Spirit* (San Francisco: Ignatius Press, 1993), pp. 15-55.

26. It is important to note that the child cannot be lacking altogether in a prior capacity to receive the mother's smile — or else the smile would never, in fact, reach him intelligibly. As we will clarify below, there *is* a prior capacity, but this capacity is by its nature a capacity to be surprised, which is to say that the prior capacity *cannot* suffice on its own to account for the possibility of encounter (as it necessarily does in Kant). It is, after all, a capacity that is originally and ontologically receptive: it is received from God, and also from the parents, and the former reception is mediated through the latter.

> Since, however, the child in this process replies and responds to a directive that cannot in any way have come from within its own self — it would never occur to the child that it itself had produced the mother's smile — the entire paradise of reality that unfolds around the "I" stands there as an incomprehensible miracle: it is not thanks to the gracious favor of the "I" that space and the world exist, but thanks to the gracious favor of the "Thou." And if the "I" is permitted to walk upon the ground of reality and to cross the distances to reach the other, this is due to an original favor bestowed on him, something for which, a priori, the "I" will never find the sufficient reason in himself.[27]

But the mother, through her smile, does not invite the child merely into a personal relationship with her; rather, as the passage just cited suggests, she welcomes him literally into the world, i.e., into reality more generally. Balthasar specifies the gradual unfolding of this event of the awakening of consciousness in an especially dense and endlessly rich section from the fifth volume of *The Glory of the Lord,* called the "miracle of being and the fourfold distinction."[28] While we cannot enter into the complexities of these pages here, we ought nevertheless to extract the salient point in relation to our present concerns. The child's first experience of both self and world in his mother's embrace is *simultaneously* personal and ontological, it is simultaneously historical/phenomenological and metaphysical. Here we see what Balthasar's starting point adds to the common response to the Cartesian problem alluded to above. It is said that the soul does not need to find a bridge to reality, because it is always already "in" the world, and its self-consciousness develops in tandem with its knowledge of the world. But this response generates the problem from the other direction: if the "bridge" problem is solved by denying the difference — i.e., by *identifying* the self and the other in the act of knowing — one is led to ask how to salvage an abiding *difference.* In other words, reason is *still* in this case incapable of being surprised, because it accommodates contact by affirming that the contact has always already been made. Incidentally, we may suggest that Heidegger's *Ereignis* ends up in the same predicament, insofar as he interprets the essential reciprocal "belonging" together of being and the human essence as consisting ultimately in a nothingness in which all differences are eliminated.[29]

27. Balthasar, "Movement Toward God," p. 16.

28. Balthasar, *GL5*, pp. 613-27.

29. Martin Heidegger, *Zur Seinsfrage* (Frankfurt am Main: Klostermann, 1956), p. 28.

For Balthasar, by contrast, because the original event in which consciousness is constituted is *personal* as well as ontological, the true identity that occurs between the soul and being does so at the very same time within the irreducible and generous opposition of freedoms.[30] Indeed, the difference of the opposition makes the unity possible and vice versa; the unity and difference are inseparable and irreducible aspects of the very same event. Moreover, from the beginning — a beginning that is never more to be left behind — being has a personal face, and the personal always has an ontological depth, or to use Plato's language, love both is and is not "beyond being," because being and love have from the beginning acquired their meaning only in relation to one another.[31] The importance of this simultaneity cannot be overstated; we will return to it below.

The second crucial principle in Balthasar's understanding of truth is the identity of form and freedom in the *Gestalt*. We will elaborate further the significance of the notion of *Gestalt* in chapter four. Here, we note that *Gestalt* represents the inseparable objective correlate of the awakening of consciousness in the mother's smile. If, as we shall see, Balthasar insists on beauty as the starting point for thought,[32] it is because he thinks of *form* not in the first place as abstract, universal essence, say, but rather paradigmatically as the concrete, brimming *Gestalt*, a visible manifestation of nonappearing depths, in which the particular and the universal, the sensible and the supersensible, the outward and the inward, the historical and the transcendent, are all bound together at once.[33]

This *Gestalt* is intelligible insofar as it possesses an irreducible unity that gathers up its constitutive "parts" or aspects into a meaningful whole, and yet precisely for the same reason, this intelligibility is inescapably concrete. The "meaning" is not simply a concept that the soul abstracts and

30. "Opposition," here, is not meant in the negative sense; rather, the word indicates the fact that the two freedoms "face" one another.

31. Balthasar, following Gustav Siewerth, differs in a subtle, but significant way from Jean-Luc Marion on this point. While Marion characterizes love as "beyond being," or indeed "without being" (cf. *God without Being* [Chicago: University of Chicago Press, 1991]), Balthasar insists that such a self-transcendence is in fact being's highest act. Thus, the transcendence is *not* simply outside of being, but is contained within it; however paradoxical it may seem, being *itself* is "beyond being." On this, see the two important footnotes in *TL2*, pp. 134-35, n. 10, and 177, n. 9. We will return to this point repeatedly at various places in the present book.

32. Balthasar typically insists on this for specifically *theological* thinking, but we will argue in the next chapter that it holds analogously for all thinking.

33. See *GL1*, pp. 117-19.

internalizes "according to the mode of the knower." Rather, as a *manifestation* of meaning, it lies in a decisive way "outside" of the soul, and calls upon the soul to conform itself to *it*, the concrete *Gestalt.* We see here the importance of the imagination, which we will discuss in chapter five. The fact that the manifestation of meaning lies in some respect beyond the soul does not make it for all that inaccessible. To the contrary, it *is* accessible, but only to a soul that can be "transported" outside of itself in order to enter into it. The act of understanding, then, requires the soul's self-transcendence, and in this act the difference between spontaneity and receptivity effectively falls away: the soul *receives* the meaning of the *Gestalt* by indwelling it, which means by moving "spontaneously" beyond its prior state — or, if you will, its preconceived expectations.

Although it is principally to Goethe that Balthasar claims he is indebted for his notion of the beautiful, organic *Gestalt,* we might in the present context draw on its connection with Schiller in order to understand why *Gestalt* represents the unity of freedom/spirit and form, and the significance of this unity. In his *Letters on the Aesthetic Education of Man,* Schiller defines beauty as the "living form," that is, as the determinate manifestation of freedom.[34] What he means by freedom seems related to the "light" that gives a beautiful form its radiance, insofar as they both indicate a kind of center or ground that, because it is capable of integrating all of the parts of a form into a whole, necessarily transcends those parts. But the connection between freedom and form allows us to see that the *Gestalt* that Balthasar intends here is neither (simply) the Platonic *eidos,* nor the scholastic *forma;* it is not an eternally immobile quantity or quality, not a mere content of the intellect — if that is in any event an adequate understanding of *eidos* in the first place — but includes, for example, the concrete shape of a life or the intelligible wholeness of an action or an event.

Let us return to our prior discussion of the awakening of consciousness as an illustration, and in order to see the implications of this point more concretely. When the mother smiles at her child, she is in fact presenting him with a *Gestalt* in which she makes her person accessible to him as a loving gift. The gesture is not simply an opaque picture, which can adequately be read as it were "off the surface." Instead, the whole has a *meaning* because of "something" that is both not any particular part of what she shows him and

34. See the Fifteenth Letter from the *Letters on the Aesthetic Education of Man,* trans. Elizabeth Wilkinson and L. A. Willoughby, in Friedrich Schiller, *Essays,* ed. Walter Hinderer and Daniel Dahlstrom (New York: Continuum, 2001), pp. 127-32.

at the same time transparently present everywhere within it, namely, *herself,* i.e., her freedom. This freedom is what makes the smile radiant, or in other words genuinely beautiful. The intelligibility of this event is thus grounded in this center that is both above and within the sensible phenomena.

Now, this smile is clearly not merely an image but at the same time a gesture, an action. Because the action, moreover, is a personal address, it can be received only through a reciprocating response. The child has not understood the smile, received its intelligible form, *until* it responds with a smile of its own, or better, only *in* its smiling. The child's smile is the reception of the mother's smile, which means: the child's return gift of freedom is its reception of the mother's gift of the same. What this implies, in turn, is that the ecstatic moment of action is not something that comes simply before or after understanding, but is an intrinsic part of the understanding itself. If it is true, as Aquinas says following Aristotle, that the true is the soul's taking the object into itself while the good is the soul's movement beyond itself toward its object, then for Balthasar, as we shall see at greater length in the next two chapters, these two moments are joined together in beauty, and the true itself depends on the soul's ecstatic movement toward the good.[35] All of this follows from identifying the concrete *Gestalt,* rather than simple abstract essence, as the intelligibility sought by understanding.

We are now in a position to see why such a view of the soul's grasp of truth deserves to be called "dramatic."[36] According to Aristotle, the plot of a good drama involves a reversal and a discovery, or we might say a "surprise" and a "resolution."[37] The sequence of events that constitute a drama does not proceed in a merely linear fashion, "one damn thing after another," as someone once wittily described history. Instead, we say that a plot *unfolds,* which makes sense only if the events that constitute the plot possess an intrinsic and intelligible inter-ordering. Such an organic unity, in turn, re-

35. Anton E. van Hooff is right to insist that the object of fundamental theology is not an abstract idea but a "humano-divine action," and that an object of this sort entails an appropriate method. "Facticité et argumentation: Réflexions sur la méthode en théologie fondamentale," *Recherches de science religieuse* 86, no. 4 (1998): 549-58. Van Hooff draws on Blondel to propose the concrete mediation of action, a solution similar in spirit to the "dramatic" notion of reason we are describing here.

36. The aspect of drama we elaborate here is only the one that relates directly to the problem at hand, and by no means claims to do justice to the whole of Balthasar's theory. The exceedingly rich diversity of aspects that enter into the dramatic analogy can be found in a long section called "Elements of the Dramatic," in *TD1,* pp. 259-478.

37. Aristotle, *Poetics* 11.

quires some key turn of events, some moment of decision, which ties together the disparate parts into a meaningful whole. When the drama is successful, this moment takes us by surprise, it evokes astonishment, not only because we sense the fateful significance of the moment, but also because the moment is not simply the mechanical product of the preceding events. At the same time, however, the turn of events is not *merely* a surprise, because it serves to give meaning to the plot as a whole, and thus to bring to light the significance of all the other aspects of the plot. There is a discontinuity that nevertheless preserves a continuity, though that continuity gets recast by the dramatic reversal. In contrast to predominantly physiological readings of the effects of tragedy, Goethe offered a new interpretation of the mysterious word "catharsis" in Aristotle's famous definition in relation to the objective structure of the plot: it designates, he explains, the resolution of the pity and fear generated by the drama's action, the "untying" of the knot.[38]

Now, in relation to the matter at hand, it is interesting to consider the trajectory of the expectations in the spectacle of drama. In order for there to be a genuine surprise, it is necessary for the prior events to generate a state of anticipation, which means that they must already possess an intelligible form or meaning. At the same time, however, the moment of reversal cannot simply be deducible from the prior events: it has to interrupt the claim, thwart or even shatter the expectations. But — and this is the key — the moment cannot shatter the dramatic form of the whole without undermining the very surprise it initially effected. Instead, this reversal must recast the meaning of the parts and the anticipation they produced in a manner that brings them all to a definitive fulfillment. Here is the great paradox of great drama: anticipation is fulfilled by what it cannot have expected; the turn of events that "shatters" the progressively developing intelligible form ends up crystallizing that very form in a startlingly radiant whole. The form does not become less intelligible by the disruption, but in fact it becomes far more intelligible than one could have anticipated at the outset or along the way.

Drama, thus described, provides a powerful metaphor for the act of knowledge, as Balthasar characterizes it. The paradox of the dramatic recasting of intelligible form would be an affront to the structure of consciousness only if we viewed consciousness as deriving its capacity for the reception of

38. See "On Interpreting Aristotle's *Poetics* (1827)," in Goethe, *The Collected Works,* vol. 3: *Essays on Art and Literature,* trans. Ellen and Ernest von Nardroff (Princeton: Princeton University Press, 1986), pp. 197-99.

its object solely from within its immanent potentialities, however they may be conceived regarding their details. In this case, the advent of the object to be known must already correspond to the anticipations or else simply have no place of entry. There can be no fundamental surprise within such a perspective; the mind can receive only what it is in some sense already prepared to receive. We could therefore say that, according to their usual interpretations, traditional epistemologies are constitutionally undramatic.

The principle of the mother's smile, however, offers a contrast on precisely this point. If it is the case, as Balthasar proposes, that the spontaneous activity of consciousness — i.e., the child's initial human act, his smile — arises as a gift in the reception of his mother's initiating act, then surprise is, as it were, built into the very heart of consciousness. The potential for the reception of the mother's smile does not precede that address as an *a priori* condition of possibility but arrives *with* that address; it is part of the original gift itself.[39] The child does not expect to be able to respond to his mother before she addresses him, and indeed the capacity to do so is not simply latent within him like a switch waiting to be flipped on. Rather, he finds himself responding to her in the very moment he grasps her address. We can thus affirm the Aristotelian/Thomistic principle that act precedes potency without already anticipating all possible actualities within the soul's immanent capacities, for now the act that precedes potency occurs as an event, a simultaneously immanent and transcendent encounter, in which the soul is already outside of itself in its reception of its other.

It is helpful to see how this proposal differs from the postmodern notion of "impossibility." Jean-Luc Marion, for example, describes God as "strictly impossible for man," meaning that man does not possess an *a priori* capacity for revelation.[40] If he did, it would no longer be revelation in the proper sense. Thus, the actuality of revelation precedes the possibility for it, which means that, prior to the event, revelation is "impossible." What we are describing in Balthasar, here, is similar to Marion, but the differences, though subtle, are crucial. In the first place, Balthasar would not describe the event as *impossible* before the actuality, for doing so would take as given the nonactuality of revelation, which amounts to *defining* this condition apart

39. More accurately, as we saw above, we would have to say that the child possesses certain capacities that prepare him, not specifically for the smile, but for the *surprise* that he cannot simply anticipate. The child receives the *a priori* condition of the possibility of reception.

40. See Jean-Luc Marion, "The Impossible for Man — God," in *Transcendence and Beyond: A Postmodern Inquiry*, ed. John D. Caputo and Michael J. Scanlon (Bloomington: Indiana University Press, 2007), pp. 14-43.

from revelation, or in other words making the exclusion of revelation something essential to it. This makes the closure to revelation part of the definition of the prior condition. The paradox we are describing, by contrast, would reject the alternative of possible or impossible *a priori.* Instead, it would insist — in a manner we will elaborate especially in chapter nine — that the encounter *gives* the *prior* conditions of possibility, so that there is a genuine anticipation even if this does not compromise the surprise. The primacy of beauty, moreover, is crucial here, as we will see in chapter three. Second, while Marion makes the event of revelation an incomparable case, arguably in the manner of Karl Barth, for Balthasar, as we have been insisting, this paradox occurs in an analogous way in every single act of consciousness.

We thus break open the paradox that confounded Meno: the soul anticipates its object, but because that object is not derivable from the soul itself, its anticipation gets recast in the encounter, so that its anticipation is simultaneously surprised and fulfilled. In this respect, the strangely satisfying upheaval that one experiences in great drama turns out to be — surprise! — not an exception to the normal act of cognition, but in fact simply a particularly intense instance of what occurs in every act of knowing whatever insofar as every act is the soul's grasping, and being grasped by, what is other than the soul itself.

Moreover, it becomes evident from what has been said that the act of knowledge is never a merely intellectual act. As we saw above, in Balthasar's understanding, the form to be known is not ultimately an abstract essence alone, but a concrete *Gestalt* that necessarily includes, but is not reducible to, its intelligible structure. Here again we see the significance of drama, which we sketch here but will elaborate in the chapter that follows. The soul must move beyond itself to receive its object, that is, to enter into and conform itself to that object. If the soul, then, does not simply take the object into itself according to its prior capacity, its pre-given mode of reception, but truly conforms itself to the object, it must receive the capacity for the object in some sense from the encounter: the movement is initiated by the object. But to respond to this call by the object, the soul cannot be passive (i.e., *merely* receptive), but must actively consent to the movement; it must contribute an act of the will. This spontaneity on the part of the soul, then, is not *merely* spontaneous but is a constitutive aspect of a more comprehensive receptivity. This is why the soul's spontaneity is not an imposition on the object — as it necessarily is, for example, for Kant.[41] But precisely because the sponta-

41. It is for this reason, in fact, that Kant posits an absolute distinction between

neity is an aspect of a more basic receptivity, the active anticipation it entails does not unilaterally determine the object's final meaning. Instead, the expectation is surprised by that meaning, and precisely in the surprise finds its expectation fulfilled, insofar as it sought to know the object — its other — and not merely itself or its own experience. The moment in which the soul moves beyond itself is the moment in which the object finally discloses itself.

The intellectual grasp of meaning thus turns out to be an irreducibly distinct part of a more comprehensive whole, which includes a perceptive, affective, and volitional dimension as well. Here, I believe, we can understand the significance of the order of Balthasar's trilogy, which we will explore in the next chapter: first, the experience of the form which calls forth a response: beauty; then, the will's contribution, the moment of decision and action: the good; and finally, the unveiling of the meaning of the whole, which is both anticipated and beyond all expectations: the true.[42] We are generally accustomed to think of the dramatic moment in Balthasar's work as specifically theological, that is, as the encounter of divine and human freedom. But if this moment itself is to be at all intelligible, we must understand that every cognitional act — insofar as it involves the advent of a meaning that includes the soul's capacity without being reducible to it — is something like an encounter between two freedoms. There is, in other words, from the outset an analogy between the theological and the properly philosophical act, and indeed between the act of faith and every use of the intellect, even the most rudimentary.

The Gift of Understanding and the Leap of Reason

Let us now return to the problem of fundamental theology with which we began. In order to affirm its genuine gratuity, revelation must be in some basic

---

noumena and phenomena: taking for granted that the understanding effectively constructs its object, Kant avoids idealism by insisting that we do not in fact know the thing itself, but only our experience of it. See *Prolegomena to Any Future Metaphysics,* trans. Gary Hatfield (Cambridge: Cambridge University Press, 1997), pp. 40-41.

42. On this, see the section titled "Dramatic Theory between Aesthetics and Logic," in *TD1,* pp. 15-23. The notion that, at the center of revelation lies not *merely* an aesthetic/intelligible form, but in fact a *deed,* and thus that dramatic engagement lies at the center of the response to revelation, suggests the possible inadequacy of a merely aesthetic approach. See, e.g., David Bentley Hart, *The Beauty of the Infinite: The Aesthetics of Christian Truth* (Grand Rapids: Eerdmans, 2003).

sense discontinuous with the demands of human thought. But in order to affirm the integrity of reason and its natural aspiration to ultimacy, there must be some continuity between reason in its "natural" functions and reason in its grasp of revealed truth. *Prima facie,* we seem to be facing a straightforward contradiction: How can discontinuity and continuity be anything but mutually exclusive? But we cannot resolve the problem of fundamental theology unless we can affirm both at the same time, and we cannot affirm both unless we have something like a dramatic understanding of truth as the foundation not only for fundamental theology, but for all thinking.

The simultaneity of continuity and discontinuity is the very definition of drama.[43] The event of revelation — and we might say the advent of grace, the moment of the act of faith — can take reason wholly by surprise, even shatter its expectations, demand a rethinking of everything it previously thought from top to bottom, and yet remain perfectly rational, or indeed show itself to be even more intensely rational, on one condition only: that it is the very nature of reason in its normal, everyday constitution, to be taken by surprise. If this is the case, then on the one hand no matter how discontinuous revelation is with respect to the "horizon of human reason," no matter how radically surprising, it will represent a fulfillment of what reason is by nature. Insofar as reason in its natural functions aspires to know what is other than itself, it expects to be "overturned" to some degree — as slight as the reversal may happen to be in ordinary circumstances — by the object it seeks to know. And in aspiring to ultimacy, it naturally aspires to be overturned by what is ultimate.[44] On the other hand, this reversal, though it corresponds in some respect to the nature of reason, is in no way reducible to the immanent structure of reason, because what reason itself demands is in fact the priority of its irreducibly other: in the natural order, it is the priority of the object to be known, and in the supernatural order, it is the priority of

43. And we might add that it is also the very essence of analogy as defined by Lateran IV: similarity within a greater dissimilarity. The line of argument in this chapter suggests, indeed, that a proper view of analogy requires a dramatic sense of truth, and that drama might therefore provide a test for analogy in one's thinking: To what extent does one simply carry over some aspect of one's thinking from one term to the other (univocally) without an intrinsic reversal? The doctrine of analogy reveals the inadequacy of the view that insists on "clarifying concepts" philosophically, and then applying them within theology.

44. Here we see an epistemological version of the paradoxical relationship between nature and grace that de Lubac articulated in his interpretation of Aquinas: the human being naturally desires something that surpasses human nature, namely, the supernatural invitation to share in God's triune life. See *The Mystery of the Supernatural* (New York: Crossroad, 1998).

faith. There is thus something analogous to faith operating in every act of reason, which is precisely why its being surprised by faith is a perfection of its nature.[45] Faith corresponds, we might say, by not corresponding. We will return to the relationship between faith and reason in our final chapter.

Moreover, the same paradox explains how Christianity can lay claim to the assent of reason, can lay claim, in fact, to the very roots of reason, while at the same time arriving as a sheer gift of grace. Understood dramatically, the inner spontaneity of consciousness is constituted in the advent of a gift, namely, the mother's smile. If this is the case, the advent of revelation, as a gift from above, recapitulates the constitutive aspiration of reason and in this sense directly "speaks to" reason in its most inward core precisely as an unanticipated event.

This simultaneity has two further implications. First of all, at the outset of this chapter, we insinuated that far from being difficult to reconcile, the integrity of reason in its encounter with revelation and the gratuity of revelation *require* one another, so that we cannot affirm either without affirming both. To the extent that reason aims at understanding, it aims at attaining an object that is in some sense other than itself. There is therefore some degree of self-transcendence demanded of reason for the completion of its most basic acts. But such a self-transcendence requires a moment of discontinuity and therefore gratuity. In this respect, the encounter with revelation turns out to be, not a limit question that can be attended to *after* reason has figured out how knowledge of the world is possible, but the paradigm that is approximated in all of its acts. Thus, the gratuity of revelation is intrinsic to, constitutive of, the integrity of reason, whether it be the revelation of being in its natural self-disclosure or the revelation of the triune God in history.

On the other hand, revelation can be gratuitous, that is, it can be a surprise, only in relation to a reason that in fact aspires to ultimacy, and that means only in relation to an integral conception of reason. Surprise requires expectation. One can impose oneself from the outside, "from above," on an inanimate object, but one cannot surprise it. If we think of the constitutive aspiration of reason from the beginning in dramatic terms, we no longer need to affirm an inverse relation between expectation and surprise. To the contrary, the deeper one's anticipations, the greater one's capacity for surprise. As Heraclitus said long ago, "Whoever does not expect will not dis-

45. According to Aquinas, "All knowing beings know God implicitly in whatever they know." *De ver.* 22.2ad1.

cover the unexpected."[46] The gratuity of revelation in some sense "depends on" the integrity of reason.

The second implication concerns the operation of reason within the revealed order, within theology itself. We typically think of the problem of the encounter between reason and revelation as essentially a "bridge" problem: Can reason appropriate revelation, and if so, how? The terms in which this problem is articulated prepare what may be an even more serious difficulty once the problem finds its resolution. If reason *can* appropriate revelation, does its appropriation eliminate the gratuity and thus render revelation mundane?[47] Is it therefore the case that what we understand of revelation has now entered into the immanent system of rational necessity, while we can yet be surprised only by what has not yet been appropriated? If this is the case, faith is a reality only *in via*, and just so far a provisional imperfection that will be eliminated *in fine*. But St. Paul affirmed faith as one of the three theological virtues that "will abide." Once again, the significance of a dramatic sense of truth becomes apparent. We need only oppose faith and reason if we interpret reason wholly in terms of immanent potentialities and conditions of possibility. In this case, reason can appropriate only by eliminating the "otherness" of its object. If reason is constituted dramatically, by contrast, the more it internalizes, the more it is expropriated and joyfully immersed in a luminous mystery.[48] Faith therefore need never lose its character of surprise in theology, even in the most rigorous and penetrating of rational reflections. It is not, then, only the apologist's dialogue partner who ought to expect to be surprised, but also and first of all the theologian himself.

In conclusion, let us consider a possible objection from the philosophical side: while we may have articulated a notion of reason that can accommodate the demands of theology, someone could argue, we have done so at the cost of severing any continuity with the philosophical tradition. In other words, can we really claim to do justice to reason's demands if, after all, we have to formulate what seems to be a novel conception of reason precisely in

46. Hermann Diels and Walter Kranz, *Die Fragmente der Vorsokratiker* (Zürich: Weidmann, 1985), p. 18.

47. "L'assunzione del *novum*, non si limita al dato rivelato, ma prosegue nella sua stessa comprehensione che si sviluppa nel corso dei secoli" [Appropriation of the *novum* does not stop at what has been revealed, but continues as it is more deeply understood through the centuries] (R. Fisichella, "Oportet Philosophari in Theologia (II)," *Gregorianum* 76, no. 3 [1995]: 503-34; here, 528).

48. "Finally the knowledge faith offers does not destroy the mystery. Rather it makes it more evident and proves it to be almost a necessary element in human life" (*Fides et ratio*, 13).

order to meet those demands?[49] I propose that this objection can itself be answered *dramatically.* While the vision of reason we can distill from Balthasar's work does indeed present a certain novelty, and therefore discontinuity, with respect to the philosophical tradition, it also turns out to confirm that tradition, to recast the epistemologies of previous thinkers in a way that fulfills them. This fulfillment is perhaps easiest to see with respect to Aristotle and Aquinas: we can affirm that truth is the actualization of a prior potentiality in the soul while insisting that this potentiality is nevertheless in some sense a gift of the truth itself, and likewise we can affirm that truth is an "adequation" between the mind and thing while insisting that the capacity for adequation is given in part by the thing.

But is the dramatic notion of truth simply the opposite of Kant's epistemology? In fact, from a dramatic perspective, we can affirm, with Kant, that the immanent structures of reason and the understanding possess conditions of possibility that establish, so to speak, the horizon *within which* truth takes place, but we must insist on the proper understanding of a horizon. As Hegel argued in response to Kant, a horizon can exist only in relation to what lies beyond it; its limits are defined in a decisive sense by what lies beyond those limits. It is true that there can be no understanding without a "predetermined" limit or horizon because limit and definition are essential to order. But it is the very nature of a limit not to be the final word; the notion of limit itself is unintelligible without the open space into which it is projected — the open space of transcendence and therefore surprise. Revelation, we might say, does not obliterate or ignore the human horizon. Rather, we might better conceive it as the in-breaking of dawn, which needs the world's horizon, and in fact gives that horizon a sharper definition than it could possibly have had at night. Grace will often arrive with a certain irony.

What seems to be the limit between two disciplines turns out to lie close to the center of each, as we will see in this book's concluding chapter. The engagement with fundamental theology becomes an occasion to develop a notion of truth with profound and wide-ranging significance not only for theology, but perhaps even more directly for philosophy. It is a particularly precious occasion in an age that is witnessing a growing contempt for reason and a growing disillusionment regarding its capacity to know.

49. Bernhard Blankenhorn, O.P., raises just such an objection against Balthasar in "Balthasar's Method of Divine Naming," *Nova et Vetera* 1, no. 2 (2003): 245-68.

3 The Primacy of Beauty, the Centrality of Goodness, and the Ultimacy of Truth

"Beginning," observes Hans Urs von Balthasar in the paragraph that opens his sixteen-volume *Trilogy*, "is a problem not only for the thinking person, the philosopher, a problem that remains with him and determines all his subsequent steps; the beginning is also a primal decision which includes all later ones for the person whose life is based on response and decision."[1] It is, in other words, a problem for both the person occupied with the true and the one occupied with the good. The problem, specifically, is to find a starting point ample enough not to preclude from the outset anything that will eventually be necessary in both orders. This problem faces anyone who would wish to affirm a catholic notion of reason, since the aim of such a notion is, we might say, total inclusiveness. What is to be "included," here, is of course not only the realities of the world, but, paradoxically, what cannot be included in any straightforward way as one reality among them, namely, God himself. Balthasar raises this problem as the first consideration in the development of his theology, the primary aim of which is to understand God in the world in a manner that respects God's infinite difference from the world. He responds to this problem with the notion of *beauty*, which, he goes on to explain, represents, on the one hand, the unity of truth and goodness, and, on the other hand, a mysterious point of intersection between the orders of nature and the supernatural. He thus develops a theological aesthetics through a reading of the intellectual history of the West in the seven-volume *The Glory of the Lord* (beauty) to set the stage, as it were, for his five-volume *Theo-Drama* (goodness), which is followed by a three-volume *Theo-Logic* (truth) and a slim *Epilogue*.[2]

1. *GL1*, p. 17.
2. The English publication of Balthasar's *Meisterwerk* is articulated differently from

Balthasar's decision to order his main systematic work around the traditional "transcendental properties of being" — beauty, goodness, and truth[3] — rests on a conviction that these properties are *analogous* in a paradigmatic sense, that is, that they may be used meaningfully to describe both God and the world without compromising God's radical transcendence. We might, in this respect, call them "catholic": "If there is an insurmountable distance between God and his creature, but if there is also an analogy between them that cannot be resolved in any form of identity, there must also exist an analogy between the transcendentals — between those of the creature and those in God."[4] Such a conviction has a firm basis in the Christian tradition: not only does Aquinas mention them as proper names for God which have significance also for creatures, as distinct from metaphorical language that is founded first on the created order,[5] but the terms

---

the original German, which presents the aesthetics in just three volumes (the latter two of which being "triple" sized) and the dramatics in four.

3. There is some scholarly dispute, both over whether the beautiful ever belonged to the "medieval canon" of the transcendentals, as it were, and also specifically whether Aquinas ever recognized it as a transcendental. Although two of the three earliest discussions of the transcendentals included it (the *Summa fratris Alexandri,* attributed to Alexander of Hales, and the *Tractatus de transcendentalibus entis conditionibus,* by an unknown author whom some believe to be the young Bonaventure), the third, which became the most influential of the three, by Philip the Chancellor, mentioned only being, one, true, and good. Neither Albert the Great nor the mature Bonaventure included it on his "official" list. As for Aquinas, he also did not include it, though in his later commentary on the *Divine Names* he seems to characterize it in the same way he characterizes the others. There are some, then, who take Aquinas to have embraced beauty as a transcendental, albeit of a peculiar sort: see Francis Kovach, *Die Ästethik des Thomas von Aquin: Eine genetische und systematische Analyse* (Berlin: De Gruyter, 1961); Winfried Czapiewski, *Das Schöne bei Thomas von Aquin* (Freiburg: Herder, 1964); Günther Pöltner, *Schönheit: Eine Untersuchung zum Ursprung des Denkens bei Thomas von Aquin* (Freiburg: Herder, 1978); Jacques Maritain, *Art et scholastique* (Paris: Librairie de l'Art Catholique, 1947); Mark Jordan, "The Grammar of *Esse:* Re-reading Thomas on the Transcendentals," *The Thomist* 44 (1980). One of the most comprehensive studies on Aquinas's notion of the transcendentals, Jan Aertsen, *Medieval Philosophy and the Transcendentals: The Case of Thomas Aquinas* (Leiden: Brill, 1996), refuses to admit beauty onto the list. See also his "Beauty in the Middle Ages: A Forgotten Transcendental?" *Medieval Philosophy and Theology* 1 (1991): 68-97.

4. Hans Urs von Balthasar, *My Work in Retrospect* (San Francisco: Ignatius Press, 1993), p. 115.

5. The reason these stand as "proper names" is that they do not include any imperfection (i.e., limitation) in their definitions and do not imply any dependence on matter. See Aquinas, *De ver.* 2.11. On the difference between the classical "divine names" approach to natural theology and the modern "divine attributes," see Janet Martin Soskice, "Naming

are also presented in Scripture itself as belonging in a particular way to God.[6]

In spite of this foundation, the better part by far of discussions in the twentieth and twenty-first centuries of God's relationship to philosophy and reason's capacity for knowledge of the divine have focused on the question of the *analogy of being.*[7] This preoccupation is no doubt due to two powerful moments in recent intellectual history that have served to reawaken broad interest in the problem of reason's relation to God even as they have narrowed the scope of the problem: from the theological side, there is Karl Barth's vehement rejection of the analogy of being as the "invention of the antichrist" in his endeavor to rethink theology from the ground up in a resolutely christocentric fashion,[8] and from the side of philosophy there is Martin Heidegger's critique of the essential ontotheological constitution of metaphysics, which charges the traditional philosophical thinking of the West with absorbing the divine into a perfectly closed causal system through the identification of God with the being that grounds all beings.[9] To be sure, the analogy of being presents the heart of the problem of reason's relation to God insofar as Aquinas is correct that the other transcendental properties are ultimately derived from being as what is most basic,[10] but it is worth asking, precisely because the transcendental properties thereby represent, as it were, an unfolding of the meaning of being, whether they do not therefore unfold the problem of reason's relation to God into a more ample register.

God: A Study in Faith and Reason," in *Reason and the Reasons of Faith,* ed. Paul J. Griffiths and Reinhard Hütter (New York: T. & T. Clark, 2005), pp. 241-54.

6. This is clearest regarding goodness: see Mark 10:19. Jesus claims truth for himself, and also associates it with the Spirit: John 14:6; John 4:24. On beauty, consider not only Psalm 27:4, but also, as Robert Louis Wilken points out, the prevalence in Scripture of terms such as "glory," "splendor," "light," "image," and "face." *The Spirit of Early Christian Thought* (New Haven: Yale University Press, 2003), p. 20.

7. Erich Przywara's classic treatment, *Analogia Entis,* to be sure, mentions the transcendentals *verum-bonum-pulchrum* as the actualization of the "subjective relation" in his discussion of Aquinas, but they represent a relatively small part of his overall development of the notion. *Analogia Entis. Metaphysik: Ur-Struktur und All-Rhythmus* (Einsiedeln: Johannes Verlag, 1962), pp. 180-84. (English translation, Grand Rapids: Eerdmans, forthcoming 2013).

8. See his "Preface" to the first volume of the *Church Dogmatics* (New York: Continuum, 2009).

9. Martin Heidegger, "The Onto-theo-logical Constitution of Metaphysics," in *Identity and Difference,* trans. Joan Stambaugh (Chicago: University of Chicago Press, 1969), pp. 42-76. We will discuss this essay at length in chapter eight.

10. *De ver.* 1.1.

How, in other words, does the question of reason's relation to God appear when thought through the nature of beauty, goodness, and truth rather than simply through the analogy of being?

There would be a number of ways to approach this question — one might, for example, explore more fully the biblical evidence for these names of God or interpret the perichoresis of the transcendentals as an image of the Trinity[11] — but one interesting entry into the theme is to reflect philosophically on the nature of these transcendentals in the light of their analogical adequacy, so to speak, for Balthasar's general theological project in the *Trilogy*. Even more specifically, it is worth asking, again from a philosophical perspective, what significance lies in the unconventional order in which Balthasar places these properties: Why beauty first, goodness second, and truth last? As we will see, this ordering is in fact crucial to the analogical role Balthasar gives to the transcendentals, and so crucial for a catholic notion of reason.

But in raising this question, we immediately encounter a problem. In the opening section of the *Trilogy* we cited above, Balthasar goes on to say that the philosopher, in contrast to the theologian on this point, "cannot" begin with beauty, "but can at best conclude with it (always assuming that he has not forgotten it underway)."[12] This seems to suggest that the ordering Balthasar presents has a theological, but *not* a philosophical, justification, and, indeed, in one of the main places that Balthasar explicitly comments on the particular ordering he follows in the *Trilogy*, he explains it in specifically theological terms.[13] On the other hand, however, excluding philosophy on this particular point would contradict the intrinsic role that Balthasar consistently gives, throughout his work, to philosophy in theology, and would seem to turn against Balthasar the very criticism he himself raises of Barth's position on the analogy of being.[14] It is not enough to say, in light of the text

11. See Juan Sara, "Knowledge, the Transcendentals, and Community," *Communio* 28 (2001): 505-32.

12. *GL1*, p. 17. Cf. *My Work*, p. 80: "But for the great thinkers of the West . . . beauty is the last comprehensive attribute of all-embracing being as such, its last mysterious radiance." Balthasar's judgment, which he does not justify here, may reflect his observation later that philosophy, in contrast to theology, has to begin with the "barest concepts." See *TL2*, p. 23.

13. Balthasar, *TD1*, pp. 15-23.

14. On the significance Balthasar gives to philosophy in relation to theology, see Martin Bieler, "Meta-anthropology and Christology: On the Philosophy of Hans Urs von Balthasar," *Communio* 20 (1993): 129-46. In his book on Barth, Balthasar raises the question whether Barth's exclusive centering of analogy on Christology leaves any room for analogy to have any meaning outside of Christology. *The Theology of Karl Barth* (San Francisco:

cited, that beauty represents the point at which philosophy ends and theology begins, in the sense that theology would pick up precisely where philosophy leaves off, for this would abandon the two spheres to a merely extrinsic relationship.[15] Rather, whatever *de facto* truth there may be regarding philosophy's tendency to overlook beauty, Balthasar's aim in the *Trilogy* would fail if a specifically philosophical account of his ordering principle were impossible. Balthasar briefly suggests such an account in his concluding *Epilogue*, but does not develop it in detail.[16]

The purpose of the present chapter, then, is precisely to develop such an account according to the relationship between being and the human soul that is designated by each of the properties, by showing how Balthasar's characterization of the phenomenon of beauty at the beginning of the *Trilogy* can be extended into the spheres of goodness and truth.[17] It should be noted that, by virtue of the nature of the theme at hand, what will be offered here is a philosophical argument for the "fittingness" of the order, rather than an argument for its necessity (as if the order presented here is the only one possible). It will be shown to be "fitting" both as an account of reason's encounter with its object and specifically in relation to the problem of opening reason up from within to God in a manner that does not compromise

---

Ignatius Press, 1992), p. 55. I take him to mean that the exclusion of a specifically philosophical sense of analogy empties in fact the significance of Christology, because the meaning disclosed in Christ can no longer resonate, as it were, beyond him.

15. Paul Gilbert seems to move in this direction in "L'articulation des transcendentaux selon Hans Urs von Balthasar," *Revue Thomiste* 86 (1986): 616-29, in which he addresses the question why Balthasar, in the structure of the *Trilogy*, reverses the order he had presented in his early text, *Wahrheit der Welt* (which was eventually republished as volume 1 of the *Theo-Logic*). There, the order given is: truth, goodness, beauty (which, incidentally, follows his early mentor Erich Przywara). Gilbert explains that Balthasar's different approaches can be explained as a transition from the transcendentals as an unfolding of *esse commune* in the first (philosophical) text, and of *esse ipsum subsistens* in the specifically theological work. As *esse subsistens*, God is transcendent and supremely free, so that he initially presents himself to the world as *glorious*.

16. *E*, pp. 83-86. Here, he presents the three transcendentals in primarily metaphysical terms as being's "self-showing," "self-giving," and "self-saying," which forms a hierarchy similar to the classical one of being, life, and intellect. Our aim in the present chapter is to make an argument for Balthasar's ordering more directly along the lines of Aquinas's "anthropological" deduction of the transcendentals in *De ver.* 1.1.

17. Our approach may be said to complement that of Peter Henrici, who sketches out a philosophical *dramatics*, inspired by Blondel, between a philosophy of beauty and of truth. "La dramatique entre l'esthétique et la logique," in *Pour une philosophie chrétienne* (Namur, Belgium: Culture et Vérité, 1983), pp. 109-33.

God's infinite transcendence of the created order. We will proceed, first, by sketching briefly what might be called the traditional ordering of the transcendentals in the *locus classicus,* namely, Aquinas's *De veritate* 1.1 (section I). This will provide a fruitful way to interpret Balthasar's ordering, which will prove to be, not a simple contrasting alternative to the traditional ordering, but a novel approach that nevertheless brings to light a dimension implicit in the traditional order (section II). In our final section (III), we will reflect on the implications of this ordering for the relationship between philosophy and theology.

Circular Logic

Aquinas's most extensive treatment of what came to be called the "transcendentals"[18] occurs at the outset of the *De veritate,* in which he attempts to elucidate the nature of truth.[19] To come to understand what anything is, he explains here, we must re-duce it, lead it back, to its most original principles, which, because of their "intrinsic evidence," do not require any further reduction to something even more intelligible *(oportet fieri reductionem in aliqua principia per se intellectui nota).* The most irreducible of all, because it is the very first thing to fall into the intellect, is being *(ens).* But being can be understood in a variety of ways, the most fundamental of which — unlike the categories, or genera and species — are strictly coextensive with what ex-

18. The term became standard only later. As Aertsen shows, Aquinas himself only uses it sparingly. Aertsen, *Medieval Philosophy and the Transcendentals,* p. 104.

19. Michael Waddell has helpfully observed that, if we recall that this text is not meant as a treatise on the transcendentals *per se,* but rather as a discussion of the nature of truth, we will be less inclined to read it as an exhaustive presentation, and so will allow the possibility that Aquinas would in fact include beauty if he had written a complete treatise on the matter. "Truth or Transcendentals: What *Was* St. Thomas's Intention at *De Veritate* 1.1?" *The Thomist* 67 (2003): 197-219; here, 216. Of course, to open the possibility one must deal with the substantial question of what room it would have, i.e., whether there is a distinct place in Aquinas's conception of the order of the transcendentals. In other words, while Kovach may be right, for instance, that beauty fulfills all the conditions of transcendentality in Aquinas's thought (see Kovach, "The Transcendentality of Beauty in Thomas Aquinas," in *Miscellanea Mediaevalia,* vol. 2: *Die Metaphysik in Mittelalter,* ed. P. Wilpert [Berlin: De Gruyter, 1963], pp. 386-92), Aertsen is right to insist that, in order for it to qualify, it would have to "add" something that the others do not. Aertsen, *Medieval Philosophy and the Transcendentals,* p. 336. To respond to this question, one would have to show how its synthesizing the whole, so to speak, is decisive, i.e., that the unity is more than the sum of the parts, which is essentially how the defenders of beauty in Aquinas tend to proceed.

ists, so much so that all of these terms are convertible with being, and so with one another: *res, unum, aliquid, bonum,* and *verum.* The first two express being as it is in itself, whether positively as a *thing (res)* or negatively in its indivisibility as *one (unum).* The other three indicate being specifically as relational, being taken *in ordine ad aliud.* Negatively, each thing is distinct from all others as *something (aliquid);* but each is also positively relational, and the deceptively rich mystery of this last possibility requires us to slow down this rapid review and dwell on the point for a moment.

One of Aquinas's most innovative contributions to the medieval conversation regarding the transcendentals was, on this point, to introduce anthropology into what was previously simply a metaphysical or theological issue.[20] He thereby gave human existence a role in co-determining the most basic meaning of reality — which, we must admit, is a noble risk, insofar as within this elevation of man there lies the threat of the subordination of reality to human projects, a threat that arguably becomes real in the Enlightenment.[21] However this may be, there is something paradoxical in the very notion of a *positive* relational transcendental property. Aquinas had just affirmed earlier in the text what he says even more explicitly elsewhere, namely, that "nothing is extraneous [to being] except non-being,"[22] and now says that being bears a positive relationship to what is other than itself, i.e., extraneous to it. What is this other? Clearly, it cannot simply be some *thing* in the world adjacent to everything else within the same order so that it would "compete" with being, as it were. Drawing on a phrase from Aristotle, Aquinas explains that this "other" is the human soul, which is "other" in a unique way: it is not opposed to the beings in the world, but is "in a certain sense all things." The soul, in other words, transcends being, but precisely in the mode of being open in principle to all being whatsoever, and, indeed, to the "all" as such. The positive relational transcendentals have their root in the essential relationality — the "intentionality" — of the soul. The reason there are two such transcendentals, according to Aquinas, is due to the nature of the soul. The human soul relates to the world according to irreducibly different powers, the cognitive power and the appetitive power, or as Aquinas calls these powers elsewhere, the intellect and will: the

20. Aertsen, "The Philosophical Importance of the Doctrine of the Transcendentals in Thomas Aquinas," *Revue internationale de philosophie* 52 (1998): 249-68; here, 261.

21. J. B. Metz presents Aquinas in fact as the precursor to modern thought, that is, as effecting the "Copernican revolution" even before Kant. *Christliche Anthropozentrik. Über die Denkform des Thomas von Aquin* (München: Kösel, 1962).

22. Aquinas, *De potentia Dei* 7.2.9.

conformity of being to the intellect is truth *(verum)* and to the will is goodness *(bonum).*

Let us reflect further on the significance of Aquinas's deduction of these positive relational transcendentals. A negative relation of being to its other is not difficult to conceive, since such a relation would "add" only a negation, that is, nothing more than what is already there. It would thus not compromise being's total comprehensiveness. A positive relation, on the other hand, means that there *is* something "in addition" to being, that being has a genuine, positive other to which it relates. At the same time, however, Aquinas insists that there can be nothing other than being, as we saw above. There is clearly a paradox here.[23] One might try to avoid the paradox by pointing out that any particular being may have an other, which still remains within the scope, as it were, of universal being.[24] But the relation designated by truth and goodness is not a relation between two beings within the same order, but between a being *in* its being, on the one hand, and on the other hand its genuine other. This becomes even clearer when we consider that, for Aquinas, it is not just all beings that are good and true, but being itself. This is possible, again, only if there is some other to being even in the "universal" sense. The paradox cannot be avoided. It implies that being both has and does not have an other to itself, an apparent contradiction that can be resolved only if we think of being, not so to speak as what Hegel, for example, would call an abstract identity, a simple object for the subject, but rather as a reality that includes genuine otherness within itself: being, as what is boundless, always turns out to be in some sense "more" and precisely in this way to be comprehensive. In this case, it is the nature of being to be more than itself; the properties of truth and goodness, in contrast to the other transcendental properties but nevertheless as transcendental as they, are those in which being in a certain real respect *exceeds itself* towards its other. Aquinas does not develop this point explicitly, but it has a logic that imposes itself. As we will see in the second and third sections of this chapter, it is precisely this aspect of the excess *within* the transcendental properties that Balthasar develops in a dramatic key, and which explains the fittingness of the ordering principle of Balthasar's work.

23. The question what the transcendentals, as Aquinas understands them, can possibly "add" to being is a complex one, which we cannot address in depth here. For a discussion of this problem, and Aertsen's attempt to resolve it, see *The Dramatic Structure of Truth*, pp. 351-61.

24. Aquinas himself raises this interpretation, but dismisses it as a solution to the problem. See *De ver.* 21.1.

Now, the meaning of being, which unfolds in the soul's reception, has, for Aquinas, a particular structure or logic. The true comes to light in the relationship between being and intellect, and the good in the relationship between being and the will, but there is a relationship between these relationships. While Aquinas argued in the *De veritate* that the good is prior to the true from the perspective of that which is perfectible *(ex parte perfectibilium)*, i.e., in relation to creatures, in the *Summa* he comes to the opposite conclusion.[25] "Absolutely speaking," Aquinas says here, the true has priority over the good, and he makes two succinct arguments for this claim: first, he says, the true is related to being in an absolute and immediate way, while the good, as appetible, is subsequent upon being. If what Aquinas means here is not altogether evident, it receives some light from the second argument: the true is prior to the good also because cognition naturally precedes desire.[26] We do not strive after something unless we know what it is. Even nonrational creatures are ultimately directed to an end by cognition since the presence of the teleology that runs through the natural world cannot but imply ultimately an intelligence as principle.[27] This argument illuminates the first insofar as it suggests that the true is, as it were, being's speaking to the soul, which is why the true is more immediately related to being, while the good is then the soul's response to what it grasps of this address.

This image of call and response evokes the image that Aquinas himself uses in a variety of contexts,[28] which he draws from Aristotle: Aristotle had spoken of the "circle of the acts of the soul," in which the soul cognitively "takes in" the intelligible species of a thing through abstraction, and then moves toward the real existence of the thing through the will. If Aquinas affirms that truth resides primarily in the mind and goodness primarily in the thing, it is not because one is "out there" and another "in here"; rather, residence in this case indicates, not a static place, but a *terminus ad quem*, the destination of a movement: truth occurs, as it were, in being's initiating movement toward the soul, and goodness occurs in the soul's countermovement: "It is for this reason that the Philosopher, in the third book of *The Soul*, places a kind of circle in the acts of the soul, according to which a thing outside the soul moves the intellect and the thing apprehended moves

25. Cf. *De ver.* 21.3, and *ST* 1.16.4. On the differences between these two texts, see Aertsen, *Medieval Philosophy and the Transcendentals*, pp. 284-89.

26. *ST* 1.16.4; cf. 1.27.3ad3; 1.82.4ad3; 1-2.27.2.

27. See *De ver.* 22.1ad2; *ST* 1.2.3; 1-2.26.1; 1.19.4.

28. In addition to *De ver.* 1.1, he mentions it, for example, at *ST* 1.16.1 and 1.27.4.

the appetite, and the appetite then leads to the attainment of the thing whence the motion started."[29]

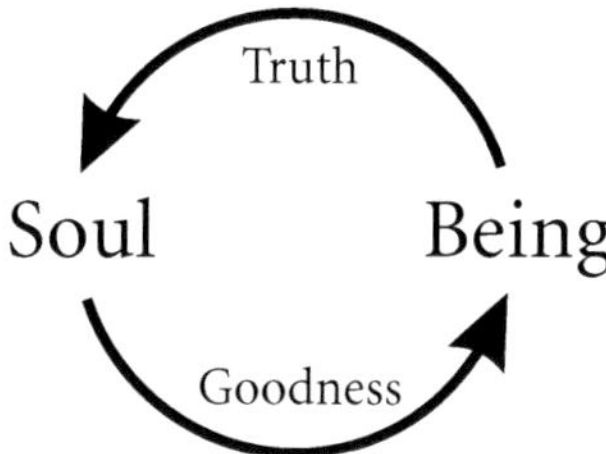

This tracing out of the circle of the acts of the soul brings us to the primary point I intended to make in relation to Aquinas as a point of entry into our discussion of Balthasar. Because the transcendentals are coextensive with reality itself, it follows that there is nothing in our experience of the world, nothing that we encounter, that does not in some sense exhibit this logic. In this respect, we may think of the circle of the acts of the soul as describing in a nutshell the essential narrative, for Aquinas, of the soul's engagement with the world, the basic plot structure of reality. When we come to face any particular thing in the world, our initial engagement with it is the essentially receptive one of the cognitive act; we first apprehend it. And once we have come to understand it, we react, we pursue whatever good it represents in a spontaneous movement toward it — or, conversely, given the circumstances, we may pursue the good negatively by shunning the evil it represents.[30] This is, perhaps, not the most exciting plot structure, but it certainly reveals something crucial, and often overlooked, namely, that all of our spontaneous action in the world takes place inside of a meaning that precedes us, and that our relationship to the world is receptive/contemplative before it is active/productive.[31]

Upon closer scrutiny, however, the plot turns out to be more complex than it seemed at first blush. Circles are notorious for their paradoxes, as

29. *De ver.* 1.2.

30. The free choice of the will, for Aquinas, is not an independent power, but is rather a relative "part" of the will more generally, which Aquinas defines as an *intellectual appetite:* thus understood, choice always operates within a pre-given horizon that already determines what the good is to which the choice is directed (see *ST* 1.83.4). As Aquinas puts it here, following Aristotle (*Nicomachean Ethics* 3.2), choice concerns means, not ends.

31. On this, see David L. Schindler (Sr.), "God and the End of Intelligence: Knowledge as Relationship," *Communio* 26 (1999): 510-40. Note, even our practical intellect does not operate in a void, but takes its bearings from the given nature of things.

Heraclitus already saw:[32] in a circle, what seems to be the end is a new beginning, and what seemed to be the beginning always proves to have been preceded by something else. Although true from an absolute perspective that the true is prior to the good, Aquinas nevertheless recognizes that, in the concrete order, any particular act of the intellect is preceded by an act of will, just as much as the reverse, and so, as far as human action goes, the intellect never sets the will in motion without already having been itself moved by the latter.[33] It thus follows that we are oversimplifying if we think of these acts as separate moments in a merely linear sequence: that we first know something, without any engagement of the will in its regard, and only then, after the cognitive act is complete in itself, do we engage it willfully. Not only would this make knowledge something completely abstract, and not only would this fragment the soul into a mere aggregate of individual faculties, but it also isolates truth and goodness from each other as separate objects that bear no intrinsic relation to one another. Such a separation, however, would offend against the doctrine of the transcendentals, which implies that, in their unbounded extension, each property inheres within the other, in a way that does not blur their distinction. In what Balthasar calls the circumincession of the transcendental properties, using a term typically employed in Trinitarian theology, each of the various transcendental properties bears intrinsically on the meaning of the others.[34] The significance of this circumincession also appears in Aquinas's conception of the faculties, even if he does not make this aspect thematic as such:[35] for him, the dimension of the cognitive act that is most properly intellectual is not the *ratio,* but the intellectual assent to reality that he calls *intellectus,*[36] and the heart of the will's

32. Hermann Diels and Walter Kranz, *Die Fragmente der Vorsokratiker* (Zürich: Weidmann, 1985), p. 103: "The beginning and end is the same on the circumference of a circle." Aquinas refers to circular motion as that which has "neither beginning nor end." *ST* 2-2.180.6ad2.

33. See *ST* 1.82.4. There is no act of will not preceded by intellect, nor any act of intellect not preceded by will. The reason this does not entail an infinite regress, Aquinas explains in response to the third objection, is that God's intellect determines man's ultimate end. This does not end the regress, however, by making intellect first in an absolute sense insofar as God's intellect does not "precede" his will, but is simultaneous with it in the simplicity of his nature. See, e.g., *ST* 1.19.4ad2. We will return to this problem in the following chapter.

34. See, e.g., *My Work,* p. 116.

35. He does, however, explicitly use the term *circumincessio* to describe the relationship between the true and the good in *De ver.* 3.3ad9: "Verum et bonum se invecem circumincedunt."

36. Aquinas defines the proper act of the intellect, *intelligere,* as "adhering to the

activity is not the power of choice but is the *voluntas* that is always already ordered in a receptive way to the good, by virtue of which prior ordering the will is defined precisely as an intellectual appetite.[37]

Beauty as Plot Thickener

What was implicit in Aquinas, namely, the mutual inherence of the transcendental properties and therefore the mutual inherence of the intellect and will, becomes explicit in Balthasar, and it does so precisely because of his thematic introduction of the beautiful. The beautiful, for him, *is* in fact the unity of truth and goodness.[38] In his mature work,[39] he appeals to the medieval interpretation of beauty as the union of form and splendor:[40] in beauty, we per-

---

formed judgment *with approval*" (emphasis added): *ST* 1.79.10ad4. This gives to the intellect itself something analogous to the assent that he ascribes in his discussion of faith, specifically to the contribution of the will. *ST* 2-2.1.4, and 2-2.2.1ad3. A much broader argument would be required, of course, in order to explain and justify how *intelligere* represents the integration of will "into" intellect, especially in light of a more common argument to the contrary, namely, that the will is most active in *ratio* (see, e.g., Reinhard Hütter, "The Directedness of Reasoning and the Metaphysics of Creation," in *Reason and the Reasons of Faith*, pp. 160-93; here, 160, n. 1). The point I wish to make here is simply that, if the will is more explicitly engaged in *ratio*, it is more profoundly integrated in the ec-static quality of *intellectus* — just as reason is more explicitly active in the deliberations of *liberum arbitrium* but more profoundly integrated in the *voluntas*. In other words, intellect and will are most fully themselves not in separation but in their union, that is, insofar as they more closely resemble the simple oneness of intellect and will in God.

37. *ST* 1.83.4.

38. *GL1*, p. 18, also *TL1*, pp. 221-22. See Gilbert, "L'articulation des transcendentaux," pp. 617-18.

39. His earlier substantial treatment of beauty, alongside goodness and truth, in the *TL1* (originally published in 1947 but included in 1985 as volume 1 of the *Theo-Logic* in his later *Trilogy*) explains it in the more Hegelian terms as a dynamic relation between essence or ground and appearance (and indeed Balthasar's first published work adopted directly Hegel's definition of beauty as the sensuous manifestation of truth; see *Die Entwicklung der musikalischen Idee*, 2nd ed. [Einsiedeln: Johannes Verlag, 1999], p. 42), but the essential core of his understanding remained the same: a determinate figure perceived as the luminous expression of something beyond that figure. It should be noted that, although Balthasar made use of these Hegelian notions, he interpreted them always in a decidedly non-Hegelian sense. For Balthasar, ground and image always remain distinct within the overall unity of the expression. This is why we can insist on a continuity between the earlier formulations and the later description of beauty in terms of an irreducible polarity between form and splendor.

40. Albert the Great, in his commentary on the *Divine Names* titled *De Pulchro et*

ceive a determinate figure, but within that figure shines out a kind of excess, a mystery, a light that signals that the form is the free expression of something greater.[41] According to Balthasar, while classical aesthetics might give more emphasis to the form (beauty) and romantic aesthetics more emphasis to the splendorous excess (the sublime), precisely the aesthetic character would be destroyed if either simply excluded the other:[42] we would have a sterile, desiccated form on the one hand and an a-cosmic chaos on the other, but in either case no beauty. In what Balthasar calls the "primal phenomenon" of beauty, there is a polarity of irreducibly different and yet interdependent aspects: "We are confronted simultaneously with both the figure and that which shines forth from the figure, making it into a worthy, a love-worthy thing."[43]

Balthasar in fact associates this polarity in beauty with the essential polarity that runs through all of created being.[44] To use Thomistic language, if not that of Thomas himself,[45] there is a real distinction between the essence and existence of all creatures, which is precisely what gives them their contingent nature, their character as *creatures* distinct from and dependent on the perfectly simple Creator himself.[46] As Balthasar sees it, just as this ir-

---

Bono, defined beauty as the "resplendence of form." Following this influential formulation, medieval aesthetics, according to Umberto Eco, can be divided into an aesthetics of proportion or an aesthetics of light, depending on which aspect receives emphasis. *Art and Beauty in the Middle Ages* (New Haven: Yale University Press, 1986), pp. 25, 28-51.

41. The reference to freedom, which is crucial to Balthasar's understanding of beauty (see, e.g., *Glaubhaft ist nur Liebe,* 6th ed. [Einsiedeln: Johannes, 2000], p. 34), is not in fact an explicit part of medieval aesthetics. Rather, Balthasar here draws on Schiller, who defines beauty as the appearance of freedom, as "lebende Gestalt"; see his "Kallias or Concerning Beauty: Letters to Gottfried Körner," in *Classic and Romantic German Aesthetics,* ed. J. M. Bernstein (Cambridge: Cambridge University Press, 2003), pp. 145-83.

42. See *TL1,* pp. 224-25.

43. *GL1,* p. 20.

44. In the *Epilogue,* Balthasar elaborates the polar structure of the transcendentals, which reflects the polar structure of created being in general. *E,* pp. 55-86.

45. Although the phrase "real distinction" has become common among Thomists to refer to the difference between *esse* and essence in created things, Aquinas himself never used it (he refers instead to a "real composition" or a "real diversity" in *De ver.* 1.27ad8 and *In sent.* 1.13.1ad3). The absence of this phrase has led to some controversy among his interpreters, beginning directly after his death, over whether the phrase in fact accurately represents his thinking. See John Wippel, "Essence and Existence in Later Medieval Philosophy," in *Cambridge History of Medieval Philosophy* (Cambridge: Cambridge University Press, 1982), pp. 385-410.

46. This is not to say that there is no foundation already in God for the distinction. See Balthasar's brief discussion of this question in *TL2,* pp. 179-86.

reducible polarity describes being, so too does it have significance for being's fundamental properties. We may fail to see this polarity, however, in goodness and truth if we think of them as separate "things," connected to each other, if at all, only extrinsically. But the polarity lies right at the heart of beauty, and if we interpret truth and goodness in their unity with beauty, this polarity becomes more evident in each of them individually.[47] We might say that their unity in beauty reveals more directly their transcendentality, that is, their being the expression of being, which in the created order is thoroughly polar.[48]

If, to repeat, we interpret the positive relational transcendentals in the light of their inward connection to one another, i.e., their circumincession, which is mediated to them by beauty, our understanding of each of the transcendentals is transformed. I would like to reflect on this transformation here specifically in terms of their acquiring a dramatic character, which reveals itself in two respects: first, in the essential polarity that each thereby possesses, just alluded to above; and, second, in the fact that each thereby involves a kind of dialogical interchange between subject and object, which we will elaborate here specifically in relation to the transcendental truth. As we will see, this elaboration will provide a demonstration of the "fittingness" of the order Balthasar follows in the *Trilogy.* It is important to note that the new character we suggest that each of the transcendentals acquires as a result of the unifying mediation of beauty is not something added to what each already is in itself. Rather, interpreting goodness and truth in terms of their unity in beauty brings to light what always already belongs to each by nature, and the new perspective opens this dimension to our experience and understanding.

The polar structure of beauty is essentially dramatic in the sense that it cannot be sufficiently grasped as a fact apart from a witness of it as an event. Beauty is *epiphanic,* and this implies the conjunction of the two aspects we mentioned above, namely, form and splendor. Each of these taken simply in itself would be undramatic: a detached form can be grasped in detachment, as so to speak a piece of information: one can register on paper the fact that a melody dances up and down a scale, that it is suspended for a moment and then resolved; but to perceive this specifically as beautiful requires the actual experience of the melody, which involves, however consciously, receiving each of the moments and movements as the communication of some myste-

47. This has been treated at greater length in *The Dramatic Structure of Truth,* pp. 403-11.

48. *E,* pp. 55-57.

rious whole, of a unity that is present but does not lie exposed on the surface. It requires, in other words, a glimpse of the splendor *in* the form. Similarly, splendor that lacked form would simply be inaccessible, ultimately indistinguishable from the void: pure light without anything to reflect it is the blackness of space. The convergence of the two is a dramatic event in which this "excess" is made determinately manifest, and indeed the more clearly and distinctly one perceives the form of the disclosure the more aware one becomes of the great, and ultimately ineffable, mystery just now and just here coming to expression.

When Balthasar says both goodness and truth ultimately threaten to lose their particular compellingness when they become separated from beauty, and so separated from each other,[49] it seems to me that he has in mind the loss of this polar character. It is this that makes each transcendental *meaning*-ful; because this is what makes each in its own way a communication of something, and indeed something inexhaustible and so always interesting. The union in beauty, in other words, makes both goodness and truth *diaphanous* in our experience of each, the shining through of something that does not simply appear on the surface and so of something that resists any cheap possession and consumption, as it were. There is no single way to formulate this polarity, and Balthasar himself never absolutizes any particular account of it.[50] Here, I would like to set into relief the paradox of the expressive "more" that is nevertheless given, as this paradox comes to expression in each.

One of the age-old questions about goodness appears in Aristotle's qualification of Plato: while Plato seems to give the good, which all things desire, an absolute, i.e., nonrelative, character,[51] Aristotle insists that what motivates each of our actions is not the good *per se,* but rather specifically the good *for us.*[52] Is goodness absolute or is it relative? If it is merely absolute, it is not what each of us perceives, since perception is always in some respect relative; but if it is merely relative, it makes no sense in the end to speak of goodness in any way that transcends the perception — we would have instead nothing more than goods of the moment, and indeed of a moment the duration of which dwindles to nothing under scrutiny. Note how goodness

49. *GL1,* p. 19.

50. Compare Balthasar's formulation of the polarity in beauty, for example, in *GL1,* pp. 19-20; *E,* pp. 59-67; and *TL1,* pp. 223-24. We elaborate the polarity differently in *Dramatic Structure of Truth,* pp. 364-65.

51. Plato, *Symposium* 205e-206a.

52. See Aristotle, *Ethics* 8.2; cf. 3.4.

loses any intrinsic interest in either case. The best answer to the question is "both/and"; goodness is essentially polar, and its two aspects — *both* its absolute goodness in itself *and* its relative goodness for us — are related in a paradoxical and so dramatic way: the good gives itself to us in a particular event, but in this gift there is a "more" that expands beyond our initial grasp and so in turn makes a claim on us. We perceive what is *our* good, but it is ultimately our *good*, and the perception eventually entails a real growth on our part.[53]

We see something similar in truth, which, when interpreted in the light of beauty, contains a marvelous polarity between clarity and distinctness on the one hand and mystery on the other. Heidegger had something of this polarity in mind when he interpreted truth as *alētheia*, disclosure, in which dark hiddenness remains just as primordial as what is brought to light in the disclosure.[54] But, as we see in Balthasar,[55] and will elaborate in the following chapter, mystery has a positive sense from the beginning; it is not in the first place an opaque darkness but an excessively luminous one, and it is so precisely because the mystery bears a relationship of polarity, rather than of tragic opposition, to the sure grasp of knowledge. This relationship is a positive one because it arises through the unity truth enjoys with goodness — and the self-diffusiveness goodness implies — by virtue of the primacy of beauty. When we view the matter thus, we come to experience truth as essentially diaphanous: the mystery of being is a "holy open mystery," to quote the phrase from Goethe that Balthasar loved; it lies, not behind or otherwise outside of what we know, but *within* it, because the mystery results from the expressiveness of reality rather than from being's relentless withdrawal. The abiding "more" in everything that is given in both the orders of the true and of the good, that is, their polar character, is due to the inward relation each bears to the other, and this inward relation is, as it were, mediated to each by beauty. If we think of the circle of the acts of the soul, we see that the relations of truth and goodness move in opposite directions. To say that each includes the other in itself means that each movement is as it were dramatically complexified by a countermovement

53. *E*, p. 69.

54. "The disclosure of beings as such is simultaneously and intrinsically the concealing of being as a whole. In the simultaneity of disclosure and concealing errancy holds sway. Errancy and the concealing of what is concealed belong to the primordial essence of truth." Heidegger, "On the Essence of Truth," in *Basic Writings* (New York: Harper, 1977), p. 137.

55. See, for example, *TL1*, pp. 206-25. Interestingly, his explicit discussion of the transcendentals occurs within this section on mystery.

within itself, which is to say that there is a resistance in each case to a tension-less collapse into a single direction.[56]

This non-negative resistance becomes especially evident when we consider the second way that beauty makes evident the dramatic character of the transcendentals, namely, the dialogical interchange it initiates between subject and object. The word "dialogue," in this context, indicates that we have, not just the acts of the soul, but an encounter between the acts of the soul and reality's acts of self-disclosure, a many-staged encounter that follows a somewhat different course for each transcendental. Here, we will limit ourselves to a presentation of the logic of truth, because it is this that explains the order of Balthasar's *Trilogy*, which, although it is no doubt better known for its aesthetics and dramatics, is after all specifically a work of theology, and so is ordered most basically by the true.[57] Let us recall what we flagged as a danger of the "circle of the acts of the soul," namely, looking at the true and good as merely successive and so overlooking their circumincession. As we observed, this leads, among other things, to an abstract conception of truth, in which we understand a thing prior to, and so separate from, our desiring it as good and for this reason without our personal engagement with it; moreover, and for the same reason, whatever personal engagement we might have subsequently with a thing would in this case strictly speaking not enrich our knowledge of it, because that act was already necessarily brought to completion before our movement toward the object in the good. At best, the engagement would elicit a new act of knowledge subsequent to the willing of the thing, but this would be in fact a new object and indeed would itself occur in the same wholly abstract way as the precedent cognition.

When we acknowledge the primacy of beauty and the circumincession it brings to light, the narrative plot described by the circle "thickens," so to speak. We may thus reinterpret Aquinas's "anthropological" deduction of the

56. In other words, the movement of truth, which according to Aquinas begins with being and terminates in the soul, must be seen as including within itself the opposite movement of the soul to being, which is the relation of goodness. This means that truth is not a unilateral movement, with a single beginning (being) and a single end (the soul), but is rather a single, complex movement, with *two* points of departure and *two* termini, although of course one set remains primary in each case. What is said for the relation of truth holds equally for the relation of goodness.

57. Balthasar makes a similar observation in *TD2*, p. 9, n. 1. It would be possible, by contrast, to think through the circumincession of the transcendentals specifically within the order of the *good*, in which case love follows understanding. See Balthasar's mention of something resembling this order in *TL2*, p. 32, speaking of the progressive unfurling of "faith, knowledge, and love" in the Gospel of John.

transcendentals in the light of Balthasar's understanding of them in a way that explains the fittingness of the order of his *Trilogy.* In Balthasar's conception of the intellect, our knowledge of reality strictly speaking comes last, rather than first. The cognitive act is first set in motion by the epiphany of the object's beauty, which elicits our intellectual interest, and it is then mediated through the drama of the good before the act comes to completion in truth. This view avoids irrationalism — of which it might be suspected to the extent that it places the willing of the good before the knowledge of the object's truth — because the good, here, is preceded by the *beautiful,* which is an intellectual perception of form even if it is not yet a perception in the mode specifically of comprehended truth.[58] According to our ancient tradition, and as we will explore in chapter seven, philosophy begins, not with knowledge simply, but with *wonder,* which we might see as the subjective correlate to beauty: Balthasar here is simply making what has too often become a gratuitous and sentimental slogan into a rigorous methodological principle. Moreover, he adds to this tradition an explicit affirmation of the personal engagement in the act of knowing, which is implied by the good, a dimension of knowledge that comes to light in a particular way in the light of Christian revelation.[59]

But this is as yet simply a general sketch; the plot thickens even further when we enter more concretely into the relations and see the implications of the polarity discussed earlier, which reveals a twofold moment in each transcendental property. We will trace the lines of this "thickened" plot in the present context in light of Aquinas's circle, and therefore specifically from the perspective of philosophical anthropology, but it is important to acknowledge that a variety of other perspectives are available, no one of which excludes the others.[60] As Balthasar explains in the opening section of the

58. See Andrea Brugnoli, "Rifondazione del 'verum' a partire dal 'bonum' nella filosofia di Balthasar," *Sensus communis* 3 (2002): 267-86. Brugnoli shows that Balthasar draws on Levinas, Newman, and Scheler for the importance of the *bonum* to the *verum,* but avoids the problem of simply reversing the order through the primacy of the *pulchrum.* Though he indicates that beauty plays a role here, he does not elaborate the nature of that role.

59. Balthasar observes that there is a "dramatic character" in "that which is Christian." *My Work,* p. 29 (he adds later that "you can never take away its dramatic character," p. 100). One of the clearest distinctions, perhaps, between Balthasar and Heidegger turns precisely on this sense of drama: although Heidegger affirms the central significance of *freedom* in the clearing of truth (see his essay "On the Essence of Truth," pp. 126-30), he specifically rejects the personal character of freedom that, according to Balthasar, is essential to drama. According to Heidegger, "Man does not 'possess' freedom as a property. At best, the converse holds: freedom, ek-sistent, disclosive Da-sein, possesses man" (p. 129).

60. For example, there is the more directly metaphysical perspective of the *Epilogue*

Trilogy, the experience of beauty contains in a unity two irreducibly distinct moments, the moment of *vision* and the moment of *rapture,*[61] by which he means the transport of the beholding subject outside of himself, the moment, that is, of ec-stasis. These two moments are so profoundly interdependent it is impossible to say which moment comes first: "no one can really behold who has not already been enraptured, and no one can be enraptured who has not already perceived."[62] In other words, the subject is not moved aesthetically without *aisthēsis,* i.e., without a *perception;* there is no such thing as an unconscious experience of beauty.[63] At the same time, this perception occurs only insofar as the beholder has been captured by it and so elevated to it. As we mentioned before, beauty in Balthasar's understanding contains within itself both truth and goodness; the classical characterization of beauty — *id quod visum placet* — reveals it to be simultaneously "conceptual" and "appetitive." Since beauty contains both of these, and so holds together at once the two acts running in opposite directions, we may think of it as a tension-filled suspension *between* the subject and object. In beauty, there is a "truth-like" movement of the object's being taken spiritually into the subject (vision), though this is not truth *per se;* it is truth trans-formed by goodness, which means the grasp is not an explicit comprehension. The "not-quite-conceptual" quality of beauty has been a regular theme of reflection on the matter from the beginning.[64] At the same time, there is a rapture, a movement of the subject *toward* the object that imitates the good,[65] but is

(pp. 59-86), or the specifically theological approach that Balthasar explains in *TD1,* pp. 15-23, which itself could be specified further into a more man-centered or a more God-centered approach. Our argument in the text, once again, is not that the order of the *Trilogy* — beauty, goodness, and truth — is the only legitimate way to articulate the order of the transcendentals, but rather that one can show the reasonable fittingness of this order, given Balthasar's aim in this work.

61. *GL1,* p. 120.

62. *GL1,* p. 10.

63. According to Aquinas, the light in which beauty is perceived is specifically the light *of reason. ST* 2-2.180.2ad3.

64. While this theme is quite explicit in the modern "refounding" of aesthetics in German philosophy — Baumgarten, for example, interpreted beauty as a "vague concept," which is then clarified in truth; Kant coined the phrase "purposiveness without purpose," which could be translated as "conceptuality without concept"; and Schiller described the aesthetic *overcoming* of logical form — it has its roots in fact in the classical Platonic aesthetics of light.

65. Commenting on Aquinas, Balthasar observes that the order of goodness thus represents a more radical self-transcendence than the order of truth. *The Grain of Wheat: Aphorisms* (San Francisco: Ignatius Press, 1995), p. 41.

not the good *per se;* it is goodness trans-formed by truth so as to be, not a real possession or enjoyment, but specifically a disinterested pleasure. This has also always been observed in aesthetic experience.[66] In short, beauty is not merely conceptual and not merely enjoyable; it is both simultaneously.

Now, the very movement toward the object designated by the moment of transport is in fact a claim that the object makes on the subject, and it therefore calls on a response from the subject. Failing to make this response, the subject would flatten beauty out into an effete aestheticism, which Kierkegaard, for example, has described with incomparable insight. In making the response, the order shifts from the beautiful now to the good. What is the response required? It has (unsurprisingly) two distinct moments. First, there is the moment of appropriative choice, by which the subject deliberately makes the movement in which he is already engaged through beauty properly his own. Because it is a recapitulation of a movement already begun, this choice has the basic structure of a *yes,* of an assent to the good that has, so to speak, presented itself *in* the beautiful. But the meaning of goodness does not exhaust itself in this appropriation: the absoluteness of the good always exceeds the relativity of its deliberate appropriation. At the same time, however, this excess does not lie adjacent to the appropriation as extraneous to it, but as we observed above, it indwells what is given. The subjective correlate of this internal excess is therefore not something in addition to the choice but is rather a deepening of the meaning of that choice, or, if you will, an unfolding of its implications. We may thus call the second moment of the good *fidelity,* an abiding with what was chosen wherever it may lead, and perhaps significantly beyond what one initially expected.

But fidelity absolutized in an exclusive way would degenerate into the obsessive self-regard we find, for example, in Rousseau's sincerity, or more subtly in Kant's moralistic appropriation of Rousseau in his deontologism, if it fails to understand itself as fidelity, not in the first place to one's choice, i.e., to the subject himself, but ultimately to the object. *With* this development, by contrast, fidelity becomes *trust,* and in this moment the order of the good passes to the order of the true. Interestingly, while the experience of the good began with a relativity to the subject and moved toward the in-itself aspect of the object, in truth there is a primacy of objectivity, which is then appropriated by the subject; in other words, we see here a kind of retrieval of the

66. Descartes is a telling exception: in his *Passions of the Soul* (Indianapolis: Hackett, 1989), pp. 67-69 (article 90), he explains, or rather "explains away," aesthetic pleasure by reducing it to the anticipated fulfillment of natural needs.

directionality described by the circle of the acts of the soul, but now the movements acquire a more textured logic. The true begins in trust, a word etymologically connected with "truth," and ends with *disclosure.* As Aquinas affirmed, with reference to Hilary, truth is "manifestive and declarative being."[67] The fruit of one's constancy is a revelation of the reality of that to which one has bound oneself. Knowledge thus understood is anything but abstract; it exhibits something of the "concreteness" that Hegel pursued throughout his philosophical speculation, namely, a comprehensiveness that cannot come to light in the discreteness of a mere "result" but instead requires a patient suffering of the object, a laboring and living-through in which disparate aspects of a reality finally reveal how they "fit" together, that is, reveal their otherwise hidden unity. We might compare the three moments of beauty, goodness, and truth in Balthasar fruitfully to the three moments in Hegel's dialectic: while Hegel alternates, as it were, between positivity and negativity — first, something is posited, then what is posited is negated, and finally the negation itself is negated, which returns us to the positive, but now in a mediated form — in Balthasar the positive and negative aspects are held together in a dramatic tension in *each* of the moments. Because for Balthasar the positivity of the givenness is paradoxically one with the negativity of excess (what one grasps is *not* the whole of what is given), the fruit of a faithful dwelling with the object comes to term, as it were, in an abiding spirit of receptive wonder, and the resulting disclosure thus includes a promise of an inexhaustible "more." The clarity of the perception of truth is one with the hopeful expectation that keeps knowledge endlessly interesting. As Josef Pieper puts it, truth is an *unaustrinkbares Licht,* an inexhaustible light.[68]

As we argued earlier, the order of the transcendentals presents the narrative structure of the soul's encounter with reality; we now see the dramatic shape this narrative acquires when we include the property of beauty. We have, not just apprehension and then pursuit, as the simple circle of the acts of soul may suggest, but first, vision and rapture; then, choice and fidelity; and finally, trust and disclosure. If all of these are ultimately one and the same "*in re,*"[69] they nevertheless reveal themselves in successive moments in

67. *De ver.* 1.1.

68. See Pieper, *Unaustrinkbares Licht* (München: Kösel, 1963). For Pieper, the inexhaustible truth of things is due to their resting in the unfathomable creative knowledge of God. While Balthasar would ultimately agree, it is significant that he roots mystery more proximately in the very nature of finite being, specifically in its polar character.

69. According to the classical view of the transcendentals, the properties are identical with one another *in re,* i.e., in the thing itself, but can be distinguished according to our un-

our encounter with reality, which is a drama of aesthetic wonderment, a grappling with the good, and finally the resolution of truth.

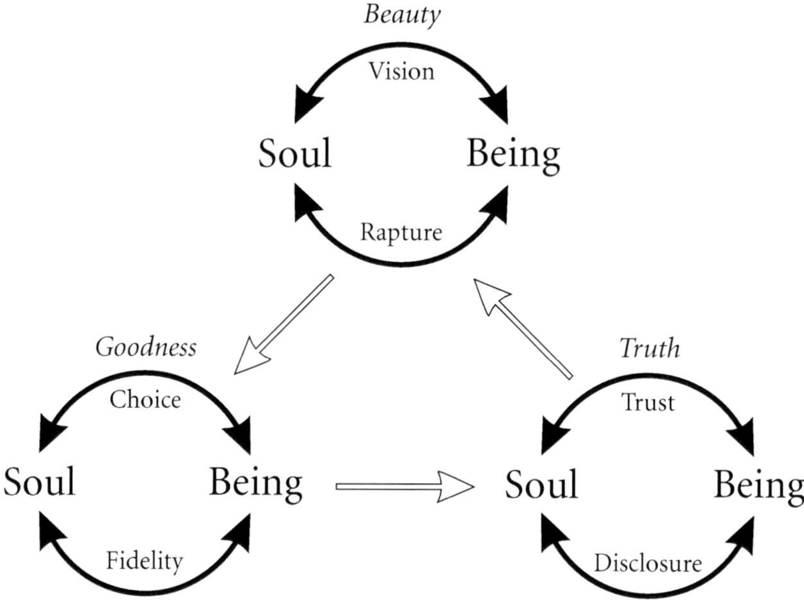

There are three observations to make about this narrative structure, viewed as a whole: in the first place, we note that each *overlaps* the other in the different transitions; more specifically, the moment of rapture *is* the moment of choice, seen from within the order of the next transcendental property, and, similarly, fidelity *is* trust, it is the entrusting of oneself to the other. This overlap is in fact just what we would expect from properties that are internally related to one another. Second, this structure does not simply come to an end with the disclosure to the understanding, but, because this approach reveals truth to be diaphanous, to be the communication of a reality that re-

derstanding. This is what makes the transcendental properties "convertible" with one another. Balthasar offers a reason for the identity of the transcendentals *in re,* based on the nature of being. For him, being is essentially self-disclosive. This can be seen as being *giving* itself (the good); as its *presenting* itself (beauty); or as its *articulating* itself (truth). It is one and the same reality, here, but can be interpreted in three distinct ways. Our point in describing this narrative structure according to the order of the *Trilogy* — beauty, goodness, and truth — is to describe the unfolding of these aspects in a succession that brings to light the abiding transcendence of being in its genuine giving of itself, which is essential to the analogy of truth that opens metaphysics to biblical theology.

tains its integrity as an objective *Gestalt* abidingly distinct from the soul and so abidingly mysterious, this expression is just as much an epiphany. In this case, the moment of disclosure is itself a vision of beauty, and the dramatically complexified circle begins once again. Third, this plot structure begins and ends with a certain priority of the object, but this priority nevertheless precisely includes a central — a pivotal — place for the full engagement of subjectivity in all of its freedom. Balthasar's dramatic conception of truth allots a role to the spontaneous activity of the knowing subject without in the least endangering the real objectivity of intelligibility.

Because we are indeed talking about the order of the transcendentals, we are describing in fact the structure of every encounter with reality whatsoever insofar as the encounter is cognitive. The path we have traced is the essential shape of the act of the intellect, as Balthasar sees it. While words like "choice" and "rapture" perhaps evoke high drama, it is crucial to see that even our most banal, everyday experiences exhibit this same structure in an analogous way, often no doubt hidden from us or scarcely conscious. But what becomes explicit in a perhaps overwhelming way in the truly dramatic, "life-changing" moments of existence — for Balthasar, a former Jesuit, the most dramatic moment is the choosing of a state of life — is simply the basic truth of our constant being-in-the-world. These great moments are *paradigmatic* in the strict sense; they reveal the dramatic structure of the life of the mind *tout court.*

Analogia veritatis

In the foreword to his concluding *Epilogue,* in which Balthasar looks back — with some surprise, it must be said[70] — on the *Trilogy* he had just brought to completion, he states that the reason he ordered the work around the transcendentals, rather than the traditional parceling into "treatises," is to allow the most "trouble-free" *(mühelos)* transition from a true philosophy to biblical theology.[71] He goes on to insist, however, that this cannot imply that the truth of Christianity should be nothing more than the culmination of philosophy, as it is in Hegel (where in fact philosophy turns out to be the culmination of Christianity). There must be, instead, a radical discontinuity between revelation and philosophy, but one that nevertheless retains suffi-

70. When he began the trilogy, Balthasar took for granted that he would not be able to bring it to completion himself. *My Work,* p. 79.

71. *E,* p. 9.

cient continuity that it does not present itself as something altogether foreign, and so nothing but a violence, to reason. This continuity within discontinuity, or unity in ever-greater difference, is what the Fourth Lateran Council defined as the essence of *analogy*.[72] Balthasar adds to this definition a note in this notion that he learned from his early mentor, Erich Przywara, namely, the ascent (ἄνα) of reason (λόγος), though he added to his mentor's insight an indispensable complementary downward movement (κατά) from above.[73] As we will explore at greater length in chapters nine and ten, genuine analogical reasoning does not transcend toward the divine without reciprocally casting a new light on what lies, so to speak, below.[74]

In this regard, Balthasar makes two points in the *Epilogue* regarding the analogical character of the transcendentals, both of which rest on their essential polarity. First, he notes that this pervasive phenomenon of "ununited unity" *(nicht-einen Einheit)* points to an Absolute simplicity as its ground, which is "*the* True, *the* Good, *the* Beautiful."[75] And yet, as truly absolute unity, it is not simply the opposite of finite polarity. In other words, we may not arrive at this unity simply by subtracting the difference of polarity, since this would both reduce the transcendent unity to a unity relative to finite difference and thus undermine its absoluteness, and at the same time it would render the difference of the polarity a simple fall away from unity and so an essential imperfection. But the polarities, as we have seen, are constitutive of the transcendental properties of being, and thus of its essential perfection as such. This means, then, that the polarity cannot owe itself to something *outside of* the source of all perfection, but must instead be grounded therein just as much as the unity of being. In other words, the difference of the polarity must reflect something of the ground of being insofar as it is a perfection. Absolute unity is thus not the opposite of created difference, but transcends *both* the unity and difference in finite being, and so reveals *both* to be irreducible expressions of God's perfection. Precisely how God "contains" both unity and difference, Balthasar observes, is something we can learn only in revelation.[76] The *discontinuity*, and so freedom, of the

72. In the words of the Council, analogy means "maior dissimilitudo in similitudine."

73. See, e.g., *TL2*, pp. 171-218.

74. This is how Plato characterizes it in what is certainly the first attempt to think through the meaning of analogy that we have recorded in philosophy. See D. C. Schindler, *Plato's Critique of Impure Reason: On Truth and Goodness in the* Republic (Washington, DC: Catholic University of America Press, 2008), pp. 145-64.

75. *E*, p. 85.

76. *E*, p. 56.

Absolute in relation to the finite, here, proves to be, not a compromise or threat to finite intelligibility, but in fact *reinforces* it, makes it luminous. At the same time, it "prepares" for the supra-rational event of revelation without presumptively anticipating it and thereby blunting its gratuity, because this *preparatio,* so to speak, comes not by "extending" finite concepts into God but rather by introducing (a fulfilling) discontinuity into the basic form of reason. It is thus that analogy allows one to evade the related problems of ontotheology and ontologism; we will return to these themes below.

Balthasar's account of the "analogicity" of the transcendentals is quite brief and formal in the *Epilogue;* indeed, the argument he makes in this context apparently could be made simply on the basis of the polarity of being; it is not evident what specific role the transcendentals as such play here apart from simply indicating the perfection of created polarity. But the previous discussion of the transcendentals in Aquinas and Balthasar allows us to approach this theme from a richer phenomenological perspective. The essence of analogy is the affirmation of a unity in difference. In Aquinas, we saw that the positive relational transcendentals imply just this, insofar as both goodness and truth describe being in its surpassing itself, so to speak, toward its other. Goodness and truth reveal being to be "inwardly self-transcending." The otherness that each relation implies therefore does not compromise being's unity, nor does that unity foreclose abiding difference. By introducing beauty in a position of primacy, Balthasar sets into relief the fact that being's self-transcendence in the transcendentals is *also* reason's self-transcendence, or perhaps we could say, both being and the soul are ecstatically immanent to one another in the transcendentals. In this respect, the primacy of beauty belongs to the specifically catholic character of reason. The fact that the epiphany of beauty sets in motion the appropriating acts of the intellect and will prevents these acts from any reductive collapse, for it shows that these acts of the soul are elicited in every case, so to speak, "from above," that is, from beyond themselves. One might interpret Balthasar, here, as recovering Plato's insight, expressed in the *Phaedrus,* that beauty initiates the soul's transcendence to truth, and indeed that it is the *sole* entryway into the truth of being.[77] Conceived as rooted in beauty, both goodness and truth likewise imply the soul's ec-static movement beyond itself. They both therefore remain just as "epiphanic" as

77. Plato, *Phaedrus* 250d-e. Plato calls beauty the ἐκφανέστατον and the ἐρασμιώτατον of the forms: it is so radiant, as it were, that it is *also* visible to bodily sight and for that reason provokes the *erōs* that Plato describes in the *Symposium* as mediating between the human and the divine.

beauty, which is why Balthasar describes them, respectively, as a "self-giving" and "self-saying" in similarity to beauty's "self-showing."[78] Each of the transcendentals is a unity-in-difference in which the soul finds itself in a *positive* relation to its *other* — which remains abidingly "other" in this relation.

The "plot" that we have traced is crucial here: we see the importance of the ordering of the transcendentals: the *truth* of being reveals itself "explicitly" only through the mediation of the expropriative moment of goodness, and this moment, in turn, does not make its demands except within the "rapture" in which the soul already receives a "foretaste," we might say, of being's good truth. Balthasar would agree with Jean-Luc Marion, for example, who overcomes ontotheologism by thinking God most basically in terms of the *good,* and yet he disagrees that this brings us somehow "beyond" the analogy of being.[79] While this isolation of the good leads Marion to overemphasize the *reversal* the absolute implies, and so its violence to reason, Balthasar's insistence on the circumincession of the transcendentals leads him to a significantly different perspective: the radical transcendence of goodness is not *opposed* to the clarity of concepts that belongs essentially to truth because it has its roots in the "formosity," so to speak, of beauty. By the very same token, truth does not have to be relativized in order to protect transcendence as something that reduces the object to the subject's idea — a criticism one finds, for example, in Nietzsche[80] and in Levinas[81] — but it, too, implies an

78. Reviewing his discussion of the three transcendentals, Balthasar observes: "The basic phenomenon in all three of them was their epiphanic character, which permeates everything that exists: self-showing (beauty), self-giving (goodness), self-saying (truth) were seen to be various aspects of this appearing." *E,* p. 83.

79. Balthasar explains this point in *TL2,* pp. 134-35, n. 10. We will discuss it further in chapter eight.

80. "What is it that the common people take for knowledge? What do they want when they want 'knowledge'? Nothing more than this: Something strange is to be reduced to something *familiar.* And we philosophers — have we really meant *more* than this when we have spoken of knowledge? What is familiar means what we are used to so that we no longer marvel at it, our everyday, some rule in which we are stuck, anything at all in which we feel at home." *The Gay Science,* trans. W. Kaufmann (New York: Vintage Books, 1974), p. 300.

81. "When, in the philosophical life that realizes this freedom [of autonomy], there arises a term foreign to the philosophical life, *other* — the land that supports us and disappoints our efforts, the sky that elevates us and ignores us, the forces of nature that aid us and kill us, things that encumber us or serve us, men who love us and enslave us — it becomes an obstacle; it has to be surmounted and integrated into this life. But truth is just this victory and this integration." Levinas, "Philosophy and the Idea of the Infinite," trans. Alphonso Lingis, published in Adriaan Peperzak, *To the Other: An Introduction to the Philosophy of Emmanuel Levinas* (West Lafayette, IN: Purdue University Press, 1995), p. 94; emphasis added.

elevating transformation of the subject, an echo of the transporting rapture we find in beauty. Balthasar can avoid the postmodern exaggeration of negative theology because he thus deepens and enriches the notion of analogy through the transcendentals. There is an essential connection, in short, for Balthasar between the primacy of beauty, the circumincession of the transcendentals, and the analogy that runs through all of the divine names.

It is, finally, just this connection that allows a transition from true philosophy, as Balthasar put it, to biblical theology. The dramatic structure of truth prefigures, in a sense, the Christian encounter with grace, and yet it is not in any direct sense derived from revelation. Instead, it has a plain intelligibility that speaks to reason as such. For this very reason, it allows revelation to resonate all through the structures of worldly being all the way to their core, something that one cannot say of Barth's analogy of faith. This metaphysical resonance is what makes revelation, for Balthasar, profoundly meaningful: "How can someone who is blind to Being be other than blind to God?"[82] By rooting the intellectual act in beauty, and thereby connecting it most intimately with the dramatic engagement with the good, Balthasar provides what we might call a natural path of reason to God, but one that, for all its naturalness, does not compromise God's transcendence or the pure gratuity of his revelation. Nor does it allow reason, on the other hand, to turn away from the *positivity* of that revelation, once it comes, as a threat to its abiding openness. Within the perichoresis of the transcendentals, their dance in and through each other,[83] truth reveals its inherently analogical character: it lies at the center of philosophy, but is no less a properly theological notion insofar as it represents at the same time a name of God. The light of faith therefore does not need to blind reason in order to demonstrate its sovereignty. Rather, a recognition of the *primacy* of beauty, the *centrality* of goodness, and the *ultimacy* of truth[84] — reflected in the order of the trilogy — in the end enables us to make sense of St. Paul's promise that, in grace, we will come to know the love that exceeds all knowledge.

82. Balthasar, *My Work,* p. 85. Balthasar famously claims that the formal object of theology lies within the formal object of philosophy. *GL1,* p. 145.

83. On the original meaning of "perichoresis," see Juan Sara, "Knowledge, the Transcendentals, and Communion," *Communio* 28 (2001): 515.

84. This is how Mario Saint-Pierre characterizes the position of each of the transcendentals in *Beauté, Bonté, Vérité chez Hans Urs von Balthasar* (Paris: Éditions du Cerf, 1998), p. 349. This formulation perfectly captures the simultaneity of the absoluteness and relativity of each in Balthasar's thought.

4 Does Love Trump Reason? Toward a Nonpossessive Concept of Knowledge

Which Comes First, Intellect or Will?

Determining whether the intellect or the will enjoys an ultimate superiority over its counterpart is a distinctively Christian problem. While it is true that ancient Greek thinkers reflected in depth on the various relationships between reason and virtue, the passions, appetite, and choice, once the issue of a unified anthropology became a central and thematic concern for philosophy, the problem for the Greeks consisted primarily in specifying how these other dimensions of the human animal were to be subordinated to reason.[1] Even Aristotle's refutation of the Socratic identification of knowledge and virtue ultimately turns on a distinction between types of knowledge.[2] It is not until the introduction of a distinct notion of will as a spontaneous principle of action and thus as sovereign — in some respect — within its own order that the monarchy, as it were, of reason comes to require justification, if not critical reconsideration. Although one finds what appears to be the first affirmation of such a principle in Stoic thought, St. Augustine is typically credited as the "author of the will," since this power represents such a basic, and indeed, decidedly positive, dimension of the soul for him.[3] There

1. It is not insignificant that Socrates, who represents a sort of "anthropological turn" in early Greek thought, introduces the reduction of the ideal of virtue to knowledge. While the celebration of virtue in pre-philosophical thought exhibits an aspiration to unity in some respect, it is not what we would call an anthropological unity in the more technical sense of the term.

2. Consider Aristotle, *Nicomachean Ethics* 7.2.1147a8-10; cf. 7.2.1146a6-8.

3. Hannah Arendt calls Augustine the "first philosopher of the will." *The Life of the Mind*, vol. 2: *Willing* (New York: Harcourt Brace Jovanovich, 1978), pp. 84-110. Cf. Albrecht

are good grounds to believe that a view of the will as an irreducibly distinct principle in the soul depends on seeing Will as a principle of the world, or, in other words, a notion of the world owing not only its organization but its very existence to an act of creation *ex nihilo*.[4] Arguably, if there is no spontaneous or "free" agency at the world's origin, then relation to this origin, and thus the highest activity in the universe, will not itself be a free response and therefore act of the will, but will ultimately reduce to some mode of rational conformity to natural order.

A notion of will as an irreducibly distinct power of the soul, however, entails the need to order it in relation to the intellect if we are to keep the soul from disintegrating. Now, if we designate the will's order as that of love, in contrast to the wisdom or knowledge that relates to the intellectual order, Scripture gives us many reasons to subordinate the intellect and give primacy to the will. Of the three things that abide, St. Paul tells us, the greatest is love; the love expressed in the Cross of Christ renders all pagan wisdom foolish; it is indeed a love that surpasses understanding. In the end, it is not knowledge or wisdom that justifies love, but always love that justifies knowledge, so much so that I ought to count any wisdom that lies outside the order of divine love as loss rather than gain: if I have wisdom, but not love, it is the clanging of cymbals — in other words, not wisdom at all but senseless noise. If there are characterizations of God in Scripture that echo insights of the Greek sages, St. John offers one that has no obvious pagan counterpart, one that expresses the summit of revelation: "God is love." We are thus not surprised to discover that, when presented with the di-

---

Dihle's similar judgment in *The Theory of Will in Classical Antiquity* (Berkeley: University of California Press, 1982). Miklos Vetö, by contrast, refers to Seneca as the "first great philosopher of the will." *La naissance de la volonté* (Paris: L'Harmattan, 2002), p. 28. To be sure, it is true, as Vetö argues, that the significance the Stoics give to submitting to, rather than simply suffering, the inevitable — and the role this implies for "intention" — marks a major step in the development of a distinct notion of will, but the will here is simply the power to conform to the cosmic Logos. In Augustine, we have a creaturely will that responds in freedom to the Creative Will. It is crucial to keep in mind that the irreducibility of the will in Augustine is different in profound ways from the sheer indeterminacy of modern conceptions of the will, a difference that Dihle seems to overlook.

4. Plotinus's notion of the absolute dependence of all reality on the One is no doubt the closest one can come to a notion of *creatio ex nihilo* without a distinct doctrine of will. But, if there is no trans-formal activity as "part" of the structure of things, creatures will be in no wise distinct from God, their exemplar cause. This problem is one of the reasons Aquinas affirms the Divine Will (which corresponds to the *esse* as distinct from the — formal — essence of things) as essential to the act of creation. See *ST* 1.19.5 and 1.44.3.

lemma of giving primacy to the order of love or the order of wisdom, the majority of Christian thinkers have sided with St. Paul. Anselm's formulation is the classic expression of this decision: *Pervesus ordo esset, velle amare ut intelligeres.*

But the issue cannot in fact be settled so easily. Not only are there passages in Scripture that clearly esteem knowledge or present it as the end of Christian existence — St. Paul, after all, speaks precisely of *knowing* the love that surpasses knowledge, while St. John refers to Christians as those who know,[5] and declares that "this is eternal life: that they may *know* (γιγνώσκωσιν) thee, the only *true* (ἀληθινὸν) God" (John 17:3) — and not only are there great figures in the Church's history that characterize Christianity essentially as a kind of γνῶσις,[6] or otherwise privilege the intellect over the will, but there are also strong philosophical reasons to suggest that affirming an ultimate primacy of the will would generate profound difficulties. Briefly, to the extent that the will exceeds the intellect in its exercise, it would be a-rational, if not outright irrational; in any event, it would be blind.[7] And if the will were to exceed the intellect in its highest activity, the heart of human life would be opaque absurdity and chaos.[8] Moreover, insofar as the will represents a "movement toward," and thus a dynamism, rather than a completion, the absolutization of the order of the will would imply the rejection of the ultimacy of unity as a principle of the universe, which would imply in turn the undermining not only of epistemological, but eventually also of ontological coherence. As we shall see more fully in a moment, reasons such as these led St. Thomas Aquinas, one of the great defenders of the dignity of intelligence both in his person and in his work, to insist on the ultimate superiority of the intellect over the will.[9]

5. See 1 John 2:20: "But you have been anointed by the Holy One, and you all know." Some ancient manuscripts have: "you all know everything."

6. This was a theme especially of Alexandrian theology. See Balthasar's brief discussion in *GL1*, pp. 131-41.

7. It is interesting to consider that this is precisely how Descartes accounts for the possibility of error: "Whence then come my errors? They come from the sole fact that since the will is much wider in its range and compass than the understanding, I do not restrain it within the same bonds, but extend it also to things which I do not understand." *The Philosophical Works of Descartes*, vol. 1, trans. Elizabeth Haldane and G. R. T. Ross (Cambridge: Cambridge University Press, 1973), pp. 175-76.

8. Which is just the conclusion that Sartre draws from his view of the priority of existence (the order of the will) over essence (the order of the intellect).

9. Although they both refer to the commonplace Thomist position on the superiority of the intellect over the will, H.-D. Simonin and F. Russell Hittinger, in different ways, point

Where, then, does Hans Urs von Balthasar stand with respect to this problem? There can be no question that he resolutely accords ultimacy to love.[10] For this reason, there are some who affirm that Balthasar falls within what is sometimes referred to as the "Augustinian" tradition, which privileges love, *rather than* within the Thomistic tradition that sees intellect as supreme.[11] In fact, Balthasar has recently come under criticism, no doubt because of this alleged "Augustinianism," for failing to do justice to philosophy or man's natural, rational relation to God. Within theology proper, he is criticized, especially in relation to his Christology and soteriology, for affirming a kind of "surprise" within the immanent Trinity, and the apparently corresponding "blind" obedience, a love to the end beyond all understanding, in the Son's economic relation to the Father, which seems to imply just the sort of irrationalism we alluded to above.[12] Now, it is true that Balthasar speaks of a moment of non-knowledge in the Son's mission of redemption, and moreover that he affirms this moment of darkness, as it were, not in stray passages, but at what is arguably the center of his theology. But what I wish to propose — and here we come to the thesis of this chapter — is that it is equally true that Balthasar's insistence on the absolute priority of love (and, indeed, obedience in love) is *not* a concession to

---

out neglected lines of argument in Aquinas that present the primacy of love over reason. See Simonin, "La Primauté de l'Amour dans la Doctrine de saint Thomas d'Aquin," *La Vie spirituelle* 53 (1937): 129-43, and Hittinger, "When It Is More Excellent to Love Than to Know: The Other Side of Thomistic 'Realism,'" *Proceedings of the American Catholic Philosophical Association* 57 (1983): 171-79. We will make reference to some of the points these articles make as we proceed.

10. Balthasar, *TL1*, p. 125: "truth serves love, while love embraces and transcends truth. Truth is the unveiling of being; the laws of love are its limit and measure. Love, on the other hand, has no measure and no limit other than itself." Cf. p. 127.

11. Jörg Disse and Pascal Ide, for example, both interpret Balthasar as esteeming the will, i.e., love, as higher than reason. See Disse, "Liebe und Erkenntnis: Zur Geistesmetaphysik Hans Urs von Balthasars," *Münchner Theologische Zeitschrift* 54, no. 3 (1999): 215-27, and Ide, *Être et mystère: La philosophie de Hans Urs von Balthasar* (Brussels: Culture et Vérité, 1995), pp. 157-59.

12. See, most notably, Bernard Blankenhorn, "Balthasar's Method of Divine Naming," *Nova et Vetera* 1, no. 2 (2003): 245-68, and Matthew Levering, *Scripture and Metaphysics: Aquinas and the Renewal of Trinitarian Theology* (Oxford: Blackwell, 2004), pp. 120-32. Cf. Guy Mansini, "Balthasar and the Theodramatic Enrichment of the Trinity," *The Thomist* 54 (2000): 499-519, and Richard Schenk, "Ist die Rede vom leidenden Gott theologisch zu vermeiden? Reflexion über den Streit von K. Rahner und H. U. von Balthasar," in *Der Leidende Gott: Eine philosophische und theologische Kritik,* ed. Peter Koslowski and Friedrich Hermanni (München: Wilhelm Fink Verlag, 2001), pp. 225-39.

voluntarism and the irrationality it entails, but is ultimately due to a significantly different notion of reason than is generally assumed, a notion of reason that is, I will argue, ultimately necessary to *overcome* irrationalism once and for all. Indeed, I want to suggest that the terms in which the problem is generally framed make an ultimate irrationalism inevitable, *even if one affirms, with Thomas, the supremacy of the intellect.* As we will see, Balthasar approaches the question of the intellect's relation to the will from a rather different point of departure, which recasts the terms of the problem in a fundamental way, and which in the end allows a view that integrates both of the seemingly opposed traditions.

To be sure, these are vast claims, which would require a much more elaborate treatment than is possible here. What I propose to do in the following is to focus on one basic aspect of the problem, namely, the philosophical dimension, and simply suggest in very general terms how the philosophical dimension illuminates his theological position. To understand Balthasar properly, it is crucial to see that he does not simply offer, as some believe,[13] a theological "corrective" to a philosophical position — a response of this sort would, indeed, give some warrant to the charge of fideism and theological reductionism — but rather offers a more adequate philosophical position in the place of a problematic one. In order to show this, I will first set up the problem of the relation between the intellect and will through an interpretation of texts from Aquinas's *Summa* that reveal a possible tension in his affirmation of the superiority of the intellect, at least as this superiority is conventionally understood.[14] Next, I will suggest how Balthasar's view of the relation between the intellect and will can resolve this tension, and finally allow for an affirmation of the supremacy of love that nevertheless includes an abiding priority of the intellect over the will, and thus responds decisively to the charge of irrationalism.

13. See Blankenhorn's final question regarding Balthasar's approach to God, in "Balthasar's Method," p. 267: "Is theology still using philosophical concepts and categories, or is it creating its own?"

14. We take for granted the axiom André Hayens introduces in his interpretation of Aquinas: "'True Thomism' surpasses the thought of all Thomists and even that of St. Thomas himself, somewhat in the way that humanity surpasses each of the human beings that instantiate it individually." *L'Intentionnel selon saint Thomas* (Paris: Desclée de Brouwer, 1954), 18-19.

Aquinas on the Circle of the Acts of the Soul in Its Relation to Being

What follows does not intend to be a full and nuanced interpretation of this complex theme in Aquinas, but rather a sketch, in broad strokes, of the straightforward meaning of certain texts from the *Summa.* A more interesting and adequate view of Aquinas's notion of reason has been developed over the last century, and we will indicate some of these openings, where appropriate, in the footnotes. The purpose of this section, however, is primarily to show the difficulties that arise from a simplistic view of reason and knowledge in order to bring out more dramatically the significance of Balthasar's insights. We discussed the order of the transcendentals in the last chapter; here we will focus on the relationship between the powers of the soul.

In his response to the question of superiority in the relation of intellect to will, which he raises directly at *ST* 1.84.3, Aquinas begins by stating that the issue can be approached either absolutely — that is, in terms of the order of the powers considered in themselves — or relatively, that is, in terms of a relation to a particular object. Let us follow out these two approaches in succession, first outlining the logic of these powers in anticipation of their final end, and then considering them specifically in the relation to God that constitutes man's final state.

To describe the logic of the intellect-will relation, Aquinas adopts what might be called the "circle of the acts of the soul" from Aristotle, which we sketched in the previous chapter.[15] The soul is ordered to being; however, it does not relate to being simply as such, but rather always under a certain aspect, most fundamentally: as intelligible (truth, the object of intellect), and as appetible (goodness, the object of will). In the normal operation of these powers, the intellect precedes the will, for the will, as a "rational appetite," always acts under the representation of an object. One does not will, in other words, without willing "something," and that something is a determinate "what" *(nihil appetitum nisi praecognitum).*[16] Thus, Aquinas says that the soul *first* apprehends a concept of its object, by abstracting the intelligible species — the essence — of the thing, becoming "intentionally" identical with it through the act of understanding *(intelligibile in actu est intellectus in actu),*[17]

15. He elaborates this in most detail in *De ver.* 1.1; see also *ST* 1.16.1 and 1.27.4.

16. *ST* 1-2.27.2.

17. *ST* 1.14.2. As Rousselot puts it, "*Veritatem videre est eam habere,* said Augustine; Scholastic analysis would add, *et quodammodo esse.*" *Intelligence: Sense of Being, Faculty of*

and thus quite literally "internalizes" its intelligible form. This is why Aquinas insists that, if all operations have a *terminus* in which the act comes to rest, the operation of the intellect terminates in the soul. To put it another way, the adequation between mind and thing that defines truth in its essential sense[18] presupposes a mode of existence of the thing that is capable of identity with the immaterial intellect. But insofar as the proper object of the mind is in fact *material* being,[19] some immaterial "aspect" of it must be abstracted from it for such an adequation to be possible: this is the form, which is distinct from the object's matter, and thus can be distinguished by the active power of the mind (active intellect) as an intelligible species.[20] Because it is the matter, and not the form, that makes the thing a particular entity located in time and space, abstracting the form is the same thing as universalizing it, or, more accurately, liberating it from its limiting conditions. Thus, Aquinas affirms that the proper object of the intellect is the "quiddity of material things,"[21] and that this object resides in the soul that knows it rather than in the thing itself: "For it is quite true that the mode of understanding, in one who understands, is not the same as the mode of a thing in existing: since the thing understood is immaterially in the one who understands, according to the mode of the intellect, and not materially, according to the mode of a material thing."[22]

God, trans. Andrew Tallon (Milwaukee: Marquette University Press, 1999), p. 68. Cf. Gilson, *The Philosophy of St. Thomas Aquinas* (New York: Dorset Press, 1948), pp. 265-66. We are using the term "intentio" as Simonin defines it, namely, as not a physical act but an object of intellection, the intellectual representation of a given reality. "La notion d'intentio dans l'oeuvre de saint Thomas," *Revue des Sciences Philosophiques et Théologiques* 19 (1930): 445-63; here, 451.

18. *ST* 1.16.1. Cf. *De ver.* 1.1.

19. *ST* 1.84.7.

20. *ST* 1.85.1ad3.

21. *ST* 1.88.3; 1.84.7; 1.85.8; 1.87.2ad2. See Gilson, *The Philosophy of St. Thomas,* p. 249.

22. Here we reach a decisive moment in Aquinas's theory of knowledge, one that presents an ambiguity. On the one hand, as we have seen, Aquinas states quite clearly that the movement of cognition terminates in the soul. On the other hand, he seems to insinuate a certain movement *outward* to the thing in the completion of the intellectual act: it is not the formation of the quiddities of things — which he repeatedly calls the proper object of the mind — that represents truth in its most proper sense, but the *actual* combinations that arise in judgment (see *De ver.* 1, 3). On this, see Gilson, *The Philosophy of St. Thomas,* pp. 272-73, where he insists that the mind has to reach "out" to a term outside of the mind itself, namely, the really existing thing, in order for there to be an adequation at all. André Hayens, by contrast, points to the fact that *judgment* presents truth most properly, not because it attains to the actually existing thing, but because the mind most completely returns to *itself* therein. "Le lien de la connaissance et du vouloir dans l'acte d'exister selon saint

But being is not merely intentional, it is also real; or as Aquinas puts it in the *De veritate,* "in any being there are two aspects to be considered, the formal character of its species and the act of being by which it subsists in that species."[23] That which the intellect grasps of being is not the whole of being precisely insofar as it excludes being in its reality, i.e., in its existential dimension. It is just this "aspect" of being that Aquinas connects with goodness. If truth exists primarily in the mind, goodness, for its part, exists principally in the things themselves.[24] It is precisely for this reason that goodness is being, specifically under the aspect of appetibility, for the appetite is, as it were, a tendency outward.[25] While the soul "internalizes" the truth of a thing by grasping it in the intentional order, to *enjoy* it requires the reality itself. For all of the profound intimacy with the being of things that truth denotes, the one thing that the knowing soul cannot internalize is the thing's actual existence. The goodness of being lies *outside* the soul, and the soul must move to *it* in order to attain this goodness. If the intellect's operation terminates in the soul, the will's operation terminates in the really existing thing. Once again, we see why the act of the will has to follow upon the act of intellect: in order to move *toward* its object, the will has to be moved *by* its object in a basic respect. We discussed this aspect in the previous chapter. As an appetite, the will is drawn by its object, which means it is principally receptive. But to be receptive means that it must first receive in order to act, and, as we saw above, the active reception of being, the "internalization" of a thing, is precisely what defines the intellectual act. To sum up the basic logic of the relation between the powers of the soul, we would say that the soul relates to being first by taking it into itself intentionally as true and then moving beyond itself to being's real existence as good: "a thing outside the soul moves

---

Thomas d'Aquin," *Doctor communis* 3 (1950): 54-72. However that may be, Thomas is clear that the abstracted species themselves are not the *object* of knowledge, but that *by* which the actually existing *thing itself* is known (*ST* 1.85.2). But the complexity and ambiguity do not end here: the actually existing thing, he goes on to qualify, is nevertheless *not* the object of knowledge itself, since knowledge is of universals and the real thing is an individual. Instead, the mind knows the quiddity *of* the materially existing thing, but not *as* thus existing. *ST* 1.85.2ad2.

23. *De ver.* 21.1.

24. *ST* 1.16.1; cf. *De ver.* 1.2. The distinction between the *loci* of truth and goodness ought not to lead one to divide being, as it were, into two halves, for doing so would undermine the transcendental nature of both. The distinction between essence and existence is not a separation; in the same way, truth and goodness each concern the *whole* of being, though from a different perspective.

25. *ST* 1-2.28.3.

the intellect, and the thing known moves the appetite, which tends to reach the thing from which the motion started."[26]

Though this describes the basic logic of the operations, however, as we suggested above, the relation between the two powers is never in reality simply unilateral, with the intellect moving the will and the will never in turn moving the intellect. In fact, Aquinas affirms that their relation is always *reciprocal.*[27] The reciprocity arises, in part, from the circumincession of goodness and truth as transcendental properties of being, and therefore strictly convertible with it. In this sense, the good and the true mutually include one another: while the good is true, because it is intelligible and contains an idea, the true is also itself a good — in fact, for Aquinas it is the highest good.[28] But if the objects of the powers of the soul include one another, so do the activities of those powers:[29] though it is true that the will can act only under a conception of its object, it is nevertheless true as well that the intellect can understand only because it is good to understand! — which is to say that (with a qualification that will be entered in a moment) there is no act of the intellect that is not willed by the will. When the will *does* move the intellect in this sense, it does so as a real activity and thus as a particular species of good; in other words, because it is good in this particular case to understand something, and every act of understanding is in fact a particular act of understanding.

Of course, the moment we affirm the intellect's dependence on will, we encounter a problem: the will can will this act of the intellect only if it *understands* it as good, which means once again only as subordinating itself to an act of the intellect. But even that act must be itself willed. And so on. We seem, then, to run into an infinite regress problem. In order to resolve it, Aquinas insists that we must "stop at the intellect as preceding all the rest. For every movement of the will must be preceded by apprehension, whereas every apprehension is not preceded by an act of the will; but the principle of counseling and understanding is an intellectual principle higher than our intellect — namely, God."[30] Though this principial act of intellect is not

26. *De ver.* 1, 2.

27. Winfried Czapiewski presents a host of texts from Aquinas illustrating this reciprocity in *Das Schöne bei Thomas von Aquin* (Freiburg: Herder, 1964), pp. 106-11. Cf. Pierre Rousselot, *The Eyes of Faith,* trans. Joseph Donceel and Avery Dulles (New York: Fordham University Press, 1990); David L. Schindler, "History, Objectivity, and Moral Conversion," *The Thomist* 37 (July 1973): 569-88; and Hayens, "Le lien de la connaissance et du vouloir."

28. *ST* 1.82.3 and 1.

29. *ST* 1.16.5 and 1.

30. *ST* 1.82.4ad3.

moved by the will, it is nevertheless not a purely spontaneous act: rather, Aquinas says that God, as intellect, first moves the will, and thus sets in motion all the rest.[31] We will see that Balthasar offers a significantly different response to this problem.

However that may be, we are now in a position to understand why the intellect, absolutely speaking, is higher than the will. In *ST* 1.82.3, Aquinas offers a basic argument for its superiority. First, if not its *adequate* object, the natural object of the soul in general is material being.[32] As true, material being is elevated, as it were, to an immaterial mode of existence, while, as good, it exists concretely through the various compositions that constitute material being (substance and accidents, form and matter, essence and existence). But simplicity and abstraction are nobler than complexity; therefore, truth is nobler than goodness. If we were to ask precisely why the simplicity and abstraction of the intellect's object make it "nobler" *(nobilior)* than the will, the answer seems to lie in the universality this simplicity implies. The word Aquinas uses to characterize the universal here is "higher" *(altior):* the universal is higher than the individual, and insofar as abstraction frees a thing from the limitations that make it individual, whereas appetite tends toward the thing as an individual, truth is for that reason higher than goodness. Thus, Aquinas adds, the *idea* of goodness is in fact nobler than its individual reality, presumably because this idea in its formality includes more than any particular instance of good.

To the arguments Aquinas offers in this question of the *Summa,* we may add another derived from his discussion of man's ultimate end:[33] because the good lies in the real thing, which possesses its individual existence *outside* of the soul, there cannot be unity in an absolute sense with a thing qua good, but only qua true. The will, Aquinas explains, is a movement, whether it be the movement of appetite prior to the attainment of a thing, or

31. See Gilson, *The Philosophy of St. Thomas,* pp. 299-300, and Mark Jordan, "The Transcendentality of Goodness and the Human Will," in *Being and Goodness: The Concept of the Good in Metaphysics and Philosophical Theology* (Ithaca, NY: Cornell University Press, 1991), p. 170.

32. As Gilson explains, for Aquinas, the human soul is naturally embodied, and its natural intellectual object is therefore corporeal. Nevertheless, material being does not satisfy the mind, which was made to know God himself, who is purely immaterial. Thus, we have the paradox that the human mind was made for an object that exceeds its nature. On this, see the chapter "The Intellect and Its Object," from *The Spirit of Medieval Philosophy* (New York: Charles Scribner's Sons, 1940), pp. 248-68.

33. We are referring here to *ST* 1-2.3 and 4.

the movement of enjoyment subsequent upon the attainment. But it is not the attainment itself, which is most properly speaking an intellectual act.[34] As we saw above, it is the immateriality of the object known that allows the soul to be *identical* with it in act, which indicates a unity that can only be approximated, better or worse, by the will's pursuit of the good.[35] This is why Aquinas, in contrast to many of his confrères in the Franciscan — or we might say, Augustinian — tradition, affirmed that man's final end, the eschatological vision of God, is not essentially an act of love (i.e., of the will), but an act of intellect: "The essence of happiness consists in an act of the intellect."[36] If the union of love, rather than the unity of knowledge, were the essence of happiness, that happiness would perpetually remain something *sought* rather than *attained,* insofar as attainment, in its perfect sense, indicates the kind of possession that can occur only intellectually; and, as Aquinas puts it, the movement of the will refers to the pursuit of that attainment or the subsequent delight in it, but is not the attainment itself.[37] To be sure, even this point is more complicated than initially appears, for Aquinas in fact states, in his treatment of the effects of love, that "the union caused by

34. In *ST* 1-2.1.1ad2, Aquinas affirms that the willing *itself* cannot be an end, but the will must command the attainment of the last end, which is itself other than an act of will — i.e., it is an act of intelligence. To affirm the contrary is to fall into a vicious circle.

35. Aquinas says that love brings about a "suitable and becoming union," which is more "real" than intellectual unity, but is not unity itself. See *ST* 1-2.28.2ad2. Moreover, in 1-2.16.4, he affirms that to possess an end thus is to have imperfectly. No matter how close they may become or how perfect their bond, lovers, indeed, remain existentially distinct from one another. In knowledge, by contrast, their existential distinction does not prevent absolute intentional unity.

36. *ST* 1-2.3.4. In his treatment of grace, however, Aquinas also says that "everlasting life consists in the enjoyment *(fruitio)* of God" (*ST* 1-2.114.4). Simonin reconciles this text with the better-known one cited above by saying that Aquinas here is referring to the order of *merit* in which goodness (and thus love) takes priority, and that the recompense of this merit is the intellectual act in which God is *received* to be enjoyed (see Simonin, "La Primauté de l'Amour," p. 132). Gallagher offers, to my mind, a better account of the larger picture: contemplation is not the *end* but the essence of beatitude. One does not love the contemplation, but *God,* even though contemplation is the essential means of realizing this love. If one loved the contemplation, one would degrade the love of God into an *amor concupiscentiae.* See David Gallagher, "Person and Ethics in Thomas Aquinas," *Acta Philosophica* 4 (1995): 51-71; here, 70.

37. See the contrast Rousselot draws between the union of love and the unity of knowledge through a juxtaposition of texts from Aquinas (and others) in *The Problem of Love in the Middle Ages: A Historical Contribution,* trans. Alan Vincelette (Milwaukee: Marquette University Press, 2001), pp. 205-6, n. 116.

love is closer [*magis unitivus*] than that which is caused by knowledge."[38] But here he is talking about union from the perspective of the *real* order, as opposed to the intentional order, and refers to material being, which we cannot possess intellectually as it really (materially) exists — in which case, the union of love brings us, as it were, closer to the reality of the thing than does intentional union. In other words, if the union of love is "closer" to the *real* thing, intentional union is nevertheless more perfect *as union.* The union of love is real, not formal, while the union of knowledge is formal, not real, and only formal union can be unity in an absolute sense. Aquinas regards the formal, nonmaterial union as the noblest type of union.[39] Elevating real over formal unity would be absolutizing the relative and relativizing the absolute. In the eschaton, however, the material conditions that keep formal unity from being real will fall away, and there will no longer be anything preventing the intellect from uniting itself perfectly to the reality it knows, which would thus make the intellectual act the best of all possible acts.

We can now return once again to the distinction we started with in Aquinas's discussion in *ST* 1.82.3, regarding which of the two, intellect or will, is the higher power. As we saw, Aquinas observes that this question can be approached either absolutely or relatively. Considered in themselves — for the reasons we elaborated above — intellect is higher than the will. However, when we consider the soul in relation to a particular object, we find two responses to the question. If, on the one hand, the soul's object is a lower good than the soul itself, then the intellect is higher, because its act "elevates" the object by appropriating it into itself. Indeed, for Aquinas, it is sinful to love what is lower than the soul insofar as this would imply the soul's debasement. On the other hand, if the object is higher than the soul, then the will is higher than the intellect. As we have seen, the act of will is the soul's movement beyond itself. If that to which the soul moves itself through the will is higher than the soul, then the act elevates the soul. This insight brings Aquinas to a conclusion that is startling in light of his affirmation of the absolute superiority of intellect to will: "Wherefore the love of God is better than the knowledge of God." As De Finance explains it, "To know God would be to lower him to us; to love God raises us to him."[40]

Now, though the intellect is intrinsically higher than the will, and

38. *ST* 1-2.28.1ad3.

39. See *In caus.* 1.18. Cf. *De ver.* 22.11.

40. Joseph de Finance, *Être et agir dans la philosophie de saint Thomas* (Rome: Gregorian University Press, 1965), p. 340.

though the beatific vision consists essentially in the act of the intellect, Aquinas affirms that, in the particular case of the soul's relation to God (and presumably its relation to those other immaterial substances, the angels), the will is higher. This particular case is the most basic one. There is clearly a tension here: the most fundamental relative case turns out to be the opposite of the absolute one. It will not do to resolve this tension by affirming that this superiority of the will holds for the will's relation to God *in via*, but not *in fine*.[41] Such a qualification would succeed in dissolving the problem only if the soul were capable, finally, of appropriating the whole of God without remainder into itself in the sense of a total comprehension, so that there would in fact be no "beyond" left to require the soul's volitional movement above itself. But Aquinas is unequivocally clear that this is never the case, and never will be the case for all eternity: God is infinite, and the human intellect, as created, is and will remain finite.[42] If Aquinas in principle says that reason is higher than love, it seems that this principle gets reversed in the end, and love turns out in fact to "trump reason" after all.[43] Nor is this merely a particular and accidental case. If it is true, as Aquinas also affirms, that this final state is that for which the human being was created, then we have an essential end that overturns man's essential nature.

Now, the reason for laying emphasis on this tension is not in the least to undermine Aquinas's philosophy. Rather, I mean to suggest only that the conventional reading of Aquinas will ultimately encounter a tension, if not an outright contradiction, when pressed to the most fundamental levels of reflection, and that, in order to avoid such a tension, one must develop a much more paradoxical interpretation of the texts of Aquinas. As I mentioned above, I believe that the depth, complexity, integrity, and honesty of

41. In *ST* 2-2.27.4ad2, Aquinas says "to love God is something greater than to know him, *especially* in this life" (emphasis mine), which suggests that the superiority of love holds in some sense also in the eschaton.

42. *ST* 1.86.2ad1: though we will be able to see God in the state of glory, we will still not be able to "comprehend" him.

43. Hittinger, in fact, proposes that love, i.e., charity in this case, will be superior to reason in all of those acts concerning God specifically: thus, if reason (and truth) is superior in relation to the natural virtues, love (and goodness) is superior in relation to the theological virtues. Unless we qualify this affirmation further, however, we have a case wherein the order of grace simply reverses the order of nature, which would entail a fideism/voluntarism/irrationalism in the order of the theological virtues. It does not suffice simply to affirm that this reversal does not imply "any sort of voluntarist or irrational subjection of the intellective union to the appetitive," as Hittinger remarks in conclusion, unless one offers an explanation *why* it does not. See Hittinger, "When It Is More Excellent to Love Than to Know," esp. pp. 177-78.

Aquinas's thought provide ample resources for such an interpretation, though we will not pursue it here.[44] Instead, I propose that the vision of the transcendentals, being, and love that we find in Balthasar serves to resolve this tension in a fruitful way, and would claim in fact that a rereading of Aquinas in the light of this tension will ultimately result in a position basically similar to the one Balthasar adopts. In other words, Balthasar is not "opposed" to Aquinas, as some have charged, but opposed only to a simplistic reading of Aquinas, which entails problems of its own; at the deepest level, there is a harmony between the two thinkers, and Balthasar helps to orient one's interpretation of Aquinas in a fruitful direction.

In order to appreciate the significance of Balthasar's contribution to this particular problem, it is good to state more clearly the potential difficulties generated by a standard interpretation, which simply contrasts the immanence of the intellectual act to the ecstasis of the appetitive act.[45] To

44. For example, there is Aquinas's fundamental notion of the *actus essendi, esse creatum,* which is inherent to all existing things, and which, as actuality, is intelligible, but as "super"-formal cannot be subsumed intentionally by the soul. Though this act is central to Aquinas's metaphysics, it does not seem to figure so centrally in his epistemology. (For an incorporation of the significance of this act into epistemology, see Gilson's chapter "Knowledge and Existence," in *Being and Some Philosophers* [Toronto: Pontifical Institute of Medieval Studies, 1952], pp. 190-215, and especially De Finance, *Être et agir dans la philosophie de saint Thomas,* pp. 305-7. Kenneth Schmitz offers a speculative development of this line of thinking in "Enriching the Copula," *Review of Metaphysics* 27 [1974]: 492-512.) To make it central, one would have to develop, for example, what it would mean to know singulars (or at least in what sense knowledge is "more" than simply universal), and thus to develop Aquinas's principles in a direction different from the one he followed. We see something of this move, for example, in Hayens, who argues for a *dynamic* interpretation of intentionality, whereby the real objectivity of knowledge is secured by the mediation of the act of the will (*L'Intentionnel selon saint Thomas,* pp. 222-25), or also in Rousselot, who develops the principles for knowledge of singulars in Aquinas through an analysis of the nonidentity between concept/definition and the actual essence of a thing, and the corresponding analogical movement *within* the intellectual act toward the really existing thing as it is in itself (*Intelligence,* esp. chapter 3, pp. 91-109). It would also be possible, finally, to put more "flesh" on the standard interpretation of species, and thus bring out its aesthetic dimension (along the lines of the *Gestalt* we elaborate below) and its mediating role between the mind and reality. See Aquinas's comments on the "intellectual conception" in *De ver.* 4.2ad3. For a recent attempt to respond to the potential problem we lay out here, see Michael Waddell, "Aquinas on the Light of Glory," *Tópicos: Rivista de Filosofia* 40 (2011): 105-32.

45. Aquinas often enough states this contrast himself in a cursory fashion: "the act of a cognitive power is completed by the thing known being in the knower, whereas the act of an appetitive power consists in the appetite being inclined towards the thing in itself" (*ST* 2-2.27.4). Cf. 1.82.3 and 1.84.7. The point is that this contrast needs significant qualification.

put it more specifically, they stem from a reading of the form of knowledge as wholly "possessive." I will mention four of these difficulties. (1) Aquinas describes the eschatological vision of God not as the soul's taking God into itself intellectually, but rather as God's elevating the soul to himself through grace.[46] But this response leaves in place a problem: if the intellectual vision of God is a movement *exactly the contrary* of the soul's natural exercise of intelligence, then — without a radical rethinking of the meaning of natural intelligence — the vision of God is, strictly speaking, the opposite of rational — i.e., it is irrational.[47] Aquinas, apparently aware of this implication, suggests a kind of analogy between this supernatural vision and the natural operation of the intellect in terms of the soul's capacity to abstract the form (and thus a certain natural aptitude for the immaterial),[48] but the deeper problem, it seems to me, is not so much the capacity to know an immaterial substance as it is the movement of soul required for such knowledge.

(2) If the previous point indicated the danger of the analogy between knowledge and supernatural vision collapsing into contradiction, we also face the opposite problem of the analogy of being collapsing into identity. Aquinas goes on to say that created grace strengthens the natural power of the created intellect to allow it to see God, an act that would otherwise simply be disproportionate to it.[49] If, in knowledge, the knower becomes identical to the known in act, so too in the beatific vision, the blessed become "deiform" *(deiformes),* that is, as one form, with God. The question is: Does this "deiformity," as it were, preclude any difference? It would seem necessary for it to do so if Aquinas had rejected love as the essence of beatitude precisely on account of the abiding difference, and thus the incompleteness

46. *ST* 1.12.4ad3; 1.12.5.

47. Hittinger observes that the eschatological "vision" is structurally more like the appetitive than the intellectual relation. "When It Is More Excellent to Love Than to Know," p. 177: ". . . a new medium is introduced [in the eschaton], and the created intellect is made dependent upon the medium of the 'other,' in a fashion similar to the natural structure of the appetitive relation to any sort of entity."

48. *ST* 1.12.4ad3: "Since therefore the created intellect is naturally capable of apprehending the concrete form, and the concrete being abstractedly, by way of a kind of resolution of parts; it can by grace be raised up to know separate subsisting substance, and separate subsisting existence." The crucial problem is how one *knows* something that remains in a decisive sense beyond the soul if knowledge *means* possession: the analogy that Aquinas presents here between the abstracted species and the immaterial substance, while it resolves one problem, by the very same token deepens this other.

49. *ST* 1.12.5.

of the unity, it entails.[50] Moreover, *if* it were true that, in spite of the assimilation to God that this created grace enables, God still remained in some sense "more" than the soul, then the logic of Aquinas's position would require him to affirm love as the ultimate act, because the act of will is nobler than the act of intellect whenever that to which the soul relates is higher than the soul. But to affirm this would, in turn, require a radical reconsideration of his philosophical anthropology, as we saw above. If we were to deny that God remained forever greater than the soul, on the other hand, then the *analogia entis* would founder into a substantial identity between the soul and God, which, as Aquinas would say, is "repugnant to the faith."

(3) To specify the problem in the philosophical anthropology just alluded to: one of the reasons Aquinas had affirmed the supremacy of the intellect, absolutely speaking, over the will was to avoid the purely spontaneous and thus irrational use of the will, which we could call voluntarism. As we have seen, Aquinas follows Aristotle in characterizing knowledge as a movement of, as it were, spiritual internalization of the intelligible form of the object, which terminates in the soul of the knower. Knowledge, in this case, is not complete to the extent that that which is to be understood remains somehow beyond the soul: comprehension means that a thing is known to the extent that it is knowable,[51] and to be known means to be appropriated into the knower, to be "included" within him:

> "To comprehend" means, as it were, "to grasp all at once," i.e., to lay hold of; and therefore something is properly comprehended when it is laid hold of all at once, i.e., with everything that belongs to it. Hence, it is necessary that every comprehended thing must be enclosed within the one comprehending. . . . Now, just as something bodily is said to be contained in another because it does not exceed any of the container's bounds according to dimensive quantity, as wine in a cask, so something is said to be contained by another spiritually when it stands under its power and in no way exceeds that [container]. And therefore something is said to be comprehended by knowledge when the thing known stands under the act of the knowing power and does not exceed it.[52]

50. See *ST* 1-2.3.4ad4: "Love ranks above knowledge in moving, but knowledge precedes love in attaining: for *naught is loved save what is known,* as Augustine says (*De Trinitate* x, 1). Consequently, we first attain an intelligible end by an act of the intellect; just as we first attain a sensible end by an act of sense."

51. *ST* 1.14.3.

52. *Sent.* IV, 49.2.3.

Knowledge, in other words, means possession, and a person either possesses something or he does not. But this implies that the use of the will in relation to anything not possessed by the soul, anything that "exceeds" the soul, is irrational.[53] It would follow that the affirmation of something on the basis of authority, for example, is not *intrinsically* a rational act, even if one has good reasons for giving one's assent.[54] In this case, because the revelation which is the object of faith cannot be *possessed* in its truth in the manner generally accorded to reason, there will always remain something fundamentally irrational, or at least "a-rational," about faith.[55] If we define reason wholly in terms

53. Aquinas *does* affirm that something can be loved perfectly even if it is imperfectly known: "wherefore it suffices, for the perfection of love, that a thing be loved according as it is known in itself. Hence it is, therefore, that a thing is loved more than it is known; since it can be loved perfectly, even without being perfectly known. This is most evident in regard to the sciences, which some love through having a certain general knowledge of them: for instance, they know that rhetoric is a science that enables man to persuade others; and this is what they love in rhetoric. The same applies to the love of God." *ST* 1-2.27.2ad3. Does this mean that the completion of the act of will does not depend on the completion of the act of intellect, so that the quality of one's knowledge is irrelevant to the quality of one's act of will? It would generally seem to be the case that the better I know something, the more I am capable of loving it. The precise wording Aquinas chooses here is significant: love is directed to a thing *insofar* as it is known, which means that I can exercise a "perfect" (i.e., complete) act of will with regard to a thing as long as I know *that* it is, without having to know much about it in particular. In this case, my act of will is still altogether governed by my understanding. According to Gallagher, the will "tends primarily towards the *formality* under which an object is willed, and only secondarily toward the object itself." David Gallagher, "Thomas Aquinas on Will as Rational Appetite," *The Journal of the History of Philosophy* (1991): 559-84; here, 576.

54. See, e.g., *ST* 1.1.8ad2. To say *simply* that the argument from authority, generally a less dignified form of argument, is strong in this case because the authority is God himself, and those to whom he originally revealed himself, does not yet show why revelation has any *intrinsic* bearing on reason. Compare this approach to the one Balthasar outlines: he interprets (as we shall see below) reason and its knowledge in a nonpossessive manner as rooted in and ecstatically ordered toward the truth of Being. Because reason is, as it were, obedient (rather than essentially possessive) in its structure, the movement into faith is a deepening and elevation of what is *proper* to reason: "It is this alone which makes it possible for the believer to submit to an external authority" (*GL1*, p. 164). We will elaborate this view of reason at greater length in our concluding chapter on philosophy and theology.

55. One might argue that there *must* be something a-rational about faith if we are to avoid collapsing the distinction between faith and reason. Indeed. But it would be better to say "suprarational" in a sense that does not indicate irrationality. If we preserve a difference between the two precisely by insisting on an essential opposition, whereby the soul-transcending assent to authority is strictly speaking extrinsic, and just so far *foreign,* to the normal operation of intellect, and vice versa, we will ultimately end with a dualism that generates in its turn a host of insoluble problems. Instead, we must find a way to affirm an essential and abiding *difference*

of possession or intentional identity, we will ultimately have no alternative but an essentially fideistic conception of faith, and of anything else that transcends such identity. Any relation, in fact, to the soul's ultimate end — and thus the order of grace, revelation, the theological virtues, and so forth — will, because the ultimate end cannot simply become identical to the soul without simply deifying the soul, inevitably have an irrational and positivistic character. By the same token, the love for God that transcends the possession of God in knowledge, whether we consider it *in via* or *in fine,* will itself, from this perspective, be intrinsically irrational precisely because it is ordered to an object that exceeds reason's grasp. Unless we modify what we mean by reason, we can avoid an ultimate irrationality only by collapsing into the comprehensive possession that the analogy of being does not permit.

(4) Finally, this same conception of knowledge as immanent possession threatens the positive value of mystery in a number of respects. First of all, according to the straightforward interpretation of the acts of the powers of the soul we have presumed in these criticisms, there cannot in principle be any genuine mystery about the created order — except perhaps for the angels. It is not possible for something that I possess simply and exhaustively, indeed, something with which I am intentionally identical in act, to be mysterious to me. And, because human beings are the noblest beings in the material universe, there is no meaningful part of this universe that I cannot take into intellectual possession once and for all. To be sure, because the aspect that the soul becomes identical to in knowledge is solely the intelligible species, one could say that the matter, qua matter, of things remains forever outside the soul, and thus in that sense will always be mysterious; but matter is, so to speak, a negative mystery, an unintelligible darkness. If it is true that the human being, by virtue of the soul, is nobler than any other reality in the material cosmos, then one could never speak of a worldly truth that is in any sense "bigger than me." I cannot participate in a truth that exceeds me, because truth after all has its "locus" in the soul: it cannot exceed me because, as we saw above, I contain it. That which is contained cannot be mysterious.

There is, of course, the Divine Essence, which cannot be contained in this sense by the human intellect. It exceeds the intellect as a power of intelligibility greater than the soul's power to comprehend,[56] and therefore is essen-

that nevertheless does not exclude an analogy, whereby reason would exhibit something of the "ecstasis" of faith, even while faith exhibits something of the "possession" of knowledge. Balthasar's view of reason, as we will elaborate it below, points in just this direction.

56. *ST* 1.86.2ad4. We will indeed know God in the state of glory, but without being able to "comprehend" him.

tially mysterious to it. Thus, it would seem to follow that whatever mystery we might wish to affirm of the world is never a mystery that belongs to the world as a created reality, but can only be the mystery of God that we somehow glimpse *through* the world. In the last chapter we alluded to Pieper's notion of truth on this score, according to which things are mysterious because they are created by God, who is Mystery itself. But there is something that still remains to be said about the divine mystery, thus conceived, and, however subtle it may be, it is decisively important: though this mystery arises from an excess of intelligibility rather than an absence (matter), it nevertheless remains in a significant respect a *negative* mystery with respect to the human soul, insofar as the mystery is due precisely to the soul's *deficiency.* If knowledge is the possession of truth, mystery can only be what is not (yet) possessed. But this entails a dialectical relationship between knowledge and mystery: what is known is not mysterious, and what is mysterious is not (yet) known. To make progress in knowledge, then, is just so far to conquer mystery, except insofar as one uncovers more to be taken into intellectual possession.[57] What we lose, in this case, is a depth dimension in both knowledge and mystery. Truth, evacuated of any *essential* mystery, becomes flat.

Now, to repeat once again, there are resources in Aquinas to respond to these problems, but to do so would require a reconsideration and qualification of the thesis that the operation of the intellect terminates simply in the soul, and that knowledge is therefore possession. It is in just this direction that Balthasar takes his understanding of reason and love, in their relation to truth. If there are aspects of his view that may appear to bear traces of irrationalism, it is only, as we shall see, because he espouses a more ample notion of reason than the one that creates the problems we have just enumerated. In the light of these problems, we turn now to consider some of the basic features of Balthasar's view of the relation between love and reason.

Balthasar on the *Gestalt* in the Circumincession of the Transcendentals

For simplicity's sake, we will sketch the basic features of Balthasar's philosophy relevant to this particular question in five theses; the first two will be stated briefly, since they were addressed in the previous chapter.

57. In *Sent IV,* 49.2.3, which we cited above, Aquinas goes on to explain that the intelligibility of a finite thing can exceed the human intellect in *quantity,* if not in quality, and offers the example of the impossibility of knowing an infinite numerical series.

(1) *Love is the meaning of being.* The first thing — determinative of all the rest — to be pointed out is that, for Balthasar, love does not principally name the act of the will, but instead indicates the meaning of being as a whole and therefore includes not merely the order of goodness, but all of the transcendentals in their circumincession.[58] The importance of this point of departure cannot be overstated. The emphasis Balthasar gives to love, indeed, the absolute supremacy he accords it, cannot therefore be interpreted as a sign of voluntarism, as it would necessarily be if it came from the medieval thinkers who identify the order of love with the order of the will *as distinct from,* say, the order of the intellect.[59] Thus, Balthasar is able to give full weight to the traditional exaltation of love in Scripture and the Christian tradition without collapsing into a problematic one-sidedness.[60] Love, as the meaning of being itself, is not merely a moral matter.[61] Instead, the correlation of love and being allows us to recover the idea that love has an aesthetic, i.e., is a matter essentially of beauty (the so-called "lost" transcendental), and — perhaps insufficiently affirmed in the tradition — that love has a logic, i.e., is a matter essentially of truth.[62]

(2) *Truth is simultaneously an object of intellect and will.* If love is absolute, truth is inseparably bound to the other transcendentals — which

58. Balthasar, *TL1,* p. 9. Note that, in his critique of Balthasar, Levering is compelled to distort Balthasar's own affirmation of the coincidence of love and being by adding to a citation precisely what Balthasar himself denies in the footnote to the passage: Levering adds "more fundamental than being or knowing" to Balthasar's affirmation of love as the "'transcendental par excellence'" (*TL2,* p. 177, quoted in Levering, p. 125), while Balthasar himself in a footnote adds: "Groundless love is not prior to being but is the supreme act of being" (*TL2,* p. 177, n. 9).

59. Here we see the significance of Balthasar's response to Rahner's critique of the importance he gives to beauty. *TL1,* pp. 19-20. Rahner wishes to preserve the duality of reason and love as a reflection of the two processions in the Trinity, while Balthasar insists on a more thoroughly circumincessive view of both the transcendentals and the divine Persons. Love is not a *part* of being, but is the full integration of all of the "parts" of being.

60. Consider the depth that this simple point opens up: for example, to say that God is love would not mean simply that he is good and wills good, but that God is the ultimate meaning of being (the New Testament revelation fulfills both the Old Testament and Greek metaphysics), and that this meaning is not merely substance but also the communion of persons, i.e., comprehensive of both nature and freedom.

61. In *Love Alone Is Credible* (San Francisco: Ignatius Press, 2004), for example, Balthasar follows the chapter on "Love as Deed" with "Love as Form."

62. See the section titled "The Logic of Love" in *TL2,* pp. 29-33. Cf. E. Tourpe, "La logique de l'amour: Propos de quelques volumes récemment traduits de H. U. von Balthasar," *Revue Théologique de Louvain* 29 (1998): 202-28.

means not only that one *ought* not to consider it apart from the others, but one *cannot* without somehow distorting its own nature.[63] But this inseparability has implications for how we understand the relationship between the intellect and will. If truth is *essentially* inseparable from goodness, then goodness is part of the intrinsic structure and meaning of truth *as* truth (and vice versa). If this is the case, it follows that the will is intrinsic to the intellect *as* intellect (and vice versa). As we saw in the last chapter, this means that the order of truth is not a unilateral movement, but a "dialogical" one, with two termini. The soul's act of intellection cannot come to completion simply within the soul itself, but must in some respect find its home, as it were, beyond the soul. This brings us to the next thesis.

(3) *The "locus" of truth is the concrete* Gestalt. *Prima facie*, there seems to be something strange about a transcendental relation with two termini: How can a movement come to rest in two different places at once? Such a movement would not be possible if it had a single principle, for the movement would then resolve in a single end. For Balthasar, the act of understanding is *not* a unilateral act, which a soul performs, so to speak, upon a passive object,[64] but is itself a *co-act,* a single act that is shared between the asymmetrical and irreducibly different activities of the soul and the object operating in conjunction with one another. Being — as love — is not a static fact but *gives* itself, *makes itself known,* in its manifestation to the soul, a manifestation that is in fact possible only through the appropriately attentive, and reciprocally generous, engagement on the part of the soul that knows. The intelligible manifestation, then, is not due to the object or the subject alone, nor is it the mere addition of their respective activities, but is rather the single fruit of their encounter or reciprocal interaction.[65] Balthasar calls this fruit the *Gestalt.*

A *Gestalt* is a whole greater than the sum of its parts; at the same time,

63. "Die Transzendentalien, die alles Sein durchwalten, können nur ineinander sein," *E*, p. 52. Cf. *TL1*, p. 225.

64. According to Balthasar, there is no such thing in the universe as a merely passive object. Even purely material things possess a kind of inner depth that gives itself in appearance, and thus all things share analogously in freedom. See *TL1*, pp. 80-107.

65. *TL1*, p. 61: "We have until now been considering the two poles of knowledge [subject and object] separately, looking at their equipment and readiness for the act of cognition. Such an inquiry resembles an investigation of the masculine and feminine that attends mainly to the functions and inclinations that predispose them for their union. The union itself is a new, third thing in which the purpose of these inclinations is truly unveiled for the first time."

it is itself a part that makes concretely manifest a greater whole. First, it is greater than the sum of its parts because it represents a distinct "third" in relation to the knowing soul and the thing known. It is not simply an idea immanent to the mind, nor simply an aspect or part of the thing, but has its own reality distinct from each. As an irreducible and thus distinct whole, it has a clear radiance that makes it a fitting object for the intellect, an intelligible "unity," which, though it can be to some extent explained in terms of its constitutive elements, ultimately resists dissolving back into them. Aquinas, following Aristotle, had insisted on the soul as the locus of truth because the intelligible species of a thing, as a universal, must be distinct from the materially subsisting and thus individualized form of the thing itself, and this species can thus exist only intentionally. For Balthasar, by contrast, the *Gestalt* is in part the fruit of spirit, i.e., the soul's perceptive and cognitive activity, and thus has an intelligibility that is "more" than the material being by itself, but this *Gestalt* nevertheless — because truth terminates in some respect beyond the knower — has a concrete existence "independent" of the knowing soul.[66] To say that the *Gestalt* is thus irreducibly distinct from the soul means that the soul can "appropriate" it only by going beyond itself "into" the meaning. This does not mean, we must realize, that the *Gestalt* is already there before the mind's activity, and that the mind must subsequently rise up to make contact with it, as it were. Instead, the *Gestalt* exists only in the medium of the soul's having risen up to meet the object it seeks to know.[67] It is therefore not merely in the act of will that the soul transcends itself toward a real object, but also in the act of understanding itself. In the encounter between the knower and the known designated by the *Gestalt*, the real thing that is known simultaneously enters into the subject and remains, so to speak, above him.[68]

At the same time, the *Gestalt* is also distinct from the reality known. As Balthasar explains, the *Gestalt* does not merely designate the reality of being as it is in itself, but includes the *appearance*, being "for" us, in its irreducible distinction from that being — even though he constantly insists that the appearance is always only *of being* (and here he is decidedly different from

66. See *GL4*, pp. 28-29, and *TL1*, pp. 202-3.

67. See the interplay between the reciprocally generous and receptive activities of the subject and object that Balthasar describes in *TL1*, pp. 61-78.

68. See *GL1*, p. 119: "We 'behold' the form; but, if we really behold it, it is not as a detached form, rather in its unity with the depths that make their appearance in it. We see form as the splendour, as the glory of Being. We are 'enraptured' by our contemplation of these depths and are 'transported' to them."

Kant).[69] By affirming this distinction, Balthasar intends to preserve what we might call the "ever-greater" *(je-mehr)* character of the *Gestalt.* The reality that comes to manifestation in the *Gestalt* is a reality "beyond" the manifestation. The nonappearing depth of being cannot be juxtaposed to the appearance as one thing next to another, because the appearance is of nothing *other* than those very depths; but neither can they be simply identified with one another.[70] No matter how immediate our relation to being may be, this relation is nevertheless always mediated by some "appearance." It is in this sense that we speak of a *Gestalt* as being an expression of the whole in the part: the *Gestalt* is the particular, and thus finite, manifestation of a depth that transcends it, and every *Gestalt* therefore possesses an intelligibility that is inexhaustible to the extent that the difference between being and appearance cannot be eliminated.[71] In sum, the *Gestalt,* as the locus of truth, as a "third" distinct from both the knower and the known, is at once more than and less than each of them taken in isolation. It is an intelligibility that the soul can comprehend, and thus include within itself, but which represents more than the soul can articulate (in knowing a *Gestalt,* the soul always knows, as it were, more than it knows);[72] and at the same time, while the *Gestalt* lies beyond the mere material existence of the thing, the *Gestalt* remains a relative partial expression of that reality: the reality could have appeared differently, and it does not simply exhaust all that it is in the particular appearance.

Affirming the *Gestalt* as the locus of truth keeps us decisively from a reduction to either idealism or empiricism, and by the same token keeps truth connected with goodness and beauty by integrating the elements of volition and perception. In other words, identifying the *Gestalt* as the place where truth essentially occurs preserves the *ontological* dimension of truth, precisely because it resists a reduction of truth to the subject or to the object. To put it another way, it brings to light the genuinely transcendental character of truth, as a property of being, which includes both subject and object in their relation.[73] Moreover, locating truth in the *Gestalt* holds together its re-

69. *TL1,* pp. 37-38.

70. *TL1,* p. 208: "Thus, insofar as the appearing essence never coincides with its appearance, it is always, and at the same time, nonapparent, held back, kept in reserve in its very veiling — though not purposely denied to, or withheld from, knowledge."

71. *GL4,* p. 31.

72. Michael Polanyi makes a similar point from the perspective of a *Gestalt*-founded epistemology in *The Tacit Dimension* (London: Routledge, 1966), as we saw in chapter one.

73. It is interesting to note that Laurence Dewan has recently argued that, based pri-

lation to the other transcendentals. If truth had a merely intentional existence, and the transcendentals were distinct not *in re* but *in ratione,* truth would be identified specifically in terms of its separateness from goodness. As "really" existing in the *Gestalt,* by contrast, truth remains within its circumincessive relation to goodness and thus to being. Here we understand Balthasar's criticism of the tendency to approach the transcendentals primarily from the vantage of their relation to the distinct powers of the soul: "The intimate connection was seen, and indeed emphasized, between the true and the good as the transcendental properties of the one being, but it was looked at more from the human standpoint, in the mutual presupposition of intellect and will (ST I, 16, 4 and ad 2), than in their objective mutual inclusion, or real identity."[74] This real identity is found in the *Gestalt.*

(4) *Mystery is convertible with truth.* To say that the *Gestalt* is the locus of truth is to say that the place wherein being actualizes its intelligibility is in this whole greater than the sum of its parts, this concrete manifestation of (ever-greater) being. The *Gestalt* is not merely the *appearance* of being, the immediately accessible surface of things, but is the *whole:* it is the *coincidence* of appearance and being, taken both in their unity and in their difference — and thus in their complex interplay.[75] But if this is the case, then we no longer have to make truth simply identical to that which is made accessible, that which is brought to light, and therefore to set truth in opposition to mystery. Instead, since the *Gestalt* is both the appearance of being (i.e., the immanence of being in the appearance) and the distinction of being from appear-

---

marily on a reading of the *Summa* (which he claims develops the notion of truth beyond the *De veritate*), truth, for Aquinas, is not in fact an ontological transcendental, but simply a *logical* one, since it, in contrast to the good, does not refer to anything *in* the really existing thing itself. See "Is Truth a Transcendental in Aquinas?" *Nova et Vetera* 2, no. 1 (2004): 1-21. But any interpretation that weakens the significance of the convertibility of truth and being cannot be said to do justice to Aquinas's thought. He himself considers the implication of the Aristotelian circle of the acts of soul and corrects it: "The true resides in things and in the intellect, as said before. But the true that is in things is convertible with being as to substance; while the true that is in the intellect is convertible with being, as the manifestation with the manifested; for this belongs to the nature of truth, as has been said already. It may, however, be said, that being also is in things and in the intellect, as is the true; although truth is primarily in the intellect, while being is primarily in things; and this is so because truth and being differ in idea" (*ST* 1.16.3ad1).

74. Balthasar, "Theology and Sanctity," in *Explorations in Theology,* vol. 1: *The Word Made Flesh* (San Francisco: Ignatius Press, 1989), p. 185.

75. There is some connection between Balthasar and the Hegelian notion, expressed in the *Phenomenology of Spirit,* that "the true is the whole."

ance (i.e., the abiding transcendence of being with respect to appearance), it follows that mystery and manifestation are in reality interdependent aspects of a single thing. Mystery thus acquires here a decidedly *positive* character: it is not the *withdrawal* of being from the illumination of reason,[76] or simply that which, as exceeding the intellect, is not given to it. Rather, it is for Balthasar precisely the *givenness* of being that is mysterious, insofar as the generosity at the heart of the act of manifestation is the reason for the mystery.[77] *Because* being does not hold itself back, but *appears,* it reveals itself as gloriously transcendent of the appearance — *in* the appearance. Being overwhelmed by the mystery of something, its ever-greater character, can occur only through the clear and certain grasp of the *Gestalt* in which that transcendence comes to expression. The very same thing is intelligible and mysterious;[78] although we might distinguish *in ratione* between the thing in respect to its being known and the thing in respect to its lying beyond knowledge, these two aspects are simply identical *in re* — that is, in the *Gestalt* itself where truth properly occurs. The "closure" that a genuine *Gestalt* brings about is, for Balthasar, always at the same time a new kind of openness.[79] Balthasar explains that a fundamental purpose of his most extensive

76. To be more precise, Balthasar qualifies the scholastic notion of the light of reason, significantly, by pointing to its more fundamental source in Being's own light: "for even this light [i.e., the light of reason] (as *lumen intellectus agentis*) is not properly speaking man's own light, but rather his openness to the light of Being which illumines him" (*GL1,* pp. 164-65). In this, Balthasar stands quite close to Heidegger. Heidegger seems to differ from Balthasar, however, and in this respect to be closer to conventional epistemologies, in affirming a predominantly *negative* notion of mystery. In other words, according to Heidegger, it is precisely the *concealment* of Being that makes it mysterious: compare, for example, Heidegger's description in "Vom Wesen der Wahrheit," in *Wegmarken* (Frankfurt am Main: Klostermann, 1996), pp. 193-94, in which Heidegger relates concealment and thus mystery to the untruth that is "older than" (and essential to) the disclosedness of truth.

77. See *TL1,* p. 223: "[T]ruth itself irradiates mystery, and it is of the very essence of truth to manifest this radiant mystery through itself."

78. It is no doubt Blankenhorn's imposition onto Balthasar of the understanding of mystery as simply opposed to knowledge that leads him to accuse Balthasar of contradiction when Balthasar affirms that the Trinitarian Persons know each other perfectly without eliminating something like "surprise." See Blankenhorn, "Balthasar's Method of Divine Naming," pp. 266-67.

79. See *TL1,* p. 39: "Truth as *emeth* does two things. On the one hand, it is conclusive, in the sense that it puts an end to uncertainty and endless seeking, to conjecture and suspicion, so that this condition of ever-shifting vacillation can give way to the clearly formed, solid evidence of things that are unveiled as they actually are. On the other hand, this closure of uncertainty and its bad infinity is the unclosing and unsealing of a true infinity of fruitful

philosophical work, the relatively early *Wahrheit der Welt,* was to "deal centrally and *in extenso* with the paradox that unveiling is perfectly compatible with veiling and mystery, in other words, that the mysteriousness of being has absolutely nothing to do with irrationality."[80] In this sense, the evermore character of a thing is a positive presentation of its intelligibility, and the more directly the mind has access to this presentation, the more wonderfully clear will its mystery be. From this understanding of being's self-revelation, mystery is due not to the finite mind's *deficiency,* but to its *power* and *perfection.* Animals know very little mystery, precisely because they "know" nothing at all. We will return to this point at length in chapter seven.

Now, it is helpful to see that this thesis requires the previous one. If truth did not occur most properly in something distinct from the soul, there would be no way to avoid making truth and mystery opposites in principle, for in this case my grasp of the truth of a thing would be my appropriation of it, my intentional identity with it, and thus the *elimination* of any distance the intelligible object has from me. By the same token, we see that the very same thing that makes truth coincident with mystery makes the appetitive power of the will intrinsic to the intellect. Intellect itself, in other words, is a kind of desire, and at the same time a kind of self-gift, insofar as its act comes to a close beyond itself, and this generous desire cannot simply take the form of a will to closure precisely because it is set on what is essentially open *in* its intelligibility. And here we come to the final thesis.

(5) *Knowledge is essentially nonpossessive.* If we think of truth as having its home in the *Gestalt,* which is relatively distinct both from the soul and from the thing known, it means that the various elements that constitute the "event" of truth *(adequation)* converge and thus come to their irreducible unity primarily beyond the intellect. It is crucial to see that, in affirming this, we are not saying that the mind does not grasp truth (also) within itself or that the soul has no immanent possession of its object in knowledge.[81] Instead, we are insisting that this immanent unity of intellect and thing within the soul is, as it were, a received or participated unity. The unity in which it

---

possibilities and situations. Once truth has become present, a thousand consequences, a thousand insights, spring from it as from a seed. Once being has become evident, this evidence immediately harbors the promise of further truth; it is a door, an entrance, a key to the life of the spirit."

80. *TL1,* p. 9.

81. In *TL1,* pp. 62-67, Balthasar describes truth as the object's immanence within the subject; but this does not prevent him from making the corresponding point, namely, that truth also designates the subject's immanence in the object (67-71).

shares, once again, is located in the *Gestalt*, and it takes this unity into itself precisely by transcending beyond itself *into* the *Gestalt*. But if this is the case, then the very act of appropriation is an act of expropriation: the mind, one might say, leaves its own home, its mother and father, in order to cleave to its object and become one with it. The identity that the mind thus achieves with the thing that it knows is therefore not the elimination of its difference from it, but instead an *appropriation of that difference as difference*. It is just this that allows us to say that a knowledge of truth is the realization of mystery. In a word, it is not only the will that represents the soul's movement beyond itself, but reason, too, is *essentially ecstatic*.[82]

The ecstatic notion of reason has three immediate implications relevant to our present context. First, it entails the affirmation of a moment of "discontinuity" in the operation of the intellect. The mind must let go of itself, as it were, in order to take hold of its object. Here, we could speak of the significance of dramatic surprise and wonder. They are not, from this perspective, mere instigators to reflection that are ultimately destined to be left behind, but are *intrinsic* elements of genuine thought, and thus abide within the intellectual act within its very completion. Here, again, the appetitive and striving aspects proper to the will, with the "distance" they imply, prove to belong intrinsically to understanding as well. And once we see that a moment of discontinuity is intrinsic to the completion of understanding, we can say that discontinuity, as such, is not in principle a threat to rationality. Indeed, if this moment is properly integrated within a comprehensive notion of the circumincession of the transcendentals, there is no limit to the possible extremity of the discontinuity — all of the suffering and alienation, for example, that Hegel intended by the "labor of the negative," all of the dread *(Angst)* that Heidegger associated with the thinking of the "nothing" — that can be embraced by the ever-greater truth of being.[83] Truth by its very nature gives space for the drama of existence.

82. Aquinas, too, accounts ecstasis as an effect, not only of the appetitive power, but also of the "apprehensive power" (*ST* 1-2.28.3). Perhaps the difference between Balthasar and Aquinas is one of emphasis here: for Balthasar, some form of ecstasis is part of the *normal* operation of reason, while for Aquinas it is only when man is "placed outside the knowledge proper to him," as in prophetic inspiration.

83. Of course, it remains necessary to distinguish the discontinuity in the ecstasis proper to the intellect in its grasp of truth from the sheer negativity of falsehood. One could ask whether Laurence Hemming and Susan Parsons do not perhaps concede too much to Hegel and Heidegger (who in different ways make falsehood *essential* to truth) by overlooking this difference: see their editors' introduction to *Restoring Faith in Reason* (London:

Second, we see that, by the same token, the ecstatic character of the will poses in principle no threat to its intelligent use. If understanding is simply the soul's appropriation of the intelligible species of its object, then the act of the will is rationally governed, as it were, only within the bounds designated by the appropriated essence. But, as we saw above, this makes assent to anything not perfectly comprehended by the soul a-rational, if not irrational, thus raising questions about the rational integrity not only of the assent of faith or obedience to authority, for example, but also to the love of God. But if reason is *itself* ecstatic, then the ecstasy of the will in its assent to such things is by no means opposed to the natural movement of the intellect. We can thus affirm that, rooted most primordially in beauty, the will's striving in and toward the good is governed all the while by intelligible form even if it has not yet fully appropriated that form as such.[84] And, by the same token, to know God would not be, as De Finance said, simply to "lower him to us," but would in fact be a way of raising us to him.

Third, knowledge thus acquires an essentially nonpossessive form. From the perspective of a conventional reading of Aquinas, *either* one knows something *or* one does not; the whole question of knowledge and truth turns around the individual soul and its particular appropriation of form.[85] But if truth essentially resides not in the individual soul, but in the objective *Gestalt,* the question becomes more complex and paradoxical. A monk in a religious order possesses nothing at all, and yet at the same time he has everything he needs. What belongs to the community belongs also to him precisely because he makes no private claim on it. Analogously, the *adequatio*

SCM Press, 2002), pp. vii-xii; here, viii-ix. They are correct that truth is not a "mere binary" opposite of falsehood, but in its being *more* than this, it nevertheless includes this opposition. On the one hand, it is indeed the case that falsehood cannot be reified into an opposite of truth without undermining the transcendental character of truth. But on the other hand, and though there is insufficient space here to reflect on this very delicate problem, we may at least point out that overcoming the opposition requires a clear judgment of the falsity of the falsehood.

84. In citing Siewerth's affirmation of goodness as "more transcendental than being and the true," Balthasar also cites Siewerth's qualification that this "does not oblige us to sacrifice the priority of truth and its ontological transcendence." See *TL2*, p. 177, n. 7.

85. It seems that Levering (*Scripture and Metaphysics,* p. 132) assumes precisely such a view of knowledge when he sets in opposition Balthasar's claims that the Father gives all things to the Son, and that the Father also "conceals" knowledge about his divine Mission in the economic order. For Balthasar, the discontinuity of obedience is the most perfect way for the Father to give all things to the Son. This affirmation simply cannot make any sense if one takes for granted an essentially possessive form of knowledge.

that constitutes truth, for Balthasar, exhibits the same paradox. Its ground is not the individual soul but the more public and thus freer space of the *Gestalt.* There need be, therefore, no anxiety about holding all things together in one's own mind in order to safeguard rationality; instead, truth is held together *for* the individual soul, and so it can entrust itself much more openly and confidently to the more encompassing reality of truth and truth of reality. One enters *into* knowledge and so one need not keep it nervously for oneself. It is thus that the act of knowledge is itself, in its very structure, a generous act. To know is a very precise, indeed perhaps the most profound, way to love.[86]

Love as Absolute

With these last observations concerning the ecstatic nature of reason, we have already begun to reply to the difficulties we pointed out in the conventional reading of Aquinas, as well as to the charge that Balthasar shows a certain tendency toward voluntarism and irrationalism. We may thus make the conclusion rather brief. All of the difficulties arise from identifying the intellectual act too simply with the soul's internalization and thus truth with intentional identity *in* the soul. Balthasar's conception does not *reject* this understanding, but merely insists on integrating it within a more comprehensive view.[87] Doing so, we can see that it is possible to know something without simply subordinating it to oneself. Aquinas had identified love of God as higher than knowledge of him precisely because the act of will relates to its object as *beyond* the soul. It is just this point that creates difficulties regarding man's eschatological state. The dynamism of the will, it seems, cannot be affirmed as ultimate without collapsing into irrational absurdity. But knowledge represents an end — from this perspective — precisely by closing the difference

86. See *TL2,* pp. 28-29: "In the Bible, knowledge has a comprehensive meaning that, far from being purely theoretical and abstract, comprises the full range of man's concrete cognitive possibilities, including sexual experience ('the man knew Eve, his wife': Gen 4:1). All of *these* possibilities are to enter the service of love."

87. Speaking now from a theological perspective, Balthasar puts the same point thus: "Only when truth is conceived in christological-trinitarian terms can it be linked with the notion of 'fullness.' For it then includes, not only the other transcendentals on the ontological level ('glory,' 'goodness,' and in the definitiveness of the enfleshed display of the divine Word, 'unity'), but also the Son's constitutive, indissoluble relationship to the Father and to the Spirit on the trinitarian level" (*TL2,* p. 21).

between the soul and its object; and thus, to affirm it, rather than love, as ultimate would seem to resolve the analogy of being into simple identity. Balthasar avoids both horns of the dilemma by making intelligence an act that preserves the difference of analogy and thus leaves room for an eternity of wonder and surprise as a restful *end* rather than as a ceaseless chase. It is this view of the understanding that lies behind Balthasar's making service the form of beatific vision,[88] and we can affirm this form even while retaining the superiority of reason over the will. In the end, it is the *whole soul,* with all of its faculties in their properly ordered integration, that reaches out to, enjoys, celebrates, and serves God. Moreover, the ultimate ecstasis of the understanding in relation to God is therefore *not,* for Balthasar, the opposite of its movement in its natural operation, but turns out to be the most perfect form of its natural operation, no matter how gratuitous and unanticipated this ultimate revelation may be. Grace, after all, does not destroy nature, but, as we elaborated in chapter two, elevates it and thus perfects it. We can affirm this perfection only if, in fact, a moment of discontinuity is constitutive of the very *nature* of human reason. But if this is the case, then the endless mystery that God presents, and will always present, to the human intellect is not the opposite of the simple intelligibility of creatures, but is in fact reflected in the mystery that inheres *properly* within them. It is not, in other words, only the truth of God that is greater than I; in some respect, *every truth* is and will always remain greater than I.

The perfection of this reverence before truth comes to expression in Jesus' relation to the Father: "The Father is greater than I." Somehow, the absolute unity in being between the Father and the Son does not preclude the distance of wonder, for it is the divine Person who says this and not merely the human nature. It will have been noticed that we have not said a word here about Balthasar's theology. A more thorough theological investigation would be necessary to show why the radical obedience of Christ to the Father in the economy of salvation does not imply a voluntarism or irrationalism on his part, or why Balthasar's radical interpretation of the dereliction on the Cross does not imply the fragmentation of the absolute simplicity of the triune God. But the theological explanation itself, I suggest, will fail to be completely compelling without the sorts of philosophical de-

88. *TL1*, pp. 293-95. Here, Balthasar shows that, insofar as we make the subject the measure of the eschatological act — which we necessarily do to the extent that we make it an act of knowledge and we define knowledge in terms of a kind of possession — we will be faced with the equally problematic alternatives of ontologism or an absolute dynamism.

velopments that we have roughly sketched out here. As we have seen, a moment of discontinuity and expropriation follows from the ontological and thus transcendental character of truth, and it is in fact only the *reality* of truth as a transcendental, the fulfillingly gratuitous objectivity of truth, that ultimately provides the adequate defense against voluntarism. The startling glory of beauty and the intense drama of the good are intrinsically necessary to the rationality of truth. To juxtapose these as extrinsic to the order of the intelligence will ultimately make knowledge — no matter how certain, no matter how clear and distinct — senseless.

So: Does love trump reason? Yes and no: if truth is a transcendental, and love is the meaning of being, to say that love trumps reason is to say that truth trumps truth. And indeed it can and it should: a smaller truth must always yield its place to a greater, more encompassing truth. To refuse to yield in this case would in fact be itself irrational in a radical way. But if the comprehending truth is truly true, the smaller truth will invariably find itself not supplanted, but surprisingly fulfilled. In the end, *the absolute supremacy of love is precisely what makes reason ultimate* because it is what allows reason to embrace the very totality that remains, even in the embrace, ever-greater than it.

PART TWO

Causality

5 The Iconoclasm of the Intellect in Early Modernity

Feeding the Imagination

In an essay on the enduring significance of Dante, the poet Paul Claudel wrote of the age that had just passed: "The crisis that reached its peak in the nineteenth century . . . was the drama of a starved imagination."[1] It may strike us as odd to show such concern over what would seem to be nothing more than a faculty of aesthetic creativity in relation to an age in which man was being radically redefined in abstraction from any supernatural destiny or transcendent horizon of meaning, when an antihuman industrialization grew with the waning of an organic and cultural Christian faith, which left the West vulnerable to the two world wars. But what is at stake in the imagination is in truth far more than a mere aesthetic faculty, conventionally understood. The imagination is, if not the center of the human being, then nevertheless that without which there can be no center, for it marks the point of convergence at which the soul and body meet; it is the place where faith in the incarnate God becomes itself incarnate and therefore truly becomes faith; it is — pace Hegel — where reason becomes concrete, and the bodily life of the senses rises to meet the spirit. It lies more deeply than the sphere of our discrete thoughts and choices because it is the ordered space within which we in fact think and choose. Far more than a mere faculty, the Christian imagination is a way of life, and this is because we might say it represents the point of intersection be-

1. Paul Claudel, "Introduction à un poème sur Dante," in *Positions et propositions* (Paris: Gallimard, 1928), pp. 174-75. For an English translation, see "Religion and the Artist: Introduction to a Poem on Dante," *Communio* 22, no. 2 (Summer 1995): 357-67.

tween Christianity and the world. In this case, a starved imagination represents a crisis indeed.

Now, it is no doubt the case that the almost maniacal multiplication of images in the technological explosion of the twentieth century has done nothing to nourish the imagination, but instead has fed it with unwholesome food. But it is not enough simply to issue a call for the reinvigoration of the imagination or for the Christianization of the media. We need instead to address the problem at its roots. We propose that one of the sources of the starved imagination lies in the general impoverishment of the notion of truth, through which all our human experience is mediated and thus formed. In the present context, it is of course not possible to lay out a satisfactory argument regarding the history of the notion of truth, so we will instead offer in this chapter a philosophical reflection on one aspect of the issue, though it may initially seem tangential to the question of the health of the imagination. We intend to reflect on the transformation of the notion of causality in the seventeenth century and what this transformation implies for the significance of sense experience, which represents of course the foundation of the imagination. Our thesis is that a mechanistic conception of the natural world evacuates sense experience of meaning, and therefore that the effort to cultivate the Christian imagination will be vain unless it is accompanied by a recovery of the ontological significance of goodness and beauty and thus by a critique of the popular view of the world inherited from classical physics. This is a task we might call a "reimagining of the natural world."

Body as Image

Every fall and spring, in Introduction to Philosophy classes all over the world, René Descartes is presented to young, impressionable imaginations as a more systematically rigorous proponent of "Rationalism," the philosophy that Plato supposedly brought into being. According to Rationalism, sense experience lacks the qualities required to furnish a reliable object for the mind: it is neither necessary nor universal, as rational objects must be. The inference generally drawn is that the senses are deceptive, and thus present at best indifferent stepping stones to reach the true life of reason, and at worst obstacles that actively seduce the mind away from such a life. If the Intro class includes a bit of intellectual history, one learns that the contempt for the body implied in Platonic Rationalism and taken over by Plotinus and his followers made Neoplatonism the philosophy most suited to the early Christian thinkers, who (as Nietzsche sneered)[2] added to Plato's primarily epistemological motivation a more directly moral reason to reject the sense world.

There are indeed texts in abundance from Plato, Plotinus, and the Church Fathers that would seem to confirm this interpretation beyond any doubt, texts that cause contemporary Christian thinkers a good deal of embarrassment. A closer inspection of these texts, however, and a consideration of them in the light of the general view of the world they express, would reveal that the antipathy toward the senses in the ancient world is radically different from that in the modern world, and that only the former is compatible with a loving embrace of the sense world as marvelously filled with meaning. A genuine contempt for the senses requires their being emptied of any significance at all, and this, as we will see, follows from the changes in our understanding of nature that occur during what is known as the Scientific Revolution, of which Descartes was both a participant and an immediate heir. To see this, we will compare Plato's and Galileo's response to the question, What is the cause of our sense experience? The first aspect of this question that we must attend to here is the notion on which it turns: What, first of all, does it mean to be a *cause?*

The Greek word for cause (αἰτία or αἴτιον) is a broad one, i.e., it does not initially have a univocal technical meaning. The Greek word for cause comes from αἴτιος, meaning "blameworthy," "responsible," "to blame," and which in turn is derived from the verb αἰτιάομαι, "to blame," or "to accuse." The verb is the middle voice form of the verbs αἰτέω and αἰτίζω, meaning "to ask," "to request or petition," or "to call for." The root sense that appears to unite all these verbs is a turning toward one who is responsible or capable of providing. It indicates a kind of dependence. Used in a philosophical context, the term indicates anything that accounts for a thing's being the way it is, that which is responsible for the how and why of a thing.[3] In his late dialogue, the *Timaeus,* Plato begins his account of cause in the cosmos by mak-

2. Speaking of the ancient philosophers, Nietzsche wrote, "Now they all believe, desperately even, in what has being. But since they never grasp it, they seek for reasons why it is kept from them. 'There must be mere appearance, there must be some deception which prevents us from perceiving that which has being: where is the deceiver?' 'We have found him,' they cry ecstatically; 'it is the senses! These senses, which are so immoral in other ways too, deceive us concerning the *true* world'" (*Twilight of the Idols,* in *The Portable Nietzsche,* trans. Walter Kaufmann [New York: Penguin Books, 1976], p. 480).

3. See Joe Sachs, *Aristotle's Physics: A Guided Study* (New Brunswick, NJ: Rutgers University Press, 1995), p. 245.

ing two fundamental distinctions. He first distinguishes between that which is and never becomes (being, τὸ ὄν) and that which becomes and never is (becoming, τὸ γιγνόμενον) (27d-28a). "Everything which becomes," he goes on to say, "must of necessity become owing to some cause; for without a cause it is impossible for anything to attain becoming" (28a). Among those things that come to be by virtue of a cause, Plato next distinguishes between those that are beautiful and those that are not. The former are modeled after that which is, the latter after that which has come to be. If we ask, then, where among these distinctions we would place the cosmos as a whole in which we live, i.e., the world that is manifest to the senses, we would have to say that, "as visible and tangible and having body" (28b), it has come to be, and, as evidently beautiful and well ordered, it has been modeled after what is eternal and perfect. To suggest otherwise, says Plato, is "impious": "It is clear to everyone that [the maker's] gaze was on the eternal; for the cosmos is the fairest of all that has come into existence, and he the best of all the causes" (29a).

As straightforward as this passage may seem, it is filled with meaning that it would be good to unfold. As we see here, Plato affirms that causality always occurs according to a model, which is another way of saying that what comes to be is not simply a self-contained entity, but a revelation or manifestation of something else: to say that the causal agent always makes according to a model means that *agency is the communication of form.* Causation is not, in other words, simply the bringing about of a thing or the setting of something in motion, i.e., an essentially formless event or activity, which may or may not *subsequently* give rise to something with form and therefore something intelligible. If the cause is what accounts for a thing, it is form for Plato that is most fundamentally cause, most fundamentally responsible for the way things are. This simple insight is magnificent: it leads to a particular way of characterizing absolutely everything that exists: "Since these things are so," Plato writes, "it follows by unquestionable necessity that this world is an image of something" (29b). To say that agency is the communication of form means that all of the things that come to be have the character of image — the Greek word is εἰκών, whence the English "icon" — or, in other words, that they reflect a meaning of which they are not themselves the source. It is crucial to see that there is no dualism here, as it were, between being and significance, as if things had a sort of opaque reality that subsequently indicated an intelligible content. To posit such a bifurcation would be to deny the meaning of cause as Plato clearly intends it, namely, as the communication of form in the bringing about of a thing. We could say that, for Plato, ontology *is* semiotics. Being an image is what makes a thing *real.*[4]

But if form accounts for the *way* things are, it does not yet account for the fact that there is a sensible world in the first place. It is significant that Plato distinguishes in the *Timaeus* between what he calls the models (παραδείγματα), and the agency that "reproduces" them, as it were, in nature — the famous "demiurge," or craftsman. To ask after the ultimate cause of the world is to ask why the agency makes it at all. Plato's response to what Heidegger refers to as the most radical question for metaphysics, Why is there something rather than nothing? is again both simple and endlessly rich: "Let us state the reason why. He [the maker and father of the universe] was good, and one who is good can never become jealous of anything. And so, being free from jealousy, he wanted everything to become as much like himself as was possible" (29e). Plato's statement here accords with his well-known claim in the *Republic* that the Idea of the Good is the ultimate cause of all being.[5] We have in this the first expression of what would become a basic axiom in Neoplatonism, and was embraced by the Fathers and the medieval theologians: it is the very nature of goodness to be self-diffusive.[6] Indeed, it is just this character that requires us to see goodness as the ultimate cause: according to the ancient axiom, what is perfect cannot come from what is imperfect, but only the reverse, which means that the ultimate cause of everything cannot be imperfect in any respect. But what is perfection itself cannot act so as to become more perfect, which implies that its causation must be a consequence of the perfection it always already is rather than a means to accomplish that perfection.

Moreover, for the very same reason, what is brought about by goodness must necessarily reflect its cause, since perfect causality cannot be anything but the communication of its own perfection, i.e., its *self,* to another.[7] In this respect the form that is communicated by agency is necessarily a reflection of goodness. And, finally, insofar as this form most basically determines what a thing is, and is itself an imitation of the first cause, the gift of

4. I am indebted to Eric Perl for my understanding of this point.

5. *Republic* VI, 509b.

6. Cf. Dionysius, *DN* IV.1; Thomas Aquinas, *ST* 1.5.4.

7. According to Eric Perl, an attentive reading of the *Timaeus* reveals that the forms by which the Demiurge makes the world are nothing but the Demiurge himself, that is, the content of his mind which is identical with himself. This, he shows, was the standard interpretation of Plato in antiquity. "The Demiurge and the Forms: A Return to the Ancient Interpretation of Plato's *Timaeus,*" *Ancient Philosophy* 18 (1998): 81-92.

the being of each thing is at the very same time the gift of the ultimate purpose of each: namely, to be what it is by imitating in its particular way the ultimate source of all that is, i.e., by pursuing goodness. In a word, what would eventually be differentiated by Aristotle into three causes, as we will see in the following chapter, appears first in Plato in its unity: the *what* of things is inseparable from their goodness, their purpose, and indeed their "thereness." For this very reason, goodness represents the paradigm of causality — the goodness at the origin of the cosmos, as we saw, is the "best of all the causes" — and thus all causes in the cosmos are, *as* causes, a reflection of goodness. Nothing is so causal, for Plato, as goodness and the beauty he takes to be essentially identical with it.[8]

What, then, does this view of causality imply for the status of sense experience? In the *Phaedo,* Socrates recounts his puzzlement at his encounter with the early philosophers who attempted to account for the way things are through what we would call "mechanistic causes," namely, through the pushing and pulling of material bodies acting upon one another extrinsically. Although he does not deny the reality of such activity, he explains that the name "cause" "does not belong to it."[9] In the *Timaeus,* he refers to what we would call mechanistic causes as ξυναίτια, that is, that which accompanies (ξυν) the cause, though he adds that the majority of people confuse them with the causes themselves. In the context of the *Phaedo,* Socrates insists that there is a distinction between that which is a cause *in reality* (τῷ ὄντι), and that without which the real cause could not be a cause. The mechanical interaction of bodies is, of course, necessary for things to be the way they are, but it does not *account* for them, it is not what explains them or reveals *what* they are.[10] What is lacking in the mechanistic explanation (or better: what prevents this account from *being* an explanation), as Socrates

8. A word should be introduced here in relation to the obvious objection that thinking of the maker of the universe as "the best of all the causes" is a textbook example of ontotheology. What Plato means by the best is the ideal or the form, which cannot itself be numbered among the things in which it is present (or it could not be present to them, but would simply be juxtaposed to them), but as present in each is transcendent of them all. Thus in this case it would be more proper to call the good the "causality of all cause." On an interpretation along these lines, see John McGinley, "The Doctrine of the Good in the *Philebus,*" *Apeiron* 11 (1977): 27-57, esp. 34-35. As he explains, it is for Plato precisely goodness that makes a cause a cause. We will explore this notion further in chapter seven.

9. *Phaedo* 99b.

10. In the *Timaeus,* Plato refers to the (mechanical) *necessity* that must be taken into account in one's explanation of the cosmos, but, precisely as opposed to intelligence, is not a cause in the strict sense. See, e.g., 46e and 47e-48a.

goes on to say, is the *goodness* that "holds [things] together,"[11] because goodness *is* in fact the causality of all cause. As Dionysius would affirm, many centuries later, every sort of cause whatsoever exists for the sake of, by means of, and in the beautiful and the good.[12] We will elaborate Dionysius's notion of cause in chapter seven.

It is at this point that Socrates offers his counterproposal for the operation of cause: what makes things beautiful, for example, is not some physical thing such as color, shape, the arrangement of parts — though of course these may be necessary conditions of beauty — but it is *beauty itself* that causes it. It is, more specifically, the presence (παρουσία) or communion (κοινωνία) of beauty "itself" in things (100d) that makes them beautiful. The sensible reality of beauty, in other words, is *caused* by the intelligible form of beauty. Now, it is difficult for us to hear this claim without imagining a "thing" called beauty, which *acts on* another thing, i.e., exerts a force on it, so as to bring about beauty in it. But this is precisely the sort of activity that, as Socrates has just affirmed, fails to warrant the name "cause," because it in fact fails to account for things. How, then, are we to understand the kind of causality Socrates is offering in its place?

To say that the presence of beauty is the cause of beautiful things qua beautiful is simply to say that the sensible beauty we perceive in things is the intelligible form of beauty manifest in space and time; in other words, it is to say that sense experience is the expression of a *meaning,* that it has intelligible content, which, *as* intelligible, cannot simply be identified with the particularity of its manifestation. If we recall the point made in the *Timaeus,* namely, that whatever comes to be is the result of the communication of form, we see that what Socrates says about beauty here ought to be extended to all things in the cosmos: physical objects, insofar as they are intelligible, are the expression of *meaning,* intelligible content, in a spatial and temporal mode. We can go further: there is, in fact, no content whatsoever in our sense experience that is not an expression of intelligible meaning. The word that this observation demands is the word we saw Plato use at the outset, a word that will forever be associated with Plato's philosophy: εἰκών, image. The sensible world is image, through and through, which is to say the sensible world is an expression of meaning, i.e., a reflection of goodness. In the divided-line image of Plato's *Republic,*[13] we see this point made with all de-

11. *Phaedo* 99c.
12. See *DN* IV.10.
13. *Republic* VI, 509d-511e.

sired clarity: here, Plato divides a line into unequal segments, the upper two representing different modes of intelligibility, the lower two representing different modes of sensible perception, but it is a continuous line from top to bottom, which is to say that the idea and the sensible reality are not two different things, but a single meaning grasped either intellectually or grasped with the bodily senses.[14] The upshot of all this is that there is nothing in what we would call the "physical" world that is not derived from form except its not being itself form, and this is simply a way of saying that the physical world is nothing but meaning made tangible.

What, then, accounts for Plato's notorious depiction of philosophy as a liberator from the deceitful senses that imprison the soul in a body?

> The lovers of learning know that when philosophy gets hold of their soul, it is imprisoned in and clinging to the body, and that it is forced to examine other things through it as through a cage and not by itself, and that it wallows in every kind of ignorance. Philosophy sees that the worst feature of this imprisonment is that it is due to desires, so that the prisoner himself is contributing to his own incarceration most of all. As I say, the lovers of learning know that philosophy gets hold of their soul when it is in that state, then gently encourages it and tries to free it by showing them that investigation through the eyes is full of deceit, as is that through the ears and the other senses. Philosophy then persuades the soul to withdraw from the senses insofar as it is not compelled to use them and bids the soul to gather itself together by itself, to trust only itself and whatever reality, existing by itself, the soul by itself understands, and not to consider as true whatever it examines by other means, for this is different in different circumstances and is sensible and visible, whereas what the soul itself sees is intelligible and invisible. The soul of the true philosopher thinks that this deliverance must not be opposed and so keeps away from pleasures and desires and pains as far as he can . . . because every pleasure and every pain provides, as it were, another nail to rivet the soul to the body and to weld them together. It makes the soul corporeal, so that it believes that truth is what the body says it is. (*Phaedo* 82d-83d)[15]

14. See the classic article by Henry Jackson, "On Plato's *Republic* VI 509d sqq.," *The Journal of Philology* 10 (1882): 132-50.

15. For contrasting interpretations, it is interesting to read Catherine Pickstock's "The Soul in Plato," in *Explorations in Contemporary Continental Philosophy of Religion,* ed. D. Baker and P. Maxwell (New York: Radopi, 2003), pp. 115-26, and James K. A. Smith's critique in *Introducing Radical Orthodoxy: Mapping a Post-secular Theology* (Grand Rapids:

For all the talk of the beautiful cosmos, is not Plato nevertheless a dualist in the end who relegates the material world to a ghostly unreality? Doesn't he make the imagination, εἰκασία, a trivial power of the soul that needs to be transcended to the purity of reason alone?[16] The interpretation we have just laid out, which brings out the significance of sense experience and the supreme beauty of the physical world, is not only able to be harmonized with the passages expressing a kind of hostility toward the senses, but in fact *explains* them.

The passage from the *Phaedo,* which is one of the clearest "anti-body" texts in the Platonic *corpus,* makes two points that are especially significant given our discussion thus far: first, he does not say that the body imprisons the soul, but rather that the soul imprisons *herself* in the body,[17] which is what constitutes the worst feature of this predicament. Second, what characterizes this imprisonment is the inversion by which the corporeal aspect of experience is taken to be more real than the noncorporeal dimension. To put this point in the language we have been using, it amounts to saying that the expression is given priority over what is expressed. But this inversion would in fact by that very stroke eliminate the body's and thus the senses' expressive character. In other words, to take the natural world *in* its materiality as a positive thing in itself separate from its subordination to meaning and thus its expressiveness is to destroy it as image, to render it mute. It thus becomes dead "stuff." The world surrenders its meaning, and the soul becomes entangled in the push and pull of pleasure and pain as so many mechanistic and therefore unintelligible, noncausal, forces. Indeed, if the body is no longer "expression," then the soul is no longer that which expresses itself. It thus becomes itself a "thing," alongside the thing called "body," and of course it will necessarily be an impotent sort of thing, for what kind of corporeal force can the soul exert in comparison to bodies? It is because of this unintelligibility that Plato describes this inversion as a state of ignorance — to fail to see the world as significant already in its being is to be ignorant in the perfect sense — and it also makes clear why this is not something the body can qua body impose on the soul: to think that it can is already to assume that the body is a thing in itself over against the soul, which is to say, it is to take the state of ignorance to be the best vantage

Baker Academic, 2004), pp. 201-4. Smith's interpretation represents just what the present chapter intends to critique.

16. See *Republic* VII, 532a-534b.

17. *Phaedo* 82e.

from which to see the truth of things. To a soul that sees because it knows, by contrast, the world is nothing but epiphany.

The irony now ought to be clear: owing to the paradoxical nature of image, the inversion of the body-soul relationship is deeply problematic, not (only) because it trivializes the soul, but because it subsequently trivializes the body. In other words, the absolutizing of the physical fails to accord the physical its due goodness — i.e., it empties it of the goodness it can possess only as receiving, and thus only in its subordinate station as mediator, as image. But this means that the sometimes vehement condemnations of the body's tendency to claim ascendency over the soul that we find in classical literature, both pagan and Christian, may indeed be a zealous affirmation and protection of the body's *significance.* The decisive question is whether the body and the soul, and thus the senses and the intellect, are taken to be opaque things juxtaposed to one another, or whether body is presented as image, and thus as an expression of spirit. One cannot insist on the body's significance without at the same time insisting on a hierarchical relationship to spirit. As we have seen, behind this question lies the even more fundamental question of whether causality is understood first and foremost in terms of goodness and beauty. As Hans Urs von Balthasar has taught us, one of the most important considerations when evaluating an intellectual epoch is the status it grants to beauty. Here we find a way in which Christianity deepens, and gives an ultimate foundation for, one of the highest truths in pagan thought. The beauty that Augustine loved late was a beauty that ran through the cosmos, a beauty that called him *in* sensible things *to* God.[18] We recall that it was precisely Augustine's encounter with Neoplatonic thought — most likely Plotinus and Porphyry in Victorinus's translation — that liberated him from the flesh-condemning Manichees.[19] It is not at all accidental that the liberation consisted in the discovery that spirit must be understood in nonmaterial terms, and thus not as a thing opposed to the thing called body. Only thus can the body, and therefore the material world, be *expressive* in the way Augustine celebrates in the *Confessions.* Plotinus himself, who may be notorious for passages that seem to demean the body, wrote what is one of the most passionate attacks on Gnosticism in the ancient world.[20] Anyone who hates the body, he writes, blasphemes because he

18. Augustine, *Confessions* X.xxvii (38). Augustine refers here to each of the five senses in recounting God's calling to him through the created world.

19. Augustine, *Confessions,* book VII.

20. Plotinus, *Ennead* II.9.

shows contempt for its Creator.[21] It is, indeed, goodness and beauty that lie directly in the center of what we may for that very reason call Plotinus's "cosmos." But the Christian thinker who adopts and adapts this view most decisively is no doubt Dionysius the Areopagite, for whom God is *cause,* i.e., creator, precisely *as* goodness and beauty,[22] and thus whose relentless *via negativa* takes place from beginning to end within a world whose very stones proclaim the Lord precisely in their stoneness.[23] Along with Augustine, Dionysius was passed on to the great thinkers of the Middle Ages as the authority on such matters, and these thinkers can therefore be said to be arguably the most decisive formers of the Christian imagination.[24] Dionysius will thus be a primary focus for us in chapter seven.

Cause as Force

The light of our discussion so far will set into relief the differences between Cartesian rationalism and the so-called rationalism or spiritualism of the Greek and Christian Neoplatonists. In the first place, Descartes explicitly distinguishes between body and spirit as between two *things:* the *res cogitans* and the *res extensa.*[25] In this, he is much closer to the Manichees, or in any event to the materialist philosophers of late antiquity, than to the Platonic or the Augustinian tradition.[26] One might object that Descartes is using the term "res" here in a wholly equivocal sense, since the mind is clearly for him in no way a "thing" like matter extended in space, which is precisely why it becomes so difficult for him to explain how they would interact in a living human being. Though it would not be difficult to show how this objection is mistaken, it is in any event beside the point. The crucial thing is this: the

21. Plotinus, *Ennead* II.9.16.

22. Dionysius, *DN* IV.7.

23. On a "theologically aesthetic" reading of Dionysius that interprets the negative moment within the positivity of manifestation, see Balthasar, *GL2,* pp. 178-84.

24. On the ultimate significance of the corporeal in a Christian vision of the world, see Nicholas J. Healy, *The Eschatology of Hans Urs von Balthasar: Being as Communion* (Oxford: Oxford University Press, 2005). For a study of Aquinas's treatment of the body along the same lines, see Graham McAleer, *Ecstatic Morality and Sexual Politics: A Catholic and Nontotalitarian Theory of the Body* (New York: Fordham University Press, 2005).

25. Descartes, *The Principles of Philosophy,* I.8; II.4. Cf. also *Meditations on First Philosophy* II and VI.

26. See the excellent argument in this regard in Michael Hanby, *Augustine and Modernity* (London: Routledge, 2003), chapter 5, pp. 134-77.

body for Descartes is no longer *image*, which is to say that it is no longer expressive of a meaning which, as meaning, cannot be body in any sense.

Descartes' relationship to the world of the senses is therefore quite radically different from what we saw in Plato. For Plato, truth is *present* (παρουσία) in sense experience, if not qua sense experience, so that transcending the senses means seeing them as images, i.e., "windows" of meaning. Body is *meaning*-ful, we recall, precisely by not being meaning itself, or, rather, substituting for it. For Descartes, by contrast, everything qualitative (i.e., expressive of meaning) in sense experience must simply be set aside as subjective, for reasons we will investigate in just a moment. What is left is nondescript "stuff," bereft of any nature and reduced to its measurable dimensionality, perceivable by the mind alone.[27] It is noteworthy, in relation to our general theme, that this stripping of sensible objects precisely of their sensibilia coincides with the elimination of the imagination as an essential part of the soul.[28] We suggested at the outset that the imagination operates as a sort of middle term connecting the body and the soul and for that very reason connecting man and the world. Lacking an imagination, Descartes reduces the real to a pure mathematical abstraction, which neither he nor anyone else will ever encounter. Arguably, Descartes finally resolves the haunting problem of knowing whether the world exists in the *Meditations* simply by eliminating the world.

Now, these observations regarding Descartes echo criticisms that have been made of his philosophy for centuries. But we wish to suggest that this destruction of the imagination in Descartes is not the introduction of the problem, but rather itself an expression of a deeper transformation that was to have a far more pervasive impact on Western civilization than even Cartesian dualism, and that is the Scientific Revolution. Descartes' "reformation" of philosophy, through the introduction of a method that would allow indifferently anyone to make progress in the understanding that was previously reserved for the few,[29] is itself a repetition of Galileo's reformation of physics through the introduction of a technique that allows experiment to take the place of insight:

27. Descartes, *Meditations* II, 31.

28. "Moreover, I find in myself faculties for certain special modes of thinking, namely the faculties of imaging and sensing. I can clearly understand myself *in my entirety* without these faculties" (Descartes, *Meditations* VI, emphasis added).

29. See, e.g., Part One of Descartes' *Discourse on Method,* which begins: "Good sense is the best distributed thing in the world. . . ." In Descartes, intelligence becomes homogenized in the same way that motion becomes homogenized in Galileo.

> Profound considerations of this sort belong to a higher science than ours. We must be satisfied to belong to that class of less worthy workmen who procure from the quarry the marble out of which, later, the gifted sculptor produces those masterpieces which lay hidden in this rough and shapeless exterior.[30]

Our thesis has been that an appreciation of the meaningfulness of the senses rests on the primacy of goodness and beauty in the order of causality and therefore of understanding. It is no doubt true that the roots of this loss of primacy lie quite deep — one might point to goodness's loss of explanatory power in the new political philosophy of Machiavelli,[31] to the ascendancy of power over goodness in the nominalist theology of divine attributes, or even to the medieval appropriation of an Aristotelianism that separated goodness and truth because it had little place for beauty[32] — but, however that may be, Galileo's work gives the reformation of causality decisive and culture-changing expression.

The heart of the matter lies in Galileo's reinterpretation of causality in strictly dynamic terms. According to Galileo, "that and no other is in the proper sense to be called cause, at whose presence the effect always follows, and at whose removal the effect disappears."[33] The difference between cause as defined here and in the classical view is striking. Cause for Galileo is not what *accounts* for an effect, but what *produces* an effect, and indeed does so wholly through direct, material contact. Moreover, the only relationship that holds in an essential way between cause and effect is *temporal succession.* It would require another generation or so before it was discovered, by David Hume, that such a relationship is not in fact intelligible in the strict sense, as we shall see in the next chapter. But Galileo already himself recognizes that this view of causality — which to be sure unlocks the door to a new charac-

30. Quoted in Edwin Arthur Burtt, *The Metaphysical Foundations of Modern Physical Science: A Historical and Critical Essay* (London: Routledge, 1932), pp. 94-95.

31. Pierre Manent gives a brilliant account of the shift in the "causal" status of goodness that occurs in Machiavelli in *An Intellectual History of Liberalism* (Princeton: Princeton University Press, 1995), pp. 10-19. For Machiavelli's rejection of the significance of the imagination, see *The Prince,* chapter 15.

32. See Balthasar's discussion of the subtle beginnings of the separation of the true and the good in his "Theology and Sanctity," *Explorations in Theology,* vol. 1: *The Word Made Flesh,* trans. A. V. Littledale with Alexander Dru (San Francisco: Ignatius Press, 1989), pp. 181-86.

33. Quoted in Burtt, *The Metaphysical Foundations of Modern Physical Science,* p. 92.

ter of the material world, namely, one that, in its predictability, allows a kind of mastery never before possible — comes at the price of renouncing insight *into* the essence of things. As he says, for example, while we might inquire into the "essence" of the thing, it is

> not as if we really understood any more, what principle or virtue that is, which moveth a stone downwards, than we know who moveth it upwards, when it is separated from the projicient, or who moveth the moon round, except only the name, which more particularly and properly we have assigned to all motion of descent, namely gravity.[34]

An "effect" is not an image; it does not reveal the nature of its cause. To *produce* the effect, the cause must be of the same order as the effect, and thus has to be equally material. Cause and effect fall on the same horizontal line, which means, as we saw, that there can be no manifestation of meaning: revelation necessarily implies a hierarchy, insofar as what reveals must be in some fundamental sense subordinate to what it reveals. Investigating effects, therefore, does not teach us anything about the causes, no matter how precise and thorough our knowledge of the effects may be. Thus, as Galileo explains, the word "gravity" is a mere name. We do not know what it is. We are left, instead, with the task of calculating the quantity of the motion it produces through controlled observation of its effects.

For Plato, goodness is the paradigm of causality because it represents self-communication, and, since all other causality reflects to some degree this ultimate causality, what principally characterizes cause, as we saw, is the communication of form. For Galileo, by contrast, we might want to say that force is communicated from cause to effect, as revealed in the motion produced in the effect. But in the strictest terms, we would have to deny that *anything* is communicated. Communication implies that something is shared, that there is something that therefore unifies the communicants. According to the mechanistic view of causality we find in Galileo, however, nothing is "shared": the only thing joining cause and effect, as we saw, is succession in time and space. Physical motion (mechanistically understood) by its nature is not something that can be shared; it is atomistic of its essence. One thing can set another in motion, but the connection between them is extrinsic; it is the nature of force to operate from the outside — as opposed to, say, attraction, which operates simultaneously externally and internally.

34. Burtt, *The Metaphysical Foundations of Modern Physical Science*, p. 93.

We do not have room to pursue the theme here, but we note how the quantification of the study of motion results naturally from this transformation of the notion of cause. In this respect, Heidegger is profoundly right: the advent of empirical science is a result of a more fundamental shift in understanding; praxis is always and without exception rooted in and expressive of theory.[35] Whereas, for Aristotle, motion is the actualization of a potential, and in this respect represents the unfolding of a nature, so that we have to describe it in the first instance as relative to that nature and thus in qualitative terms — e.g., Aristotle demonstrates why circular motion is the most perfect and thus expected of the highest things — motion can have no intrinsic significance for Galileo: it is the homogenous monotony best described by number, successive units of the same.[36]

It is at this point that we can assess the implications of the reformation of causality for the significance of sense experience. In the popular scientific imagination, Galileo stands with Francis Bacon as the one who rescued science from the groundless and sterile fancies of late scholastic Aristotelianism by bringing it "down to earth," and chastening it to remain more modestly within the bounds of the empirical. Though this judgment is in a certain respect true, the respect in which it is true rests on the radical reversal of the meaning of terms, so that the empirical loses any meaningful connection with sense experience. It is not simply that Galileo's insistence on the empirical did not prevent him from wild and presumptuous speculation about things he could never in fact determine through sense experience[37] — a fact that suggests that what "empirical" means in the first and most fundamental sense is a cast of mind, a philosophical disposition, before it designates a real practice — but in point of fact this empirical method requires one to do violence to sense experience in a systematic fashion. In his book, *The Two Great Systems,* Galileo expresses a boundless admiration for rea-

35. See Heidegger's "Modern Science, Metaphysics, and Mathematics" (which is an excerpt from his lecture *Die Frage nach dem Ding*), in *Basic Works,* trans. David Krell (New York: Harper & Row, 1977), pp. 247-82.

36. Heidegger, "Modern Science, Metaphysics, and Mathematics," p. 261. Simon Oliver contrasts the hierarchy of motion in Aristotle (and Aquinas) to the homogenization of motion in Newton, in relation to the theological presuppositions underlying this shift in understanding. *Philosophy, God and Motion* (London: Routledge, 2005).

37. In addition to his rather fanciful conjectures concerning sunspots, it is known, for example, that the instruments available in Galileo's day for time measurement were not precise enough to justify his general inferences regarding the nature of motion. His theories, therefore, possessed an *a priori* character, to which he accommodated the discrepancies in his experimental data.

son's capacity, "in Aristarchus and Copernicus, to commit such a rape on their senses, as in despite thereof to make herself mistress of their credulity."[38] Notice: the very image is wholly unnatural. But it offers a revealing point of contrast with what we saw earlier. The violation of the senses that this passage commends is foreign to the Platonic tradition, which would never imagine reason and the senses as two "things" set over against one another: for Plato, if anything, reason must keep vigil over itself, because the deception of the senses always turns out in the end to be reason's self-deception. But in Galileo, reason and sense experience are *necessarily* opposed in their nature even if they are brought into accord in practice.

The reason for this opposition follows straightforwardly from the transformation of the understanding of cause. Sense experience is an *effect* produced in us by some external cause. But effects are not images that disclose the truth of their cause. Rather, they are individual motions that bear no relation to their causes apart from the fact of having been initiated by them. Thus, after discussing the way the sensation of tickling comes about in us through the touch of a feather, Galileo concludes:

> Now this tickling is all in us, and not in the feather, and if the animate and sensitive body be removed, it is nothing more than a mere name. Of precisely a similar and not greater existence do I believe these various qualities to be possessed, which are attributed to natural bodies, such as tastes, odours, colours, and others.[39]

Galileo's inference applies to *all* of what are now called the secondary qualities of sense experience: it is all a subjective illusion, because it communicates nothing intelligible regarding the real. There is nothing in our experience of heat, for example, that reveals the nature of the objective reality of heat. What is real are bodies in motion, which lie as it were behind, but not in, our sense experience. The world of perceived qualities that fills our conscious life, and indeed our imagination, has nothing meaningful to *say* to us. It has to be mute, because — to speak somewhat anachronistically but no less accurately — it is in itself nothing but the separate motions of particles, the interplay of forces, in the material substance of the brain. Our only relationship to the world, in this case, is contiguity in time and space. There is clearly only a small step — if there is any step at all — between Galileo's

38. Quoted in Burtt, *The Metaphysical Foundations of Modern Physical Science*, p. 69.
39. Burtt, *The Metaphysical Foundations of Modern Physical Science*, pp. 75-76.

mechanism and Descartes' mind-body dualism, which turns out to be an invincible monism of rationalistic intelligence.

We observed, earlier, the irony that the passionate language used in the ancient texts to "condemn" the flesh may represent in fact nothing less than a safeguard for its significance. The converse irony can be observed here: we often hear that modernity, with its "this-worldly" religion, is the first epoch in the history of the West to come to terms with the body and make peace with the flesh. But our discussion here suggests that what looks superficially like peace and a respect for the world of the senses arises in fact from a contempt that runs so deep it has grown cold to the point of indifference. The life of the senses can be enjoyed in detachment, or, conversely, the senses can be dispassionately exploited — "raped" — ultimately because sense experience does not mean anything in itself. In this case, imagination becomes simply trivial, and so too does the natural world the imagination mediates. The imagination is where the world can have a sort of spiritual home in us, and for that same reason is what allows us to have a home in the world. The destruction of the imagination — let us call it the iconoclasm of the intellect[40] — will thus necessarily coincide with an alienation and its attendant anxiety, which drives man to the apparently more certain but literally hope-less scheme of self-redemption through productivity.[41] A more detailed investigation would be necessary to develop and justify the observation, but it is worth reflecting on the fact that the reformation of science in Galileo and the reformation of philosophy in Descartes — not to mention the reformation of political philosophy previously in Machiavelli or the subsequent reformation of logic and education in Peter Ramus,[42] and arguably even the ecclesial reformation in Luther, Calvin, and Zwingli — all seem to share different versions of the same characteristics: they deny the substantial causal significance of goodness and beauty, i.e., the metaphysical reality of the transcendentals; they excise the whole of the mediating tradition which they subsequently affirm piecemeal on the basis of a new criterion applied

40. The term was inspired by Frances Yates, who refers to the "inner iconoclasm" effected by Peter Ramus's reform of logic and education. See *The Art of Memory* (Chicago: University of Chicago Press, 1966), pp. 231-42. Yates notes that the Ramist reforms were most successful "in Protestant countries like England" (p. 234).

41. On the connection between the loss of a sacramental sense of the world and the growth of an anxious "work ethic," see Max Weber's *The Protestant Ethic and the Spirit of Capitalism* (New York: Charles Scribner's Sons, 1958).

42. See Catherine Pickstock's discussion of Ramus in *After Writing: On the Liturgical Consummation of Philosophy* (Oxford: Blackwell, 1998), pp. 49-57.

immediately by the individual; they develop a technique or method that is meant to produce practical results rather than engender insight and understanding . . . and they all eliminate the significance of the imagination.

In sum, the root of what Claudel called the crisis of the late modern world, namely, the starvation of the imagination, is the eclipse of goodness and beauty from the order of cause. If this is true, it follows that the recovery of Christian art, Christian literature, and indeed Christian culture more generally is not sufficient on its own to address this crisis. Or perhaps more adequately the recovery of a genuine Christian culture — the world and Christian imagination — requires a recovery of beauty in its theological, metaphysical, and ultimately even its physical significance. Anything less will no doubt unwittingly trivialize precisely what it seeks to restore. It is not just the Word, but the Word made flesh, who was sent by the Father to dwell among us, the Word made flesh who enjoined us to carry the Good News to the ends of the earth — i.e., to the very extremities of being. It is Christ who said, "Behold, I make all things new," and who thus revealed himself to be, as the scholastics put it, the "perfect image," of the Father, or as we might say, the Truth of the Father's Imagination.

6 Historical Intelligibility: On Creation and Causality

When David Hume denied the objective basis for the concept of causality in the eighteenth century, a denial that sent forth philosophical waves forceful enough to wake the sleeping giant, Immanuel Kant, it appeared that he was upsetting a tradition as old as philosophy itself. Even more explicitly than his teacher Plato,[1] Aristotle affirmed in the fourth century BC that the determination of causes constituted the essence of knowledge, and then proceeded to develop a theory of causality that attempted to account for the variety of ways the mind seeks to explain the real.[2] For his part, Hume accepted the essential connection between causality and knowledge, but pointed out that this connection rests in turn on what he claimed to be an as-yet-unexamined assumption, namely, that it is possible to experience causality in such a way that it would provide an empirical foundation for our claim to know. When we expose these roots to the direct light of scrutiny, Hume claimed, they wither. For Hume, this means that what we call knowledge cannot ultimately be distinguished from belief, and so an honest philosopher is in the end forced to become a skeptic. Curiously, Hume's own honesty did not reduce him to forfeiting all speech and simply wagging his finger, like Cratylus, the radical disciple of Heraclitus;[3] indeed, Hume wrote a good deal of philosophy, and not only on this topic. His skepticism did not prevent him from developing arguments on behalf of skepticism.

We will reflect on the reason for Hume's eloquent skepticism further on; for the moment, we suggest that the difference between Aristotle and

1. Plato offers a discussion of the nature of causes especially in *Phaedo* 96a-102a.
2. Aristotle, *Metaphysics* 1.2. See also *Metaphysics* 1.3983a25-983b6; *Physics* 2.3.
3. See Aristotle, *Metaphysics* 4.5 1010a10-15.

Hume on the question of knowledge and causality is not due in the first place to the degree of "optimism" regarding the stability of things in themselves, on the one hand, or regarding the adequacy of the human mind, on the other. Instead, as we will propose in this essay, their differences in these matters stem more fundamentally from a transformation in the meaning of causality, which appears to have taken place over the course of the sixteenth and seventeenth centuries, and which in turn betrays a fundamental shift in the meaning of being.[4] In the previous chapter, we considered the displacement of the good by power as the essence of causality; here, we shall investigate a related change, which may be described as a reductive temporalizing of being.[5] While this transformation succeeds in giving a new weight to history, we will see that it entails a notion of cause that combines a radical skepticism with a positivistic empiricism. One does not need to be particularly gifted with powers of observation to see that this superficial certainty coincident with a profound anxiety characterizes the temper of our age still. But to respond to the problem that this notion of causality represents, it will not do to eliminate the philosophical significance of history and simply reject the "temporalizing" of being altogether,[6] not least of all because the significance of history is one of the fruits of Christianity. Not only is salvation effected in history — in contrast to the teaching of the Neoplatonic tradition, for example — but the being of the world is *created in time,* and this origin cannot but leave an indelible stamp on its most fundamental meaning.

The question we intend to address in the present chapter is how the doctrine of creation in principle allows the affirmation of the historical dimension of being without sacrificing intelligibility. In the sections that follow, we will begin by reflecting on the meaning of causality in Hume in contrast to the classical notion of causality represented by Aristotle, in order to show how it undermines intelligibility, and does so even more radically than Hume himself acknowledged. We will then argue for the need to maintain an integrated notion of causality, which will present us in the end with two

4. Kenneth Schmitz, "Analysis by Principles and Analysis by Elements," in *The Texture of Being* (Washington, DC: Catholic University of America Press, 2007), pp. 21-36.

5. It should be noted that the "temporalizing" of being, here, is significantly different from the temporalizing of being that Heidegger calls for, which we will be discussing at length in the following chapter.

6. One of the most classic arguments against the degeneration of philosophy into history can be found in Leo Strauss's *Natural Right and History* (Chicago: University of Chicago Press, 1965). There is arguably a connection between Strauss's rejection of history and his insistence on keeping reason and revelation separate.

alternatives: either we affirm, as did Aristotle, the unchanging permanence of forms in the manner of eternal species, or we affirm the supra-temporal and -spatial notion of creation, along with a supra-formal notion of act that it implies, which is compatible with genuine change in the historical order. In other words, acknowledging the genuine reality of history forces a choice between the collapse of intelligibility, on the one hand, or a metaphysics of creation on the other.

Ontological and Dynamic Causality

In a succinct account of the argument he first presented in the *Treatise on Human Nature,*[7] David Hume claims that the "cause-effect" relation possesses three essential elements: first, *contingency* in time and place (i.e., cause and effect must be immediately "adjacent" to one another, both temporally and spatially); second, *priority* in time of the cause to the effect; and, third, the *constant conjunction* of the two, that is, the unvarying experience that "every object like the cause, produces always some object like the effect."[8] For our purposes, the first thing to notice about this description is that it takes for granted the essentially "dynamic" character of causality. In other words, it thinks of the causal relation as an event that takes place in time, and indeed is defined precisely by its temporal succession. It is significant that what Hume presents here as the paradigm of such a relation is the collision of billiard balls. His view of causality reflects a change that occurred perhaps most decisively with Galileo, as we saw in the previous chapter, even if the seeds of this change go back much earlier.[9] In this change, a *dynamic* sense of cause came to take the place of the classical view, which, as we will explain in

7. As an attempt to draw attention to the work that he lamented "fell *dead-born from the press,* without reaching such distinction as even to excite a murmur among the zealots," David Hume published an anonymous review of his own work, titled *An Abstract of* A Treatise on Human Nature, published in Hume, *An Enquiry Concerning Human Understanding,* 2nd ed. (Indianapolis: Hackett, 1993), pp. 125-38.

8. Hume, *An Abstract,* p. 129.

9. One could point, for example, to the reductive emphasis on a certain kind of efficient causality in late scholastic nominalism, to the univocal notion of being in Scotus, which removed the ontological foundation for a richly analogous notion of causality, to the temporalizing of the notion of cause in John Philoponus's transformation of Aristotle, or indeed to the proto-mechanism and atomism in the very first philosophers, which Plato criticizes in the *Phaedo* and Aristotle criticizes in the *Physics.* The point, here, is not to determine the historical provenance of the change, but rather to characterize its *nature.*

a moment, could be more properly characterized as an "ontological" sense. The word "dynamic," here, is meant to capture two features of this new interpretation of cause. In the first place, it indicates that this view conceives of cause principally as a kind of motion; secondly, if the content of this relation is motion, that which brings it about, as we saw in the previous chapter, is simply a producer of motion, i.e., it is *force.*[10] In the context of this notion of cause, "explanation" comes to mean the identification of the agent or agents that initiate the event of change, and the circumstance under which it or they thus operate. An explanation is complete if all such agents for a particular change are identified, and it is called "exact" precisely to the extent to which the amount of force can be quantified and thus rendered in the form of mathematical formulae.

It is commonly said that the essential difference between the modern and classical notion of science is that the ancients pursued four causes in their search for understanding, while the moderns cast aside final causes — which Aristotle had taken to be primary — as a hindrance to the progress of the knowledge of nature, and, in doing so, lost the formal cause that always accompanies it. According to this interpretation, modern science limited itself to the material and efficient causes, conceiving of the natural world as constituted by extended matter set in motion by extrinsic forces, in the manner we described a moment ago. While this characterization is evidently not altogether false, it does not get to the heart of the matter. The reason for the change is not simply, as it were, a reduction or limitation of *attention* to some factors in the explanation of a reality to the exclusion of others. As we intend to show, the redirection of attention is itself due to a change in *understanding.*

We contrasted the dynamic view of cause with what we called an "ontological" sense. What does this mean exactly? One of the first challenges a person tends to face in teaching undergraduates Aristotle's notion of causality is the difficulty students have in thinking of the term "cause" as referring to *things* rather than to *events.* Indeed, the Greek term that is translated as "cause," namely, αἰτία, has no verbal form that would mean what we mean by "to cause," namely, "to make something happen." In Aristotle's sense, a cause is not an event that produces a subsequent event, but is rather anything that accounts for a thing — what, how, or why it is. Moreover, it becomes immediately evident in Aristotle's presentation that cause is an essentially analogous term, which is to say that the term covers an essential

10. See E. A. Burtt, *The Metaphysical Foundations of Modern Philosophical Science: A Historical and Critical Essay* (London: Routledge, 1932), p. 89.

diversity within unity or unity in diversity: the four causes that Aristotle describes are all the same in the sense that they all serve to account for the reality of a particular thing, but they do so according to orders so basically different as to be irreducible one to the other. As we will elaborate in a moment, the causes are principles that, while absolute in respect to the particular order they designate, nevertheless subsist in interdependence on the others according to a more general determinate, asymmetrical order. They describe the complex and unified ways that things *are,* and not in the first place how they *happen.* This is what it means to speak of causality in Aristotle as ontological as opposed to dynamic.

We are going to argue that the bracketing out of formal and final causes is a natural result of a more fundamental shift, the dis-integration of the causes from one another, the isolation and thus absolutizing of each of the respective principles in itself. This shift coincides exactly, as we will see, with the loss of the primacy of things in favor of a primacy of extrinsic relations, so that formal laws or patterns become the basic residence of intelligibility rather than what Aristotle called the οὐσία. In order to understand how this shift was not simply an exclusive focus on two causes, but in fact a reinterpretation of all of them on the basis of a new sense of being, it is helpful to see how even the efficient and material causes that the new science affirms underwent a transformation that stripped them of the richness they enjoyed in the earlier conception.

As Kenneth Schmitz explains it, whereas efficient causality originally indicated an *ontological* principle, so that it would be defined as the *communication of being* — in Aquinas's words, "A cause is that from whose being another being follows"[11] — it comes in the sixteenth and seventeenth centuries "to mean an active force or impulse that initiated change by transference of energy to another, resulting in displacement of particles in a new configuration and with an accelerated or decelerated rate of motion among the particles."[12] In both cases, the notion of efficient causality indicates a relation between two entities. One of the ways we could describe the difference between these two characterizations of efficient causality, however, is that the newer understanding "exteriorizes" this relation. A communication implies — as we will explain further in relation to formal causality — a sharing, which means that there is some (identically) one "thing" in common uniting the two shar-

11. Aquinas, *De principiis naturae,* ed. J. J. Pauson, trans. V. J. Bourke (Fribourg: Société Philosophique, 1950), quoted in Schmitz, "Analysis," p. 34.

12. Schmitz, "Analysis," p. 34.

ers. What the two are individually includes, then, the reality in which they are united. In the modern conception of efficiency, by contrast, there is no sharing: force is precisely an *extrinsic* imposition of determination.[13]

Similarly, the material cause, in the older analysis, did not indicate an individual entity, but a principle, specifically that "out of which" a thing was, a principle that makes sense only in relation to an "into which," so to speak. In other words, matter was understood as potency, which for Aristotle always relates to some actuality, and the potency exhibits different levels of determinacy at different levels of being. Thus, at the higher levels, the material cause would represent a relatively formed substance, a physical body, which possesses in itself a particular nature but which is still capable of being formed (not in a separate temporal moment, but ontologically relative to a higher nature) at a higher level of being. At the lowest level, it is "prime matter," no substance at all in itself but rather the pure capacity to receive determination. Regardless of the level, in this older view material cause always has a relationship to an actuality distinct from it. In other words, it is not intelligible, and does not have its existence, merely in itself, but only as itself in relation to a determining act that is distinct from it. To put it even more simply, matter is relatively determinate openness, or receptivity, to order. This view of matter contrasts sharply with, say, the Cartesian view of "res extensa," which possesses no such openness. It is, rather, opaque "stuff"; it designates inert objects of the forces that push and pull it in one way or another. In this case, we can see that it is still possible to affirm what we did above, namely, that matter is not intelligible in itself, but only in relation to what is distinct from it — in this case, force — and yet now the meaning of this affirmation changes by virtue of the new context: while in the first case matter itself receives meaning insofar as it relates to actuality, and does so because it itself is a potentiality on which actuality depends, in the second case matter remains always outside of meaning, just as meaning remains outside of matter.

But it is not only the efficient and material causes that are carried over into the newer analysis in a transformed state. It is important to see that form and finality are likewise present, though equally changed. Regarding formal cause: in both the older and the newer understanding, form represents a kind of determination or intelligible order. The two differ most directly in the "place" of that determination, though this difference has immediate implica-

13. See Aristotle's discussion of violent motion as change resulting from an external principle in *Physics* 8.4. Cf. *Nicomachean Ethics* 3.1 1110a1-5.

tions for the nature of that order. In the classical understanding, form determines a being *from within;* it is an internal principle of order, because it is "that by which a thing has existence" and that which "makes something to be actually."[14] Aristotle observed that form is most directly connected to nature precisely because he defined nature as an internal principle of change and rest. Now, the association of form with actuality is crucial. There can be no act without some *thing* that is actualized, and that thing must possess the specific potentiality for the actuality of a particular form, a potentiality that is distinct from the form that actualizes it. There is a connection between the rejection of the subsistence of forms as such and the interpretation of them as actuality. The meaning of form as act depends on the meaning of matter as potency. Only if we understand them both thus in relation to one another are we able to affirm the determination or intelligibility that form provides as *internal* to the being in question. Now, because, as we have just seen, the modern view of causality no longer thinks of matter in terms of potency, it is no longer possible within this conception to think of order as anything but *extrinsic* to things. "Formal" comes to mean separation from any particular content. In this case, it is of course natural, indeed necessary, to conceive of order in terms of law, or extrinsic pattern or structure, which, precisely because it is no longer understood analogically, comes to be expressed in terms of mathematics. It is not accidental that Aristotle, directly after presenting his most elaborate discussion of the nature of causality in *Physics* II, distinguishes the one who studies the natural world specifically from the mathematician along these lines: while both study form, the latter studies it as *separate* from natural bodies and thus in abstraction from any relation to motion, motion being in its principal sense the activity that springs from the internal principle that defines things: i.e., their nature.[15]

Now, if one is willing to admit that modern science retains formal causality, even if in an altered form, it would seem difficult to affirm that any trace of final cause remains, not least because those in whom modern science most clearly "came to be" explicitly understood themselves to be *rejecting* final causality.[16] While it is clearly true that one of the things that most

14. Schmitz, "Analysis," p. 33.

15. Aristotle, *Physics* 2.2.

16. See, for example, F. Bacon, *Novum Organum,* book 2, aphorism 2: "It is a correct position that 'true knowledge is knowledge by causes.' And causes again are not improperly distributed into four kinds: the material, the formal, the efficient, and the final. But of these the final cause rather corrupts than advances the sciences, except such as have to do with human action."

defines the revolution in understanding we have been describing is the attempt to abolish teleology from scientific accounts, final causality nevertheless stubbornly refuses to leave. We see this stubbornness in two ways. In the first place, as Robert Spaemann has shown, even analysis carried out strictly in the terms of mechanistic causality nevertheless has to isolate causes and effects, removing them from a literally endless continuum of possibly significant facts. Such an isolation cannot occur without some reference to final causality, since causes stand out as causes only in relation to the relevant effect that they are taken to produce.[17] If we eliminated even this minimalistic teleology, we would simply have no understanding whatsoever. Intelligibility of *any sort* always requires at least some modicum of purpose — which is a plausible way of interpreting Plato's claim that whatever we understand, we invariably understand by reference to the good.[18]

At a more general level, final causality remains in modern science by virtue of the fact that science is a human activity, and there is no human activity that occurs without some reference to purpose, however implicit. Thus, if final causality is removed from the inner constitution of things, it nevertheless has to go somewhere, as it were. The purpose of modern science and therefore the source of its intelligibility according to its founders is the improvement of the human estate. Scientific study and the gathering of data make sense insofar as they serve this larger goal. For Aristotle, by contrast, the purpose of science is the science itself, or in other words, it is good — indeed arguably one of the highest human goods — simply to know. What is crucial to see in relation to our general argument is that, in *this* case, the final end of human activity perfectly coincides with the final end of things themselves, insofar as absolutizing knowledge means affirming the intrinsic meaning of things, the simple integrity of the way things are. Conversely, there is a necessary connection between depriving things of an internal finality and subordinating them, not to the act of knowledge (because knowledge as such does not subordinate), but to human praxis: if we make the improvement of the human estate the end of science, we displace the intelligibility of things themselves, and the more we reduce the meaning of things to data to be gathered, the more suitable they become to be used as instruments of human praxis.

The point of the foregoing, in short, is to see that the essence of the Scientific Revolution, viewed specifically in relation to the issue of causality,

17. Robert Spaemann, *Die Frage Wozu?* (München: Piper-Verlag, 1981), pp. 243-49.

18. Plato, *Republic* VI, 505e-506a.

is not that it retains only some of Aristotle's causes and rejects others, but that it retains *all* of them in some sense even while it radically transforms the meaning of each. What we wish to suggest is that this transformation is not arbitrary, but itself reflects a change in the understanding of being. The next point in our argument, however, is to show that the meaning of each of the causes changes, and indeed *has* to change, precisely to the extent that each is interpreted in abstraction from the others. More precisely — because there is a sense in which any act of understanding involves some kind of abstraction — the change occurs insofar as the causes are no longer understood as *intrinsically dependent* on one another, so that one would have to understand the other causes at least implicitly in order to have a proper understanding of each one individually. The transformation at issue can be described as the dis-integration of the causes. In order to see this it is necessary to consider in what sense the causes depend in each case on an implicit reference to the whole for their own integrity. We will then go on to consider, in the fourth section, what sense of being is required for an integrated notion of causality and the "conditions of possibility" for this sense of being.

The Interweave of the Causes

Let us briefly consider each of the causes in turn with a view to at least some aspect of their interdependence.[19] As we saw above, classically understood, the efficient cause is not a force that sets a mechanistic event in motion, but in the first place is a *communication of being:* the paradigm of such causality for Aristotle would be the generation of progeny; for Aquinas — as we will explore further in a moment — the only "instance" of efficient causality in the strictest sense, which establishes the meaning for every other analogical instance, is God's act of creation. This act is a communication of being *simpliciter.* It is worth pointing out that, in contrast to the modern notion of cause which is necessarily a temporal event, this act designates in the first place an ontological relationship; it is not a change that occurs within the world. Now, setting aside the act of creation for a moment, and considering efficient causality in a general sense, the word "communication" implies that something is shared, which as we suggested above means that there is some unity between the cause and

19. The discussion that follows is not meant to be an exhaustive account of the interdependence of the four causes on one another; rather, it is meant only to say enough to establish the fact of that interdependence.

the effect. This unity lies in the *form:* a father and mother "cause" a child by passing on to him the human form, and they have a unity with him because this form is in some respect identically the same. The general principle in classical thought, *omne agens agit sibi simili,* holds by virtue of this unity in form, so that there would be no unity were there no form. This means, then, that the efficient cause cannot be what it is, namely, the communication of being *sibi simili,* without reference to form: the formal cause, in other words, *belongs* to the efficient cause properly understood. As we argued in the previous chapter, if it is separated from the formal cause, the efficient cause cannot *communicate* anything, but can only transfer energy, which, precisely because it is necessarily extrinsic in this case, takes the form of *force.*

While matter in the modern conception means mere extension in space, and so designates "physicality," we might say, bereft of any inherent qualities apart from measurability, matter in the classical understanding was an essentially relational term. Specifically, as a potency, it always referred in some sense to form or actuality, in two respects. On the one hand, matter is, in itself, *aptitude* for form, so that, as we explained above, its intelligibility derives in part from the form that actualizes it and thus determines it in a certain way. Matter is openness upwards, we might say. On the other hand, what is potentiality in one respect will always be actuality in another: the body that represents the material cause of a living organism with respect to its animating principle, namely, the form or soul, is itself the form with respect to its own material principles, namely, the flesh, blood, and bones, and so on down the line. In this sense, matter — understood as formed body — will always have a qualitatively determined nature, in one respect, even while it will remain in another respect open to higher determinations. Although this inference was rarely drawn in classical accounts, it follows in fact that the more relatively determinate matter is, the more receptive it is capable of being for a higher form. But this means that, if matter is defined as a potency for form, the higher, more organized instances of matter, which by virtue of their complexity are more capable of receiving higher-order actualities, represent more fully *what* matter is than the lower instances. Thus, for example, a human body is a better representative of the nature of matter than, say, a stone, which has little intrinsic potency to receive form.[20] Thus, in short, we

20. It would be interesting to compare prime matter to organized body in relation to the question that best reveals the *meaning* of matter: while prime matter would seem most receptive in one sense, insofar as it is a kind of pure indeterminacy, it nevertheless is not immediately capable of being actualized at a high level precisely because of that very indeterminacy. A full reflection on this issue lies beyond the scope of our discussion in this chapter.

do not speak of matter, simply, as a thing in itself, but always of the material principle *of* a particular being. The natural being as a whole is in each case the subject, the fundamental reference point, in relation to which we are able to judge what in fact the material cause is. The material cause alone, without any reference to form or nature, would be simply unintelligible.

Next, we may consider the dependence of form on matter. The key to this dependence is that, if form is not the actualization of some potency, as we noted above, it cannot be the *intrinsic principle* that it in fact is. Instead, it becomes an abstract formality, so to speak, which must remain by definition superficial, since it does not bear any internal relationship to the thing of which it is the form. In other words, it necessarily turns into a purely extrinsic structure, pattern, or law.[21] We thus no longer speak of *things* as *formed*, in the sense of being "in-formed," but rather we speak of form as the external patterns *to which* things are *con-formed*. To speak of form as an internal principle requires, once again, a reference to a real being — or as Aristotle puts it, a "natural body" — *of* which it is the form, and a real being is such only by virtue of the relation between form and matter: "nature is twofold, and is both form and matter."[22] We can explain this essential relation by saying that, in order for form to be internal to a being, it must be received into it, and it can only be thus received if there is an intrinsic potency for that actuality, i.e., if there is a material principle understood as we have just described it. There is thus a relationship of reciprocal dependence between form and matter: matter, as a "potency for," implies the priority of form, and form cannot exist as such except as received by matter. This means that there cannot be a temporal priority of one or the other, so that they are then added together in a subsequent "moment." Instead, they must always already be involved with one another, so to speak. This is why Aristotle presents organic form, which is always already intrinsically related to its matter, as the paradigm, and treats the form of an artifact, which is to some degree simply

21. See, e.g., Bacon's observation in the *Novum Organum*, book 2, aphorism 2, which is the continuation of the passage we quoted in footnote 16: "Nor have I forgotten that in a former passage I noted and corrected as an error of the human mind the opinion that forms give existence. For though in nature nothing really exists besides individual bodies, performing pure individual acts according to a fixed law, yet in philosophy this very law, and the investigation, discovery, and explanation of it, is the foundation as well of knowledge as of operation. And it is this law with its clauses that I mean when I speak of *forms*, a name which I rather adopt because it has grown into use and become familiar."

22. Aristotle, *Physics* 2.2; J. Sachs's translation, *Aristotle's Physics: A Guided Study* (New Brunswick, NJ: Rutgers University Press, 1995), p. 52.

imposed on matter that is in a certain respect independent of it, as an analogous sense of the term.[23] An intrinsic relation to matter is part of the meaning of form in its strict sense.

As for final causality, it represents an explanation of the meaning of things, and not simply an arbitrary imposition, only insofar as teleology is taken to be most fundamentally intrinsic. If there is no intrinsic relationship between a being and the purpose it serves, if, in other words, the purpose is simply extrinsic to a being, then it becomes wholly accidental that it happens to be this particular being that serves the purpose, and not some other. Things become interchangeable with respect to their purpose, and represent nothing more than instruments in its service. The purpose, in this case, does not illuminate the meaning of the being, which is to say it has no strictly theoretical role, but as we saw above dissolves into a kind of positivistic pragmatism that is never truly self-explicating but only ever endlessly self-justifying, and indeed, always in terms other than itself. For teleology to have an essentially theoretical dimension, the end must be internal, which is another way of saying that natural things must be their own end. Aristotle coined the term "ἐντελέχεια" to refer to organisms: they possess *(echein)* their end *(telos) in (en)* themselves; they are, so to speak, "enpurposed." But this simply means that the first aim of an organism is to be itself, to actualize as fully as possible *what* it is. It follows, then, that final causality, if it is to be something other than external manipulation, requires a reference to formal causality, the essential "whatness" of a thing or its most basic determinate act, and more specifically to an internal notion of form, which as we saw above, is such only with reference to an internal potency. In the paradigmatic case of the organism, once again, the "reference" is so intrinsic as to be materially identical, to represent one and the same thing under a different aspect.[24] Finality as a *cause* is inconceivable without formal causality.

The Unraveling of Intelligibility

There would be other ways to show the interdependence of the four causes, but the brief account given already establishes the principle that the causes cannot be understood in isolation from one another, so that to separate them is to distort them. Before we raise the issue of what understanding of

23. *Aristotle's Physics,* 2.1.
24. Aristotle, *Physics* 2.7.

being is required in order to be able to affirm an integrated notion of causality, we will first consider the implications of this distortion with respect to the intelligibility of things more generally. We have suggested that the modern view of causality did not so much eliminate some of the causes as it did reinterpret them in a dynamic, rather than an ontological, sense. We wish to argue now that this reinterpretation in fact undermines their intelligibility more radically than is typically acknowledged.

As we saw at the outset, Hume affirmed the dependence of knowledge on causality, which he in turn described as the regular succession of contiguous events in time. Having described things thus, he points out that the mind has no access to any necessary connection between the two, but only to the one event that precedes and the other that follows. This exhaustively "dynamic" notion of causality is, we might say, a paradigmatic expression of the dis-integration we have been describing. Unities are always *supra*-temporal — which does not mean that they do not exist *in* time, but only that their existence in time does not account for the whole of their reality. An identity, which is a type of unity, remains numerically the same over the course of a multiplicity of moments, which means that its reality transcends each one of those moments and so cannot be reduced to it. To *define* causality in strictly temporal terms is not to show that there is no basis for knowledge, but in fact to take the absence of that basis for granted at the outset, which is of course to beg the question.

It is interesting that Hume does not link knowledge to essences or forms, or to intrinsic teleology, all of which imply a unity, but rather to the physical interaction between things, an event. As a merely physio-temporal event, this encounter — if the word is appropriate at all in this context — is wholly extrinsic. Nothing about the interaction reveals the meaning of either of the things involved, or bears significantly on that meaning. Indeed, it is wholly a matter of indifference what the cause and effect are in themselves, but only that they happen to connect at this point in time and space: there is no communication (of form), which means that the effect tells us nothing about the nature of the cause. Now, it follows directly from this that there can be no essential necessity to this relation. If the two things relate to one another in a wholly extrinsic fashion, their interaction will be altogether accidental, or in other words arbitrary in relation to the meaning of things, regardless of the empirical reliability of the law to which they appear to conform. In this case, the regularity of their interaction — should it happen indeed to exhibit some regularity — is simply a matter of probability, a likelihood that always only asymptotically approaches necessity as something extrinsic to itself. Given Hume's definition of causality, he cannot *but* deny any essential difference between what we call knowledge and the belief based on custom and constantly reinforced by experience.

But Hume did not draw the full implications of his starting assumptions; more needs to be said here. It is not merely the necessity of the connection between cause and effect that gets lost the moment we reductively temporalize the relation and see them therefore as wholly extrinsically connected, but intelligibility itself founders at its root: we are in this case not simply unable to *predict* things with the absolute certainty that necessity offers, but the very possibility of any sort of understanding is undermined as well. As we mentioned above with reference to Spaemann, even a wholly "positivistic" view of causality derives whatever intelligibility it possesses from an implicit affirmation of teleology. One cannot distinguish a cause from the essentially infinite number of conditions preceding the effect without some minimal reference to final causality: this reality differs from the others in that it acts "for the sake of" this effect; its activity has the purpose of producing such and such an effect. If there is nothing but wholly extrinsic relations, it would make no sense to distinguish a "post hoc, propter hoc" fallacy from a valid analysis of a causal relation, because there would *be* only "posts" and no "propter." Thus, not only would we lack a basis for attributing any necessity to the connection between cause and effect, but we would in fact have no way of identifying any causes, which means we would also lose the ability to identify something as an effect, insofar as doing so depends on identifying a cause. Along with necessity, there would be no such thing as probability.

At an even more fundamental level, the reduction of cause to an event not only precludes the possibility of knowing the necessity or even probability governing the relations between things, but it eliminates the understanding of the things themselves at all, since no "thing" whatsoever can be a "thing" unless it is an intelligible whole. If there is no form as an internal principle of unity that identifies a thing as what it is and distinguishes it from everything it is not by gathering up the multiplicity of parts and aspects and ordering them around a center, then the mind seeking understanding has, as it were, no place to go in its relation to things. It is interesting to note that, addressing the question of the possibility of knowledge, Hume immediately speaks of the connection *between* things, and considers whether it is possible to affirm necessity of this connection. But he does not first raise the question of our knowledge of the things themselves that connect. He evidently takes it for granted that we are able to identify the first billiard ball, and then the second, even if he rejects the claim that we can identify anything in experience that we could call their causal connection. It is only later that he introduces the issue of substance, and of course denies that we can have knowledge of it, since our experience of things is limited to their accidents: our relation to things is, indeed, just as extrinsic as the colliding billiard balls. For Hume, the mind seeking understanding is drawn outward, away from things and toward their external relationships.

The implications of this turn however extend further than Hume seems to have realized. He denies substance, and speaks instead of accidents; he denies knowledge, and speaks instead of experiences and impressions that give rise to belief of varying degrees of compelling power. But isn't an accident also an object with its own form, a meaningful whole that is not merely the sum of its parts, and couldn't we say the same for any experience or impression, not to mention the notion of knowledge or belief? The strictures that Hume demands would render unintelligible the very language in which he demands them.

Or apparently, at any rate. It turns out that a strategy remains for salvaging at least a *kind* of intelligibility in the face of a fundamental skepticism with respect to any intelligibility, whether in the world or in the soul. In a book published in 1969 titled *Two Logics,*[25] Henry Veatch describes the supplanting of Aristotelian categorical logic by the symbolic logic represented by Russell and Whitehead, and claims that much more was going on here than simply the expansion of logic's scope and power: symbolic logic, according to Veatch, is essentially a "relating-logic," which in contrast to the Aristotelian "what-logic," is "unable to say what anything is." Although we unfortunately cannot enter into the details of his interesting argument, it is helpful, in relation to our theme, to note one feature of it. At the heart of this transition to symbolic logic, which we find for example in the analytic philosophy that dominates the Anglo-American academy, lies a radical reconception of the basic instance of human thought, namely, the simple proposition: S is P. Whereas in the traditional view, this presented an articulation of the subject and its accident, whereby the accident reveals something about the nature or the reality of the subject, in the modern view this simple proposition represents a relation between two terms, which relationship is conceived as a logical function. In this case, the predicate is not understood to disclose something about the meaning of the subject, but instead represents simply a

25. Henry Veatch, *Two Logics: The Conflict Between Classical and Neo-Analytical Philosophy* (Evanston, IL: Northwestern University Press, 1969).

property that is posited as belonging in this case to the subject. In other words, it assumes an extrinsic relationship between the two terms, so that either the predicate is already contained in the subject and so is not different from it (analytic statement), or the predicate is separate from the subject and can be connected either formally by the logic of categories (synthetic a priori) or materially by experience (synthetic a posteriori). But this way of conceiving things leaves us, on the one hand, the sphere of necessity that is limited to a logical analysis of "what we mean" by the language we use to describe the world or the necessary relations between concepts, and on the other hand the contingent sphere of empirical facts, which can be recorded and organized according to patterns (i.e., form understood extrinsically as law) but not intellectually *penetrated* as an essential, intrinsic meaning (form as ontological principle). Intelligibility is therefore "saved" in this case by separating thought altogether from things, allowing it the much more modest goal of coherence and consistency, and subsequently extrinsically reconnecting it to the world only in the apparently equally modest mode of a positivistic empiricism. It is just this that we find in both in Hume and in a more sophisticated form in Kant. What Veatch does not say here, but what our previous discussion allows us to see, is that the root of this development in twentieth-century philosophy is a dis-integration of the notion of cause; a metaphysical problem lies at the basis of the epistemological problem.

The question often arises, with respect to this detachment of thought from the world, which is itself a reflection of the displacement of intelligible form from the center of things, whether it does not harbor within itself outright contradiction, along the lines we indicated above with respect to Hume: even within this apparently modest self-limitation of reason, he necessarily speaks of the *nature* of concepts, of propositions, of reason, and even of the things whose nature is unknown to us. Indeed, this is clearly self-contradictory. But it is crucial to see why the very separation of thought from the world renders this charge gratuitous, at least in a certain respect. The problem in a nutshell is that this contradiction lies too deep to create a difficulty for self-limiting thought; it lies, we might say, in the very realm that reason restrains itself from entering. The result of this self-restraint is that a new criterion for judgment takes the place of truth, namely, a necessarily utilitarian concept of the good. Although this pragmatism cannot justify itself theoretically, it can always persuade itself to take solace in the fact that the essentially contemplative vision of truth presupposed by the ancient science cannot justify itself practically — at least not according to the terms set by pragmatism: i.e., it does not appear to produce anything of immediately utilitarian benefit. The key is that, along with its being shifted from a theoretical to a pragmatic register, the criterion for judgment is simultaneously "temporalized," in the sense that an idea justifies itself by pointing to its consequences *here* and *now.*[26]

What is at stake in the question of the proper measure of truth is nothing short of the basic meaning of the cosmos, the meaning of human nature, and indeed ultimately as we will see in a moment the meaning of the God who created both. The fragmentation of causality not only eliminates necessity, but it undermines intelligibility so radically that intelligibility no longer matters, so radically that intelligibility can be "used," even if it does not in fact have a basis in reality or ultimately mean anything, as long as its use brings about desired results — "desired" meaning here only what the utterly arbitrarily imposed final cause determines it to mean in any given case.[27] This is a nihilism far more profound than that expressed by Friedrich Nietzsche, who suffered extreme loneliness as a result of his convictions. It is a nihilism compatible with the various truth claims required for efficient living in the contemporary world. The fragmentation of causality puts reality wholly at the service of human aims, and indeed at the service of aims that have become so bourgeois they are no longer human, but merely "all too human."

Substantial Meaning

To respond to this nihilism, we must ask what understanding of being is necessary for an integrated notion of causality. As we have seen, each of the causes has its proper meaning only in relation to the others. But this interdependence would seem to create a logical difficulty: if A cannot be A without B, but B cannot be B without A, then it would seem to be impossible to have either, for each would await the other to attain to its own meaning, which entails an infinite regress with no absolute place to start. But if it is true that

26. There is an analogy between this pragmatism and the replacement of philosophy by sociology in political theory represented by Montesquieu. According to Pierre Manent, this replacement, which he takes to be the precise moment of the emergence of the modern age, does not justify itself theoretically in comparison with the ancient world, but simply supplants it on the strength of the authority of the "present moment." History takes the place of nature. See *The City of Man,* trans. Marc A. LePain (Princeton: Princeton University Press, 1998), pp. 11-49.

27. For an elaboration of the significance and implications of the shift from a theoretical to a pragmatic criterion for judgment, see my *Plato's Critique of Impure Reason* (Washington, DC: Catholic University of America Press, 2008), pp. 1-21.

one could never move sequentially from A to B, or from B to A, insofar as the two are reciprocally dependent, it is possible to have both of them at the same time, or in other words to take as the starting point the reality of a *whole* in which A and B are reciprocally dependent as constitutive parts. And here we are brought to the sense of being required for an integrated notion of causality: as Aristotle saw, the essential meaning of being is *substance;* what are absolute are concrete, natural things, the most basic of which are organisms, and the most derivative of which are in some sense elements and in another sense artifacts.[28] A substance is a whole, which is simultaneously complex and irreducibly one. A substance cannot be divided, properly speaking, without ceasing to be the substance it was (homogenous elements come closest to this possibility, but for that very reason are the least deserving of the name "substance"). In it, the constitutive principles — efficiency, matter, form, and finality — interweave in a reciprocally dependent and asymmetrical manner, as we described above. They exist together in some respect "all at once."

Now, the complex unity of substance has a difficult implication, which could scarcely be entertained today, but which follows from Aristotle's view with strict logical necessity: it is impossible, according to this understanding of the interdependence of causes, for new forms to come to be. Aristotle affirmed the eternality of the species, and it should be clear that he could do nothing else. A whole that is in the strictest ontological sense greater than the sum of its parts cannot be "cobbled together" from those parts. Take a frog: an organism of this sort represents the integration of causality to such an extent that the efficient, formal, and final cause are in this case one and the same (it is the *frog,* the *what* of the thing, that moves itself, and it does so in order to be a frog in the fullest sense it can). The material cause, though not in any genuine sense identical to form, nevertheless remains intrinsic to it so that there never exists frogness "as such," but only as individual frogs. Because of this integration, it would be impossible to assemble a frog in the manner of Frankenstein's monster, and to the extent that one could approximate such a thing, it would inevitably serve an extrinsic purpose, which means it would not be an "entelechia," as properly befits an organism. In a proper substance, none of the four causes, in other words, has its being, so to speak, in itself. Rather, each is a cause *of* the being in both the objective *and* subjective sense of the genitive. The substance is the absolute to which the causes are relative, it is the essential reference point for the understanding of

28. Aristotle, *Physics* 2.1.

each. Thus, for Aristotle, substance must be eternal, a frog cannot be produced out of something more basic, but can come only from other, already actualized, frogs. If it *did* come from something more basic, it would be reducible back to that or those most basic things, which would then represent eternal substance themselves. In this case, what *appeared* to be the reality would not be the genuine reality.[29] Strict novelty, in any event, is impossible for Aristotle; even the creation of apparently original artifacts is the expression of forms that have been derived from other more basic forms, and cannot be said to have been generated from nothing.

We thus appear to stand before a dilemma. On the one hand, we have an integrated causality that represents the condition of possibility for all intelligibility, but to affirm this would require us to accept the eternal reality of substances, for any whole greater than the sum of its parts cannot simply be constructed step by step out of its parts. But this is an essentially "static" notion of the cosmos; it denies development, and very clearly denies the possibility of anything like an evolution of species. It would seem to deny, moreover, the possibility of creation, if one thinks of this divine act as an *alternative* to the eternality of species. There thus appears to be good reason to reject this understanding of being. On the other hand, actually to do so would present an even more obviously problematic implication: it would entail the dis-integration of the causes, and therefore a purely mechanistic conception of the universe and all things in it, coincident with the loss of any foundation for intelligibility, so that, if there is to be meaning at all, it is forced to fix its outer limits at the hermetically sealed borders of self-enclosed reason. What, in this situation, are we to do?

29. Interestingly, the truth of this line of argument reveals itself in Richard Dawkins's neo-Darwinianism, as he expresses it in *The Selfish Gene* (Oxford: Oxford University Press, 2006): he explains that *genes* are the basic units of natural selection. He thus makes them the absolute to which the organisms are relative. This leads him to claim, (1) that organisms are not real in themselves, but are simply genes' "survival machines"; (2) that organisms ought thus to be understood as instruments by which genes replicate themselves; and (3) that it is genes that are (relatively) "immortal." In other words, Dawkins does not ultimately eliminate Aristotelian substances, but simply transfers the properties of substance to mechanistically conceived units. His account fits exactly Aristotle's criticism of the "naturalistic" pre-Socratic thinkers: "For whatever from among these [physical elements] anyone supposes to be [the nature of things that are], whether one of them or more, this one or this many he declares to be all thinghood [i.e., substance], while everything else is an attribute or condition or disposition of these, and whatever is among these he declares to be eternal (since for them there could be no change out of themselves), while the other things come into being and pass away an unlimited number of times." *Physics,* 2.1; Sachs, *Aristotle's Physics,* p. 50.

One might anticipate that it was precisely the worldview brought by Christianity that undid the integration of Aristotle's eternal substances, insofar as the doctrine of creation means that *all* things in the cosmos "come to be," at least in some respect. But this would only be the case in principle if indeed the sense of being entailed in the doctrine of creation were incompatible with the absoluteness of substance. As Thomas Aquinas shows, there is no contradiction in principle between the world's being created and its being eternal. As he indicates in the short treatise *On the Eternity of the World*, it is a mistake to think that efficient causality can operate only according to temporal succession.[30] While it is true that efficient causality implies a "before" and an "after," he explains, these terms need not indicate an order of time (as they *essentially* do in Hume, and "before" him in Galileo), but can also indicate an order of nature.[31] In other words, the causality of creation does not necessarily imply an event in time, but can simply mean absolute metaphysical dependence — even, in principle, of eternal things. In this respect, Aquinas affirms that the Platonic notion that the world is both eternal and wholly dependent on God is not offensive to reason.

There are some who believe that Aquinas means to present this an-

30. "First, we should show that it is not necessary that an agent cause, in this case God, precede in time that which he causes, if he should so will. This can be shown in several ways. First, no cause instantaneously producing its effect necessarily precedes the effect in time. God, however, is a cause that produces effects not through motion but instantaneously. Therefore, it is not necessary that he precede his effects in time. The first premise is proved inductively from all instantaneous changes, as, for example, with illumination and other such things. But the premise may be proved by reason as well. . . ." *On the Eternity of the World,* trans. Robert T. Miller.

31. "Further, let us even suppose that the preposition 'out of' imports some affirmative order of non-being to being, as if the proposition that the creature is made out of nothing meant that the creature is made after nothing. Then this expression 'after' certainly implies order, but order is of two kinds: order of time and order of nature. If, therefore, the proper and the particular does not follow from the common and the universal, it will not necessarily follow that, because the creature is made after nothing, non-being is temporally prior to the being of the creature. Rather, it suffices that non-being be prior to being by nature. Now, whatever naturally pertains to something in itself is prior to what that thing only receives from another. A creature does not have being, however, except from another, for, considered in itself, every creature is nothing, and thus, with respect to the creature, non-being is prior to being by nature. Nor does it follow from the creature's always having existed that its being and non-being are ever simultaneous, as if the creature always existed but at some time nothing existed, for the priority is not one of time. Rather, the argument merely requires that the nature of the creature is such that, if the creature were left to itself, it would be nothing." *On the Eternity of the World,* trans. Robert T. Miller.

cient view as a possibility for reason; guided by the Christian faith, however, which affirms the creation *in time* of all things and so denies the eternity of the world, we ought to reject this possibility in favor of the other reasonable possibility, namely, that all things come to be in time. If this were the case, one would wonder why he would write an entire treatise on behalf of a position he considers false.[32] But there is another way to interpret Aquinas regarding this question. If we consider Aquinas's metaphysical exposition of creation in the *Summa,* we realize that, for Aquinas, this ancient philosophical notion regarding the eternity of the world is and remains in some respect *true,* even if this truth does not contradict the affirmation that all things have come to be. We are approaching the height of paradox here, but it is reason that is leading us to it. One of the constant themes in Aquinas's exposition of the notion of creation is that the proper *terminus* of God's creative act is the particular subsistent being, what Aristotle calls the substance: "Creation does not mean the building up of a composite thing from pre-existing principles; but it means that the *composite* is created so that it is brought into being at the same time with all of its principles."[33] The reason for this is that we can attribute being to parts — for example, to form and to matter — only analogously insofar as they contribute to the reality of things. But being belongs in the *proper* sense "to that which has being — that is, to what subsists in its own being."[34] Aquinas in other words affirms Aristotle's notion that it is *wholes,* composite beings, that are what is most real, and that other aspects of the world have their reality always *relative* to these wholes. In this respect, a human being would be more real, for example, than the genes that make him up. He is more real than an atom, or indeed even more than a rock or a tree, insofar as a human being has more independence than they. Composite wholes — whether we call them substances in Aristotle's sense or subsistent beings in Aquinas's — *remain absolute* in the doctrine of creation, which means that this doctrine entails an integrated notion of causality.

The question that arises, here, is whether this absoluteness of wholes

32. Moreover, this interpretation tends toward an instrumentalist view of reason and an extrinsicist view of the relationship between reason and faith: if reason leads to one conclusion, and faith then simply introduces a different one without including a rational critique of the first, then we are left with a decidedly un-Thomistic dual truth theory. We intend to suggest that the truth that faith brings, which reason cannot anticipate by itself, nevertheless integrates the whole of what reason itself affirms.

33. Aquinas, *ST* 1.45.4ad2.

34. *ST* 1.45.4.

presents a difficulty for the temporal coming to be of the world that is entailed in the Christian belief in creation *in time.* On the one hand, Aquinas affirms that *substances* as such imply the *transcendence* of time — "time does not measure the substance of things"[35] — and for this reason, because demonstration concerns the essence of things (which represents their non-temporal aspect), creation in time cannot be demonstrated. This implies that a "supra-temporal" aspect of being is essential to its intelligibility, which is what we have argued with respect to the notion of causality. Indeed, Aquinas specifically distinguishes eternity from time by the principle of wholeness: eternity is simultaneously whole, while time is not.[36] We may infer from this that, *insofar as something is whole, and to that extent it represents something essentially greater than and irreducible to its parts, that thing transcends time.* It is important to see the implication: it is not simply a *part* of a substance — for example, the abstract form or the "ideal" reality of the thing — that transcends time, but that each individual substance must transcend time precisely to the extent that the substance represents an irreducible unity. This does not mean the thing does not exist in time, but only that its temporal reality is not the whole of its reality. Again, it is just this transcendence of time that makes it intelligible. But faith does not contradict reasoning; the light of faith does not obscure the light of reason. This means that the new context into which faith introduces the being of the world preserves the intelligibility, and therefore the time-transcending character, of being even as it transforms it. The sharpest question we must ask, then, is how does the origin *in time* of things not eliminate the supra-temporal integrity of their intelligible reality?

We cannot here explore this question in all the depth that it demands, but we may nonetheless draw principles of a response to it from Aquinas. Precisely because substance necessarily has an "all at once" quality, it cannot as we said come into being incrementally. Moreover, insofar as creation is a divine act, it does not itself take place *in time,* as a movement or a change, which always implies the succession of moments. Thus, Aquinas affirms that the world is created simultaneously with time: "Things are said to be created in the beginning of time . . . because together with time heaven and earth were created."[37] Indeed, God does not "take time," as it were, to create, but rather "He must be considered as giving time to His effect as much as and

35. *ST* 1.46.3 obj. 1. See also 1.46.2.

36. *ST* 1.10.4.

37. *ST* 1.47.3ad1.

when He willed."[38] It is manifestly not the case that, for example, the matter is first created as a potential to receive at a later moment the form that actualizes it. This would leave form and matter extrinsic to each other in a way that would not allow us to make sense of organic beings, the epitome of the real. To the contrary, not only is no matter present prior to God's creation of subsistent beings, but no possibility is present — or rather, if there is a possibility it lies wholly in God's will.[39] God does not operate within the limits of the conditions of possibility, but he *gives* those conditions in giving being. It is in this sense that each real, subsistent being is created "all at once," specifically *as* a whole.

Now, while we might be able to imagine in some distant way that God created the world together with time in the distant past, it does not seem to be the case that individual beings are created "immediately," in the manner described. If they were, we would expect to see beings "pop up" into existence literally "out of nowhere." Is it not the case that the beings that make up the world have come to be gradually insofar as they evidently did not exist at the beginning of the universe — something that not only modern science, but Aquinas too seems to have held?[40] If this is the case, it seems to contradict the claim we have repeatedly made that substances have an absolute character that does not allow them to be reduced back to anything less than they. There are two points to make in response to this difficulty: first, the absoluteness of substance precludes a "coming to be" from below, but does not preclude a coming to be, so to speak, from above. But such a "coming to be" requires a kind of actuality that is distinct from, and indeed superior to, the actuality of form. Aquinas presents this kind of actuality in his notion of *esse,* the existence that God shares with the beings he makes be, or the act by which all forms themselves are actualized.[41] *Esse,* according to Aquinas, is formal with respect to all form because it is the actuality of all (formal) acts.[42] In this respect, it is that to which the actuality of real beings can be reduced. It is not a potentiality out of which forms are generated "from below," but is rather an excess, so to speak, of actuality that is limited

38. *ST* 1.46.1ad6.

39. *ST* 1.46.1ad1.

40. See *ST* 1.46.3.

41. On the significance of the supra-formal act of being for historical intelligibility and the relationship between being and time, see F. Wilhelmsen, *The Paradoxical Structure of Existence* (Irving, TX: University of Dallas Press, 1970), pp. 127-55.

42. "*Esse* is what is innermost in each and every thing, and what is deepest in them all, for it is formal in respect of all that is in a thing." *ST* 1.8.1.

"from below" by the forms to be actualized.[43] Because *esse,* moreover, is not itself a subsistent being, but is rather a substantial-*izing* act, the reducibility of form to *esse* does not eliminate the absoluteness of individual substances. To the contrary, it is precisely what *makes* them absolute.

The second point to make is a more speculative development: it is true that no substance can exist merely temporally; the sheer multiplicity of time is incompatible with any sort of subsisting being. *A fortiori* a subsistent being does not come to be merely in time. Once we recognize this we are able to say that, if there is a subsistent being at all, its conditions of possibility were not given merely in the temporal moment prior to its actuality, but rather that its possibility is given simultaneously with its actuality, which transcends time by definition. What this means is that we cannot think of the coming-to-be of substances merely "horizontally," but must rather think of them "vertically" as unfolding in time *from above.* We will explore this notion more fully in the following chapter. The condition of possibility, in any event, does not precede in time but rather *in nature,* and the reference point for understanding the process lies not in the first moment, and then each succeeding moment thereafter, but in the form that lies above the temporal process altogether. At the same time, of course, the form reciprocally depends on the temporal process for its coming to be in reality, but this dependence is asymmetrical: the substance's dependence on its history lies so to speak *inside* the history's dependence on the substance. The passage we cited above expresses this point quite nicely: God *gives time* to the effect that he creates, which we may read as generously allowing it to develop gradually into what it has always been meant to be.

The inclusion of the horizontal dimension of being within the vertical dimension allows the possibility of a kind of evolution in the biological sphere, even though it precludes a purely mechanistic account of that evolution. It should be noted that, despite claims to the contrary, evolution cannot in any event be accounted for in wholly mechanistic terms insofar as mechanism excludes the possibility of natural forms and therefore of genuine substances.[44] This means, ironically, that not only are creation and evo-

43. This does not imply a unilateral relationship, which would make the form nothing but a "negative" quantity in relation to the positivity of *esse.* Instead, there is a reciprocal (though asymmetrical) dependence between *esse* and the essence within the unity of God's creative act. For a clear statement of this point, see Adrian Walker, "Personal Simplicity and the *Communio Personarum:* A Creative Development of Thomas Aquinas's Doctrine of *Esse Commune,*" *Communio* 31 (Fall 2004): 468, n. 11. See also Balthasar, *GL5,* pp. 619-24.

44. See Hans Jonas, "Philosophical Aspects of Darwinism," in *The Phenomenon of*

lution not opposed in principle, but in fact evolution *requires creation* to be intelligible at all as the gradual coming to be *of real beings.* Chesterton captures this point quite well:

> Evolution is a good example of that modern intelligence which, if it destroys anything, destroys itself. Evolution is either an innocent scientific description of how certain earthly things came about; or, if it is anything more than this, it is an attack upon thought itself. If evolution destroys anything, it does not destroy religion but rationalism. If evolution simply means that a positive thing called an ape turned very slowly into a positive thing called a man, then it is stingless for the most orthodox; for a personal God might just as well do things slowly as quickly, especially if, like the Christian God, he were outside time. But if it means anything more, it means that there is no such thing as an ape to change, and no such thing as a man for him to change into. It means that there is no such thing as a thing. At best, there is only one thing, and that is a flux of everything and anything. This is an attack not upon the faith, but upon the mind; you cannot think if there are no things to think about. You cannot think if you are not separate from the subject of thought. Descartes said, "I think; therefore I am." The philosophic evolutionist reverses and negatives the epigram. He says, "I am not; therefore I cannot think."[45]

The reason that there cannot be evolution without creation is because, as we have seen, there can be no intelligibility of any sort without the absoluteness of substance, which the supra-temporal and indeed the supra-formal act of creation alone — if one does not affirm the eternity of species — makes possible. As we have come to see, this acknowledgment of intelligibility requires an inversion of our normal way of thinking that limits physical being to the flux of time, and demands instead that we see time as *belonging to things,* as unfolding from above in reference to what transcends things. The physical world does indeed exist in time, but not reductively so: all real beings "stick out" ec-statically into the eternity of the God who made them from nothing and "continues" so to make them. The dis-integration of causes is a natural

---

Life: Toward a Philosophical Biology (Evanston: Northwestern University Press, 2001), pp. 38-63, esp. 51-52. Cf. Michael Hanby, "Creation without Creationism: Toward a Theological Critique of Darwinism," *Communio* 30 (Winter 2003): 654-94.

45. G. K. Chesterton, *Orthodoxy,* in *The Everyman Chesterton* (New York: Knopf, 2011), p. 287.

result of the failure to interpret creation thus metaphysically and the subsequent temporalization of being. A recovery of their integration, a restoration of the wholeness of things and thus the basis of any thinking whatsoever, will therefore require a restoration of a proper sense of being as created.

7 Giving Cause to Wonder

In 1829, Goethe observed to Eckermann:

> The highest that man can attain . . . is wonder [*das Erstaunen*], and when the original phenomenon [*Urphänomen*] causes him to wonder, then let him be content; it can grant him nothing higher, and he should not seek anything further behind it, the limit is here. But men are usually not content with the perception of an original phenomenon; they think there must be something further, and they are like children, who, when they have looked into a mirror, immediately turn it over to see what is on the other side.[1]

What Goethe says here itself causes us wonder, if we consider it from the perspective of the classical tradition, for two related reasons. First, Goethe presents wonder as a final state, as that-than-which-nothing-further-ought-to-be-sought, whereas Plato, for example, characterized wonder, τὸ θαυμάζειν, specifically as an ἀρχή, a beginning, origin, or first principle:[2] in other words, that which precedes as giving rise to, generating, something else. Thus understood, wonder would not be a destination, but a starting point, not a place at which to come to a contented rest, but an initiation. According to Aristotle, the resting place into which wonder initiates one is *knowledge*. As he explains, to philosophize is to learn, learning represents a change, and change is always a movement between two contraries. The line of philosophy, accordingly,

1. 18 February 1829; J. P. Eckermann, *Gespräche mit Goethe*, 6th ed. (Leipzig: F. A. Brockhaus, 1885), vol. 2, pp. 50-53.

2. Plato, *Theaetetus* 155d.

stretches between wonder and knowledge as its defining poles: if philosophy begins in wonder, it must end in knowledge.[3]

Second, Goethe presents wonder as the "highest that man can attain," whereas Aristotle, apparently by virtue of the reasoning just mentioned, had presented wisdom as the highest excellence possible, and defined wisdom as the unity of knowledge and the grasp of first principles.[4] The highest act, from this perspective, would appear to be precisely a movement *away* from wonder, an overcoming of wonder. According to Aristotle, the reason people first began to philosophize is "to escape ignorance [τὸ φεύγειν τὴν ἄγνοιαν]."[5] As Thomas Aquinas puts it in his commentary on this point in Aristotle, "the philosophers themselves were moved to philosophize as a result of wonder. And since wonder stems from ignorance, they were obviously moved to philosophize in order to escape from ignorance [*Et quia admiratio ex ignorantia provenit, patet quod ad hoc moti sunt ad philosophandum ut ignorantiam effugarent*]."[6] Insofar as it is the contrary to knowledge, wonder would be inseparably bound to ignorance, and would apparently represent an imperfection precisely to the extent that knowledge is a perfection.[7] Just as Plato said that eros does not belong among the gods, since eros implies a desire and so a lack,[8] and therefore an incompleteness that is incompatible with divine perfection, so too we might say that the gods do not wonder. And indeed this has been said.[9]

3. Aristotle, *Metaphysics* I.1.982b12-23.

4. See Aristotle, *Nicomachean Ethics* VI.7. Of course, there is some question whether *sophia* is a properly *human* excellence, or whether, instead, *phronēsis* is the highest human virtue, while *sophia* in fact belongs to the gods. This question does not concern the point we are making above.

5. Aristotle, *Metaphysics* I.2.982b20.

6. Aquinas, *In metaph.*, book I, lesson 3, 55.

7. Aquinas himself classifies wonder *(admiratio)* as a species of fear, which, in contrast to the stupor that prevents one from pursuing inquiry, is nevertheless, precisely as a kind of fear, something negative: it is a reluctance to make a judgment about something that exceeds one's mind in some respect: see *ST* 1-2.42.4ad4 and ad5. According to Aquinas, Jesus possessed wonder only with respect to his "empirical" knowledge, and not with respect to his divine knowledge, which, as perfect, excludes wonder. *ST* 3.15.8. On Aquinas's notion of wonder, see André Guindon, "L'émerveillement: Étude du vocabulaire de l'admiratio chez Thomas d'Aquin," *Église et Théologie* 1 (1976): 61-97.

8. Plato, *Symposium* 201aff.

9. See, e.g., Josef Pieper's observation: "He who feels wonder, does not know, or does not know completely, does not comprehend. He who knows, does not feel wonder. It could not be said that God experiences wonder, for God knows in the most absolute and perfect way." *Leisure: The Basis of Culture* (South Bend, IN: St. Augustine's Press, 1998), p. 106.

But in a disenchanted age, Goethe's observation strikes a chord that seems to resonate irrepressibly. The subordination of wonder to knowledge has implications both broad and deep if it is taken in the most obvious sense: to the extent that the experience of wonder indicates an encounter with something "greater" than one, however this may be interpreted,[10] then to represent wonder as an imperfection ordered to the perfection of knowledge would seem to imply that knowledge has the form of domination, and that the intellect's most proper relation to reality is one in which the real is trivialized, made something that precisely ceases to be greater than one. But this presents us before a dilemma: if we reject Goethe's observation that wonder is "the highest," we would seem to justify the Enlightenment conception of knowledge as power that we have been criticizing from various angles over the course of this book. A model of such thinking, Descartes justifies wonder by the knowledge it yields and describes remaining in wonder as a kind of dull stupefaction.[11] If, by contrast, we accept Goethe's observation, we not only appear to reject the entire classical tradition, which affirmed the desire *to know* as the basic trait of human nature,[12] we also seem to embrace unthinkingly what proves fairly quickly to be an empty and ultimately meaningless circle: a desire, not to know, but simply to go on desiring. Is it in fact possible to conceive of desire at all that does not want satisfaction? Can there even be such a thing as a lack without some reference to a corresponding fulfillment? Doesn't the positing of wonder simply for its own sake belie a hidden nihilism? Is there not a similarity between wonder so conceived and the narcissism that Denis de Rougement diagnosed in the cult of unrequited love?[13]

In chapter four, we concluded that truth and mystery, properly understood, are ultimately convertible terms. The aim of the present chapter is to show that a correlate claim also obtains, namely, that knowledge and wonder

10. Thomas Carlyle famously wrote that "wonder is the basis of worship." *Sartor Resartus,* book 1, chapter 10.

11. Descartes, *On the Passions of the Soul,* part 2, articles 70-78, esp. 73. On Descartes' "appropriation" of wonder for mastery, see Mary-Jane Rubenstein, *Strange Wonder: The Closure of Metaphysics and the Opening of Awe* (New York: Columbia University Press, 2008), p. 15, and the contemporary echoes of the same spirit she cites, p. 202, n. 51.

12. Aristotle, *Metaphysics* I.1.980a22; Plato indicates, in metaphorical language, that a soul cannot be human unless it has at some time enjoyed a vision of truth. *Phaedrus* 249b.

13. See the general argument made in Denis de Rougement, *L'Amour et l'Occident.* One need not subscribe to the dubious historical account de Rougement presents to acknowledge the truth of the psychological insight he develops.

are likewise two sides, as it were, of the same coin: rather than say that wonder is simply an impetus that propels one toward knowledge, or merely reverse these terms and make knowledge a means to greater desire — rather, that is, than oppose presence and absence to each other in one direction or the other — we will argue that wonder and knowledge perfectly coincide. Our aim will be to show that, in its ideal instance, the philosophical act does not represent a change from wonder to knowledge, but instead always a change from less perfect knowledge to more perfect knowledge, which coincides with a change from less perfect wonder to more perfect wonder. This reflection will take as its starting point the classical definition of knowledge as an understanding of causes, a definition that has prevailed through the different periods of intellectual history, and accordingly attempt to show that causality is generative of wonder just as it enables knowledge. Martin Heidegger is well known for having criticized the modern interpretation of wonder as an impetus for knowledge that is left behind once knowledge is attained.[14] But Heidegger has also mounted one of the most profound criticisms of the causal thinking that he rightly claims is inseparable from the Western philosophical tradition. According to Heidegger, causal thinking is incompatible with genuine wonder, and so is in part responsible for the trivializing of reality that one witnesses in the modern world. For Heidegger, the fateful moment in this history is the coming together of biblical faith with the causal thinking of metaphysics in the Christian doctrine of *creatio ex nihilo.* An engagement with Heidegger's claims is thus particularly appropriate in a book on the catholicity of reason.

Our reflection will thus involve an *"Auseinandersetzung"* with Heidegger's critique of causality, primarily on the basis of the "causality of creation" we have in Dionysius the Areopagite's *Divine Names.* In terms of the larger argument of the present book, this chapter seeks to deepen the classical sense of causality presented in the previous two chapters, to provide a deeper context for the discussions of ontotheology in chapters eight and nine, to confirm the convertibility of truth and mystery proposed in chapter four, and, finally, to show why the encounter with being takes place *first* under the sign of beauty, which sets the stage for the drama of knowledge that was described in chapter three.

14. See, e.g., Martin Heidegger, *What Is Philosophy?* (Albany, NY: NCUP, Inc., n.d.), pp. 78-89.

Preliminary Reflections

To prepare for this study, let us first reflect on the nature of wonder and what it requires. Wonder is a kind of astonishment or surprise, but it also has a positive character missing in a simple shock. If one wonders, one is struck by something, but specifically in such a way that one is at the same time drawn to it. Wonder implies a kind of desire. Thinking of it thus brings us immediately to Socrates' discussion of eros in Plato's *Symposium*, in which he indicates that desire rests on a paradoxical relation of poverty and plenty: it implies an absence, but not a simple absence, since a total lack of a relationship to something is an inert indifference.[15] Complete ignorance has no desire for knowledge. As we suggested in our first chapter, one can remain genuinely open to something, one can desire it and genuinely seek it, if one knows not only *that* one does not know, but also in fact in some sense *what* one does not know. What this paradox means here is that wonder is not an inarticulate stupefaction, but a "directed," and in some sense therefore a "predetermined," openness. One's ability to formulate one's questions quickens one's wonder. Questions are an essential part of philosophical wonder — which is wonder in its fullest and most perfect sense — but they have, as it were, a point, an end. As opposed to the kind of questioning one sometimes observes in children, who repeat the question "why" at every response in a kind of mechanical, automatic way, wonder's questions are *disciplined*, i.e., they follow a matter — into its heart. Philosophical wonder is a kind of inquiry, an "in-quest," so to speak.

At the same time, to turn to the *Symposium* again, desire is — perhaps more obviously — never a simple presence. One does not desire, Socrates says, what one already has except in the sense of wanting its continued possession, which means, in this case, one desires what one does not (yet) have, namely, the future possession of a thing. We note here that possession can coexist with desire if possession is understood in temporal terms, i.e., as a state that extends in time. Desire necessarily implies a lack of some sort, and by analogy so too does wonder. We cannot be surprised at something we already know (though this statement will have to be qualified below). But there is an ambiguity in the notion of "lack" that is crucial for our discussion to follow. To use the language of "subject" and "object" for a moment, a lack can be due, on the one hand, to a deficiency in the subject, in the sense that a subject happens not (yet) to be in possession of what there is to possess. Or,

15. Plato, *Symposium* 204e.

on the other hand, it can be due to an excess on the side of the object: the object may always exceed what the subject possesses of it, and indeed such an excess may happen to belong to its very nature. If it does, the subject may be in perfect possession of an object, but that object would continue to lie beyond the subject by virtue of its excessive nature, the very nature that the subject "possesses" in possessing the object. These two senses of "lack" will clearly overlap to a significant extent, but there is evidently a different emphasis in each case. The difference bears directly on our aim in this chapter. If the reality that one is to know is, for example, what Hegel calls a simple identity, or Descartes describes as a clear and distinct idea, or positivism conceives as a straightforward fact or definable state of affairs, then wonder can only have provisional significance, because it can only have a negative meaning. In this case, we could sustain wonder only by keeping a distance from reality, by holding ourselves back from an in-quiry *into* reality. Wonder in this case becomes, we might say, something wholly subjective, which is threatened by the knowledge of the real. If, by contrast, the lack is due to an excess on the part of the object, and specifically an excess that unfolds in time, then in fact wonder would increase the closer we got to reality: the intimacy implied by knowledge, and the fidelity implied by the unfolding in time, would entail no diminishment in principle of the distance implied by wonder. Wonder, in this case, would not require that one "artificially" — i.e., in an *a priori* way — set limits to one's knowledge. Quite the contrary, it is just a setting of limits that would obstruct wonder, because to the extent that the limits separated one from an object, they would separate one precisely from that which provokes wonder. Conversely, then, the intimacy with the object that knowledge represents would coincide with wonder.

Specifically philosophical wonder is desire disciplined by reality in its most *essential* sense. In the "intellectual autobiography" that Socrates presents in the *Phaedo,* he describes his beginnings as a "most wonder-filled desire for the wisdom they call an inquiry into nature [θαυμαστῶς ὡς ἐπεθύμησα ταύτης σοφίας, ἥν δὴ καλοῦσι περὶ φύσεως ἱστορίαν],"[16] and proceeds to recount his search for *causes,* which led him to be both attracted to, and then dissatisfied with, what we would call the materialist accounts of the first philosophers. To seek the causes of a thing is to seek what most fully accounts for it, with respect to *what* it is, *how* it is, and *why* it is at all. In the broadest sense, as we have seen, cause (αἰτία) is whatever is *responsible* for a thing in all these respects. As we saw in chapter five, the ultimate "responsi-

16. Plato, *Phaedo* 96a.

ble" or ultimate cause, for Plato, is the good, which has a particular relationship to form. It is well known that Aristotle discovers an irreducibility of causes to account for a thing: the matter (τὸ ἐξ οὗ), the form (τὸ εἶδος), the "source of change" (ἡ ἀρχὴ τῆς μεταβολῆς), and the end (τέλος), which we discussed in the last chapter.[17] We will consider below the connection between the two different accounts of causality given by Plato and Aristotle. For the moment, we wish to point out that there can be a convergence between wonder and knowledge only if the answers to the questions what, how, and why indicate realities the meaning of which cannot be exhausted in a single, momentary grasp.

To sum up our preliminary reflections, wonder requires some excess, however it may be determined: a more, a difference, a distance, "otherness," transcendence, etc. The quality of the wonder will depend on the nature of this difference. It has to be a difference that provokes interest, that is accessible without being simply evident, that invites in rather than keeps out. What this brief reflection on the nature of wonder shows is that the relationship between wonder and knowledge is not in the first place an epistemological question (What is the nature of knowledge?, or indeed even more narrowly, What can we know?), but rather an ontological question: What is the nature of reality? It is for this reason that the question of causality lies at the center of this inquiry.[18]

Heidegger: Time for Wonder

Our preliminary reflections have put us in a position to explore fruitfully what Heidegger means by wonder. His most extensive treatment of the theme can be found in his *Basic Questions of Philosophy*,[19] the lectures he delivered in Freiburg during the winter semester of 1937-1938, while he was composing what is considered by many to be the most decisive text in the development of his mature thought, the posthumously published *Beiträge*

17. Aristotle, *Physics* II.3.194b24-195a3.

18. It is on this score that our study differs most significantly from the recent book by Rubenstein, *Strange Wonder*, with which it nevertheless shares a basic aim, namely, to recover the positive and abiding role of wonder in philosophy: Rubenstein focuses above all on the subjective disposition, attributing the loss of wonder to the advent of a "will to mastery" in Western thought, while we wish to suggest that even this will is due to a reconception of the nature of reality.

19. Hereafter cited as *BQ*.

zur Philosophie. In these lectures, Heidegger inquires into the essence of philosophy and the questions that most properly belong to it. His aim is both to retrieve the original experience of philosophy in the classical tradition, beyond the sedimentation of the basic concepts of philosophy in contemporary thought, and to open up a new origin proper to our own time. The reflection on wonder occurs, somewhat surprisingly, at the end of the lectures, which are devoted, in the first place, to a sustained investigation of the essence of truth and then the more basic question of the nature of essence (i.e., the truth of essence). These reflections form a necessary background for understanding the nature of the experience that Heidegger says defines philosophy, though we cannot explore them in detail in the present context. To enter into a discussion of the original experience (πάθος), Heidegger quotes the classic texts from Plato and Aristotle wherein wonder is affirmed as the ἀρχὴ of philosophy, and explains that it can be the beginning only to the extent that wonder describes the *most basic disposition,* or fundamental attunement *(Grundstimmung)* in which philosophical thinking takes place. He defines the disposition in an unusual way, which requires some unpacking to become comprehensible: for Heidegger, wonder is essentially the "distress of not knowing a way in or out," and so it signifies a being caught up "in the midst of beings," or even more properly, in the "open 'between' in which beings and non-beings stand forth as a whole, though still in their undifferentiatedness" (*BQ,* 139).

Heidegger clarifies what he means by "distress" in two decisive ways. First of all, he explains that this "is not a lack and not a deprivation but is the surplus of a gift which, however, is more difficult to bear than any loss" (*BQ,* 133). Second, he says that "distress . . . is a characteristic of Being and not of man, as if this distress could arise 'psychically' in man as a 'lived experience' [*Erlebnis*] and have its proper place in him" (*BQ,* 133). These two points are intimately connected. Heidegger wishes to avoid a reduction of wonder to an emotion or feeling, a mere psychological, and so essentially subjective, state.[20] It is rather, for him, something *into which* man enters, something that is greater than the human being. This is precisely why Heidegger characterizes it as a gift rather than a lack. If it were essentially a lack, it would

20. Cf. Heidegger, *What Is Philosophy?* pp. 80-85. In this text, Heidegger translates the πάθος of wonder as a *Stimmung,* in which he intends the words *"Gestimmtheit"* and *"Bestimmtheit"* to be heard: the latter in particular expresses the fact that it is an experience that comes to, and so determines, man from the outside. The point here is that a pathos is *not* a subjective experience, i.e., an experience circumscribed within man's consciousness *(Erlebnis).*

represent a specifically human need, and so would be measured by that need, which would inevitably entail a reduction of its significance back to man. But its proper place, Heidegger says, is Being, not man, so that if man experiences this distress, it is because it has been *given* to him, because he has been brought beyond himself in some sense. There is a certain gratuity, a surpassing of necessity, in this experience, as Heidegger understands it. To be sure, it carries the aspect of need — he describes it, after all, in negative terms as a distress, and so as hard to bear — but this aspect lies within its more basic character as gift.

As *basic*, the disposition of wonder is distinguished from the related experiences of amazement, admiration, and awe: each of these, Heidegger explains, is a reaction to a particular being or set of beings, which stand out as unusual over and against the general background of the usual, either carrying one away in excitement (amazement), provoking the free act of evaluation (admiration), or overwhelming one (awe). The first two, according to Heidegger, are superficial because they imply a kind of subordination of the being to the person, whether it be to the subjective "lived experience" *(Erlebnis)* of excitement, or in the case of admiration to the powers of critical judgment. But even the third, "awe" — an experience that opens one to something greater than one — remains different from wonder because it is bound to a particular being or set of beings. The experience of awe thus preserves a difference between the usual and the unusual, and so a ground outside of the experience: a way out and a way in. We are struck by awe when some thing or things stand out from against the background of what does not so strike us. By contrast, wonder concerns the whole of reality: in this experience, it is *precisely what is usual* (namely, that which exists: *das Seiende*) that comes to reveal itself as unusual. It does so because beings are taken, not simply as already there, given, things that are complete and so unworthy of thought — in Heidegger's own language, as already unconcealed — but rather in their being unconcealed, in their emerging, presencing, or, in short, in their Being.

Wonder thus occupies the place of the "as" in the phrase "being as being" *(das Seiende als das Seiende, ens qua ens,* τὸ ὂν ᾗ ὄν) that defines metaphysical philosophy (*BQ*, 146). This being "between" Being and beings has two meanings for Heidegger. On the one hand, it indicates that, in wonder, man is "thrown" "into the midst" of beings. This is simply another way of saying what we mentioned above, namely, that man does not enter deliberately, as a matter of his own choice and so as a function of his own will, into the experience from a more secure ground. Instead, this "place" is more primordial than any secure ground, that is, any already unconcealed realm. On the other hand, it reveals that beings are received here from the perspective of Being, which Heidegger describes as presencing. In other words, in this experience, one is, so to speak, "catching beings in the act" of emerging into presence rather than encountering them "after the fact." Wonder is *basic* because it does not concern beings that already exist (this is the realm of logic, in which the affirmation is given priority over the negation), but rather precedes the distinction between beings and non-beings (*BQ*, 132), which is, as it were, the only perspective from which one could catch sight of things in their "arrival," their standing forth in being.

We ought to dwell for a moment on the strangeness of the notion that wonder's "object" is the unusualness of everything that is usual as a whole. It is hard to grasp what "unusual" might mean except in contrast to the usual, but this is precisely what Heidegger is attempting to convey. The difference is not, we might say, a horizontal one between types of being within the same order, but rather a vertical one, between two orders. The unusual is not something "out of the ordinary" in the sense of something that arises out from within the backdrop of the ordinary, but if anything the relation goes the other way: the ordinary is so to speak "out of the extraordinary." The unusual is originality itself, a "novelty" that comes before — and so is paradoxically "older" than — anything that is old. Wonder is an attunement to the origin, which is not a beginning relative to what comes later, but is ab-solute, so that in fact the words "usual" and "unusual" lose their typical meaning. The paradox here is similar to the one we described above, namely, that of the "gratuitous need" of wonder, and these two are due in fact to the same thing: that the experience belongs to Being first and is then open to man.

Along the lines we are at present following, wonder represents a "between" in yet another sense, namely, between man and beings as beings, i.e., *in their Being*. Heidegger describes wonder as a disposition that acts, so to speak, bilaterally. On the one hand, "[w]onder — understood transitively — brings forth the showing of what is most usual in its unusualness" (*BQ*, 145). In other words, the disposition of wonder is what allows things genuinely to manifest themselves, to be, so to speak, not just beings that then manifest themselves, but rather to be "manifest being," or indeed "being manifest." This, of course, is precisely what Heidegger means by truth as the Greeks understood it: unconcealment, the self-showing of beings. On the other hand, man is not the *agent* of wonder, which thus works transitively on beings; rather, he is in himself its patient: man is *moved by* wonder (*BQ*, 146), and specifically to the "acknowledgment of what has erupted" (*BQ*, 146). He is thus called, in this experience, to sustain ἀ-λήθεια, the "unconcealment" of beings, which is to say to remain open in this acknowledgment of beings in their Being. As Heidegger often repeats in his late philosophy, the carrying out of this task is what is essential to man, is that whereby he exists essentially. It is for this reason that Heidegger describes the distress of wonder as "more essential than [man] himself": "man himself first arises out of this distress, . . . for he is first determined by it" (*BQ*, 133).

It is crucial to hold on to the fact that presenting wonder as a kind of task to be "carried out" does not mean that it can be accomplished in the sense of a discrete activity that is begun at a certain point and then brought to an end. Rather, as we saw above, there is no beginning or end, no way in or out, to wonder as Heidegger conceives it. In other words, wonder is not a gate through which one passes in the pursuit of truth. Instead, we ought to say that wonder is the act in which truth is received, it is the reception of truth itself, or better, the "attunement" defined by the manifestation that truth is: there is truth only insofar as there is wonder; there is truth *while* there is wonder.[21] Truth for Heidegger, like Being, is "temporal."[22] Truth is not an "object" that exists in the world, much less a property of beings or indeed of propositions. It is instead an event, the self-showing of beings, to which wonder corresponds as the witness, so to speak, of the unconcealment. Heidegger therefore calls the "aim" of wonder a "pure acknowledgment of beings as beings" (*BQ*, 150), an acknowledgment that is pure only to the extent that it sustains itself "in questioning what beings as such are." But this is *not* a question that seeks resolution in an answer. As Heidegger puts it, this questioning is "not a desire for explanation or for the elimination of the most unusual, that beings are what they are. On the contrary, this question is an even purer adherence to beings in their unusualness" (*BQ*, 150-51). In other words, this questioning about the "what" does not seek a definition or a form, i.e., a circumscribable quiddity, but simply attends, as it were, to the

21. Josef Pieper says something similar: "For wonder is not merely the beginning, in the sense of *initium*, the first stage or phase of philosophy. Rather, wonder is the beginning in the sense of the 'principle' *(principium)*, the abiding, ever-intrinsic origin of philosophizing. It is not true to say that the philosopher, insofar as he philosophizes, ever 'emerges from his wonder' — if he *does* depart from his state of wonder, he has ceased to philosophize" (*Leisure*, p. 106).

22. Not, of course, in the sense of a thing that exists "in time," but in association with time. As he puts it in the lecture *Time and Being*, "Being is not a thing, thus nothing temporal, and yet is determined by time as presence." *On Time and Being*, trans. Joan Stambaugh (New York: Harper, 1972), p. 3.

"that" of the "what" as the unusualness of the usual. This can be the case only if the essence of things is something other than a mere datum.

With this interpretation of wonder, Heidegger is seeking to get back "behind," as it were, Plato and Aristotle, for whom wonder was connected in a direct way with desire, to what he takes to be the more originary Greek experience of Being (and as we will see shortly, he eventually intends to go behind even this to what he claims has yet to be experienced). On this score, it is interesting to note that Heidegger elsewhere contrasts Heraclitus (in whose writings the term "philosophy" first appears), for whom the name meant someone who lived in a (desire-less) friendship or harmony with wisdom, to Plato for whom philosophy acquired the character of a yearning (ὄρεξις) that strives *(streben)* after wisdom, and so is essentially determined by eros.[23] However this may be, Heidegger insists that the primordial questioning of wonder is not a seeking after something external to itself, i.e., knowledge as the contrary to wonder, but rather "[h]ere questioning already counts as knowledge" (*BQ*, 7), i.e., questioning is itself "the most constant being-in-proximity to what conceals itself" (*BQ*, 6).[24]

Heidegger describes the content of the task of wonder as a "suffering in the sense of the creative bearing-with-ness for the unconditioned [*der schaffende Ertragsamkeit für das Unbedingte*]" (*BQ*, 151, translation modified). Each part of this phrase is essential for us. First, the word "suffering" *(Leiden)* is meant to prevent us from understanding the carrying out of this task as an active accomplishment, as a result that comes about by virtue of our deliberate agency. As we will see in greater depth below, deliberate agency, for Heidegger, can never capture what is essential because it always takes place *within* the sphere of what is already unconcealed. At the same time, Heidegger goes on to explain, "suffering" ought not to be interpreted simply as *passive,* as the opposite of activity, because this remains within the same sphere as activity. Heidegger describes this view as the "Christian-moralistic-psychological" notion of "submission to woes." Note, wonder cannot be *either* active *or* passive because it would thereby cease to be a *basic*

23. *What Is Philosophy?* pp. 50-53. According to Heidegger, philosophy acquired this character in Socrates and Plato because of the attacks on the "most wondrous wisdom" by the sophists, who thus disturbed the peaceful friendship with wisdom.

24. In his famous Rectorship Address, Heidegger had said: "Questioning will then no longer simply be the surmountable, preliminary stage to the answer as knowledge, but questioning will instead itself become the highest form of knowledge." "The Self-Assertion of the German University," in *The Heidegger Reader,* ed. G. Figal (Bloomington: Indiana University Press, 2009), p. 112.

disposition in relation to beings as beings and become a relation to particular beings in one respect or another. It therefore has to be in some sense "both" active and passive, deeper than their distinction.

This brings us to the second part of the phrase: "creative bearing-withness" *(schaffende Ertragsamkeit)*. Here we have an echo of the twofold character of wonder: there is, first of all, the receptive dimension of the acknowledgment of beings in their emerging; but, secondly, this acknowledgment is something things need in order to show themselves properly. Beings in the world are relative to one another in various ways, but they can be *unconcealed,* they can reveal their beingness *(seiend-sein),* only to man. This is what Heidegger had described, earlier in the lectures, as a "productive seeing of the essence" of things, which is simultaneously a grasping of the essence and a bringing it forth (*BQ*, 74-77). As he explains it, there is a twofold unity, here, between the essence being brought forth before us and our bringing ourselves before the essence. These two are irreducibly different aspects of a single, whole event. The essence of beings, then, is not a fact lying exposed, so to speak, out in the open, but is rather what presents itself to the proper attunement, or in fact the presencing itself in the "what" that presents itself.[25] Again, this unconcealment of beings lies between mere fabrication on the one hand and mere discovery (as an encounter with what is already simply there, present-at-hand [*vorhanden*]) on the other. We will return to the precarious ambiguity of this understanding in a moment.

The third part of the phrase is "for the unconditioned." This part is perhaps the most crucial of all for our purposes, though Heidegger does not elaborate in this context what it means. To grasp what Heidegger has in mind here we must see that to be unconditioned is to be "uncaused," that is, not to be dependent on any condition outside of itself for what it is. For Heidegger, there is an essential tension between wonder and explanation. "All explanation," he says, "is directed to some being, already unconcealed, from which an explanatory cause can be drawn" (*BQ*, 147). To explain, that is, is to advert to a cause in relation to which the explanandum is an effect. But an effective cause, to be able to bring about an effect, has *already to be,* it

25. This is why Heidegger, in his late thought, tends to use the verbal "Wesung" in place of the nominal form "Wesen," essence. In *BQ*, he writes: "The essence of truth is not a mere concept, carried about in the head. On the contrary, truth is alive; in the momentary form of its essence it is the power that determines everything true and untrue; it is what is sought after, what is fought for, what is suffered for. The essence of truth is a happening, more real and more efficacious than all historiographical occurrences or facts, because it is their ground" (p. 41).

has to be already concealed. For Heidegger, then, this means that the cause-effect relationship is one that holds between beings that are already present. It is an "ontic" activity that occurs — to use Heidegger's language — *within* the "clearing" of Being, and so "comes too late," we might say, to concern the basic disposition of wonder that lies at the root of philosophy. This is why Heidegger says that to explain beings necessarily reduces the unusual back to the usual — and we must understand these terms in the technical sense that Heidegger gives them here: no matter how strange or surprising or even *sui generis* a cause may be, to the extent that it is a cause, an efficient agent, it already *is* and so it already stands among and within the horizon of the usual, i.e., *das Seiende.*[26] That which provokes amazement, admiration, or awe may be "inexplicable" in the sense that one does not (yet) know the cause — in this case, the inability to explain is due to the subjective condition of ignorance rather than to the nature of the reality itself — but what brings about wonder is inexplicable simply; it is inexplicability itself: "We fail to realize how decisively the reference to θαυμάζειν as the origin of philosophy indicates precisely the inexplicability of philosophy, inexplicability in the sense that here in general to explain and the will to explain are mistakes" (*BQ*, 136). There is an absoluteness, for Heidegger, about unconcealment, an inability to "get behind" it in order to discover something more fundamental, which, we will see, represents a basic dimension of Heidegger's thought. Truth, in *this* sense, for Heidegger is something absolute, not subordinate to anything more basic: it is the "unconditioned."

Now, for Heidegger, the unconditioned character of truth as unconcealment is something difficult to sustain, or perhaps better, impossible to sustain as the result of deliberate effort. It is rather what Heidegger calls a destiny *(Geschick)* and understands as the particular "sending" of Being that most basically characterizes a given age, or "epoch," in the history of the West. According to Heidegger, the presencing of what is present, the "Being" of what exists *(das Sein des Seienden),* was the destiny of the Greeks, and it is in relation to this that we need to interpret the fundamental notions of φύσις and τέχνη.[27] These two terms reflect the twofold reality of wonder we have

26. See "Letter on Humanism," in *BW,* p. 199: "Beings themselves appear as actualities in the interaction of cause and effect. We encounter beings as actualities in a calculative business-like way, but also scientifically and by way of philosophy, with explanations and proof."

27. Of course, there are other fundamental notions besides these, which are quite closely related: most notably λόγος and τὸ εἶναι. See the essays gathered in *Early Greek Thinking: The Dawn of Western Philosophy,* trans. D. Krell and F. Capuzzi (San Francisco: HarperCollins, 1984).

been discussing: φύσις, from φύειν, is the *growing* of beings, their self-showing or emerging into presence, an "event" that Heidegger explores with great depth in his important essay on the notion in Aristotle.[28] In the essay on Aristotle, he shows that the "four causes," rather than being things to which the event of Being's self-showing is referred for the sake of explanation, are the irreducibly manifold aspects of the one reality of presencing: to put oversimply what he describes there, the *form* ("formal cause") is the principle of motion (the so-called "efficient cause") — understood most profoundly as the perfection of the act of a thing's being what it is — and so its own end (the "final cause"). Εντελέχεια is the meaning of nature, a difficult word that Heidegger interprets as a thing's "having of itself in its end" (ἐν τέλει ἔχει).[29] And, finally, this having of itself includes in its meaning the possibility of its not having itself, just as life includes in an essential way the possibility of death, so that we can say that the self-placing into appearance (μορφή) includes absencing (ὕλη, "matter," interpreted here as στέρησις, "privation") within itself. By reducing the first and final causes, traditionally known as the "external" causes, and even in some sense reducing matter itself, back to form, Heidegger makes beings "self-explicatory," as it were. In a word, φύσις is the self-showing of beings as what they are, and this event of their unconcealment ought to be taken as unconditioned, i.e., it ought not to be referred to anything "outside of itself" as a further explanation.

Τέχνη has its place within this notion of φύσις. It is, according to Heidegger, not in the first place a doing or making (as it is implicitly at least in our term "technology"), but a particular kind of knowing, though of course it is itself, *as knowing,* a fundamental kind of action as well. Specifically, for Heidegger τέχνη means

> to grasp beings as emerging out of themselves in the way they show themselves, in their outward look, εἶδος, ἰδέα, and, in accord with this, to care for beings themselves and to let them grow, i.e., to order oneself within beings as a whole through productions and institutions. Τέχνη is a mode of proceeding *against* φύσις, though not yet in order to overpower it or exploit it, and above all not in order to turn use and calculation into principles, but, on the contrary, to retain the holding sway of

28. Martin Heidegger, "On the Essence and Concept of Φύσις in Aristotle's *Physics* B, I," in *Pathmarks* (Cambridge: Cambridge University Press, 1998), pp. 183-230.

29. Cf. this interpretation to the one we proposed in the previous chapter, namely, "to have an end within."

> φύσις in unconcealedness. Therefore, because the pure acknowledgment of beings as such, the perception of φύσις in its ἀλήθεια, is the disposing need in the basic disposition of wonder, τέχνη and its carrying out become necessary as what is wholly other than φύσις — wholly other yet belonging to φύσις in the most essential way. (*BQ*, 155)

It is interesting that Heidegger privileges the notion of τέχνη, a kind of knowing that is at the same time a caring for, and tending to, in his interpretation of the Greeks, as opposed to the more strictly theoretical "ἐπιστήμη," which seems to imply — at least as normally understood — a detachment, an unrelatedness of the knower to the known, the gaze of an isolated subject on an already complete, already unconcealed object.[30] In any event, τέχνη is an activity that nevertheless remains at the service of the unconcealment of truth.

But it is precisely here that the ambiguity lies, which accounts for the well-known "narrative of decline" in the "history of Being" that occupies Heidegger's thinking in his late period. In a nutshell, τέχνη bears within itself "the possibility of arbitrariness, of an unbridled positing of goals and thereby the possibility of escape out of the necessity of the primordial need" (*BQ*, 155). The word "arbitrariness" here has to be understood properly: the emphasis is not first on the *randomness* of the activity, as the English word most immediately suggests, but rather this aspect is derivative of the implied priority of the deliberate will (i.e., an act is still "arbitrary," *willkürlich,* in this sense even if it is perfectly rational and in conformity to some given norm, as long as it is understood as having its effective origin in the explicit act of the will). According to Heidegger, a reversal of sorts occurs such that, instead of τέχνη being at the service of φύσις, τέχνη, understood now in this new context as deliberate, willed activity in relation to pre-given goals, is made primary, and φύσις comes to be interpreted as a form of τέχνη. Truth then ceases to be the emergence of beings in unconcealment, and becomes instead the *correctness* of judgment. This can occur only where εἶδος (idea or form) has come to take precedence over unconcealment — i.e., the outward look, and so the result of unconcealment, over the event of unconcealment itself. At the same time, with the interpretation of truth as correctness, we have morality and values, as the measurement of action by the εἶδος, and finally education, παιδεία, as

30. Cf. Heidegger's criticism of the theoretical knowing that occurs only when our more organic and fluid relationship with things (with which Heidegger associates a less "objectifying" sort of viewing, namely, that of "*Umsicht*") in *Being and Time,* §§15-16.

the forming of people in relation to skills and values. This sense of παιδεία is the heart of *humanism*, for Heidegger, and why he resists this term in his philosophy.[31] Let us explore this decline, and the role the notion of cause plays in it, in greater depth.

Causality and Superficiality

In his essay, "The Question Concerning Technology," Heidegger attempts to think through the original notion of causality in the Greeks, or, better, the original notion of what came to be called causality. The point of entry into the notion is the classical doctrine of the "four causes," which has its roots in Aristotle. According to Heidegger, the four "causes" name disparate things, but nevertheless possess a unity; to understand them, we must therefore discover the unity that gathers them together, so that each can be what it most properly is. The difference between modernity and the Greeks can in fact be accounted for by the way each epoch interprets the underlying unity. For the moderns, the unity is found in the model of the maker, who represents the first cause, the *causa efficiens* ("*efficiens*" as that which *effects* or brings about a thing). The maker imposes a form on matter in view of a goal. But there is no Greek equivalent for "causa efficiens."[32] Aristotle speaks instead of an ἀρχὴ τῆς μεταβολῆς, a "source of change," and, as Richard Rojcewicz has helpfully observed in his illuminating book on Heidegger's understanding of technology, Aristotle offers a counselor, a father, and a farmer as illustrations of what this means.[33] Note: none of these is a "maker" in the modern sense just described. In none of these cases do we have an "absolutely first source" that explains the reality that comes about. Instead, the "action" of the moving cause, as illustrated in the examples, is a kind of "releasing" or "setting free" that allows a thing to come to be such as it is. Rather than im-

31. See "Plato's Doctrine of Truth," in *Pathmarks*, p. 181. See also "Letter on Humanism," in his *Basic Writings (BW)*, p. 202: "Every humanism is either grounded in a metaphysics or is itself made to be the ground of one." Cf. "Letter on Humanism," pp. 195-204.

32. See "On the Essence and Concept of Φύσις," in *Pathmarks*, p. 188. In fact, Aristotle apparently uses the word "effect" (αἰτιατόν) as a correlate to the cause (which would imply an efficient sense of causality) only twice, in the *Posterior Analytics:* I.9.76a21 and II.16.98a36. (I owe these references to Vincent Carraud, *Causa sive ratio: La Raison de la cause de Suarez à Leibniz* [Paris: Presses Universitaires de France, 2002], p. 55, n. 2.)

33. Richard Rojcewicz, *The Gods and Technology: A Reading of Heidegger* (Albany: State University of New York Press, 2006), pp. 19-29.

posing a form and goal, it enables the interplay of each of the causes in an organic coming to be. The farmer, for instance, does not make the crop, but tends to the seeds, providing the conditions in which they may grow of themselves. The original meaning of cause, αἰτία, as we mentioned above, is that which is responsible, and Heidegger interprets this "being responsible" of causality in decidedly receptive terms as a *Ver-an-lassen*, an "allowing to come forth." The unity of the "causes" for Aristotle, then, is the bringing-forth of being, which has its paradigm in nature, φύσις, the self-showing of beings.

To illustrate the difference between the ancients and moderns on this point, Heidegger offers the famous example of a silver chalice. According to the modern conception, the chalice exists as it does because a silversmith imposed the form of a chalice on silver to produce an instrument to be used for the celebration of religious ritual. From a more authentically "Greek" perspective, we would recognize that silver is not a mere passive recipient of form, but lends itself to the formation of a chalice in a manner that serves to "co-direct" the creation of the chalice. As Michelangelo famously described his own way of sculpting, he sees the statue *in* the marble, and works to release it.[34] It is active work, to be sure, but the activity is one that affirms and indeed enables a kind of self-revelation of that to which it is directed. The τέλος, thus, in this conception is not an "aim" or "purpose" — i.e., not a representation in the mind of the maker to which the thing made is ordered. Instead, it is in the first place a "limit," understood as the defined place within a larger sphere of meaning, and so a "home," as it were, wherein a thing first comes to be rather than the place wherein it stops. It is in relation to this notion of τέλος, it seems to me, that we can gain some insight into what Heidegger means in his later thought regarding the "play of the fourfold" that constitutes the "thingness of the thing."[35]

There are clearly two fundamentally different conceptions of nature that correspond to the different interpretations of αἰτία. On the one hand, there is the "poetic" (from ποίησις) view of nature as self-showing, which human τέχνη serves in the manner of assisting the coming forth through a kind of cooperative opposition. On the other hand, there is what we might

34. The most striking example of this in my experience are the concertos Mozart composed for particular instruments. It is difficult, for example, to imagine the Oboe Concerto being played by any other instrument (which is not to say it has not been tried), and the piece appears to bring out the very essence of an oboe.

35. See his "Bremen Lectures: *Insight into That Which Is*," in *The Heidegger Reader*, pp. 253-83.

call a "technological" view of nature. This view, we might say, exploits an ambiguity that Heidegger discovers in Aristotle. The term ἀρχὴ, which is decisive for Aristotle's understanding not only of nature but of being simply, originally had a variety of meanings, two of the most significant of which are "beginning," and secondly "domination": "On the one hand ἀρχὴ means that from which something has its origin and beginning; on the other hand it means that which, *as* this origin and beginning, likewise keeps rein *over*, i.e., restrains and therefore dominates, something else that emerges from it. Αρχὴ means, at one and the same time, beginning and control."[36] The reason that ἀρχὴ implies domination is because of what Schürmann, in his classic interpretation of Heidegger, has called its implied "telocracy":[37] the origin is the source of the τέλος, which is why it is not simply left behind after the beginning but rather retains a measure throughout: i.e., it "governs." The key, here, is the goal that is posited at the outset, prior to what follows from the ἀρχὴ. This is what nature looks like after the model of technological making.[38] Because in this case the self-showing of beings is no longer "unconditioned," i.e., uncaused or absolute, we have a "positing of goals" that is specifically "unbridled," as Heidegger put it earlier. Heidegger describes this as "the transformation of the character of ἀρχὴ to that of αἴτιον,"[39] and explains that the "equation of ἀρχὴ and αἴτιον" can be found already partially in Aristotle.[40]

What for Heidegger clarifies this ambiguity in Aristotle in the direction of the causal thinking that belongs to metaphysics is the force, so to speak, of Plato's conception of the ἀγαθόν, which overwhelms the return to a more originary notion of Being in Aristotle and eventually prepares the way for the Roman conception of *actualitas.* As Heidegger observes, the idea of the good for Plato is the paradigm of causality.[41] To understand how the good plays this role, it is helpful to return to our earlier discussion regarding wonder. Wonder is a basic disposition because it holds man, as it were, in the event of the unconcealment of things. Causal explanation is necessarily sub-

36. "On the Essence and Concept of Φύσις," in *Pathmarks,* p. 189.

37. Reiner Schürmann, *Heidegger on Being and Acting: From Principles to Anarchy* (Bloomington: Indiana University Press, 1987), pp. 101-5.

38. This, of course, is not how Heidegger thinks Aristotle ought best to be interpreted; rather, it brings to light an ambiguity that lies within Aristotle's thought.

39. Martin Heidegger, *The End of Philosophy,* trans. Joan Stambaugh (New York: Harper, 1973), p. 14.

40. Heidegger, *The End of Philosophy,* p. 14.

41. "Plato's Doctrine of Truth," in *Pathmarks,* pp. 174-75.

sequent to, and indeed derivative of, this event insofar as a cause is already unconcealed. To use technical terminology, it is a "founded reality." According to Heidegger, Plato so to speak "trapped" thinking at this founded level, which is the level of representational thought *(Vorstellen)* as opposed to primordial questioning, i.e., wonder. He did so by defining Being as *idea* (εἶδος), which is to say by defining the essence of being as the *look* or outward appearance of what shows itself in self-showing. This outward look is the stable presence of the present in its presencing, and so represents "that which we constantly have in sight in all our comportment to the thing" (*BQ*, 58). It is not what physically presents itself in any given thing, of course, but rather is the aspect to which our mind adverts *in advance*, over and above the thing, whenever we think about it or engage with it. Heidegger uses strong language here. He says that Plato's definition of essence as the *whatness* of things, as idea, is "perhaps the most consequential, influential, and disastrous philosophical definition in Western thinking" (*BQ*, 58). It is so decisive — "fateful" — because it closes off the original Greek experience of Being and so what we might call the *depth* dimension of truth: the ground of the acknowledgment of things as ἀλήθεια. As we can see, the depth dimension depends on a recognition of the temporal character of Being, the event of things' unfolding in presence, insofar as this recognition grasps that there is "more" to Being, as it were, than what is given in presence, what endures. By interpreting Being as εἶδος, "outward appearance," rather than as the *self-placing* of things in appearance, Plato shifts the understanding of Being into an entirely different, nontemporal register. The idea, *what* is unconcealed, henceforward becomes the standard for truth, now understood as "correctness." Plato, for Heidegger, represents the "yoking" of truth to the idea,[42] which is that by which we measure both our behavior and our understanding. In a word, the idea is a fixed object of thought and action. When truth gets subordinated to the idea, its essence changes.

Here we see the importance of the "idea of the good." According to Heidegger, "ἀγαθόν" is not a moral term in the Greek, as it is conventionally thought, though the predominance of the term will eventually lead to modern moralism. Instead, he claims, the proper sense of "good" for Plato comes to expression in the German word "*tauglich*," useful, serviceable, suitable, etc. — the sense of good, e.g., in the phrase "a pair of good skis."[43] Let us

42. See Plato, *Republic* 508a.

43. Martin Heidegger, *The Essence of Truth: On Plato's Cave Allegory and Theaetetus* (New York: Continuum Books, 2002), p. 77.

note that we hear no echo here at all, either in the conventional interpretation or in Heidegger's alternative, of the notes Plato explicitly ascribes to it and the subsequent classical Christian tradition recognized, namely, that of desirability and generosity.[44] This will be crucial for us below. Instead, goodness represents the perfection of what the idea means more generally as that which guides our thought and action, our comportment toward things. The good, according to Heidegger, is the "*Tauglichmachende schlechthin,*" that which most perfectly makes things serviceable. It is, in Plato's words, the "brightest," the most evident, of the ideas, and so, Heidegger says, the "being-est of beings" *(das Seiendste des Seienden).*[45] The superlatives indicate that it represents the extreme end of presence, and therefore lies at the furthest remove from origination, the event of coming into presence. The identification of Being with εἶδος or "whatness," and the perfection of whatness in the good, Heidegger claims, "gives more room to being itself, the *on* nominally conceived, than to the *on* verbally conceived."[46] There is a dramatic shift of centers, here, we might say, from the unconditioned character of the unconcealment of beings to the serviceable result of unconcealment, the *whatness* that enables things to be identified as one thing or another and treated accordingly. It is this shift that Heidegger identifies with causality. Causality, thus, is a kind of enabling ("Being-responsible-for as making possible")[47] — and, specifically, of activity at the ontic level. As Heidegger summarizes in his essay "Metaphysics as History of Being," "The fundamental characteristic of *idea* (cf. 'Plato's Doctrine of Truth,' 1942) is the *agathon.* Outward appearance showing itself makes beings capable of becoming present as this and that. *Idea* as whatness has the character of *aitia,* cause. Origination from its whatness dominates in every coming-to-be of beings. Whatness is the matter of every thing, that is, its cause. Accordingly, Being is in itself causal."[48]

As we indicated above, while Aristotle recovers something of the original experience of being — he is "more Greek" than Plato[49] — the "causal"

44. See *Republic* 505e; *Symposium* 206a; *Timaeus* 29d-30b. Adriaan Peperzak has criticized Heidegger for neglecting the evidently ethical aspect of the good in Plato. See "Heidegger and Plato's Idea of the Good," in *Reading Heidegger,* ed. John Sallis (Bloomington: Indiana University Press, 1993), pp. 258-85, esp. 276-77.

45. "Plato's Doctrine of Truth," in *Pathmarks,* p. 181.

46. *End of Philosophy,* p. 55.

47. *End of Philosophy,* pp. 13-14.

48. *End of Philosophy,* p. 13.

49. *End of Philosophy,* p. 9.

sense of being comes to triumph when the Greeks are appropriated by the Romans, by which Heidegger means not only the ancient Romans, but also (and perhaps most decisively) the "Roman Church" and to a lesser extent even the modern "Romantic" movement.[50] In this appropriation, Aristotle's sense of ἐνέργεια gets translated into "*actualitas*," and with this a new epoch of the history of being takes place. In this epoch, the Aristotelian notion of ἔργον, "work" in the sense of "presencing in the open," is replaced by *opus, factum,* and *actus.* We might say that this is a replacement of being by acting, so long as we understand being here as presencing rather than a static "thereness" *(Vorhandensein).* Somewhat surprisingly, Heidegger draws a link between Plato and Roman thought on this score. This may seem strange, insofar as *actualitas,* which affirms actual beings as what is real, would seem to represent the exact opposite of the "idea" which is distinct from all real beings. And so it is. But we have to reflect more deeply to see that this opposition lies within a significant unity. The "thatness" of actuality (existence) is indeed the opposite of "whatness" (essence), but as its opposite remains within the same order. More precisely, actuality is the *presence* of what is present, so that a thing is more actual "the more the presencing being endures in a lasting manner."[51] In spite of their apparent opposition, idea and actuality are the same in two respects: first, they both represent the *unconcealed* character of beings, and so lie equally on "this" side of the event of unconcealment. In other words, they are both ontic rather than properly ontological. And second, for the very same reason, they occlude the temporality of Being, affirming instead the constancy of presence rather than the emergent character of presencing. Heidegger insists that the distinction between whatness and thatness, *essentia* and *existentia,* has always belonged to metaphysics as what is proper to it, and why metaphysics has always failed to inquire into the truth of Being as such. From the perspective of actuality, what Plato had called the idea of the good comes to be called "*actus purus,*" but these are not fundamentally different. The good is the "brightest" of being because it does not reflect light from any other source; it *is* that which shines. Similarly, *actus purus* has no shadow of potency,[52] not because it represents the unity of whatness and thatness prior to their distinction that constitutes the origin of metaphysics, but because it perfectly persists (exis-

50. *End of Philosophy,* pp. 12-13.

51. *End of Philosophy,* p. 15.

52. We recall that, according to Heidegger, the Aristotelian notion of ἐνέργεια includes δύναμις within itself.

tence) as what it is (essence), or rather what it is *is* this perfect persistence. It is significant that Heidegger refers to God in this context specifically as the *summum bonum*, which is *"prius quam ens,"* signaling the supremacy of causality that Plato had as it were instituted with the ἀγαθόν.[53]

According to Heidegger, "[w]hen Being has changed to *actualitas* (reality), beings are what is real. They are determined by working, in the sense of causal making."[54] It is this notion of Being that was so readily taken up by Christian thinkers because of the biblically based belief in creation. And, for Heidegger, it is specifically this notion of Being that persists into the modern era even when Christian faith fades.[55] One might wish to object that Heidegger's association of actuality and causal making is gratuitous, and serves only to set up a straw man for his critique of causality[56] — and indeed it would be difficult to deny that this objection has some merit. But we ought to see why this association is not simply arbitrary, and to make a case for it (which Heidegger himself does not spell out explicitly in this context). If actuality is separated from "whatness," it cannot be an internal event of a being's self-showing, i.e., its emergent essence if you will, but can only be the "that," the *enduring presence* of a being. In this case, to point to pure actuality as the origin of beings is to conceive of the origination as an act or action that has a completed actuality, a perfect presence or perfectly "unconcealed" being, as its subject. One can object, here, once again with some merit, that classical metaphysics has never conceived of the first cause as "a being," i.e., a particular being among many, because this is so obviously a contradiction. But, while Heidegger does indeed seem to attribute such a peculiar mistake to metaphysics in at least the modern era,[57] the main point for him is that

53. Heidegger appears to be quoting here from Aquinas, *ST* I.5.2, in which Aquinas asks "whether *bonum* is *prius quam ens*," and answers that it is not (!).

54. *End of Philosophy*, p. 14.

55. *End of Philosophy*, p. 24.

56. See Kenneth Schmitz's observation in this regard. "From Anarchy to Principles: Deconstruction and the Resources of Christian Philosophy," in *The Texture of Being* (Washington, DC: Catholic University of America Press, 2007), p. 44.

57. Heidegger interprets Leibniz, for example, in this sense: in Leibniz's thought, "Being's character of production appears in the sense that Being itself is made and effected by a being" (*End of Philosophy*, p. 45). In *Contributions to Philosophy*, Heidegger clarifies that the point is not so much the notion of a creator, i.e., a being that creates, as it is a conception of Being founded on a notion of causality: "Even if one refuses crudely to interpret the idea of creator, what is still essential is beings' being-caused. The cause-effect connection becomes the all-dominating (god as *causa sui*)." *Contributions to Philosophy (From Enowning)*, trans. P. Emad and K. Maly (Bloomington: Indiana University Press, 2000), p. 88. If thinking, in

such a conception makes the ultimate ground of things so to speak a being that, as pure act, is *already true,* and so, because we cannot go further back behind it, we are shut off from even inquiring into the *essence* of truth in an originary way.[58] In the doctrine of creation, a being that *is* true, in other words, is prior to the essence of truth. The essential problem, for Heidegger, is not that one fails to think of the first cause in a manner that sufficiently transcends being, but that one attributes the reality of the world to a *pure actuality,* an already "completed" (unconcealed) agent. And there is, for Heidegger, in fact no other way to think of a deliberate, "causal" agent. To put this back into the language of wonder, the first cause, so conceived, would either be "usual" in the sense of being always already present, or would be "unusual" only in the superficial sense of something rare or novel against the backdrop of the usual. What it would *not* be, in any event, is provocative of wonder as the inescapable unusualness of the totality of the usual. Heidegger thus explains that Beingness acquires in this case a self-evident character presumably because it is necessarily posited as already given, rather than seen as abidingly question-worthy.

The reason the activity of creation, according to Heidegger, is necessarily conceived as a "making" is that it cannot have any dimension of *receiving* and potentiality that is in any sense determined by something outside of itself. It cannot but be a unilateral act: what results from this act is "posited" into existence, we might say, entirely "from above." "What" a thing is, in this case is not "liberated" in the sense of being "brought forth" from its own — *unconditioned* — source, but is imposed on what makes no contribution to the "process," i.e., an inert matter. If Heidegger identifies the Christian notion of creation with the assumption of a "hylomorphic" conception of substance, in which matter is conjoined to form as if they were two distinct principles, it is not because he confuses creation and fabrication,[59] but because the two, thus conceived, would play separate roles in the constitution of a thing, form providing the determination and matter simply receiving it. For the very same reason, the first cause in such a conception can only be it-

---

other words, begins with the *true* rather than the essence of truth, which means beginning with what (already) exists rather than with "das Sein als solches," there results an inexorable drift toward the absolutizing of representational thinking.

58. See *BQ,* pp. 27-50.

59. In the "Origin of the Work of Art," in *BW,* p. 159, Heidegger explains that even if the belief in creation falls away, what is essential is simply the conception of beings as a conjunction of form and matter, which is another way to express their character as being-caused.

self the final cause of things, their end and so goal, since things have no other source. Far from being "unconditioned," they are radically dependent on this source for both their essence and their existence, their "what" and their "that." The beings that are, therefore, "co-respond" to this source: "The reality of the grain of sand, of plants, animals, man, numbers, co-responds to the making of the first maker. It is at the same time like and unlike his reality."[60] The first cause, as perfectly actual, measures beings, which is to say that their truth consists in measuring up to the divine idea. Efficient causality gets absolutized here: Form and finality come wholly from the first source, and matter becomes a mere passive ingredient of causality. The ultimate reason for this conception of causality is the absorption of Being into actuality as complete act, which can be source only as a spontaneous producer, as imposing on reality. Creation is an activity belonging to pure presence, and so all things that are *act,* in turn, by being. To say that a thing is actual means that it can act on other things and can resist their action: "The actual is the completed act or product of an activity. This product is itself in turn active and capable of activity. The activity of what is actual can be limited to the capacity of producing a resistance which it can oppose to another actual thing in different ways."[61] In such a conception of the cosmos, "the whole of beings is the effected and effecting product of a first producer," which means that the Being of beings is "effecting in the unified-manifold sense according to what effects, but also what is effected and also what is the effected-effecting and the effective being, is what is."[62] In a word, "actualitas is . . . causalitas."[63]

Now, Heidegger does not (always) suggest that Christianity *introduced* causal thinking into Western philosophy; rather, according to Heidegger, causal thinking is, as it were, "built into" metaphysics to the extent that metaphysics inquires into being qua being, that is, Being insofar as it discloses itself in beings, and so is constituted by the distinction between whatness and thatness, *essentia* and *existentia* — a distinction, as we have seen, that occurs *within* the truth of Being. What is fateful, for Heidegger, is the joining of philosophy and Christianity, which gives we might say a divine sanction to the causal character of Being such that it comes to overpower any other way of thinking. When this happens, Being becomes utterly forgotten:

60. *End of Philosophy,* p. 18.
61. *End of Philosophy,* p. 1.
62. *End of Philosophy,* pp. 18-19.
63. *End of Philosophy,* p. 15.

> Abandonment of being is strongest at that place where it is most decidedly hidden. That happens where beings have — and had to — become most ordinary and familiar. That happened first in *Christianity* and its dogma, which explains all beings in their origin as *ens creatum,* where the creator is the most certain and all beings are the effect of this most extant cause. But cause-effect relationship is the most ordinary, most crude, and most immediate, what is employed by all human calculation and lostness to beings in order to explain something, i.e., to push it into the clarity of the ordinary and familiar. Here, where beings have necessarily to be the most familiar, Being is necessarily and *all the more* ordinary and most ordinary. And now since Being "is" in truth what is most *non*-ordinary, Being here has withdrawn completely and has abandoned beings.[64]

The key is the ultimacy that one accords to causality as the Being of beings when one connects biblical belief and metaphysics. This is why Heidegger insists, as we will see in chapter eight, on keeping faith and philosophy *separate:* if faith concerns the holy, and the holy requires awe in a profound sense, then faith requires that we *not* think of God as first cause. As Heidegger puts it in his essay on technology, "where everything that presences exhibits itself in the light of a cause-effect coherence, even God for representational thinking, can lose all that is exalted and holy, the mysteriousness of his distance. In the light of causality, God can sink to the level of a cause, of *causa efficiens.* He then becomes even in theology the God of the philosophers, namely, of those who define the unconcealed and the concealed in terms of the causality of making, without ever considering the essential origin of this causality."[65] The call to consider the "essential origin of this causality" is not, for Heidegger, a "hermeneutics of suspicion" that would discredit the notion through genealogy. The point, rather, is to reconnect the ontic, representational thinking of causality to its ontological depths. Since the cause-effect relation is an activity that occurs within the unconcealment of beings, we can become open to the unusualness of the usual only if we think Being in a more essential way, more primordially than causal terms allow.

64. *Contributions to Philosophy,* p. 77. Translation adjusted for consistency. The English word "ordinary," here, translates the German "gewöhnliche," which is given as "usual" in *BQ.*

65. "Question Concerning Technology," pp. 307-8.

The End of Wonder?

Modern man, for Heidegger, is incapable of wonder. But this is not a moral failing that can be corrected in principle; it is rather due to something deeper, beyond the reach of any deliberate activity on man's part. First of all, for Heidegger, philosophy, and therefore also the wonder that belongs to it, has come to its end in modernity. Truth, for Heidegger, is historical in a radical sense: Being shows itself — or, as Heidegger puts it most often in his later thought, it "sends" or "dispenses" itself — in a particular way in different epochs in history; or better, it is Being's dispensation that constitutes these epochs. Philosophy, which for Heidegger is essentially metaphysics, had its ambiguous beginnings in Plato and Aristotle, and comes into its own with the "Romans," which includes late antiquity through the Middle Ages. This epoch, we might say, stands under the sign of "the good," and for this reason is dominated by representational thinking, which is a knowledge of causes. The primary cause in metaphysical thinking, for Heidegger, is the efficient cause, but in medieval thought this kind of causality still bore a relation to the other Aristotelian causes. At the end of metaphysics, philosophy seems to "dissolve" into the empirical sciences. The world shows itself, now, not as a cosmos of created (caused) beings, but rather merely as objects of technological manipulation, i.e., as "standing reserve," or as Rojcewicz vividly translates the term *Bestand,* "disposables."[66] In connection with this, Heidegger explains that the nature of causality changes: "This system is then determined by a causality that has changed once again. Causality now displays neither the character of the occasioning [*Veranlassen*] that brings forth nor the nature of the *causa efficiens,* let alone that of the *causa formalis.* It seems as though causality is shrinking into a reporting — a reporting challenged forth — of standing-reserves that must be guaranteed either simultaneously or in sequence."[67] And because the character of causality, taken in its broadest sense, is essentially connected with the character of knowledge, again taken in the broadest sense, the τέχνη that was replaced with causal thinking ends as modern technology, which is "knowledge," but now only as power, as "ordering" and the ability to manipulate. As Heidegger puts it, "'science' is not a knowing, but rather a mechanism of accuracies of a region of explanation."[68] Being, in this case, comes to mean what Heidegger calls "machina-

66. *Gods and Technology,* pp. 83-90.

67. "Question Concerning Technology," p. 304.

68. *Contributions to Philosophy,* p. 103.

tion."[69] Heidegger connects the predominance of machination and its necessary subjective correlate "lived-experience" with a complete absence of awe: "Knowing no limits, above all no embarrassment, and finally no deep awe — all this lies within what is ownmost to both [machination and lived-experience]," the two most basic traits of the modern age.[70]

But Heidegger had emphasized that philosophy only "seems to" dissolve into the empirical sciences in the modern age.[71] In fact, he explains, modern technology represents an end, not in the sense of where philosophy stops, but more profoundly in the sense of "completion." It is an unfolding of what was present, but hidden, at the beginning. Though we cannot here enter into the details of the continuing development of the notion of causality in the modern period, which Heidegger traces especially in relation to Leibniz's principle of sufficient reason, it is not hard to see the connection between *ens creatum,* as Heidegger interprets it, and the eventual prevailing of modern technology. In this case, cause as the *positing* of the existence of things becomes "cause" as the violent imposition of one's own ends and goals. This is a similar structure, only shifted we might say from a vertical to a horizontal position.

At the heart of this shift is the unfolding of truth, the unconcealment of Being: the self-showing of beings, attended to at its deepest level, is the disclosure of Being (presencing). To put the matters somewhat oversimply, in metaphysics Being is grasped precisely in its transcendence of beings, which for Heidegger means understood in the light of what is true, what exists (and therefore understood *causally:* ontotheology), and in the modern period Being has so to speak disappeared, so that the world appears as so many beings, without transcendent causality, but merely in their effective action upon each other. It should be clear, then, why wonder is no longer possible in this world, insofar as wonder requires an attentiveness to beings precisely in their Being, which is what Heidegger means by the "pure acknowledgment of beings in their emerging." To attempt to recover wonder in this case would be to deny the historical character of Being,[72] which means to remove oneself from an obedient listening to Being — and this in turn means simply to take oneself out of wonder. The very attempt to recover wonder in this case undermines it. Heidegger says that this attempt can therefore not avoid becoming "senti-

69. *Contributions to Philosophy,* pp. 88-90.

70. *Contributions to Philosophy,* p. 91.

71. "The End of Philosophy and the Task of Thinking," pp. 375-76.

72. See *BQ,* p. 162.

mentality," that is, a matter of a particular feeling rather than a "basic disposition." One thus clings to philosophy, he says, as a "value," as a cultural artifact, and so precisely *not* as philosophy.[73]

But if philosophy is at an end, this does not mean that thinking *tout court* is over, that there can no longer be a basic disposition in which man in his essence is attuned to Being. It *does* mean, however, that this basic disposition can no longer be characterized as *wonder*. Here we come upon the notion that most deeply characterizes Heidegger's later thought: modernity is characterized by the "abandonment of beings by Being," or more simply, "the abandonment of Being," understood in both the objective and subjective senses of the genitive. As Heidegger never tires of explaining, to unconcealment belongs concealment; Being is not a being, or even primarily what shows itself in beings, but is rather most fundamentally the "clearing" or "opening" or "lighting" *(Lichtung)* in which beings show themselves. Toward the end of his life, Heidegger began to use the term "Ereignis," "event of appropriation," to describe this, rather than the overused word "Sein."[74] When considered in this way, the very emergence of beings in their Being coincides with the "hiding" of Being itself, its "expropriation." Thus, according to Heidegger, even the "pre-metaphysical" Greek thinkers, present at the emergence of beings, did not inquire into Being as such, Being itself. They were "closer" in some sense, to Being in their experience of beings as presencing, and so we might say "co-experienced" the hiddenness of Being — all of which belongs to the basic disposition of wonder — but they did not (and we might say *could* not, because of the power of the presencing of what is) attend to Being itself. In this respect, the very abandonment of beings by Being, the perfect concealment of Being in its disclosure of beings that characterizes modernity, is a privileged moment in the history of Being, the καιρός, we might say, in which a more primordial beginning becomes possible: as the Greeks saw, what is truly first becomes apparent last. The experience of Being itself is not wonder at the unusualness of the usual, but terror *(Erschrecken)* at the abandonment of Being.[75]

73. *BQ*, p. 157.

74. See Stambaugh's introduction to *On Time and Being*, pp. ix-x. In the 1949 edition of his "Letter on Humanism," Heidegger wrote in a note that "since 1936, 'Ereignis' has been the guiding-word of my thinking." See *Brief über dem Humanismus*, in *Wegmarken*, 3rd ed. (Frankfurt am Main: Klostermann, 1996), p. 316, n. a.

75. *BQ*, p. 171: "The need of the first beginning has its own form, and as a consequence wonder is there the compelling basic disposition, and the primordial and lasting question is there the question of beings: what are beings? On the other hand, the need of the

This most primordial attunement represents for Heidegger an *absence* of wonder. In his essay on the "End of philosophy," Heidegger refers to the clearing of Being as the "*Ur-Sache,*" hyphenating the word in order to show that he does not at all mean by it "Ursache," normally taken to be the German translation of "*causa.*"[76] Rather, he refers here to Goethe's important notion of the "*Urphänomen,*" which we alluded to at the outset of this chapter, and at the same time he intends, in this particular context, a reorientation of Husserl's and Hegel's search for the *Sache selbst* as the basis of reason, a search that is very different from Heidegger's own but which has the same goal of ultimacy. Being, as clearing, is the primal "reality," if you will, that which is so basic one may not seek "behind" it for some further cause. Being cannot be an object of representational thinking, which inquires after causes, but is the "ground" of things only as itself having no ground: Being is "Ab-Grund," the abyss. It is therefore not a ground as *cause,* as an effective force, so to speak, an "activity" that makes beings be.[77] As we saw, in Heidegger's interpretation, a cause *is;* it has the status of being already true, i.e., already unconcealed. Instead, Being lets beings be as nothing itself, as the sheltering place in which things show themselves. In a certain sense, this is the very *opposite* of causality. The opening that Being is, which is a kind of self-opening, seems to have the character of generosity for Heidegger: he speaks of it in terms of the phrase "es gibt," "there is/it gives," and uses words such as "gewähren," "to grant," in addition to the "providential"-sounding words like "sheltering" *(Bergen).* But at the same time, there is always a definitive *no* in this apparent generosity;[78] in letting beings be, Being *refuses itself,* and beings likewise in

---

other beginning has the form of an abandonment by Being, to which corresponds the basic disposition of terror. Therefore even the primordial question is different in the other beginning: the question of truth, the question of the essentialization of truth." This text is from his first draft of the 1937-1938 lectures. In the completed draft, he differentiated the *Grundstimmung* as a "restraint" [*Verhaltenheit*], which contains in itself terror and awe (*BQ,* p. 4). In *Contributions to Philosophy,* Heidegger says this *Grundstimmung* "can hardly be named with *one* word, unless it be with the word *restraint*" (p. 277).

76. "The End of Philosophy and the Task of Thinking," p. 385.

77. On this, see John Caputo, *Heidegger and Aquinas* (New York: Fordham University Press, 1987), pp. 198-210.

78. "Enowning [*Ereignis*] as the *hesitating refusal* and therein the fullness of 'time,' the mightiness of the fruit and the greatness of the gifting — but in the *truth* as *clearing* for the *self-sheltering.* Fullness is pregnant with the originary 'not'; making full is not *yet* and *no longer* gifting, both in *counter-resonance,* refused in the very hesitating, and thus the *charming-moving-unto* in the removal-unto. Here [is] above all the swaying not-character of be-ing as enowning." *Contributions to Philosophy,* p. 189.

their emergence refuse themselves to us precisely in their manifestation.[79] Concealment is a withdrawal, a "negative" gesture, as it were, and it belongs inseparably to the "unconcealment" of truth. Indeed, to interpret truth as unconcealment points to concealment as more fundamental, since it is precisely that *from which* beings emerge in their "truthing" (ἀληθεύειν). Being is not present *as Being* in beings; it is their presencing, the possibility of which is given in Being's self-concealment. The "abandonment of beings by Being" is not simply an appearance due to some moral failing; it is rather the precise way in which Being reveals itself in our age. Our age is therefore, ironically perhaps, the one in which the truth of Being becomes most "explicit."

The negativity of Being's withdrawal comes to ultimate expression in Being's refusal, so to speak, to answer the question "Why?" Heidegger quotes Goethe again at the end of a 1956 lecture on Leibniz's "principle of reason": "How? When? And Where? — The gods hold their tongues!/Stick to the *Because,* and do not ask *Why?*"[80] There can be no ultimate reason given for things, but only a "groundless ground," a "because" *(weil),* which Heidegger reads in relation to the Old German verb "weilen," "to while," that is, "to linger." The ground "lingers," without a why: it "grounds." This does not mean that Being is "inexplicable," for that category already, according to Heidegger, presupposes the causal relation in denying its applicability in this particular case. It is rather prior to all explanation and so also all failure to explain. It simply "whiles," that is, it "becauses." Since this is the character of the ground, it is also the character of that which is "grounded." Explanation in every case is radically relativized by an awareness of being as "abyssal." It is significant that Heidegger quotes the famous verse from Angelus Silesius in relation to this notion of ground:

> The rose is without why; it blooms because it blooms,
> It pays no attention to itself, asks not whether it is seen.[81]

"The rose blooms because it blooms": this text evokes the blooming, the upsurge *(aufgehen)* of φύσις, which we saw earlier. The self-showing of things is

79. *BW,* p. 175: "Beings refuse themselves to us down to that one and seemingly least feature which we touch upon most readily when we can say no more of beings than that they are. Concealment as refusal is not simply and only the limit of knowledge in any given circumstance, but the beginning of the lighting of what is lighted."

80. Martin Heidegger, *The Principle of Reason,* trans. Reginald Lilly (Bloomington: Indiana University Press, 1996), p. 126.

81. Heidegger, *The Principle of Reason,* p. 41.

precisely *unconditioned,* i.e., uncaused, even if beings have a ground; things show themselves because they show themselves; they emerge from the ground, but are not "caused" by it. The clearing of Being, thus, is not a reality one would search for "behind" the self-showing of beings; it rather coincides with that self-showing, as we might say its deepest essence, the essence of Being as such, which is the origin of the Being of beings with which classical philosophy occupies itself. This means that questioning ultimately must relinquish the form of the "why," and must become instead a silent acknowledgment. In a published summary of the seminar discussion of Heidegger's essay "On Time and Being," the author writes: "one cannot speak of a 'why'. Only the 'that' — that the history of Being is in such a way — can be said."[82]

It is important to see, however, that the "other beginning," the terror and awe that Heidegger suggests represents the basic disposition possible in the modern epoch as that which corresponds to the primordial question of the truth of Being, is not meant to replace the wonder at the origin of metaphysics as the beginning of a new, alternative tradition. Heidegger presents it rather as an entry into the ground of the Western tradition, which thus is meant to allow us to appropriate that tradition in a more originary way. It seems that we might best understand Heidegger's interpretation of wonder in precisely this light: we noted above that, in his reading, wonder lacks all traces of desire, which belongs to the meaning of wonder from within the classical tradition, and which connects it in an essential way with an inquiry into causes. But wonder has a different character when approached from the perspective of terror, in which the thinker is precisely repulsed rather than attracted. The thinking of Being is a "step back" *(Schritt zurück)* from the tradition rather than an immersion in it; this thinking is a matter of restraint — and only thus does it represent a recovery of the respectful distance metaphysics seems necessarily to surrender in allowing the experience of wonder to ask "why?," to pursue causes.

To sum up, causality is an activity that transpires within the clearing of truth; causal explanation is thus "founded," not primordial. If it is made ultimate, and made to define the scope of thought, what is most primordial, the *Ur-Sache,* becomes essentially occluded, set outside of thinking. Metaphysics is the forgetting of Being. The wonder that corresponds to the (temporal) presencing of what is present can be retrieved in our age only on the basis of a more radical kind of thinking that attends to what is occluded in metaphysics, or more adequately to what conceals itself precisely *in* giving Being

82. *Time and Being,* p. 32.

to thought in metaphysics. This more radical thinking is restraint in the fundamental attunement of terror and awe. The wonder thus retrieved from the more originary ground of metaphysics is, accordingly, a pure, dispassionate acknowledgment. It is a thinking that "holds itself back" from inquiry in the end.

Heidegger had wanted to sustain wonder by rejecting explanation, but it becomes apparent that he ends up eliminating wonder from the other direction, or at the very least transforming it into something quite different by subordinating it to terror. The claim that there is, and indeed that there can be, no answer to the question "Why?" cannot help but be itself an answer to the question, which has the same effect of shutting down wonder that the facile response does. A question we must ponder is whether the closing of the question "why" in fact closes one's receptivity to what seeks to reveal itself, whether proper reception requires a positive "going forward" as much as a negative "holding oneself back." Note that the holding oneself back, the restraint, bears a likeness to the a priori setting of limits to reason, which we have been suggesting in different ways in this book cannot avoid turning into a false modesty, because it gives priority, ironically, to one's own will. Asking the question "why" in wonder, by contrast, can be a way of giving oneself over to what gives itself to be known. The question "why," asked genuinely, is reason's making itself vulnerable, its placing itself at the disposal of whatever may happen to come in response to this question. If a rejection of the ultimacy of causal thinking leads to a suspension of wonder, we are prompted to consider whether there might be a different way of understanding causality and so to enter more deeply into the nature of the causality that lies at the root of genuine questioning.

Response to Heidegger

Heidegger's philosophy demands a profound response: what he proposes is not simply an idea or theory, but an interpretation of what is most fundamental, namely, Being as such, and indeed an interpretation that challenges the Western tradition as a whole. One's response to Heidegger will thus necessarily require one to take a position with respect to the tradition as a whole.[83] Now, there are several things that Heidegger brings to light about the

83. Günther Figal justly observes that "an engagement with Heidegger has become a necessary condition for understanding philosophy. His philosophy demonstrates possibilities

nature of wonder that seem to be essential, and have to be affirmed, though perhaps on different grounds.[84] We will simply mention them here, since we have discussed the issue at length above: first, the quality of Heidegger's thinking, the depth at which he engages ideas and thinkers, reveals the fruitfulness of an "abiding with the question" rather than allowing a too-quick contentedness with one insight or another. His work, whatever judgment one might eventually formulate, makes it clear that the question of Being is truly inexhaustible. Second, Heidegger brings to light the central importance of the notion of causality — whatever judgment one ultimately makes on it — for our understanding of Being simply, and so in fact for our understanding of all things whatsoever, and moreover, he clarifies how the notion of causality turns on what we take to be the unifying paradigm of the multiple senses of the term. Third, Heidegger shows the significance of the "revelatory" aspect of truth and its "event-like" character, so that the reception of truth is an activity in which one dwells, or perhaps a relation in which one stands, rather than simply an object to be grasped.[85] It is here that the significance of the

---

for every philosophical work that understands itself from out of, and in reflective relation to, tradition. This is also true for philosophers who engage Heidegger critically. To critique is to differentiate; a critique determines in what respect, and to what extent, one wishes to follow someone. In this way, critique confirms a philosopher's significance." "Introduction," in *The Heidegger Reader*, ed. G. Figal (Bloomington: Indiana University Press, 2009), p. 2.

84. The historical basis of Heidegger's philosophy is certainly weak: not only has the adequacy of his interpretation of various thinkers been widely, and often convincingly, challenged, but even one of the most basic historical contentions has been shown to be dubious, namely, the claim that ἀλήθεια originally meant "unconcealment" (which requires interpreting it as ἀ-λήθεια, i.e., the root connected with λανθάνω preceded by an alpha privative); see Paul Friedländer, *Plato*, vol. 1, 3rd German ed. (Berlin: De Gruyter, 1964), p. 236. Heidegger himself concedes this point in a late essay (1964) ("The End of Philosophy and the Task of Thinking," pp. 388-90), admitting that ἀλήθες means "true" exclusively in the sense of "correct" and "reliable" already in the earliest instances of the word (in Homer), and indeed allows that he may no longer insist that there was a shift in the essence of truth in Plato or in (Roman) Christianity. Instead, he says in this essay that even the Greeks did not understand truth properly from the beginning. Of course, to concede this is arguably to abandon a "historical" sense of Being, since Heidegger is brought to appeal to a notion that has never appeared in history, and to make this in some sense normative. One cannot therefore hold on to Heidegger's notion of truth as unconcealment without at the same time reconsidering in a radical way his notion of the historicity of Being and truth. For a brief defense of Heidegger on this point, see Alain Boutot, *Heidegger et Platon: Le problème du nihilisme* (Paris: Presses Universitaires de France, 1987), pp. 211-16, in which Boutot contends that Heidegger's position had always been that the word contained more than the Greeks in fact understood, and so even they never understood ἀλήθεια properly as ἀλήθεια.

85. On this, see Stambaugh's introduction to *On Time and Being*, p. x.

temporal character of Being becomes evident, insofar as unconcealment is an *unfolding*, not an "already-there-ness," but an arriving. We mentioned in our preliminary reflections that Plato intuited something along these lines in his bringing into unity of possession and desire. The basic thrust of Heidegger's thought from the beginning was to show that the notion of truth as a property of propositions ultimately depends on a more essential notion of truth, which is at the same time an experience (πάθος as *Stimmung*, not as *Erlebnis*) because it is an event. Moreover, along the same lines, Heidegger shows that the persistence of wonder requires a kind of absoluteness, an "unconditionedness," of things' self-showing. He provides a philosophical argument for Goethe's primal phenomenon. If what a thing presents is an effect of a cause that, as it were, lies behind it, then one does not need to abide with the effect, but only to see through it, as it were, to its truth. And thus the "abiding" character of wonder *and* truth disappears. Heidegger's philosophy thus offers a more essential ground for Nietzsche's profound insight into the need for remaining at the surface of things.[86] The acknowledgment of things in their emergence is complete, rather than a first stage on the way to an explanation, if this self-showing *is* in some basic way their truth, what is ultimate about things. Whatever response we give to Heidegger will have to affirm this insight in a basic way.

On the other hand, Heidegger's insight comes at a cost, especially when viewed from the perspective of the claim of the catholicity of reason. There are several things to mention in relation to our present aim, which we will simply list in no particular order.

(1) First, we note that the very attempt to preserve wonder by overcoming causality ends up undermining wonder, as we just saw. It does not seem to be possible to dissociate the question "Why?" from wonder without denaturing it; it is difficult to see how a "pure acknowledgment" without desire could possibly warrant the description of a *questioning*, as Heidegger suggests it does.

(2) To the extent that one seeks to salvage wonder by discovering an *alternative* to causal thinking, one ends up abandoning causal thinking itself to pure "wonderlessness." In this case, everything that falls within the domain of causal thinking, which indeed encompasses most of the ordinary world, is abandoned to hollowness and banality. The cause-effect relationship, for Heidegger, is therefore left to the realm of the wholly "usual," and so

86. Friedrich Nietzsche, preface to *Die fröhliche Wissenschaft*, in vol. 3 of the *Kritische Studienausgabe*, ed. G. Colli and M. Montinari (Berlin: De Gruyter, 1988), p. 352.

incapable of provoking wonder. The mystery of Being will, in this case, not be found in beings, but will show itself only when they all disappear in nothingness, in the nothing of the clearing of Being (behind them, around them: open space, etc.).[87] But this wonder will then itself turn out to be quite vacuous. We will dwell on this further below. In any event, we may say that the "saving" of such a world, to use Heidegger's language, will turn out to be merely forensic: the pile of dung covered over by snow, as Martin Luther famously put it.[88] A recovery of genuine wonder, we are proposing, must occur *in* the knowledge that comes with causality.

(3) The wonder will be hollow because it can correspond only to the "whylessness" of things; their *reasons,* whatever "why" they betray, becomes in this case a threat to their wonderfulness.

(4) Along these very lines, what is most significant, or to use Heidegger's language, what is most question-worthy, what most compellingly calls for thinking, is what is *negative:* the hiding of Being, concealment, self-refusal, the withdrawal, the invisible, the unsaid, and so forth. It would not be correct to say that Being ceases to provoke thought *to the extent* that it unconceals itself in beings, because in fact the refusal of Being cannot be separated from the unconcealment, but nevertheless unconcealment is question-worthy, *not as* unconcealed, but only in virtue of the concealment that is inseparable from it. There is in other words no positive dimension in wonder so conceived, which corresponds to the rejection of causality (since a causal relation is a positive one).

(5) The joylessness implied by this total lack of positivity is connected with a quietism that critics have often identified in Heidegger's philosophy. Man is indeed the "shepherd of Being," but he exercises this task only as an obedience — a "releasement" or "detachment" *(Gelassenheit)* — that is compromised by deliberate and willed activity, eros, appetite, and so forth.[89] All

87. See, e.g., *Contributions to Philosophy,* p. 339: "Be-ing is the non-ordinary in the sense that it remains untouchable by any ordinariness. Thus, in order to know be-ing, we must step out of every ordinariness." It is true that Heidegger insists that "Wonder does not divert itself from the usual but on the contrary adverts to it, precisely as what is the most usual of everything and in everything" (*BQ,* p. 145). But the question is whether and in what precise sense the conception of Being he proposes can sustain this simultaneity.

88. On the significance of Martin Luther for the early Heidegger, see Sean McGrath, *The Early Heidegger and Medieval Philosophy: Phenomenology for the Godforsaken* (Washington, DC: Catholic University of America Press, 2006), pp. 151-84.

89. To be sure, Heidegger denies that this is "obedience" in the sense that compromises freedom. In fact, he regularly affirms that this relationship precisely *sets one free:* "being is nothing other than what sets free [*Ent-setzende*] and what calls for setting-free [*Ent-*

of the action, so to speak, takes place prior to consciousness. He is in every significant reality an instrument of something greater: man can only chatter; it is *die Sprache* that *spricht.* Man does not possess freedom, Heidegger says, but freedom possesses man.[90] And so forth. There is a connection between this problem and the first one mentioned: insofar as efficient causality bears some essential relation to agency and the will, the rejection of one will entail the rejection of the other. Heidegger equates the modern conception of freedom with causality, and so rejects both.[91]

(6) The rejection of causality also entails a rejection of *conceptual reason.* Heidegger insists that his proposal has nothing to do with irrationalism, since it concerns a listening, an openness, to the ground of reason (which is as such beyond reason in some sense).[92] There is certainly an indispensable truth to this, but — as we will see below — a ground can either *include* what follows from it or *exclude* it. The former is what is understood in the classical tradition as implied in the causal relation. In the latter case, the conceptual aspect of reason will always turn out to be a compromise of the truth that is constantly being "overcome" by a more basic disposition, rather than something that reinforces the transcendence of the ground. But this relation requires the positive — causal! — presence of the ground. Thus, the radically receptive heeding of the call of Being we described above tends to devolve at the same time, and for the same reason, into a *blind* obedience, a listening belonging-to *(das Gehör)* without any clear seeing, in the sense of representational thought.

(7) While it may be true that Heidegger does not simply reject Christianity, or at least the embrace of his philosophy does not require one to reject Christianity — he himself insists that his thinking allows for a "purer" kind of Christianity, and, as we will see in chapter eight, there are some who take his word for it[93] — it nevertheless remains the case that he *does* reject

---

setzliche]," *Contributions to Philosophy,* p. 339. But he nevertheless means "freedom" in a way that renders ultimately insignificant whatever belongs to deliberate, willed activity.

90. See, e.g., "On the Essence of Truth," in *BW,* p. 129.

91. See "Technology," in *BW,* p. 306: "The essence of freedom is *originally* not connected with the will or even with the causality of human willing." Heidegger is thus led to reinterpret the meaning of freedom in a radically new way. The point is not that there is nothing to criticize in the modern conception of freedom and its connection to the will and causality, but rather that an adequate conception will have to include this dimension (without reducing it) rather than simply substituting something else for it.

92. *Letter on Humanism,* pp. 225-28.

93. See Lawrence Paul Hemming, *Heidegger's Atheism: The Refusal of a Theological*

the Christian tradition. In other words, he rejects the Christianity that is *given,* the actual Christianity that has developed in the West in dialogue with Greek philosophy. One of the central terms of this dialogue is the notion of cause, and a failure to recognize the importance of this notion risks enshrining, so to speak, Heidegger's nihilism.

(8) Finally, the rejection of causality appears to lead Heidegger to undermine his own thinking on a central point. If there is no causal relationship between Being and beings, if Being *holds itself back* in relation to beings, then Being does not disclose itself in history. It is absent from the "Geschick" that constitutes the various historical periods — which Heidegger calls "epochs," after the Greek word ἐποχή, a suspension or holding back.[94] Indeed, Heidegger claims that "refusal" *(Verweigerung)* is the "highest nobility of gifting" *(Schenkung),*[95] which makes the *not*-giving, the concealment, the most primordial. There really is a "leap," then, not only out of the tradition, but in fact out of history, or out of time simply, in the "other thinking" that Heidegger proposes. There is terror here because one is entirely unmoored. But if we make this leap primordial, without a certain dependence on what is already given, it cannot avoid becoming arbitrary. And thus Heidegger's listening to Being will have nothing to prevent its collapse into an oppressive self-assertion, i.e., the assertion of Heidegger himself. Because it is Being itself that comes to expression in Heidegger to the extent that he genuinely *"denkt und dichtet,"* Heidegger therefore speaks *for* Being, and Being refuses to respond to the question "Why?" A radical passivity will always turn out to have as its flip side a literally boundless self-assertion, no matter how unintentional this may be.

As we observe in the next chapter regarding Heidegger's critique of ontotheology, a common contemporary Christian response has been to concede the terms that Heidegger sets, and then attempt to argue for a nonmetaphysical Christianity, to show that Christian thinking avoids the collapse into technology even more than the *"Seynsgeschichtliches Denken"* — that is, it "out-Heideggers" Heidegger. Once again, regarding the specific terms of causality, Jean-Luc Marion represents a paradigm of this approach. As he sees it, the Christian notion of creation has nothing to do with causal-

---

Voice (South Bend, IN: University of Notre Dame Press, 2002), a book we discuss in the next chapter.

94. "The history of Being means destiny of Being in whose sendings both the sending and the It which sends forth hold back with their self-manifestation. To hold back, in Greek, is *epoche.* Hence we speak of the epochs of the destiny of Being." *On Time and Being,* p. 9.

95. *Contributions to Philosophy,* p. 285.

ity, meaning not only the modern notion of efficient causes, but even the more properly interpreted Aristotelian view.[96] Thus, he takes a thinker central to the Christian tradition, namely, Dionysius the Areopagite, who speaks almost obsessively of God in causal terms, and argues that the word Dionysius uses to describe God, "αἰτία," ought to be translated as "Requisite," while the word Dionysius uses for creatures, "αἰτιατὰ,"[97] normally meaning "effects," ought to be translated "Requestants" — indicating that creatures turn to God as the object of petition and praise rather than as a "first cause," to be mastered in concepts. Separating God from causality thus "protects" him, as it were, from our knowledge. While Marion's translation would be difficult to defend even on linguistic grounds alone,[98] the more fundamental problem is that the concession to Heidegger concedes in some respect all of the problems we have just listed.

We wish to propose that there is a more fruitful response, one that affirms and deepens the tradition rather than attempts presumptuously to reorient it from the outside: instead of interpreting creation in terms of causality (Heidegger), or interpreting creation in noncausal terms (Marion), we might interpret causality in terms, first, of creation.[99] In other words, we may affirm that the act of creation presents the paradigm, establishes the deepest meaning of, causality more generally — a properly analogical notion of cause, according to the view of analogy we sketch below in chapter

96. *The Idol and Distance: Five Studies,* trans. Thomas Carlson (New York: Fordham University Press, 2001), pp. 60-61.

97. See, e.g., *DN* I.5.593D.

98. While not impossible, the translation requires attributing a use of the verbal adjective for which there seems to be no contemporary parallel (the reference Marion provides in his note is from the thirteenth century). (I owe this observation to my colleague, Paul Danove.) Moreover, to be compelling, this translation would require some explanation of the constant use Dionysius makes of the common Aristotelian and Neoplatonic philosophical vocabulary of causality (the word αἰτία regularly appears in the *Divine Names* with words and phrases connected with causality: οὗ ἕνεκα, ἀρχὴ, τέλος, and even ςτοιχεῖον, not to mention other technical philosophical vocabulary such as δύναμις and ἐνέργεια). It is difficult to believe Dionysius would use a term that had a standard meaning in this context, and intend something that was, as Marion describes it, altogether unrelated to this meaning, without some explicit signaling of this fact in the text. More generally, it is important to note that Dionysius is hardly the only classical thinker to speak of God as cause; to justify Marion's interpretation one would have to explain why the rest of the classical Christian tradition was able to take up the philosophical vocabulary of causality.

99. Kenneth Schmitz provides an excellent example of this in his interpretation of a Thomistic metaphysics of creation in *The Gift: Creation* (Milwaukee: Marquette University Press, 1982), pp. 118-30.

nine. In fact, this suggestion is supported by historical evidence: Heidegger claims that the dominance of "efficient" causality was a "Roman" event, but he does not distinguish between late antiquity and medieval thought. It is true that the Stoics reduced causality to the agent, or active cause, in a manner that corresponds roughly with Heidegger's account, and opposed to this merely the passivity of matter as what is acted upon.[100] But the Stoics did not recognize any "efficient" cause in the sense that the term had in medieval thought; this notion was explicitly introduced by Avicenna *in distinction from* agent or motor causality, as a way of characterizing the *unique* causality operating in creation: the act of creation does not designate a cause of motion but a cause of being without motion. In other words, creation is not an event in any sense *within* the world (within the clearing of Being, if you will), but is what brings it about that there is a world at all.[101] This causality was given the name *efficiens* — from *efficere*, "to effect," to "bring about," i.e., to bring *into* being — by the thinkers of the High Middle Ages.[102] In contrast to the Stoics who arguably collapsed causality into the univocity of what we may call mere "agentiality," i.e., acting on, the positing of things, the setting of and pursuit of goals, and so forth — the hermeneutical key to causality in the Stoics is moral responsibility[103] — efficient causality in this more "originary" sense necessarily included the essential diversity of Aristotelian causes in a manner that transformed them without simply making them something else. And while the explicit distinction between the cause of motion and the cause of being was introduced in the eleventh century and clarified terminologically only in the thirteenth century, it merely gave to expression what can be found echoing throughout the classical Christian tradition, and what prevailed in that tradition until the arrival of late medieval nominalism — ironically, precisely when the connection between Greek philoso-

100. Of course, the Stoics differentiated causes, but these were distinctions of the various contributions to the *physical activity* that brought about an effect. See Michael Frede, "The Original Notion of Cause," in *Essays in Ancient Philosophy* (Minneapolis: University of Minnesota Press, 1987), pp. 125-50.

101. Étienne Gilson, "Notes pour l'histoire de la cause efficiente," *Archives d'histoire doctrinale et littéraire du Moyen Age* 29 (1962): 7-31.

102. To be sure, terminological ambiguity persisted for a long time: even up through Aquinas, the phrase *"causa efficiens"* could mean either the *causa motus* or the *causa essendi* (as Carraud observes, Aquinas uses the phrase to indicate the cause of any change whatsoever; *Causa sive ratio*, p. 75). It is not until Peter of Auvergne, a disciple of Aquinas, that we have a precise terminological distinction between these two senses. Nevertheless, the understanding of this distinction preceded the clarification of terminology.

103. Frede, "The Original Notion of Cause," p. 131.

phy and Christian faith was *broken.* Arguably, what characterizes modern thought is not the absolutizing of efficient causality, but rather precisely the *forgetting* of efficient causality, and its replacement by the physical, i.e., non-*meta*-physical, "agent" cause of the Stoics, a notion that collapses the rich diversity of causality into a single sense.[104]

Our aim here, however, is not to trace out the history of the notion of causality, but instead to reflect in a more internal way on the nature of causality as it comes to expression in perhaps the most thoroughly *causal* thinker in history, Dionysius the Areopagite, as it bears on the theme of wonder and Heidegger's interpretation of the same. Heidegger's critique is a fruitful one in that it sheds a new light on traditional themes by virtue especially of a profound sense of the contemporary crisis. In what follows, we will attempt to gather some of this fruit in an interpretation of Dionysius's notion of causality against the backdrop of Heidegger's concerns, and then finally consider the implications for the relationship between knowledge and wonder.

Dionysius on the "Cause of All Things"

The most constant title that Dionysius ascribes to God is *cause;* the expressions αἰτία or αἴτιον τῶν πάντων (the causality or cause of all things) and παναιτίον (the universal cause) occur on nearly every page of the *Divine Names.* If he does not devote a particular chapter or section to this particular name, as he does for Being, Life, Wisdom, and so forth, it is only because this name is not one of the names, but the meaning that underlies them all. Each of the names, in other words, sets forth a different aspect of the singular reality of God's causality. Indeed, Dionysius characterizes the names he discusses in the book precisely as *"aitiological"* (τὰ αἰτιολογικὰ), i.e., as bearing the logos, that is, the meaning of causality.[105] The names that Dionysius discusses in the book represent what we can know of God on the basis of created realities. These are the names then that describe God specifically in relation to the world. Dionysius indicates that there are names of God that

104. Contrast this reading with that offered by Louis Dupré, for instance, who believes that the reduction of creation to efficient causality is one of the primary sources of modernity, and seeks instead to recover formal and final causality (participation) over against efficient causality. See *Religion and the Rise of Modern Culture* (South Bend, IN: University of Notre Dame Press, 2008), pp. 45-51.

105. *DN* II.3.640B.

describe him as it were in himself and in relative distinctness from the world: on the one hand, names that refer to God in his simplicity, i.e., "supergoodness," "superessentiality," and so forth, and on the other hand those that refer to God as Trinity, i.e., Father, Son, and Spirit. That there are names other than the "aitiological" indicates that God exceeds his relationship to the world, but even these are not simply separate from that relation, as we will suggest below. A complete reflection on precisely how this is so lies beyond the scope of the present context.[106]

The divine names, we said, explicate the meaning of causality, but not equally in every case. In fact, Dionysius calls "goodness" the "perfect name," and says that this one name reveals everything that proceeds from God, i.e., the whole of God's *ad extra* activity (τὴν παντελῆ καὶ τῶν ὅλον τοῦ θεοῦ προόδων ἐκφαντορικὴν ἀγαθωνυμίαν).[107] But if that activity is essentially *causal,* as we just suggested, it means that, for Dionysius, goodness — and, we might add, "beauty," which for Dionysius is so inseparable from goodness that he begins to refer to God by the end of chapter IV simply as "the beautiful and good" — is ultimately another name for causality. The names "beauty and goodness" and "causality" are convertible.[108] We saw in chapter five that Plato thinks of causality essentially in terms of goodness, and we saw above that Heidegger, too, sees an essential connection between the two, a connection that in fact represents the heart of Western metaphysics. When Dionysius identifies this as the highest name, and describes it as causality itself, he is indeed taking over a theme that is central to Plato and the Neoplatonic tradition. On the other hand, it also happens to be the name most explicitly given to God in Scripture, which is what Dionysius himself cites, rather than a Platonic philosopher, as the source for the status he accords it.[109] Heidegger had interpreted goodness as "*Tauglichkeit,*" but we have suggested that this does not do justice to Plato, and certainly not to the way the term is used in Dionysius. For the Christian Neoplatonic tradition, goodness has the character above all of generosity and desirability, though it will be-

106. For a succinct account of the way transcendence is constitutive of causality in Neoplatonic thinking, see Eric Perl, *Theophany: The Neoplatonic Philosophy of Dionysius the Areopagite* (Albany: State University of New York Press, 2007), pp. 17-34.

107. *DN* III.1.680B.

108. Aquinas explains that "Dionysius attributes good to God as to the first efficient cause" (*ST* 1.6.1), and indeed observes that the "name *good* is the principal name of God insofar as He is a cause" (*ST* 1.13.11ad2).

109. *DN* IV.1.693B. Dionysius says it is the name ascribed to God by the "θεολόγοι," the sacred writers, that is, the writers of Scripture.

come apparent that this meaning acquires further dimensions when conceived in connection with the causality of creation. As we will see, it is this meaning of goodness that unites the diverse orders of causality that Aristotle originally articulated, and which we discussed in the previous chapter; Dionysius thus brings together Plato and Aristotle.

Goodness, for Dionysius, presents itself initially along very evidently Plotinian lines as "productivity," or perhaps we might say, "generativity."[110] He begins his discussion of the names goodness and beauty in chapter IV by comparing the good (again, like Plato), to the sun, which sends the rays of its light throughout the cosmos. What is most important about this image in this context is the nature of causality it expresses, or more specifically the nature of the relationship between the being and causality of the cause: the sun is not a *thing* that subsequently *shines;* instead, it *is* shining, its activity of shining is so to speak equiprimordial with its being, so that there is no essence, no matter how deeply one goes, that is not "already" shining. This is why the light given by the sun is not something other than the sun, or something the sun "has," a surplus that is separate from what the sun is. Instead, what is given away *is* the sun; sunlight is the sun *as* given away, sent out, and indeed light is itself radiation, a shining, a going forth. By the very same token, what Dionysius calls the "cause of all things" is not a being that possesses goodness as one of its properties, but is goodness itself, and so the being of the good is in a certain respect the same as the activity of goodness, i.e., generosity or self-giving. It is even more radical in this case than the sun, because the good does not simply shed itself on a world already there, but in fact gives rise to the very world to which it gives itself, or better: gives rise to the world *in* giving itself.[111] The reason this is important, in the present con-

110. Dionysius refers to God's goodness as a "producer of form" (εἰδοποιεῖν, *DN* IV.3.697A) and a "producer of being" (οὐσιοποιεῖν, *DN* V.2.816C).

111. Obviously, we have to face the specter of pantheism here, which always haunts Neoplatonism. But it is important to see that qualifications need to accommodate the total self-giving character of the first cause, not replace it. Aquinas, for example, affirms the Neoplatonic idea that God is distinct from the world, not as an individual "being," but as the purity of goodness, i.e., God's being the good (in an unlimited way) that created beings share in a limited fashion. See his commentary on the *Book of Causes* (Washington, DC: Catholic University of America Press, 1996), p. 72. Aquinas himself affirms that "being" is a higher name than "goodness" because it indicates God in himself rather than God in relation to the world (*ST* I.13.11). This *seems* to be a criticism of Dionysius, but in fact Dionysius, too, presents goodness as the highest name of God only in relation to the world — and as we indicated above, he affirmed that there were higher names for God in himself. Perhaps the best way to qualify this is the following: God's creation of the world is not a merely natural act, which

text, is that it reveals that, for Dionysius, and indeed arguably for any metaphysics of creation that is ultimately coherent, the causality of creation is not an ontic activity in the sense that it is an activity that belongs to an "already complete," i.e., already unconcealed, agent — i.e., an agent that so to speak already has his being behind him, so that the activity of creation would be "added to" the creator as a change to his being. An affirmation of the perfect simplicity of God precludes such an interpretation. By the same token, to say that the act of creation does not come "after" the being of God does not mean the original cause is incomplete without its effects, or considered apart from them. The point is that the causing of the world is not an after-effect, but is an act that arises from the most original "point," an act that coincides in some sense with the being of God (without reducing to it). To use Heidegger's terminology, it is ontological, or it coincides with the Being of the ground of things. But at the same time, understood as the positivity of goodness, the primary generosity, the giving of all things, *includes* rather than excludes what might be classified as the "ontic" dimension of deliberate, willed agency, even as it transcends this agency. In other words, Dionysius can speak of causation in what we might call (anachronistically, of course) the *personal* terms of free self-gift, jealous yearning, providential kindness, and love, even if doing so does not then circumscribe causality within the merely ontic sphere. As we will see below, this dimension, moreover, gives causality a kind of gratuity, which is not the horror of the nothing, but the positive presence (in transcendence) of generous love.

The coincidence of goodness and causality has a direct implication for the meaning of the "effects." Created beings are not simply *posited,* as the products of a making or as the results of an act. Their being is a response to the goodness that creates them. Again in line with the Platonic tradition, Dionysius understands *desire* (the verb he tends to use in the *Divine Names* is ἐφίημι, but he will identify this with eros in section 10, as we will see), as the receptive relation to goodness. As Dionysius puts it, it is by desire that things have their existence and well-being: καὶ αὐτῆς (i.e., the divine goodness) ἐφιέμεναι καὶ τὸ εἶναι καὶ τὸ εὖ εἶναι ἔχουσι.[112] It is crucial to see, here, that the desire Dionysius describes is not simply an activity, nor even a pas-

---

would in fact reduce to pantheism, but nor is it merely an act of freedom, which would entail nominalism. Rather, it is both at once in a nonreductive way. We can imagine this as a freedom that is perfectly good, i.e., wholly given over to the good, so that there is "no hesitation" to create the world, even though this creation does indeed arise from God's freedom. We will see some of this paradox arise when we speak of *eros* in relation to God below.

112. *DN* IV.1.696A.

sion, that resides in an already constituted subject. Rather, in a manner that mirrors divine generosity, the being of the subject *is* its desiring; desire, as the reception of the creative act, i.e., the primal goodness, coincides with existence, so that we can even say that desire is a term that describes the act of existence specifically with reference to the good as its cause. The verb ἐφίημι literally means a "setting forth upon," and so a "coming out toward" (ἐπι-) — evoking Heidegger's interpretation of existence as a "standing out from" *(ek-sistere).* To compare to Heidegger, we could say that, for Dionysius, the emergence of beings, their unconcealment, *is* their desire, which from the start reaches out toward something beyond themselves.

As coincident with existence, this "primordial desire" lies deeper than sentience, which is why Dionysius ascribes it not only to living creatures, but to nonliving being, too (ἄψυχος καὶ ἄζωος οὐσία), insofar as it exists at all.[113] Indeed, as we will explain further on, primordial desire extends for Dionysius even to the nonexistent insofar as it has any bearing whatsoever on reality.[114] Thus understood, desire is "prior" to sentience, and *a fortiori* to deliberate appetite, as its enabling ground. Sentience and deliberate appetite, interpreted in this way, are the emerging into consciousness or self-consciousness of a movement that is rooted, as it were, more deeply than either. In this respect, desire is "ontological" rather than merely ontic. At the same time, however, it is not the case that appetite — and so the willed agency associated with it in the human being — as an "ontic" activity is merely subsequent to ontological desire. Instead, rational appetite is this desire expressed at the level of reason, which means that rational appetite is a "higher-level" recapitulation of ontological desire. In other words, a creature's "ontic" activities are a participation in their ontological ground; these dimensions are not separate or opposed, but reflect one another. As we will see, the "ontic" desire of one creature for another is not isolated from its ontological desire for God that lies at the root of its being (and indeed in a certain respect *is* that being).

What all this means is that creation, as "causal goodness," is not a unilateral act that posits a thing into existence, an actualizing of pre-given possibilities, but is rather a giving that includes within its own intelligibility a receiving, which is to say that it is a "unilateral" act that is so radically generous it includes within itself a reciprocity: desire is the active participation in the act of creation and indeed, by way of, inclusive of, creatures' interrelations among one another. This is what goodness looks like, as it were, from

113. *DN* IV.2.696D.
114. See, e.g., *DN* IV.3.697A.

the perspective of what is generated. In this sense, creation is not a "making," but a "letting emerge," or more adequately it is indeed a making precisely *as* a letting emerge, insofar as the activity of coming into being is *given* to creatures. But notice: the emergence of beings is not here in the first place a "self-showing," but more fundamentally a "reaching out" for what is other than the self (which nevertheless coincides with its self-showing). This point will become crucial below.

It is by desire, as reception of the good, that one exists: to exist is to receive goodness. But goodness, as we have seen, is generosity, the gift of self. This means that to be is by the same token to give of oneself, to communicate further the good that one has received, or better, that one *is:* as St. Paul said, "what you have freely received you must freely pass on." Again, it is important that we maintain the simplicity in this differentiation: it is not the case that one has first received and so one subsequently *ought* to give. Indeed, this way of seeing things moralizes generosity, and appears to be the root of the fateful split between ἔρως and ἀγάπη that was given classical expression in Anders Nygren's book.[115] Instead, the desire *coincides* with the generosity, just as it does with being: to desire is to be is to give, and though these "moments" are really distinct from one another, they are expressions of a single, simple act. In the text just cited, Dionysius goes on to say, continuing the same sentence quoted above: "and being conformed to the divine goodness according as it is received, they are 'good-like' [ἀγαθοειδεῖς], and under the guidance of the divine law, they share [κοινωνοῦσιν] with others the constant gifts that come to them from the good."[116] As received from the good, the being of creatures is "good-like," which means their being imitates the good, sharing itself with others and so enjoying community. The fact that giving is not separate from receiving means that there is no simple division between those "above" one, from whom one would receive, and those "below" one, to whom one would give. Rather, while there is a clear hierarchy of being here — indeed, Dionysius is the one who coined the word "hierarchy"[117] — there is a paradoxical interplay between the levels, which is nothing but an expression of the simplicity of the divine gift. Dionysius

115. See Perl, *Theophany,* pp. 47-48. Cf. a lengthier discussion of this theme in my "The Redemption of Eros: Philosophical Reflections on Benedict XVI's First Encyclical," *Communio* 33 (Fall 2008): 375-99.

116. *DN* IV.1.696A.

117. Dionysius appears to have coined the term ἱεραρχία specifically to describe the ecclesial and angelic ranks, but what he says about these represents a general principle of being for him. See Perl, *Theophany,* pp. 65-81.

highlights the complex order that gives expression to the simple divine cause by considering the good under the name of "beauty" in chapter 7, and henceforward referring to this cause as "the beautiful and the good" for the "cosmos" that forms in this causality.[118] The "intercommunions of all things in all things proper to each" (IV.7.704B) follows logically from the meaning of the transcendent cause of the whole. But it is not only a logical inference; it also accords with our experience that giving and receiving coincide in the most perfect instances of love: the most generous gift to another is to desire the other, both because it is a recognition, indeed an "existential and ontological affirmation," of the goodness (and so *desirability*) of the other, and also because one cannot give one's being to another except in desire, insofar as desire represents the outward aspiration of a thing's inner being.

In Neoplatonism generally, eros in the true sense is "ascending"; it is a desire of the inferior for the superior.[119] To desire what is inferior is a basic expression of disorder. But by radicalizing, we might say, the "efficient causality" — i.e., the generosity — of the first cause, Dionysius brings to light a paradox: the "movement" by which a creature comes to be, its desire turned toward the good that lies above it, is not only the same movement by which it is itself, but is also the very same by which it shares in God's "descending" generosity to what is below, which means to absolutely everything at all without exception. Interestingly, it is right here at this juncture in Dionysius's account, when he attempts to comprehend the diversity of causal relations in a single unity, that he introduces the word "eros," in the place of the word he had been using, namely, ἐφίημι, presumably because it is more ample than desire simply — more ample, it seems, than even the word "agape," though he also uses that word in this context.[120] Dionysius expresses this complex unity in the following way (because the precise vocabulary is important, the translation here is literal):

> The beautiful and good is to be desired and to be loved erotically and to be loved agapically, and it is by this [the good and beautiful] and for its

118. *DN* IV.7.704B-C.

119. See, e.g., Plotinus, *Ennead* III.5.9: love is always a desire for "the higher [τὸ κρεῖττον]."

120. Dionysius seems to privilege the term "eros" over the term "agape" because of the "ecstatic" quality that comes to more direct expression in it, which gives what we may call the structural aspect of generosity. See *DN* IV.13.712A. Interestingly, in the first line of the passage we quote below, Dionysius places eros in between desire and agape, as if it contains in itself the sense of both as the unity of the two.

> sake that the inferior love erotically the superiors by turning toward them ("epistreptically"), those of the same rank love erotically their peers communionally ("koinonically"), the superiors love erotically the inferiors providentially ("pronoetically"), and each thing erotically loves itself by holding itself together ("synektically"), and all things do and will all the things that they do and will by desiring the good and the beautiful.[121]

There are several things of special significance in this single, complex statement. First, every action and willing is simultaneously due to the good and the beautiful (δι' αὐτὸ) and to the acting and willing of creatures (πάντα . . . ποιεῖ καὶ βούλεται πάντα), the link between the two being desire (τοῦ καλοῦ καὶ τοῦ ἀγαθοῦ ἐφιέμενα), which is the "flip side" of the acting of the beautiful and good. Indeed, Dionysius identifies what is done *by* the beautiful and good and what is done *for its sake:* "καὶ δι' αὐτὸ καὶ αὐτοῦ ἕνεκα." Second, there is a single verb, namely, "they love" (ἐρῶσι), governing all of the activities in the central passage of the long sentence quoted, the different aspects of which are thus indicated, not by a different verb, nor even by a repetition of the same verb with new subjects, which would suggest a new origination of that activity in sequence, but simply a different adverb in each case ("epistreptically," "koinonically," and so forth). This makes clear that the various "activities" are in fact diverse dimensions of one and the same act, namely, love as eros. Eros represents a transcendent (ontological) activity that subsists in the (ontic) diversity of apparently opposed activities of self-love, love of other, desire of the higher, generosity toward the lower, friendship toward the same, and so forth. These dimensions, however distinct from each other at the ontic level, turn out to be inseparable from each other in their depths. It is by reciprocal giving and receiving in love that all things *are,* and this active interaction coincides with the single generous act at the root of their being.

Who is the primary subject of eros? Beyond and supporting the plural subjects, there is an original unity. It is at this point that we arrive at what is most decisive in Dionysius's metaphysics. After the passage cited above, Dionysius takes a crucial step: true reason (ὁ ἀληθῆς λόγος), according to him, "will dare to say" that the "cause of all things" *possesses eros for the world that is caused.*[122] It is perhaps not too much of an exaggeration to say that

121. *DN* IV.10.708A.

122. In the *Divine Names,* Dionysius tends to signal his departure from or, perhaps

this text represents one of the most dramatic moments in the history of Western thought. Plato had associated eros with a lack, specifically in relation to the good and beautiful.[123] Dionysius "reverses" this notion, but without simply overturning it. He says that the cause of all things *loves* (ἐρᾷ) them, not because of any lack, but just the opposite: "by an excess of goodness" (δι' ἀγαθοτητος ὑπερβολὴν). As the cause of all things in the world, God does not lack anything in relation to the world, simply speaking, but the world nevertheless represents *more* than God precisely because of the excess, the "moreness," literally, the "hyperbole," of his goodness. There is some sense in which the world "exceeds" God, but only because God himself is excessive. And if this is the case, the "moreness" of the world is already anticipated by God in his essence, as it were, which means that this "more," paradoxically, does not imply a comparative "less" or a previous lack. Dionysius had shown that desire and generosity, properly understood, are inseparable. If this is the case, it means that God's perfect causality cannot be pure generosity without being at the same time pure desire. As we said, to desire a thing is to affirm its desirability, which is to say, its goodness. We might see this insight into God's erotic goodness as a resolution of the vexing dilemma Plato raises in the *Euthyphro,* either alternative of which entails enormous difficulties: Does God will something because it is good, or is it good because he wills it? Dionysius's response is simply: "yes."

What creation is, along these lines, is as it were the comparative form of affirmation,[124] a giving of the world to itself as something good precisely in its otherness from God: it is good for the world to be. Dionysius describes the act of creation in a bold way as God's being drawn outside of himself by the goodness and beauty of the world: "And we must dare to speak the truth, namely, that, in his beautiful and good eros for all things, the cause of all things, by virtue of the excess of erotic goodness, comes outside of himself [δι' ὑπερβολὴν τῆς ἐρωτικῆς ἀγαθοτητος ἔξω ἑαυτοῦ γίνεται] in the providential acts toward all beings and is touched by goodness and agape and eros, and, abandoning the solitude above all things, comes down to dwell within all things according to the ecstatic excessive power by which he re-

better, his creative appropriation of the Neoplatonic and theological traditions, by the phrase "dare to say."

123. Plato, *Symposium* 201a-b.

124. According to Georg Simmel, "Creation is the comparative of affirmation." *Fragmente und Aufsätze* (München: Drei Masken, 1923), p. 24, cited in Pieper, *Faith — Hope — Love* (San Francisco: Ignatius Press, 1997), p. 170. Pieper interprets this claim in the context of a metaphysics of creation.

mains by himself."[125] Creation, indeed, cannot but be an "ecstatic" (ἐκστατικός) act, insofar as it represents the bringing into being of something that cannot be reduced back to its source, and because eros is a more obviously ecstatic form of love, Dionysius suggests it is in fact a "more divine" term than agape to speak of God's causality. There is, of course, a paradox in saying that God remains in himself by ecstasis, but this paradox follows logically from an understanding of essential goodness as "excessive" by nature. Dionysius gives this nature a succinct formulation in what amounts to his definition of divine eros: "And the divine eros," he says, "is indeed good desire for the good by way of the good [καὶ ἔστι καὶ ὁ θεῖος ἔρως ἀγαθὸς ἀγαθοῦ διὰ τὸ ἀγαθόν]."[126] Divine eros, he says, is the good desiring the good "through" the good, which, in addition to alluding to the Trinitarian nature of God, wonderfully expresses the paradox we have been describing: the first cause is not simply the good in a static sense, but in an excessive, ec-static sense. It is a goodness that has given itself away, which implies a true otherness (or else the good would not be good, i.e., generous), but an otherness that is always already surpassed: the "bridge" between the good in itself and its excess, i.e., the good beyond itself, is itself nothing but the good once again. Eros is thus another name for excessive goodness, or perhaps another name for the inner dynamic of goodness simply.

Insofar as it expresses this inner dynamic, excessive erotic goodness is thus the essence of causality as Dionysius understands it. Dionysius says that what constitutes the causality of every cause is the desire for beauty and goodness,[127] and of course the desire for beauty and goodness is the "flip side" of the erotic generosity of the cause. It is this radical generosity that provides the inner unity of the diverse orders of causality. Heidegger claimed that the unity of the "Roman" notion of causality as efficiency was given in *making,* the imposition of form and finality on inert matter by an external agent, and he contrasted this with the unity of "Greek" causality as φύσις/ποίησις, which is given in a "letting come forth" *(Ver-an-lassen)* of things. Heidegger's concern is to protect the "unconditioned" quality of things' emergence into presence, their showing themselves, coming forth out of themselves as it were into presence, by insisting there is literally no-thing "behind" this emerging, i.e., nothing but Being as self-concealing clearing. To posit an "agent" of the

125. *DN* IV.13.712A-B.

126. *DN* IV.12.709B; IV.10.708B.

127. "All things desire the beautiful and good in every cause [τοῦ καλοῦ καὶ ἀγαθοῦ κατὰ πᾶσαν αἰτίαν πάντα ἐφίεται]." *DN* IV.7.704B.

being of things as maker, to his mind, is to eclipse what is most profound, and while this "forgetting" of being is necessary to metaphysics, and indeed metaphysics itself a necessary *Geschick,* or dispensation of Being, it remains true that thinking is not thus brought to an end with metaphysical causality but rather confronted with a new task, to inquire into the truth of Being as such.

But the classical Christian metaphysical thinker Dionysius reveals that neither of Heidegger's alternatives is an adequate conception of the nature of causality: it is neither the imposition of the subject in technological construction nor the mere standing back, the withdrawal of the subject so that the work may work, may show itself from its own origin. Instead, it is indeed a *making,* an act of "personal" agency — and indeed of an agent that is perfect — that takes the form of a drawing forth of the other, an eliciting of the internal energies, the active participation of the other. Heidegger, to be sure, says many profound things along the lines of a generous eliciting or setting free in his own way, but there is a subtle difference between his conception and that of classical Christianity that makes all the difference in the world. For Heidegger, one allows the other to come forward precisely by stepping back, which leaves in place a dialectical opposition, and inverse relationship, between the self and the other: it is a meditative silence that allows the other to speak, or a kind of "polemic" (from πόλεμος) that provokes the other.[128] For Dionysius, the "cause of all things" gives rise to a substantial world other than himself, not by withdrawing or refusing himself (self-concealing), but rather by giving himself so radically that the other comes forth in some sense "of itself." The giving and receiving is one and the same, a single "cause." God's ecstatic reaching out to the world includes within itself an allowing himself, as the beautiful and good, to be pursued by the world, and his causing of the world is, as it were, the context in which things can, so to speak, "cause" themselves — which in this context therefore means among

128. This is certainly an oversimplification, but the aim is to bring out a central note. Clearly, Heidegger does not use the language of "self" and "other," and so forth. Moreover, the *clearing* of Being is not an empty void, but a generous space, or indeed sheltering *place* that brings things into their own. It shelters, it arranges, and it sets up, and thus gives beings to themselves, as it were. It *enables (ermöglicht)* by caring affection *(mögen).* All of these notes are to be affirmed, and bring out elements of the classical position that have been as it were "forgotten." The question is the extent to which this positive sense can be sustained if Being is denied any positivity at all, i.e., any personal quality as agent, *not* in a merely ontic sense, but ontologically *and* ontically, so to speak, in the manner we are presenting. Heidegger cannot give Being "agential" qualities (giving, sending, and so forth) and at the same time deny any agential character to Being without turning those qualities into empty metaphors, i.e., an ultimately meaningless play of language.

other things to "hold themselves together" in an eros that is at the same time goodness. Indeed, the more comprehensively things are caused, the more they "cause" themselves, because this means they are more fully sharing in their own causation and so have more fully appropriated it as their own. If it is a withdrawal alone that allows things to come forth, their coming forth can only be an ultimately opaque self-assertion — a "mere" self-showing that does not "speak," does not express anything beyond themselves. But if a *positive* giving, if causal goodness and beauty, is what calls things forth and allows them to be, their emergence will be, not a mere self-positing, but simultaneously a generous attraction to what lies beyond themselves and so a genuinely ecstatic event that is simultaneous with their genuine substantiality. As we will see in a moment, this invites thought by virtue of its abundance, its luminosity, rather than its relentless concealment.[129]

The "cause of all things" is thus the efficient cause of the world,[130] not in the "Roman" — i.e., Stoic — sense of agent cause, into which formal and final cause collapse, and outside of which is left matter simply as the *opposite* of cause, but rather as what the Germans would call the "*Inbegriff*" of causality, the perfection of all causality that involves all other causality within itself. It is the cause of all other causality, so to speak, or better: the causality of all cause. "And for its [the beautiful and good's] sake and by it and in it is every exemplary cause, every final cause, every productive cause, every formal cause, and every material cause — in a word, every origin, every integration, and every end."[131] Contrary to Marion's suggestion that Dionysius's notion of creation has nothing to do with Aristotelian causality,[132] Dionysius regularly uses Aris-

129. To be sure, the superabundant generosity *includes* a kind of withdrawal and concealment, but the point is that what gives rise to creatures' bringing themselves about is not *exclusively* this concealment.

130. Dionysius of course precedes the introduction of the term "*causa efficiens*," but it is clear that what he means by divine causality anticipates this "transformative elevation" of the "source of change" cause in Aristotle or the "motor" or "agent" cause of the Stoics. Dionysius will occasionally use the word "αἰτία" in the place of "ἀρχή" in his list of the Aristotelian causes (example), while he will also use the word "cause" to indicate not only the ἀρχή but also the εἶδος, the τέλος, and even the "στοιχεῖον" — which suggests that the "radicalized" or "elevated" ἀρχή is the paradigm of causality that includes within itself all the other dimensions. This is similar to the understanding we find, for example, in Aquinas: in the *Summa Theologiae,* Aquinas describes creation as an efficient cause (I.44.1), but unfolds this simple causality in terms of material causality (44.2), formal (exemplar) causality (44.3), and final causality (44.4).

131. Ref. *DN* IV.10.705D-708A.

132. Marion, *Idol and Distance,* pp. 160-61.

totelian vocabulary, identifying the "cause of all things" with the source, the formal, and the final cause, and, as we see here and on at least two other occasions, includes the material cause as well.[133] This last is especially significant, as we shall see in a moment. The fact that "excessive erotic goodness" is the unity of the causes means that they cannot be interpreted properly in separation from each other, but rather the relation each bears to the others informs its own particular meaning. On the other hand, it is essential to interpret the beautiful and good as the unity *of* the diverse causes, which means as having its proper unfolding — an unfolding that is not a subsequent "act" of the beautiful and good but the essential expression of its inner reality — precisely in their interplay. We cannot grasp the diverse causes except in their unity, nor can we grasp their unity except in the diversity of the causes.

Let us sketch as simply as we can the interrelation among the causes as Dionysius presents them. To be the cause of all things is to be self-giving goodness, since there is nothing else for the absolute first cause to give but itself; to create can only be to share existence, and this is what it means to be good — why, that is, there is a connection between goodness and causality. Since to be source is to give oneself, the "effect," as we have seen, cannot fail to be similar to the cause in its essence, as the scholastic dictum has it: *omnis agens agit sibi simili.* According to Dionysius, the form of all things is a participation in goodness itself, which means that beings are of their essence "good-like." As we have just seen, however, the form can also be described as a thing's holding itself together through erotic love of itself, which means its form is an "efficient cause" of itself.[134] And because their *essence* is defined by beings' sharing in the good, it represents at the same time their perfection and end. But, notice: because this perfection is also ἀρχή, it is an end only by being a beginning; the rest of completion is ultimately the same as the labor of self-giving and desire, and the identity that constitutes the form of things is coincident with the ecstatic character of goodness.

The aspect of material causality is not as obvious in all of this, but a moment's reflection reveals that it is decisive, and indeed indispensable to a proper interpretation of Dionysius on causality. The Neoplatonic tradition associates matter with nonbeing precisely because it equates being with

133. See, e.g., IV.10.705D; IV.7.704B; and IV.18.716A. This "inclusion" of even material causality distinguishes Dionysius, as we will suggest in a moment, from the Neoplatonic tradition generally (as is his wont, he indicates this by the phrase "our argument will dare to say" [IV.7.704B]).

134. It bears remarking that Plato had himself described the causality of goodness in terms of the verb συνεχειν. See *Phaedo* 99c.

form. It is this association that leads Plotinus into the ambiguity of identifying matter with evil,[135] or conversely including it within the real as the lowest level of idea.[136] But Dionysius clarifies this ambiguity by drawing a line that definitively distinguishes the two from each other. For Dionysius, the good, because it exceeds created being as its cause, provides a positive ground for nonbeing of a particular kind, and so allows a positive distinction of matter *both* from evil *and* from form: "Even non-being [τὸ μὴ ὄν] desires it [the beautiful and good] and struggles somehow to be in it and is that which produces the form even of the formless things, and even nonbeing is said to be and indeed is encompassed by the superessentiality of the beautiful and good."[137] And again: "Evil is neither included among the things that are nor among the things that are not, but is even more alien to and distant from the good even than non-being, and is even more nonexistent."[138] One of the implications of this insight is that it gives room to the positive otherness of creation.[139] It is quite clear that difference is an effect of the causality of the beautiful and good.[140] In fact, Dionysius presents "Difference" (τὸ ἕτερον) as one of the divine names of God.[141] We could perhaps say that the nonbeing, the "nihil," is that "out of which" creation arises *(creatio ex nihilo)*;[142] it is an indispensable aspect of the good and permanent distinction of the world from God. For Plato, matter is the receptacle in which the forms appear as a "this" or a "that," as distinct from their being a universal "such."[143] In Aristotle, matter is, among other things, the potency that belongs to the individuality of particular substances.[144] With-

135. Plotinus, *Ennead* I.8.8; 1.8.13. Plotinus also identifies matter with nonbeing: e.g., II.4.16.

136. See Plotinus, *Ennead* V.8.7.

137. *DN* IV.18.716A.

138. *DN* IV.19.716D.

139. Plotinus had said, looking at the beauty of the physical cosmos, that the only reproach we can make to this world is that it is not the intellect itself (*Ennead* V.8.8); for Dionysius, even this "not" is no reproach, but a kind of perfection.

140. Dionysius lists "αἱ ἑτερότητες," "differences," as one of the effects of the beautiful and good, just after explaining that God is the cause of nonbeing (*DN* IV.7.704B).

141. *DN* IX.1.909B; IX.5.912D-913B. See Perl, *Theophany*, p. 32.

142. On the meaning of the *nihil* in the doctrine of creation, see Schmitz, *The Gift*, pp. 2-34.

143. See *Timaeus* 49a; 49e-50a.

144. We have no intention here of entering into the discussion of the proposition that matter is the principle of individuation. We are saying simply that matter belongs to individuation as one of its causes, without claiming necessarily that matter alone is the sufficient cause of individuation.

out entering into the tricky question of the precise nature of matter, and the significant differences between Plato and Aristotle on this point, we may simply say here that matter is an essential aspect of the "lying in itself" and apart from others that characterizes physical beings, that which distinguishes beings of the same form from one another.[145] As Parmenides originally understood, nonbeing must in some sense be real if there is in fact to be otherness and difference at all.

Now, it may rightly be objected that Dionysius does not develop this reflection himself, but it is nevertheless the case that he establishes the principle that allows this development. According to Dionysius, the "beyond being-ness" of the Good is the *cause* of even nonbeing. This idea takes on particular significance in the light of Heidegger's critique. To speak metaphorically, we can interpret it precisely as positing the otherness that draws God "out of himself," the otherness that ignites the eros that characterizes the bringing into being of the world. To be sure, Dionysius says it is God's own goodness and beauty that draws him, but as we have insisted it is specifically the *excessiveness* of that goodness, the "moreness" it represents: eros occurs only in relation to what is *other*. What draws God to create is, so to speak, his own goodness and beauty as "already" having been given away. God is also the material cause, or more properly, the source of the material cause, precisely as generously letting the world emerge as other than himself, which is to say, in Dionysius's paradoxical image, as being stirred by the beauty and goodness of the world to create it.

Matter is "nothing" in itself, as it were, but interpreted precisely within the interplay of the causes, it is an essential part of the otherness of the beings that are caused; the positive nonbeing is what allows the form of things to be "not God," i.e., to belong truly to the beings that are caused, and so at the same time what allows beings to be from and for themselves, to be their own source and end. Because the generosity of God, as beautiful and good, includes the nonbeing that belongs to the *self*-being of things, the "cause of all" can be the source of *both* the (transcendent) exemplary cause *and* the (immanent) formal cause at once, which is to say that God's causality presents a goodness that is both something for things to strive after as ever beyond them and a good that lies within them as their very own. Thus, the inclusion of the

145. Dionysius points out, in his discussion of the divine name "Peace," that the desire for peace — i.e., unity with all things — does not at all compromise the rejoicing in opposition, difference, and distinction that belong to the irreducible individuality of each thing. See *DN* XI.3.952B.

material cause in the configuration of the causes, all of which are nothing but an unfolding altogether of the inherent complexity-within-simplicity of goodness at the source of the world, brings to light in a particular way the radical character of the generosity of divine causality, the fact that this cause is so generous that it does not give everything simply "from above," but allows itself also to receive or, better, gives everything so fully that it gives also the capacity to give (back). For Dionysius, the depth of the goodness of the first cause shows itself above all in the desire to be good, to "possess" its goodness, not by clinging to it, so to speak, and simply "rationing it," i.e., dispensing it to creatures with a miserly caution, but only by also receiving the goodness that it is *back* from its own creatures. The good possesses itself only as also receiving itself: as we recall, Dionysius defined God's causal being as divine eros as ἀγαθὸς ἀγαθοῦ διὰ τὸ ἀγαθόν. The "movement" of the good from itself to itself by means of itself passes through, as it were, the entire world. There can be no more radical affirmation of the being of the world than such a generosity, which conveys, we would have to say, a share in its own absoluteness. The world is not a mere negative to God's positive actuality, or a mere positive with respect to Being's self-refusal (nihilation), but is *good* in God's goodness, an irreducible positivity "inside" God's gracious reality. The world does indeed have an "unconditioned" character, i.e., an "uncaused" character, but — quite differently from Heidegger — this is due paradoxically to the unconditionality of its cause, i.e., the unconditionality of divine eros. In other words, there is a gratuity at the ground of the being of all things, but it is not the empty Ab-Grund of Being's ultimate concealment in unconcealment; instead, it is the gratuity of love. For this reason, the gratuity does not present a final limitation on the question "Why?," the finality of the ever-lingering *"Because!" (weilen),* but is an insurpassable "why" that, even so, never ceases to surpass itself with ever greater cause: "And from his fullness we have all received, grace upon grace [χάριν ἀντί χάριτος]" (1 John 1:16).[146]

Heidegger's refusal to accord ultimacy to causality is a kind of echo of the classical notion that one ought "not to inquire into the cause of the first principle."[147] But in Dionysius, the "uncaused" character of the first principle, precisely as eros, paradoxically includes a "being caused" in its own meaning. This is why the gratuity is *full* of reason rather than being simply

146. Cf. St. Paul's description of the "beatific vision": "And we all, with unveiled face, beholding [or: reflecting] the glory of the Lord, are being changed into his likeness from glory to glory [μεταμορφούμεθα ἀπὸ δόξης εἰς δοξαν]" (2 Cor. 3:18). A question: Is the movement from glory to glory a "metamorphosis"? The answer is both yes and no.

147. See Plotinus, *Ennead* V.8.7.

without reason ("whyless"). If we interpret this "being caused" — both with and beyond Dionysius at this point — in a Trinitarian manner, we could say that even creation itself is not an exclusively spontaneous event, but that it too is elicited by an other: the otherness of creation that draws God out of himself, as Dionysius describes it, lies within the otherness already inside of God himself, so that "being caused" comes to acquire an absolute status, however paradoxical this may appear. In this respect, a kind of "being caused" by the world, in the sense of an eros that gives to the world by receiving from it, does not "add" something new to God's immanent nature, but simply re-presents what God always already (i.e., eternally) is. From the perspective of the Trinity, we can affirm a notion of the ultimate cause as a kind of *causa sui,* without, however, sealing the whole inside the perfectly closed system that Heidegger feared in his critique of ontotheology. In fact, the *causa sui* of the Trinitarian exchange of love becomes a final guarantor that the world will never simply close in on itself.

In sum, within a view of the world as an "effect" of absolute love, of excessive erotic goodness, there is no dualistic separation between the uncaused source, on one side, and the wholly caused ("conditional") effects on the other. Instead, there is a proper analogy: the world's receiving of itself in desire shows itself, in a surprising way, to be an image of God's generous eros, and, for that reason, the world reveals itself as having its own proper share in God's "unconditionality."

Knowledge and Wonder

So, what shape do wonder and knowledge take in relation to causality so conceived? As a point of contrast, let us recall here Heidegger's understanding of wonder as the distress of not knowing a way in or out, in which the usual in its entirety reveals itself as unusual, that is, not as already unconcealed, but as presencing, as "arriving," and so as provoking thought. It is the depth of wonder that accounts for the absence of an entry or exit, since it concerns an experience of beings in their Being, in a sense "prior" to the differentiation into being and nonbeing, which occurs at the ontic level. There is no fixed place to stand; one is caught up "in the midst" of beings. For the same reason, this experience is in tension with the representational reason *(Vorstellung)* that thinks in terms of causes and explanations, for this sort of reason subordinates the unconcealment of truth to the correctness of judgment concerning beings that are true. In this case, the clarity and certainty of knowledge represent a kind of haven from the distress of not knowing a way in or out. In order to recover the experience of wonder, one has to trace one's concepts back to their origin, which means to re-view them, as it were, from within the clearing of Being, and ultimately to inquire into the clearing itself. In our age, this requires an entry into wonder from the new beginning in the abandonment of beings by Being. Let us note that, while Heidegger seeks a recovery of the temporality of Being, wonder for him has an oddly static quality to it, a kind of Buddhistic dispassionate stillness, which distinguishes it from the classical notion: one cannot move forward, for this would entail a conceptual grasp of beings rather than a "pure acknowledgment" of their arrival; and at the same time one cannot move backward, for this entails the restraint of terror at the abandonment of Being and so once again the loss of wonder.

The notion of wonder that one can derive from Dionysius[148] shares with Heidegger the sense of an acknowledgment of beings in their Being, as "presencing," but it does so in continuity with the classical association of wonder with desire, specifically, as a desire for knowledge of causes. Or, to come at it from the opposite direction, a Dionysian notion of wonder shares with the tradition the association of wonder with knowledge of causes, but it does so while affirming with Heidegger the "unconditioned," the *ne plus ultra,* quality of the experience. To understand how this is so, we must first come to see what Dionysius means by knowledge, which he describes in chapter VII under the divine names of wisdom, mind, and reason. As we might guess, the paradigm of knowledge, for Dionysius, is given in God's knowledge of his creatures. This is, of course, not a knowledge of causes, as human knowledge is, but not because it has no relationship to causality. Quite to the contrary, divine knowledge is *identical* with causality: "For if God shares existence with all beings in one cause, in this same single causality he will know all things as being from him and having preexistence in him, and he will not receive knowledge of those beings from them, but he will be the one who supplies [χορεγός: literally, he will be the 'chorus-leader'] the knowledge of each to each and of the others to the others."[149] God's knowledge of things *is* their being, it is the ontological principle that holds them together; Dionysius speaks of God "knowing and holding together [εἰδὼς

148. It is to be noted that Dionysius does not himself speak of "wonder" in the *Divine Names,* though of course what he describes therein coincides with the notion as we have been interpreting it. Dionysius presents the knowing of God as a unity of *gnosis* and *agnosis* (*DN* VII.3.872A); we are reflecting here on the implications for knowing more generally.

149. *DN* VII.2.869B.

καὶ συνέχων] all things in a single comprehensive causality" (VII.2.869B), a causality, as we know, that includes not only the formal cause, which is signaled by the two participles here,[150] but also the efficient, final, and material causes of things.

There are three things to note about this in the present context. First, there is no opposition, here, between knowledge of things and the event-character of their arrival into presence; instead, the knowing is the giving of their arrival, so to speak. Second, things have an intelligibility that is radically distinct from God, even while remaining wholly unified with that intelligibility, because of the causal character — which means, as we have seen, the radically generous character — of the knowledge that brings them into being. Nietzsche raises an important question when he slyly remarks that there is something "indecent" about divine omniscience.[151] Dionysius's view of the causal character of divine knowledge preserves a distance even in its perfect intimacy. Third, the simultaneity of intimacy and distance, of knowledge and the emergence of things from out of themselves, means that the clarity, the absolute stability of the intelligibility of things, is not in any tension with the mystery of their unconcealment. This latter is rather given in and with the clarity of their form.

It is because divine knowledge is identical with divine causality that human knowing may be defined as a grasp of causes. To know the causes of a thing, in this case, does not mean referring it to some "already true" being outside of it as an explanation. Rather, the knowability is the causality of things, and the cause is their ontological principle, which is "inside" them. Knowing thus means entering into the intimate heart of a being, making contact, as it were, with its essence, the act whereby it subsists and its subsisting act. Now, we saw above the complex-simplicity of causality, as Dionysius

150. Dionysius often describes God's causality as presenting the beginning (ἀρχὴ), the "cohesive power" (συνεχής), and the end (τέλος) of all things, signaling the efficient, the formal, and the final cause (see, e.g., *DN* IV.4.700A). The word εἰδὼς, of course, is related to εἶδος. Note that, in contrast to the static interpretation of the Platonic form that one finds in Heidegger, form for Dionysius is not a (mere) object of vision, but is at the same time, and more fundamentally, an activity: God's creative act of *knowing* — and all that it implies — is *what* we know in our knowing of things.

151. Friedrich Nietzsche, *Die fröhliche Wissenschaft*, p. 352: "We no longer believe that truth is still truth once its veils have been drawn back; we have lived too much to believe this. Today, we take it to be a matter of decency [*Schicklichkeit*] not to want to see everything naked, not to want to be present everywhere, to understand and 'know' everything. 'Is it true that God is present everywhere?,' a little girl asked her mother: 'I think that's indecent' — a hint for philosophers!"

understands it, the goodness and beauty a thing simultaneously *is,* and *seeks,* and *offers.* Knowledge, as an intimacy with this causality, will betray the same multifaceted unity. The erotic goodness, and good eros, that holds a thing together as what it is is inseparably united with the transcendence of goodness that it desires and gives, which means that the substantiality of its intelligible form is simultaneous with the translucence of its being from and for others. To know a thing in this way, then, is more intimate than the simple grasp of an object, because it is a *joining with* the being in its seeking its cause, and in the self-showing that is a generous self-giving. Moreover, knowledge is at the same time more modest than the *a priori* limitation to reason that would separate what is known from the real reality of the being of things (the division of phenomena from noumena) because it receives the self-showing, the intelligible truth, as a self-*giving,* which means as arriving from its own source, from a self-possessed origin. One does not simply take what is immediately given in the self-showing, but patiently attends to the being of the thing, the whole of it, that is offered *in* the specific "glimpse," as it were, of what is shown. Intelligibility, as a real self-communication, is received by being known and known by being gratefully received. Knowing, too, then becomes a generous self-giving, and the act of knowing comes to reveal itself as genuinely analogous to an exchange of love. If wonder is a seeking of causes, and knowledge is a discovery of causes, these two coincide in the complex-simplicity of causality as Dionysius presents it.

According to a typical interpretation of Aristotle, while we can inquire into a substance as a form-matter composite so as to discern the intelligible form, we cannot inquire beyond the form, once discerned, insofar as it is a "simple term." As this interpretation suggests, inquiry requires some dimension of difference, even the basic difference between form and matter that would make a substance something other than a simple term. As the Ross translation has it, "Evidently, then, in the case of simple terms no inquiry or teaching is possible; our attitude toward such things is other than that of inquiry."[152] For Dionysius, by contrast, simplicity is not exclusive of difference.

152. See Aristotle, *Metaphysics* VII.17.1041b9-11. Vincent Carraud also interprets this passage thus; see *Causa sive ratio,* pp. 53-54. In fact, however, the Greek does not say "ἕτερος ἤ" but "ἕτερος τρόπος τῆς ζητήσεως" — in other words, not "something other than inquiry," but "a different kind of inquiry." The *different* inquiry he intends here is a move from "internal" causes (form/matter) to "external" causes (efficient/final causes) in our interpretation of a thing. This is why Aristotle turns from form to an exploration of the potentiality and actuality of form. The question for us is whether this moves the mind *away* from the simple term, or if this pursuit belongs to the intelligibility of the simple term (which would mean

For him, the form, the "what" of a thing, is not simply a discrete object. Instead, its definitiveness includes within itself the difference of its source and end. Concretely, this means, for example, that the "what" of a bird cannot be separated from its "that" and its "why." There is no end, in other words, to the surprise of the whatness; one can never "get over" what a bird is, and there is no reason why one should. The mystery of its origin is *inside* the clarity of the concept and belongs to its intelligibility. This is not a mystification; the surprise is not an empty stupefaction. Instead, it coincides with a real, certain, in principle even unshakeable grasp of the intelligibility of the bird, and increases with the certainty of the grasp. It is a *deep* knowing of the bird, but a knowing that is always also a receiving, a letting be, and so a wondering. This interpretation of form allows us to reconcile Aquinas's famous claim that "no philosopher has ever been able completely to know the essence of even a single fly"[153] with his statement that the "knowing soul penetrates to the essence of a thing."[154] According to the perspective we are advancing here, the knowing soul's penetration to the essence of a thing is a going out into something that remains greater than the knowing soul. Note how different this is from Heidegger, even from within a similarity: the usual is seen here in its unusualness, but this is not a moorless distress. It is not a standing out into the nothing, a sort of suspension in the Ab-Grund. Instead, the unusualness lies *inside* the usual, even as it unfolds beyond the usual into genuine ontological depth. Whenever one grasps the usual, the unusual is so to speak always already inside this, and so one does not need to "let go" and turn in some other direction in order to enter into wonder: one needs instead to deepen one's grasp. There is a sure footing here, a place to stand, namely, the clear intelligibility of what is given to know. But this is a footing that allows, one might say, an even deeper spring into mystery. This wonder is shot through with desire, and indeed a non-narcissistic desire, because it is constantly brought beyond itself in genuine fulfillment. It is shot through with desire, quite simply, because it is a participation in "excessive erotic goodness," the causality that makes all things be what, how, and why they are.

One might object that what we are presenting here is an entirely equivocal notion of causality, which, if it may have some connection with an ancient sense of cause, has nothing at all to do with the modern use of the

---

the term is after all "not so simple"). Whatever ambiguity might remain in Aristotle's thought on the matter is certainly removed in Dionysius's account.

153. Aquinas, *In symb. apost.* 1 (see Pieper, *Leisure*, p. 110).

154. Aquinas, *ST* I-II.31.5.

term. This objection, however, misses one of the crucial points being made here. To be sure, "causality" has acquired a fairly banal meaning in science, as we already discussed in the previous two chapters, as the imposition of a quantity of force or energy, and more generally as change produced through direct contact. But if we abandon causality to this banal sense and attempt to think of God's relation to the world in noncausal terms, then we risk separating knowledge and wonder, privileging a kind of mystical ecstasis over the cold calculation of causal thinking. What we are arguing for here, instead, is that the "unusuality" of transcendent causality needs to be rediscovered *within* the "usualness" of the mundane notion of cause, that this latter, in other words, ought to be reconnected with the tradition at its source. Dionysius does not offer the "beautiful and the good" as a special kind of causality that is unrelated to other notions of cause, but rather refers to it as the *perfect cause* (αἰτία παντελής).[155] In other words, it is what provides the ultimate meaning of causality, which is operative in all cause. *Goodness and beauty is the causality in all cause* — whether the efficient, formal, material, or final. As he puts it, "all things desire the beautiful and good *in every cause*,"[156] and, as we know, the desire is also the self-communication of beauty and goodness. Every causal event is in fact an expression of beauty and goodness, even if it is not recognized as such, and all knowledge of any sort whatsoever, even the most mundane kind, to the extent that it is knowledge at all, is a glimpse of causality, a participation in beauty and goodness. If this sounds strange to our ears, it is arguably the most traditional view of causality, a tradition begun by Plato's association of causality with the good. The compendium of classical thought on causality compiled by an anonymous Arabic author and widely commented on in the Middle Ages, came to be known as the *Liber de causis*, the "Book of Causes," but it had a different original title: the *Liber de expositione bonitatis purae*, the "Book of the Exposition of Pure Goodness."[157] Dionysius's celebration of beauty and goodness as the causality of all causes is simply a particularly profound articulation of an insight that belongs to what might be called the perennial philosophy.

Reconnecting causality with this tradition would have many implications for thinking in science, which we cannot explore here, but we may nevertheless make two observations. First, taking beauty and goodness as "per-

155. *DN* IV.4.700B.

156. *DN* IV.7.704B. Emphasis added.

157. See Vincent A. Guagliardo's "Introduction" to Aquinas, *Commentary on the Book of Causes*, p. ix.

fect causality" and the causality of every cause allows a properly analogical notion of causality, within which the cause-effect thinking in science would have a place, but a place that is integrated into the more comprehensive context of meaning rather than isolated from it. In this case, even physical causality would open up as full of meaning, and the wonder that scientists so often talk about in personal accounts of their work but that rarely presents itself in the content of that work could find a place inside the rigor of scientific thinking.[158] Second, an analogical notion of causality founded on the simple-complexity of beauty and goodness would shift the center of scientific thinking. The determinism of simple mechanical relations is often taken as a paradigm of causality, and so as an instance of what can be more properly known. Nonmechanistic relations are then either reduced to this insofar as they are made objects of knowledge, or set aside as "subjective." The perspective offered by Dionysius flips this paradigm. God is most perfectly knowable, because he is the perfection of causality. The kind of self-causality that one finds in life, and even more evidently in personhood, reveals itself as a fuller participation in beauty and goodness, and so a more perfect example of causality. A person, then, is more intelligible than a mechanical event, more completely knowable, not because there is less mystery, but precisely because there is more. A purely mechanical event, by contrast, is both less intelligible and less mysterious.

What all of this means is that wonder is not the point of departure for a change that ends in knowledge. Instead, *ignorance* is the point of departure, which of course is never total or else, as Plato observed, it would have no impetus for attaining knowledge. This starting point is characterized by wonder only to the extent that it is also already in some sense a knowing, and the wonder increases as the knowledge does. In his *Itinerarium mentis in Deum,* Bonaventure speaks of the mind's elevation *"in admirationem"* — not "in wonder," as it is often translated,[159] but *into* wonder: wonder is the place into which the mind is brought, specifically through the illumination

158. On this, see the passages from Marco Bersanelli, "Wonder and Knowledge: Scientific Investigation and the Breadth of Human Reason," cited in David L. Schindler, "The Given as Gift: Creation and Disciplinary Abstraction in Science," *Communio* 38 (Spring 2011): 52-102; here, 63-66, nn. 13 and 15.

159. St. Bonaventure, *The Mind's Road to God,* trans. George Boas (New York: Macmillan, 1985), book V, section 7, p. 37. Moreover, in the conclusion of question 6 of his *Disputed Questions on the Knowledge of Christ,* Bonaventure describes the ecstatic knowing that occurs in the eschaton as continuous in some sense with earthly wonder, and concludes that "wonder has a place not only in via but in patria." I owe these references to my colleague Kevin Hughes.

of knowledge.[160] This knowledge is a wondering, for Bonaventure, because what is known, in this case, is the paradoxical unity of opposites found in the mystery of the Trinity: communicability and individuality, oneness and plurality, intimacy and mission, and so forth. Because the being of created things, however, is in a similar way constituted by irreducible tensions, as we have seen, what Bonaventure says of the mind's relation to God might be said in an analogous way of the mind's relation to everything created by God: the elevation of the mind in the event of the truth of things is at once an elevation into knowledge and into wonder, because the grasp of a thing is a sort of suspension that arises from the essential tension between irreducibly different aspects joined in a unity.

What are these aspects? Insofar as causality is beauty and goodness, there is a coincidence between things causing themselves, emerging into presence from themselves in a relatively absolute way, and their doing so by virtue of an ultimate cause. Second, there is a coincidence between the mysterious, inexhaustible depths of beings and their "adequate" self-showing in concepts. Third, there is a coincidence between the self-showing of things and their being known by what is other than they. And finally, there is a coincidence, in the knower that receives the self-showing, between the act of reason and the will or desire. At each of these points, the coincidence does not eliminate the abiding difference, which is what makes the event of truth inexhaustible. Now, it is not an accident that Hans Urs von Balthasar refers to these various coincidences as constitutive of the reality of *beauty.* To see the world in causal terms is to encounter it first under the sign of beauty. In chapter three, we traced in some detail the itinerary that leads from this initial encounter in beauty to truth.

Wonder as Ultimate

Let us, in conclusion, return to Goethe's claim that wonder is the "highest" that man can attain. We have seen that wonder can be eclipsed in two different directions: either by closing its questions with an answer in the form of what we called in chapter four a "possessive" notion of knowledge, or by closing its questions through a refusal to answer, by limiting it with the "*Because!*" It can be held open only if questioning receives a positive answer that is, in itself, inexhaustible. In this case, we have suggested, wonder does not

160. See, e.g., *DN* VI.6.

represent an imperfection with respect to the perfection of knowledge, but rather coincides with that perfection. Instead of interpreting wonder as a species of fear that holds one back from reality, we may see it as a positive expression of the fullness of reality, as the good itself in a certain respect.

And this leads us to the final step. If wonder in its most proper sense is not a function of imperfection, but rather coincides with knowledge, then there is no reason to deny this "highest" state of God. Plato had said that the gods do not love wisdom, do not "philosophize," because they *are* wise; indeed, they do not have eros at all, because the desire it represents depends on some lack. If God *is* the good, he does not desire it. But we saw that Dionysius reversed this idea, interpreting eros, not as a lack, but as an excess, a paradoxical "more" without any correlative "less." If the divine knowledge is identical with divine causality, which in turn is of its essence "excessive erotic goodness," does it not follow that, just as God's generous bringing the world into being includes within itself an allowing the world to emerge as other — in other words, he gives in the form of receiving what he gives from the other — so, too, his productive knowing includes in itself a wonder, a kind of surprise at the truth of the world, which is a receiving of his own truth from another? In this case, he gives things their intelligibility *also* in the form of receiving it from them as other.[161]

This, of course, is possible only if God's self-knowledge is itself a perfect wonderment, which becomes conceivable if God is a Trinity, if the simplicity of his being does not exclude the "drama" of interpersonal love. Aquinas says that the word "cause" is not appropriate to describe the Trinitarian processions: "the term *cause* seems to mean diversity of substance, and dependence of one from another,"[162] but he also says that causality is the *ad extra* image of procession.[163] We might in this case interpret the "diversity" implied by cause not as a diversity of substance but analogously here as a perfect diversity of personhood, in the perfect unity of substance. The goodness that we have seen is the essence of productive causality would in this case have its paradigm in the Father's begetting of the Son, in which he gives all, and at the "same time" receives all back. If this is true, we could say in an

161. We would therefore have to qualify Dionysius's repeated claims that God does not "learn from things" but gives them their intelligibility in the same way that Dionysius qualifies God's goodness as eros. This is *true,* but not the whole truth, or at least not exclusively so.

162. *ST* 1.33.1ad1.

163. Aquinas says that "the processions of the Persons are the type of the productions of creatures" (*ST* 1.45.6).

analogous way: the Father knows the Son, and this knowledge, which is the generosity of the Son as *perfectly* other, is at once a "wonder" at the Son,[164] and this knowing wonder and wondrous knowing transpires in the truth of the Holy Spirit, who sounds the depths of the mystery of God. If our knowing is a participation in God's knowledge, it is also the case that our wonder is a sharing — distant, to be sure — in the wonder that belongs to God, and that he has given in the excess of his goodness. Only thus can we say that wonder is the highest that man can achieve: because it reveals itself to be a gift of God's own inner life.

164. Of course, it is essential to keep constantly in mind that this wonder would be *analogous* to (and so remain infinitely different from) the human experience of wonder, which is never without some connection to ignorance.

PART THREE

God and Reason

8 The Problem of the Problem of Ontotheology

The question that Heidegger raises at the end of a seminar on Hegel given in 1957,[1] namely, "Wie kommt der Gott in die Philosophie?" ("How does the god enter philosophy?"), has been echoing and re-echoing in theology, and even more in Continental philosophy of religion, so incessantly that it may be said to have acquired something like the authority of tradition.[2] To be sure, on its face the question simply asks after the relationship between God and human thinking, or how and to what extent God is accessible to reason, but Heidegger himself raises the question as a problem specifically within the context of the profound and extensive critique of Western metaphysics that we explored in the last chapter. The question, How does the god enter philosophy?, he explains, "leads back to the question, What is the origin of the onto-theological essential constitution of metaphysics?" (*ID*, 56). As we will see more fully below, God's entering — or perhaps we ought to say his being dragged — into the ambit of human thinking is the determining event in the Western metaphysical tradition.

Heidegger's charge has provoked a variety of responses: on the one

1. The concluding lecture, titled "The Onto-Theo-Logical Constitution of Metaphysics" and delivered 24 February 1957, was published together with a lecture called "The Principle of Identity," in *Identität und Differenz* (Pfullingen: Verlag Günther Neske, 1957). References to this essay will be drawn from the English translation: *Identity and Difference*, trans. Joan Stambaugh (hereafter: *ID*) (Chicago: University of Chicago Press, 1969).

2. Anthony Godzieba observes that Heidegger's "analysis of ontotheology marks an epochal shift which has affected not only the intellectual history of the West but the history of the Catholic theology of God as well. It acts as a marker, dividing that history into periods of 'before' and 'after.'" "Prolegomena to a Catholic Theology of God Between Heidegger and Postmodernity," *Heythrop Journal* 40 (1999): 319-39; here, 320.

hand, the question has been welcomed by those who wish to be relieved, once and for all, of what has been experienced as the oppressive burden of religion (and specifically Christianity), insofar as its unmasking of the "theology" latent in the philosophical tradition opens up the possibility of (what presents itself as) more radical, and radically free, questioning. On the other hand, those who do not wish to be deprived of their faith by this unmasking tend either to embrace Heidegger's "methodological atheism"[3] as a way of purifying faith of reason's apparently incorrigible habits of setting up for itself false idols, or they attempt to show that Heidegger's critique of ontotheology does not, in fact, apply to certain key figures in the Western tradition (for example, Dionysius,[4] Bonaventure,[5] and even Aquinas[6]), however just its judgment may be regarding the conventional reception of these figures. The point of excepting these figures is for the most part to enable a renewed appropriation, rather than critical abandonment, of the Western tradition.

The present chapter addresses itself to those in this latter group, who seek to preserve the integrity of faith, whether it be with the *help* of Heidegger's critique or *in spite of* it (i.e., showing the limitation of his critique in relation to particular thinkers). We wish, in the following pages, to raise a question regarding the question itself — to ask, that is, whether the terms in which Heidegger poses the question permit a satisfactory response, regardless of the eventual content of the response. As is no doubt already becoming clear, our thesis is that they do not, and that the engagement with Heidegger's question of ontotheology threatens to impoverish our notion of reason and to render a genuine *Christian* faith in God impossible precisely to the extent that it allows Heidegger to set the terms of the engagement. If we seek to save the transcendent mystery of God from the light of reason by forcing him to retreat into the darkness of the unknown, we risk depriving God of intelligible significance and therefore any *real* bearing in the world; making faith ulti-

3. See Merold Westphal, *Overcoming Ontotheology: Toward a Postmodern Christian Faith* (New York: Fordham University Press, 2001), pp. 10, 38-39.

4. Merold Westphal, *Transcendence and Self-Transcendence: On God and the Soul* (Bloomington: Indiana University Press, 2004), pp. 93-141.

5. Kevin Hughes, "Remember Bonaventure? (Onto) Theology and Ecstasy," *Modern Theology* 19, no. 4 (2003): 529-45.

6. Jean-Luc Marion, "Saint Thomas d'Aquin et l'onto-théo-logie," *Revue Thomiste* 1 (1995): 31-66. See also Marion's preface to the English translation of *Dieu sans l'être,* in which he "recants" what appears to be an initial acceptance of the charge against Aquinas in the original text. *God without Being,* trans. Thomas A. Carlson (Chicago: University of Chicago Press, 1991), esp. pp. xxii-xxiv.

mately arbitrary, accidental, and sentimental; and casting a shadow on the "positive" aspects of God's revelation, which include the dogmatic and institutional dimensions of the Church that have traditionally been understood to be an inseparable extension of the Incarnation. In other words, if the "true" God is the hidden one, accessible only to the mystical labors of negative theology or to the moments of nonrational ecstasis, then revelation, and the particularity of Christianity that stands and falls with it, will tend to be taken for the dispensable matter the Enlightenment considered it to be.

Our thesis, thus, is that the question, "How does the god enter philosophy?" with the critique of ontotheology it implies, is something like the one put to the young Stephen Dedalus by his jeering classmates, namely, the question whether he kisses his mother: it is a question that cannot be answered one way or the other without compromise. The question, therefore, ought to be refused, at least in the terms in which Heidegger frames it, and whatever is of genuine value in the question, we will propose, ought to be recast within a question that is more radical because it begins in fact with the *prius* of God: How does man enter into theology? In other words, our first question ought not to be how we keep our thinking free from (presumption regarding) God, but how God is able to raise *even our* minds to participate in the "theo-logic" of his own mystery.

To be sure, the issues we allude to here cannot be settled or even sufficiently explored in a brief chapter such as this. Our aim, instead, is to set into relief some of what is at stake in the question of ontotheology, and to do so in a provocative manner, making a plea in the end for the recovery of a more robust and theologically oriented notion of reason. To that end, we will first give a very brief sketch of Heidegger's critique of ontotheology and the significance this critique has for him in relation to the question concerning God. We will then turn to see what Hegel, whom Heidegger presents as a paradigm of ontotheology, has to say on this theme by considering his preliminary reflections on the relationship between God and human thinking that formed the introduction to his *Lectures on the Philosophy of Religion.*[7] While Heidegger's criticism of Hegel needs to be affirmed, we will see that Hegel in turn shows up certain problematic implications of Heidegger's position. We will then offer an assessment of these two critiques in relation to

7. We will be drawing freely from the "Introduction" to his lectures as presented in his manuscript as well as in the notes from his 1824 and 1827 series: *Lectures on the Philosophy of Religion,* vol. 1: *Introduction and the Concept of Religion,* ed. Peter Hodgson (Berkeley: University of California Press, 1984).

one another, in order to suggest that what seems to be an opposition between them — Heidegger seeks to "free God" from metaphysical thinking, while Hegel insists that shielding God from metaphysical thinking leads to a problematic dualism — is merely apparent, since their differing judgments are due to what amounts to a similar assumption regarding the nature of reason. Finally, we will describe an alternative to this assumption offered by the thought of Hans Urs von Balthasar, which seems in principle able to provide a means of avoiding the pitfalls of *both* ontotheology *and* its critique.

It should be noted that the following criticism of the project of overcoming ontotheology is not intended to be a general assessment of Heidegger, who has opened up perhaps more avenues of fruitful reflection than nearly any other philosopher in the twentieth century. It is intended, instead, to be a caution regarding the "use" of his thinking in theology and the philosophy of religion. Moreover, an adequate assessment of Heidegger in this respect would require a more thorough treatment from the perspective of dogmatic, systematic, and fundamental theology; we offer here simply some initial philosophical reflections suggesting why such an assessment appears to be necessary, to complement our discussion of his critique of Western metaphysics in the last chapter.

Heidegger: Freeing God from Being

The term "ontotheology," though apparently first used by Kant,[8] initially appears in Heidegger's work in the new introduction he added in 1949 to the lecture "What Is Metaphysics?" which was first published in 1929.[9] In this new introduction, he is inquiring into the essence of metaphysics through a reflection on seminal texts from Aristotle. According to Heidegger, metaphysics is

8. Kant distinguishes between "cosmotheology" and "ontotheology," as the two theological sub-branches of the transcendental theology that thinks its object, the "supreme being," through reason alone (as opposed to the natural theology that thinks the supreme being on the basis of a concept borrowed from nature). While cosmotheology proceeds on the basis of some experience, ontotheology proceeds from a "mere concept." See the *Critique of Pure Reason*, A 631-32 = B 659-60.

9. This introduction was published in English as "The Way Back into the Ground of Metaphysics," in *Existentialism from Dostoevsky to Sartre*, ed. Walter Kaufmann (New York: Meridian Books, 1956), pp. 206-21. Heidegger had already made brief allusion to the concept of ontotheology in a typescript on "Nietzsche's Metaphysics," written in the second half of 1940. See Heidegger, *Nietzsche*, vol. 3: *The Will to Power as Knowledge and as Metaphysics*, ed. David Farrell Krell (San Francisco: Harper, 1987), p. 241.

essentially concerned with ὄν ᾗ ὄν, being qua being, which he takes to mean: the *beingness* of beings *(die Seiendheit des Seienden)*, i.e., "being" understood specifically on the basis of that which exists, as a generalization of what makes a thing a being ("the οὐσία of the ὄν"). It thus seeks to grasp being, or beings, not as this or that particular being, but as a whole, which is why metaphysics can claim to be the roots for the tree of the human sciences that study beings in various particular respects.[10] In pursuing its aim, metaphysics moves in two directions at once: on the one hand, it represents "the totality of beings as such with an eye to their most universal traits (ὄν καθόλου, κοινόν); but at the same time also the totality of beings as such in the sense of the highest and therefore divine being (ὄν καθόλου, ἀκρότατον, θεῖον)" ("Way Back," 217). There is a link, then, between the universality and "foundationality" aimed at by metaphysical thinking and its latent theological character: we might say that in seeking the "best" sense of being as a way of understanding beings as a whole it seeks being in the best sense, namely, as God. After showing the latent theological character of metaphysics in Aristotle — which indicates, as he observes, that God does not enter philosophy only with the Christian appropriation of the Greeks, but is there as soon as philosophy becomes metaphysical — Heidegger goes on to say that Christians ought in fact to have been the first to repudiate the entry: "Will Christian theology make up its mind one day to take seriously the word of the apostle and thus also the conception of philosophy as foolishness?" ("Way Back," 218; cf. 1 Cor. 1:20).

In order to see why Heidegger thinks that Christianity ought to take a distance from metaphysics (which is not to say that metaphysics ought simply to be rejected),[11] it is good to turn to his more detailed account in the lecture, "The Onto-Theo-Logical Constitution of Metaphysics." It is here that Heidegger casts the issue in terms of the question we mentioned at the outset, namely, How does the god enter into philosophy? In continuity with

10. Heidegger begins this introduction with an illuminating reference to the image Descartes presents in a letter to the person who translated his *Principia Philosophiae* into French. Heidegger uses the image to bring to light the more fundamental question regarding the ground in which the roots have their place and receive their nourishment. See "Way Back," p. 207.

11. Indeed, Heidegger tends to use the term "Verwindung" rather than "Überwindung" in this context, intending an "overcoming" that incorporates rather than eliminates. See "Overcoming Metaphysics," in *The End of Philosophy*, trans. Joan Stambaugh (New York: Harper, 1973), pp. 84-110. In *Zur Seinsfrage*, Heidegger says that the "Verwindung" of metaphysics is in fact an opening into its essence, which allows us to *restore* metaphysics. See *Zur Seinsfrage*, in *Wegmarken*, 3rd printing (Frankfurt am Main: Klostermann, 1996), pp. 385-426; here, 416-17.

his earlier description, Heidegger claims in this lecture that it is the very nature of metaphysical thinking to become theological; in other words, precisely because it is occupied with the thinking of being qua being (which is to be contrasted with Heidegger's own "being-historical" thinking *(seynsgeschichtliches Denken)* that thinks the *difference* between being and beings),[12] metaphysics is *defined* by the entry of the god into philosophy. To put it yet another way, metaphysics is the name of that manner of thinking which *forgets* its radical temporality and finitude and thereby confuses itself with what is objectified as "transcendent," i.e., elevated outside of time and change (and in that respect divinized). But if this is the case, the god that manages to fit himself into philosophy, on philosophy's terms, hardly warrants the deference due to the "godly God" *(der göttliche Gott).* As we see here, the ontotheological god enters philosophy precisely as a means of understanding the "beingness" of beings, and thus is, so to speak, enlisted to serve the project of rendering all of being intelligible, opening the whole of reality to the grasp of (calculative) thought. As part of this project, the god is named principally by his function: *causa sui.* Because he is the "self-grounding," the god becomes the ground for everything else. In other words, the god becomes that which explains everything, and he is summoned first of all by the need for an explanation.

Though they emphasize different aspects of Heidegger's critique, we see that there is a convergence between Merold Westphal's and Laurence Hemming's summary statement of that critique. According to Westphal:

> God is at the beck and call of human understanding, a means to its end of making the whole of being intelligible in keeping with the principle of reason. In order to place the world at the disposal of human theory (and practice), it becomes necessary to place God at our disposal as well.[13]

According to Hemming,

> [t]he God of metaphysics is . . . that being who precedes, founds, universalizes, and omnitemporalizes every possible being and time that my "I"

12. "Since metaphysics thinks of being as such as a whole, it represents beings in respect of what differs in the difference, and without heeding the difference as difference" (*ID*, p. 70).

13. Westphal, *Overcoming Ontotheology,* p. 12.

> might ever be, *Ens,* but only as *ens infinitum,* God, as given in metaphysics, but nothing other than a projected and transcendent "I," myself, reflected back as wholly alien to me.[14]

The Onto-Theo-Logical constitution of metaphysics may thus be said to coincide with the reduction of truth — originally the event of unconcealment: ἀ-λήθεια, or φύσις — to (self-) certainty, however unrecognizable the self may have become in the transformation. In any event, the final result of the metaphysical project is a forgetfulness of the truly sacred. As Heidegger famously remarks, after his explanation of the origins of the ontotheological god, "Before the *causa sui,* man can neither fall to his knees in awe nor can he play music and dance before this god" (*ID,* 72).

When Heidegger therefore *insists* that philosophy is a-theism, it is apparently not because he wishes to *reject* God, but rather to refuse the absorption of theology into philosophy — the absorption that constitutes metaphysics — and for that very reason is able to open a sense for the holy, to open space for prayer and for faith, without, that is, deciding anything beforehand about what is to occupy this space. As both Hemming and Westphal have claimed in different ways, Heidegger's "atheism" is essentially a repetition of Kant's denying knowledge in order to make room for faith. In Heidegger's own words, "The god-less thinking which must abandon the god of philosophy, god as *causa sui,* is thus perhaps closer to the godly God. Here this means only: god-less thinking is more open to Him than onto-theologic would like to admit" (*ID,* 72).[15] It is crucial to note that, for Heidegger, this "god-lessness" is not a movement either toward or away from faith, but is rather the clearing of a space that would presumably allow faith to arrive, if and when it does, as more authentically itself: a more faithful faith.

This is, indeed, a powerful critique, and it is clear why Hegel would present for Heidegger a paradigm of ontotheology. Although Hegel, like Heidegger, rejects representational thinking *(Vorstellen)* as an inadequate form of thought, he nevertheless ultimately identifies being — that which is both first and last — with the Absolute Idea *(Idee).* At the same time, as

14. Laurence Paul Hemming, *Heidegger's Atheism: The Refusal of a Theological Voice* (Notre Dame: University of Notre Dame Press, 2002), p. 208. Cf. also his essay, "Nihilism: Heidegger and the Grounds of Redemption," in *Radical Orthodoxy* (New York: Routledge, 1999), p. 102.

15. In the translation, "the divine God" has been replaced by the more literal "the godly God."

Heidegger points out, Hegel remarks in his discussion of the proper starting point for the *Science of Logic* that "*God* would have the uncontested right to have the beginning made with him."[16] Here we see a confirmation of Heidegger's judgment: Hegel seeks to give an account (λόγος) of the whole of reality in the most comprehensive way possible *(science* of *logic),* which leads him to seek the most original starting point, the highest standpoint, namely, Being. This standpoint, which is both first and last, origin and end, insofar as it is the highest, is at once separated from all things (perfectly empty) and for that very reason inclusive of all things (fully determinate). After determining this ultimate and primordial principle, Hegel naturally — indeed, as he confesses, *unavoidably* — gives it the name "God." If Hemming is correct that our thinking is always inescapably *ours,* and therefore that Hegel's thinking is inescapably *Hegel's,* then Hegel's "onto-theos" is in fact the absolutization of Hegel's own finite being. The upshot of Hegel's approach, from this Heideggerian perspective, is that God, indeed, becomes a servant of the human project of rendering the world fully intelligible, so much so that, when all is said and done, even God himself ends up with, so to speak, nothing left to hide from the human need to know. In the final form of religion, which fulfills the representation of the whole of reality in order then to be taken up into reason itself, Hegel states forthrightly: "The revealed religion is the revelatory or manifest religion because God has become wholly manifest in it. Here everything is commensurate with the concept; there is no longer anything secret in God" (*PR,* 184, n. 85).

Hegel: The Rational Reception of Revelation

We begin our consideration of Hegel with a concession: the enclosure of the divine wholly within the embrace of determinate reason not only undermines the possibility of faith, which by its nature has its ground beyond itself, but in fact destroys philosophy as well, ultimately subordinating it, too, to what will eventually become technological-manipulative thinking: "To help bring philosophy closer to the form of Science, to the goal where it can lay aside the title '*love* of knowing' and be *actual* knowing — that is what I have set myself to do."[17] There are few who would wish to defend Hegel on

16. From the Lasson edition, vol. 1, p. 63, cited in *ID*, pp. 53-54.

17. Hegel, *Phenomenology of Spirit,* trans. A. V. Miller (Oxford: Oxford University Press, 1977), p. 3.

this point (however many there may be who nevertheless unwittingly side with him in practice). But it is precisely here that we see the potential dangers of the sort of *Destruktion* of Western thought that comes to expression in the critique of metaphysics as ontotheology, and indeed of any primarily polemical or skeptical stance with respect to the tradition.[18] If one's first impulse toward a thinker is negative, one tends to oppose oneself dialectically to that thinker, which means that one thereby methodologically eliminates from one's own position the essential dimension that belongs to the other's. Rather than dismiss Hegel as the representative of ontotheology and therefore of metaphysics, it is good to give him a fair hearing, in order to understand his reason for insisting on the intelligibility of revelation and on philosophy's native desire for God.[19]

Although he obviously is not responding to Heidegger's clearing of thought for faith, in his apologia for a philosophy of religion, Hegel makes regular reference to something with an apparently similar spirit: the tendency in his time to hold reason in suspicion in matters of faith and to condemn attempts to understand what necessarily lies beyond all comprehension, namely, the reality of God. Hegel explains that this tendency can take two forms: the first, milder form, holds that reason can generally cognize truths, but is unable to reach into the more-than-human authority of God's self-revelation, which "lies beyond the domain of human reason" (*PR*, 134). The second regards "reason and cognition" "almost . . . as the focal point of the plague of the present age," and insists that "reason must forgo all claims and all attempts to grasp any aspect of the infinite affirmatively; for through

18. Tradition has (virtually) always been recognized as intrinsic to theology, but perhaps less often in philosophy. A serious philosophy of tradition (and not merely a philosophy of history or a history of philosophy) remains to be written. For a philosophical reflection pointing in this direction, see Ferdinand Ulrich, "Überlieferte Freiheit," in *Gegenwart der Freiheit* (Einsiedeln: Johannes Verlag, 1974), pp. 11-72. It should be noted that Heidegger's thought, precisely because it understands itself as historical in perhaps a more radical way than anyone before him, is *not* simply polemical with respect to the tradition, but indeed embraces it. At least parts of it. One may ask whether it is possible to remain organically related to the tradition if the critique of metaphysics is a basic feature of one's thought; or perhaps we could put the question more concretely: Why is it that Heidegger, who incessantly encourages one to allow the object of one's thinking to speak for itself or himself, has given rise to disciples who notoriously install not only Heidegger, but his very terminology, into a sort of judgment seat over everything else?

19. To be sure, this comment is directed, not to Heidegger himself who certainly took Hegel quite seriously, but to those who would uncritically embrace his critique of ontotheology.

comprehension the infinite is annulled and downgraded to the finite" (135). The second, then, radicalizes the first since it critically denies our cognitive grasp of any reality, much less God, but in any event the two forms agree in their rejection of the inclusion of God within the ambit of philosophy: "For the doctrine that we can know nothing of God, that we cannot cognitively apprehend him, has become in our time a universally acknowledged truth, a settled thing, a kind of prejudice" (86). Because to understand is to finitize, it necessarily follows that God cannot be understood in his essential nature: whatever we understand of God is by that very token not God.

Where does this "universal prejudice" lead? While, on the one hand, the ascetic gesture of restraining reason from making any presumptive claims of being able to attain to God arises from the desire to respect the holiness of God, the primary purpose of Hegel's introductory remarks on the philosophy of religion is to show how and why this desire cannot avoid betraying itself, however sincere its intentions may be and however vigilant its efforts. The betrayal is in fact a necessary implication of the position. We must first see that it entails a separation of God and the world. If God is simply unknowable, then whatever *is* knowable is therefore without God — it is "God-less." As Hegel puts it, the assumption of strict incomprehensibility regarding God implies that whatever relationship man may have with God occupies a sphere that is defined *precisely by its opposition* to the sphere of normal rational awareness: "Without philosophical insight, the relationship of religion to the rest of consciousness is such that the two are conceived in isolation from each other. They constitute two kinds of occupation, two regions of consciousness, between which we pass back and forth only alternately" (*PR*, 92).

The separation of the two spheres, he goes on to say, ultimately renders each essentially *boring,* insofar as the absolute loses any relative importance (i.e., importance for us in the world) and the relative loses any absolute importance. On the one hand, the sphere related to reason collapses into what one might call sheer immanence. Detached from any intrinsic relation to God, worldly occupations become *wholly* worldly, that is, they reduce to the pursuit of what Hegel calls purely finite ends, which are at their core indifferent precisely to what transcends the finite. The things in the world then appear only in relation to these finite ends, and thus, lacking any essential end in themselves, which would require a ground beyond the merely immanent sphere, they become submerged in the project of man's self-glorification through work. In other words, for Hegel, if reason is made indifferent to God, it will eventually but inescapably exhaust itself in the exact sciences and finally in technology: "Cognition of this kind, therefore, does not transcend, or even desire to transcend, the finite sphere. It is a universe of cognition that does not need God and lies outside of religion. These cognitions constitute a kingdom of what we call the sciences and special technical knowledge" (*PR*, 102).

On the other hand, Hegel explains that the critical project, insofar as it sets philosophy *against* itself in order to keep reason from trying to lay hold of God, thereby and against its purposes diminishes God's significance. Ironically, the charge Hegel brings against the *separation* of God from philosophy has some similarities to the one Heidegger brings against the *inclusion* of God in philosophy: "The consequence is that no meaning for the expression 'God' remains in theology any more than in philosophy, save only the representation, definition, or abstraction of the supreme being — a vacuum of abstraction, a vacuum of 'the beyond'" (*PR*, 126). The application of predicates to God, which would be the means by which reason would bring him into the light of intelligibility, would at the same time bind God to finite concepts. To preserve his transcendence, then, we remove him from intelligibility, but this means we deprive the notion of God of any meaningful content. The effort that "purports to set God exceedingly high in calling God the infinite for which all predicates are inappropriate and unjustified anthropo-morphisms," in reality makes God "hollow, empty, and impoverished" (124, n. 31).

The inference that Hegel draws from this position is crucial. If the concept "God" has *no determinate content,* then we cannot distinguish him from anything else. The very acknowledgment that God is *not* the world, or *not* me (or *not* the Being of beings), is already a cognitive grasp of something of the nature of God, which immediately requires the reflective — indeed, at some point also the philosophical — assessment of whether it is in fact a proper grasp. It is in this respect impossible properly to acknowledge the transcendence of God without the differentiation of rational inquiry. To refuse this reflection is to forfeit any sense of that transcendence. If God has nothing to do with reason, according to Hegel, then our relation to God will unavoidably reduce to my own self-relation because it reduces to the realm of *feeling:* "Because knowledge of God does not fall within the comprehension of reason, there coheres with this standpoint the view that consciousness of God is rather sought only in the form of *feeling.* . . . What is rooted only in my feeling *is only for me;* what is in my feeling is what is mine, but it is not what is his [God's?], is not independent in and for itself" (136-37). In short, if we affirm the sheer incomprehensibility of God, "Religion . . . shrivels up into simple feeling, into a contentless elevation of spirit into the eternal, etc., of which, however, it knows nothing and has nothing to say, since any cognizing would be a dragging down of the eternal into [reason's] sphere of finite connections" (*PR*, 103).

The core of the problem, once again, is that God is placed simply *beyond* reason, which means that the spheres of faith and reason become juxtaposed to one another as two separate realms that have, if any, only an extrinsic relation to one another. In order to overcome the problems that inescapably arise from this dualism, Hegel therefore seeks to disclose an alternative notion of reason and God, starting from the assumption that the divine and worldly spheres bear an *intrinsic* relation to one another. Thus, on the one hand, he affirms a desire for God as constitutive of the very nature of human reason, and, on the other hand, he shows that reason, so conceived, participates inwardly in God's being God, insofar as spirit is meaningless in abstract isolation, but can exist *as* spirit only *for* spirit.[20] Now, the question for Hegel will be, of course, whether he is able to affirm this intrinsic relation without collapsing it simply into identity; we will suggest in the next section that his presupposition regarding the nature of reason cannot avoid such a collapse, but we must nevertheless understand what is essential in his position.

As we have seen, one of the elements of the problematic faith-reason dualism is the assumption that reason is essentially concerned with the world alone, and is to that extent constitutively indifferent to what lies beyond the world. Hegel observes that such a view of reason is peculiar to modern philosophy:

> There was a time when all science was a science of God. It is the distinction of our age, by contrast, to know each and every thing, indeed to know an infinite mass of objects, but only of God to know nothing. There was a time when [one] cared, was driven indeed, to know God, to fathom his nature — a time when spirit had no peace, could find none, except in this pursuit, when it felt itself unhappy that it could not satisfy this need, and held all other cognitive interests to be of lesser import. (*PR*, 86, 87)

20. It is interesting to note that an analogy thus appears between the problem that confronts Hegel (God as spirit *needs* the world, because spirit is not spirit unless it can reflect itself back to itself) and the classical problem that confronts the Christian conception of God as love: if love requires an *other,* then God would need the world in order to be God. It would be fruitful to compare Hegel's rational deduction of the Trinity to the meditation offered, for example, by Richard of St. Victor in book 3 of his *De Trinitate.*

According to a transcription of the lecture, Hegel adds, "and what else, we must ask further, would be worth comprehending if God is incomprehensible?" (*PR,* 88, n. 20). Such an aspiration is inscribed within reason, not only as a reflection of man's God-given supernatural destiny, but also simply because reason is a desire for truth, and a desire for truth that is not also a desire for God will always turn out to rest on a fairly empty conception of the nature of truth.

The claim that reason *needs* God, of course, lies at the root of what Heidegger calls the essential ontotheological constitution of metaphysics, but, while there is certainly a point to Heidegger's objection, as we have seen and as we will elaborate further in a moment, it is crucial to note that Hegel's view at least in principle pushes beyond what this critique fears.[21] Reason's desire for truth, at least as Hegel characterizes it here, is not a desire for conceptual mastery, which would presuppose the subordination of truth to finite ends, but is in fact the opposite: a desire to relinquish one's immediate designs in order to become a means by which that which is greater than oneself can realize itself. As Hegel puts it in a striking formulation, philosophy in truth "is of itself the service of God" (*Gottesdienst:* worship) (*PR,* 84). Along these lines, Hegel makes the profound observation that there is a connection between the loss of metaphysics in his age and the disappearance of religious orders of monks whose lives were ordered around the sole object of giving praise to God.[22] Reason, in its most complete sense, in other words, is not ordered to some pragmatic purpose or other, but is ordered to God's own ends: in the experience of religion at the heart of philosophy, "we are not concerned with ourselves, with our interests, our vanity, our pride of

21. This is most clear with respect to Westphal's characterization of ontotheology, but it is also true in a more subtle sense with respect to Hemming's formulation.

22. "Philosophy [*Wissenschaft*] and ordinary common sense thus co-operating to bring about the downfall of metaphysics, there was seen the strange spectacle of a cultured nation without metaphysics — like a temple richly ornamented in other respects but without a holy of holies. Theology, which in former times was the guardian of the speculative mysteries and of metaphysics (although this was subordinate to it) had given up this science in exchange for feelings, for what was popularly matter-of-fact, and for historical erudition. In keeping with this change, there vanished from the world those solitary souls who were sacrificed by their people and exiled from the world to the end that the eternal should be contemplated and served by lives devoted solely thereto — not for any practical gain but for the sake of blessedness." *Science of Logic,* trans. A. V. Miller (Atlantic Highlands, NJ: Humanities Press, 1997), pp. 25-26. Balthasar also connects the existence of contemplative monasteries with the existence of metaphysics; see "Philosophy, Christianity, Monasticism," in *Explorations in Theology,* vol. 2: *Spouse of the Word* (San Francisco: Ignatius Press, 1991), pp. 333-72.

knowledge and of conduct, but only with the content of it — proclaiming the honor *of God* and manifesting *his* glory" (*PR*, 85). In the contemporary idiom, we could say that, for Hegel, reason is essentially *doxological.*

Now, if it is true that reason is not indifferent to God, it is equally true, according to Hegel, that God is not indifferent to reason. The manifestation of glory is not something simply accidental to God, but it is God's *nature,* precisely because God is Spirit. In contrast to the "dead" notion of God that thinks of him in an undifferentiated manner as "the beyond," Hegel embraced the revealed doctrine of God as Trinity, with the claim that this revelation expresses what Spirit is in truth:

> If "spirit" is not an empty word, then God must [be grasped] under this characteristic, just as in the church theology of former times God was called "triune." This is the key by which the nature of spirit is explicated. God is thus grasped as what he is for himself within himself; God [the Father] makes himself an object for himself (the Son); then, in this object, God remains the undivided essence within this differentiation of himself within himself, and in this differentiation of himself loves himself, i.e., remains identical with himself — this is God as Spirit. (*PR*, 85)

Self-revelation is therefore intrinsic to God, which is precisely why revelation is a genuine communication of God's self and not merely an offering of something else, something other than God, and to that extent *dispensable* in one's relation to him. There is a connection, then, between Hegel's understanding of God as Spirit, and the seriousness with which he takes the positive aspects of religion — i.e., the dogmatic and institutional aspects of the Church — in contrast, for example, to Heidegger's indifference toward these aspects.[23] However much we would need to qualify Hegel's notion in order to avoid making God's relation to the world necessary in a mechanical sense, the affirmation that self-revelation is not *extrinsic* is one we ought to embrace.

This understanding of God, moreover, has three immediate implications for the nature of human reason. First, human reason becomes not primarily that which makes a claim on God, but that by which God makes

23. Consider, for example, Hemming's judgment: "Heidegger remains firmly within the Western tradition to which he repeatedly returns and on which his work meditates. For Heidegger, this tradition remains a Christian one, although he refuses to acknowledge it confessionally or within the terms of *die Kirchenlehre,* Church Doctrine. His philosophical atheism is simultaneously this remaining within and refusing the institutional claims of the tradition" (*Heidegger's Atheism,* p. 281).

himself known, and therefore is a reflection and instrument, so to speak, of his glory. God's transcendence is therefore *magnified* by the existence of reason; his "majesty consists precisely in the fact that he does not renounce reason, [for then his majesty would be] something irrational, empty, and grudging, not something communicated in spirit and in the highest form and innermost being of spirit" (*PR*, 104). Second, as this passage already suggests, reason proves to be the very means by which we participate in God and not an obstacle to intimacy. Indeed, a human being can *receive* and be deeply affected by something only if his reason is involved; otherwise what is given is never "internalized" or "taken to heart," but left as an external possession: a gift must be received to be recognized as a gift, and the gift of self-communication in revelation requires the receptive inwardness of reason. Finally, it is only if revelation appeals to reason that we can say "In the Christian religion, I am to retain my freedom — indeed, I am to become free in it" (106). If revelation bypasses what is most proper to man as man, relation to God becomes a violence that cripples humanity. We might sum these three points up together with Kierkegaard's insight that the absoluteness of God is nowhere so evident as in the fact that he can create an *other* that is free in relation to him. The insight is richer, more complex and paradoxical, than might appear at first glance, as we saw in our reflections on Dionysius' notion of causality in the previous chapter.

Affirming the dignity of reason is therefore in Hegel's eyes essential to the glory and majesty of God — indeed, even to God's *mystery*. While one typically complains that reason "objectifies" what it knows, and thus cannot but compromise the transcendence of God, Hegel argues, not that reason does not "objectify," but — perhaps to our astonishment — that objectification of some sort is an essential aspect of transcendence. With no objectivity, he claims, our relation to God collapses into the subjectivity of feeling. It is in this respect that Hegel goes so far as to affirm the significance of the classical proofs for the existence of God: "It seems necessary therefore to show beforehand that God is not simply rooted in feeling, is not merely *my* God. The former metaphysics, therefore, always used to begin by proving that there is a God, that God is not merely rooted in feeling, that God is not merely something subjective but is something objective" (*PR*, 137). The point is that reason in some respect objectifies *because it mediates*, and thus *if* we eliminate reason, our relation to God becomes one of im-mediacy. But *sheer* immediacy, of course, is precisely no relation at all. By taking concepts out of religion as so many obstacles to God's divine Otherness, I paradoxically remove the means by which God's Otherness is manifest, and I reduce him simply to some feature of myself. If Hegel's judgment here carries weight, it is worth noting that the attempt to liberate God from being, made by critiques of ontotheology, to the extent that being is in fact the proper element of reason, threatens to undermine precisely the respectful distance it seeks to secure.

False Modesty and Unholy Zeal

Hegel's tracing of the implications of abandoning God to the "Beyond," no matter how piously intended the abandonment may be, is certainly sobering. On the other hand, his critique of dualism does not eclipse the force of Heidegger's critique of ontotheology. It is interesting to observe that what Hegel identifies as an essential part of resisting the collapse of religion into a kind of subjectivism, namely, conceptual proofs for the existence of God, Heidegger for his part identifies as the decisive moment of the collapse into subjectivism, insofar as the *causa sui* that results from these is God as servant of human calculative thinking: "a proof for the existence of God can be constructed by means of the most rigorous formal logic and yet prove nothing, since a god who must permit his existence to be proved in the first place is ultimately a very ungodly god. The best such proofs of existence can yield is blasphemy."[24] What then are we to do? Clearly, the only way to assess this situation properly is to see how they are both right, which is another way of saying how they are both wrong. Let us consider the two positions more closely in relation to one another.

On one reading at least, Heidegger withdraws philosophy from the theological in order to avoid the presumption of human thinking determining who or what God is: "[A]ssuming that philosophy, as thinking, is the free and spontaneous self-involvement [*freie, von sich aus vollzogene Sicheinlassen*] with beings as such, then the god can come into philosophy only insofar as philosophy, of its own accord and by its own nature, requires and determines that and how the god enters it" (*ID*, 56). The heart of the matter lies in Heidegger's characterization of philosophy as an activity carried out "*von sich aus,*" on the basis of itself. *If,* he says, we assume philosophy to be such an activity, *if,* that is, the way Heidegger characterizes philosophy here is indeed an adequate one, then the conclusion Heidegger draws necessarily

24. Heidegger, *Nietzsche,* vol. 2: *The Eternal Recurrence of the Same,* trans. David Farrell Krell (San Francisco: Harper, 1991), p. 106.

follows: the god's entry into philosophy can occur *only* on philosophy's terms, because philosophy itself operates, as it were, solely on its own terms. The god, we might say, has no choice but to accept these terms if he does indeed wish to give human reason access to himself — i.e., communicate himself at all in an intelligible manner.

It is in contrast to the philosophy thus described that Heidegger presents his essentially god-less thinking, which is god-less, he explains, not because it is atheistic or in other words because it has decided *against* God, but because it resolves to make no such presumption on God from the outset either way. As Heidegger clarifies in his *Letter on Humanism,* this thinking "can be theistic as little as atheistic. Not however, because of an indifferent attitude, but out of respect for the boundaries that have been set by what gives itself to thinking as what is to be thought, by the truth of Being."[25] In a word, the "truth of being," here, is its essential finitude, which is its historicity. Thinking in this authentic sense, then, resolutely embraces its "worldliness" and does not seek to "transcend" it to some higher standpoint. It is in this respect more open to God because it does not set conditions for God, which implies that philosophy, understood as metaphysics or as representational thinking, by contrast necessarily sets its *own* conditions, that it operates "von sich aus."

We know that Hegel is altogether determined to lead philosophy down the path opposite Heidegger's *Feldweg,* but is this because he has a radically different conception of philosophical thinking? It is different, to be sure, but, setting aside the rich complexities of their conceptions for a moment, we can nevertheless point to something crucial that Hegel shares with Heidegger: for Hegel, too, reason operates "von sich aus." Indeed, not only is self-grounding a feature of *Geist,* we ought to say that it is precisely what constitutes the essence of *Geist,* what distinguishes it most properly from everything else. Spirit is the culmination of reality because, even in the furthest extremities of alienation, it is no less at home with itself, it operates no less *von sich aus.* The reason that philosophy *must* take a systematic form, for Hegel, is that Spirit thus conceived stands, so to speak, as its governing principle and engine. As Hegel explains in the *Phenomenology,*

> That the True is actual only as system, or that Substance is essentially Subject, is expressed in the representation of the Absolute as *Spirit* — the most sublime Notion and the one which belongs to the modern age

25. Heidegger, *Letter on Humanism,* in *BW,* p. 230.

> and its religion. The spiritual alone is the *actual;* it is essence, or that which has *being in itself;* it is that which *relates itself to itself* and is *determinate,* it is *other-being* and *being-for-itself,* and in this determinateness, or in its self-externality, abides within itself; in other words, it is *in and for itself.*[26]

The perfection of the Idea consists in its complete *determination,* which means that it exists *for* itself, reflected to itself as an "other" that is nevertheless wholly "possessed" as identity. We saw above that Hegel interprets the doctrine of the Trinity in just this sense. That which is *not* thus mediated, i.e., that which exists only in immediacy, is either the pure internality of inert "substance" or the abstraction of simple exteriority, and is in either case not rational. Reason *determines,* and it does so by necessity "von sich aus."

Heidegger had prefaced his judgments with the conditional — "assuming that philosophy . . ." — but it is remarkable how little attention this assumption has received, how rarely any question has been raised regarding its legitimacy. Before turning to this question, it is illuminating to consider where it is that granting the assumption puts us. Let us take the "von sich aus" character of reason to mean that it operates essentially and wholly "from below," rather than in some sense also from beyond itself, "from above," leaving aside for a moment what this latter phrase might mean. If we grant that reason does indeed operate wholly "from below," we are faced with two, equally problematic, alternatives: *either* we limit from the outset the scope of reason so as to preserve the freedom of that which lies beyond — in this case, God — and thus fall prey to a faith-reason dualism, with all of the problems Hegel exposed in such a dualism; *or* we do not set any limitations to reason's scope, we combine its *self*-determining character with its natural desire to comprehend nothing less than God, and we thereby suck dry the whole divine mystery. *Either* God is beyond our thinking, so "beyond" that he simply can't mean anything substantial to us, and can approach us only through the superficiality of arbitrary "miracles" and bursts of enthusiasm (Westphal) or through the pseudo-depth of a mystical union that proves to be in the end a perverse narcissism (Hemming); *or* God is, at best, only provisionally beyond us, and, because spirit is spirit (as Hegel says), whether human or divine, will sooner or later reduce to our own self-understanding. There is no escape from these alternatives if we accept that reason operates simply "from below."

26. *Phenomenology of Spirit,* par. 25 (p. 14).

Indeed, if we reflect more deeply into the matter, we discover that we are not really faced with two alternatives, but in fact two sides of the same coin. We might think that Hegel presumes too much, and that Heidegger, by contrast, seeks to recover a modesty for reason, and thus could be said, at worst, to presume too little — though in the end, we might go on to add, presuming too little expresses the sort of humility appropriate for a Christian thinker. But this is a misunderstanding. Each position thought deeply enough turns into the other. First of all, while the totalizing embrace of self-determining reason in Hegel would seem to make the self master over the whole of reality, God included, in fact the individual self paradoxically becomes an utterly inert moment in the movement of history. Marxist materialistic determinism in this respect at least follows naturally from Hegel's Absolute Spirit. When one is so presumptuous as to presume *everything*, one's thinking takes on an absolute character that becomes, by that very fact, wholly indifferent to the person who thinks. Pure spontaneity turns into the complete impotence, one might say nihilism, of just passively "letting be" — which, oddly, takes on all the formal features of Heidegger's *Gelassenheit* or the obedience to the sending of being as history.[27]

More subtly, but perhaps for that very reason all the more importantly, what appears to be a modest restraint in Heidegger proves to be its own titanic self-imposition. There is a connection in Heidegger's thinking between his insistence that philosophy be god-less precisely in order not to anticipate and thus constrain genuine faith, his claim that the analytic of Dasein — i.e., the interpretation of the fundamental structures of human existence — exhibits what he refers to as a "peculiar neutrality,"[28] and his judgment that theology represents an "ontic" science in relation to the ontological interpretation of Dasein that belongs to philosophy.[29] As we have seen, according to Heidegger, the alternative to the absorption of theology into philosophy, which he takes to be the essential constitution of metaphysics, is a "god-less" thinking, which is a thinking that clears the space for faith, without deciding beforehand anything whatsoever concerning "the divine." To evince a com-

27. On this point, see Hans Jonas's essential observations on the notion of "fate" in Heidegger's thinking in "Heidegger and Theology," in *The Phenomenon of Life: Towards a Philosophical Biology* (Evanston, IL: Northwestern University Press, 2001), pp. 235-61; here, 244-49.

28. See Heidegger, *The Metaphysical Foundations of Logic*, trans. Michael Heim (Bloomington: Indiana University Press, 1984), p. 136, cited in Marion, *God without Being*, p. 42.

29. See *Wegmarken*, pp. 48-49.

mitment prior to this opening up would be, in Heidegger's eyes, to prevent its ever opening and ultimately to make the reduction to an ontotheological conception of God unavoidable. Philosophy *requires* the suspension of the question of God, and that is why Heidegger suggests, for example, that *Christian philosophy* is an oxymoron: like "wooden iron."[30] Now, because the space cannot be cleared unless the question is suspended, it is essential that the inquiry into the being of Dasein be *neutral.* As Heidegger puts it in *Vom Wesen des Grundes,* and then reiterates in the *Letter on Humanism,* "Through the ontological interpretation of Dasein as being-in-the-world no decision, whether positive or negative, is made concerning a possible being toward God. It is, however, the case that through an illumination of transcendence we first achieve an *adequate concept of Dasein,* with respect to which it can now be asked how the relationship of Dasein to God is ontologically ordered."[31] *In order to* be properly open to the possibility of God, we must *first* have an adequate conception of Dasein. The space must be cleared *before* — if — it is to be filled. It follows naturally that theology — which Heidegger is careful to insist means *not* the study of God (since any study of God would turn out to be ontotheological metaphysics), as one might presume, but *merely* a study of faith, i.e., a study of "Dasein as believer" — will be a regional science that *presupposes* philosophy's ontological interpretation.

As Jean-Luc Marion has brilliantly shown, the supposed *neutrality* of philosophy, or as Westphal has put it, philosophy's "merely methodological" atheism, thus ends up necessarily presenting itself, so to speak, as the *measure* of theology, and indeed, the measure of God's self-revelation.[32] Because

30. *Einführung in die Metaphysik,* in *Gesamtausgabe,* vol. 40 (Frankfurt am Main: Klostermann, 1983), p. 9. Note that, however one resolves the excruciatingly difficult question regarding the possibility of Christian philosophy, Heidegger's position is not adequate insofar as it presupposes a straightforward opposition between the presumed closure of faith and the open wonder of philosophy. Is the notion that faith puts an end to wonder a genuinely Christian understanding of faith?

31. *Letter on Humanism,* in *BW,* pp. 229-30.

32. Because he focuses on the question of whether Marion interprets Heidegger as assuming God to be "a being," Hemming's criticism of Marion misses the essential point of what Marion is arguing, which remains valid irrespective of whether Heidegger thinks of God as a "being" or not. See *Heidegger's Atheism,* pp. 249-69. (Strangely, Hemming's rejection of Marion's interpretation hangs on his claim that Marion translates Heidegger's phrase "Denn auch der Gott ist — wenn er ist — ein Seiender . . ." as "*when* God is," rather than the weaker and more obviously appropriate "*if* God is." Marion does not; see *Dieu sans l'être,* p. 69 ["s'il est"], as well as the English translation: *God without Being,* p. 44 ["if he is"]. The weaker expression does not affect Marion's argument.) The essential point is that Heidegger

it is *philosophy* that clears the space for the possibility of faith, philosophy by that very fact establishes the parameters within which faith must occur, if it is to occur at all. Notice the essential connection: a modesty that withdraws *a priori* is a presumption that sets the conditions of possibility. Modesty of this sort, that is, obtrusively imposes itself. There is no real mystery in this: we encounter it every day, for example, in what the psychologists call "passive-aggressive" behavior, or in the person who frustrates and fragments a group precisely by *not* (explicitly) having any preferences. In philosophy, we see this paradoxically self-assertive modesty most especially in Kant: an unavoidable logical necessity binds his intention to deny reason in order to make room for faith, and his eventual judgment that revelation strictly speaking is impossible.[33] As we have argued in different ways over the course of the book, there is in other words simply no way at all to deny knowledge in order to make room for faith without by the very same gesture eliminating any room for faith. Heidegger's critique of ontotheology is the same false modesty done up in a different costume. This inversion of radical modesty into radical presumption comes to light particularly clearly, for example, in the form of man's relationship to God that emerges from Hemming's attempt to reconcile Heidegger's atheism with Christian faith: on the one hand, Hemming collapses any encounter with God into just the sort of narcissistic self-contemplation Hegel's analyses would have predicted,[34] while, on the other hand, he simply flips the same coin over to the other side, that of an endless striving after the absent God.[35] He takes for granted, in other

makes the ontological interpretation of Dasein *prior* to theology or indeed any encounter between man and God, and therefore necessarily ensures that this interpretation sets the parameters for the encounter.

33. In *Religion within the Limits of Reason Alone,* trans. Greene and Hudson (New York: Harper, 1960), p. 157, Kant writes, "it sounds questionable but it is in no way reprehensible to say that everyone makes his own God." It is *modest* reason, in other words, that cannot avoid making idols for itself. Westphal's attempt to "save" certain figures in the tradition from Heidegger's critique of ontotheology by showing them to be proto-Kantian anti-realists is therefore misguided. See his discussion of Augustine, Dionysius, and Aquinas in *Transcendence and Self-Transcendence,* pp. 93-141. See also *Overcoming Ontotheology,* pp. 89-105, where he presents an argument along these lines that Christian philosophers ought to be "favorably disposed" to Kantian idealism.

34. Heidegger's nihilism, he says, enables the experience of faith in which "I come about in the worlding of world to find God worlding with me and so speaking and revealing God with me and as me" ("Nihilism," p. 106).

35. "What does it mean that the essence of being-human *never* reaches the place of God? The human essence never reaches it, because it is always reaching out for it. The self is

words, that the rational reception of God's self-communication reduces God to myself, and so I must defer such a reception indefinitely. But a genuinely infinite openness, as we will see in a moment, *requires* presence and encounter, and thus rational access. The silence that is supposedly the culmination of prayer turns out to be a substitute for it. To insist *a priori* on the contentlessness of silence, in other words, is to refuse the words God himself gives us ("When you pray, say these words . . ."). The endless striving turns out to be a false imitation of genuine openness — it is, indeed, endless, but only because it never really begins. It is in the end the pseudo-transcendence of the snake swallowing its own tail.

According to Heidegger, fundamental ontology precedes theology, the study of faith, because whatever encounter there is to be with God necessarily "eventuates" within being.[36] But if being is understood without any reference to God (i.e., "god-lessly"), the horizon of this meeting place will be, as it were, determined *prior to* God, and so will impose, extrinsically, its own restrictions on God. Paradoxically, a more traditional "onto-theology" — although perhaps it would be more appropriate to speak in this context of a "theo-ontology" — allows God as it were to determine most fundamentally the medium of the encounter between God and man insofar as it takes God to be determinative of the meaning of being. This is the essential role, one might suggest, of the analogy of being: to say that being is *ana-logical* is to say that it always *also* receives its most basic sense from above. The critique of ontotheology that refuses the name of being to God is forced *either* to affirm a wholly im-mediate (and so ir-rational) relation to God, or to allow that the relation is mediated by being — as all human relations are in the end — but to affirm that this being is, as it were, determined in abstraction from and therefore prior to God. Heidegger, it appears, takes this second option; and we will see in a moment that Marion takes the first.[37]

The putative "neutrality" of the philosophy Heidegger proposes as an alternative to the "ontotheologizing" of metaphysics entails a further conse-

---

the horizon where God is revealed, but every revelation is a failure, a falling short of God. Such a revelation always strives forward into silence, as the place where all distance is overcome (because all giving of things is a speaking, and speaking thereby produces difference — so that overcoming speaking is at the same time overcoming distance), and yet is forced, gabbling, back on itself, only to struggle back into silence" (*Heidegger's Atheism*, p. 280).

36. See Heidegger's famous comment in the 1951 seminar in Zurich, which is presented in an appendix to *Heidegger's Atheism*, pp. 291-92.

37. See the insightful observation Balthasar makes in this respect regarding Marion's project. *TL2*, pp. 135-36, n. 10.

quence regarding the *historical* character of thinking. From the perspective of a historically grounded theology, we could say that the inclination philosophy has tended to evince toward *mastery* is due, not to the essential nature of reason, but specifically to its *fallen form:*[38] it would be contradictory to assume, from the perspective of Christian theology, that reason as created would be in any sense *opposed* to revelation (however much revelation would nevertheless have to remain discontinuous in some respect with the order of reason, as we will show in a moment). But *precisely because* he claims a neutral standpoint, Heidegger has no grounds from which to allude to any such distinction — namely, between reason as it is in its essential nature and as it has been affected by history — and is therefore forced to *identify* the essence of reason with its historically fallen form. It therefore becomes the essential nature of reason, its "fate," according to Heidegger, to seek to dominate and control *(das Ge-stell);* the forgetting of being is not in any sense an accident of history, but is as it were an inextricable feature of the history of being, to which human nature essentially belongs. The response to this forgetting, however serene it may appear at one level (*"Gelassenheit,"* the *"Schritt zurück,"* and so forth), is nevertheless a kind of violence:[39] it is an *overcoming,* a disconcerting calling of itself into question, which oddly seems to find its governing impulse always in the end in Heidegger's own personal authority. It is in this respect the very nature of the critique of metaphysics and ontotheology to install itself in a position above questioning, and from which all questioning takes its bearings, that is, to install itself as what Marion would call an idol.

And here we encounter yet another remarkable irony: by proposing itself as *neutral,* and by that very gesture as the condition of possibility not only for all other philosophical thinking, but also for theology, the "ontic science of faith," and even for faith itself — in short, for absolutely anything else that has to do with human existence — the ontological analytic of Dasein lifts itself *outside of time,* and thereby *outside* of the finitude it claims as its most essential feature. In other words, it accords itself a certain "universal applicability," it makes itself the eternal standard by which all else is

38. To make a distinction between nature and history does not imply that one embraces an Enlightenment notion of essence. It is possible to say that essences are always without exception differentiated historically, and still to deny that nature reduces to history.

39. It is interesting to note the preponderance of terms with a negative or violent tone that Heidegger uses to describe Dasein's deepest mood or most fundamental openness to the event of the difference of being and beings: *Angst, Ent-setzung, Erschrecken, Verhaltenheit, Scheu,* and so forth.

measured, it becomes the ever-valid cipher by which to illuminate . . . the totality of beings. One can see where this is going: Heidegger hoists himself on his own petard; his god-less thinking is itself an ontotheology. Indeed, precisely because of its presuppositions concerning the nature of reason, the critique of ontotheology cannot avoid becoming itself an ontotheology. Étienne Gilson understood this long ago, but put it in different terms: metaphysics invariably ends up burying its own undertaker. In this respect, Heidegger's modesty turns out in spite of itself to be once again at least as presumptuous as Hegel's inexorable zeal: Hegel is arguably less so since he makes no presumption of being modest. Although Hegel, too, claims a universal significance for his thinking, the *historicity* of his philosophy is in the end more concrete than Heidegger's: history bears on the *content* of his thought, not just its form; he takes an interest in *history* (and thus, as we saw, in the historically revealed Christian dogma), we might say, rather than merely in "historicity" or "temporality" *(Geschichtlichkeit, Zeitlichkeit).* There is no "neutrality" in Hegel regarding salvation history — though, to be sure, he certainly falls off the other side of the horse, making Hegelian philosophy the point of that history.

We could transpose the fundamental problem into the terms of classical Christian spirituality, namely, indifference and eros. In this case it would be possible to say that Heidegger (who after all spent time in a Jesuit seminary!) affirms indifference without eros, and Hegel, eros without indifference.[40]

A Recovery of Metaphysics

As the foregoing discussion has hopefully begun to make clear, the ontotheological problematic seems to turn on a conception of reason operating

40. It is not an accident that there is a conspicuous absence of eros in Heidegger's work and of indifference in Hegel's. (The "love" that one — rarely — finds mentioned in Heidegger [cf., e.g., *Letter on Humanism,* in *BW,* p. 196] tends to resemble an "agapic" bestowal of favor rather than the generous *desire* of eros; moreover, the concept of indifference does appear in Hegel [cf. *Science of Logic,* pp. 375-85], but principally as just the *substrate* of differentiation, i.e., self-determination.) On the other hand, we are familiar with the centrality of *Gelassenheit,* for Heidegger, a notion of "non-willing" that he appropriates from Eckhart. See *Discourse on Thinking,* trans. John M. Anderson and E. Hans Freund (New York: Harper, 1966). In Hegel, the notion of love was one of the governing ideas in his early theological writings. *Early Theological Writings* (Chicago: University of Chicago Press, 1948), pp. 302-8.

essentially "from below," and therefore as inescapably anticipating and so imposing itself on whatever reality might open access to it. Such a conception of reason has no choice but to force us to embrace one of two equally inadequate alternatives: either Hegel's unholy zeal, or Heidegger's false modesty. The best way to respond to this dilemma is, of course, to refuse the assumption that produces it. In order that we may more clearly see the significance of this approach it is illuminating to consider the implications of another possible response, that of Jean-Luc Marion, who proposes to criticize ontotheology even more radically than Heidegger himself. Thus, after having shown the way that Heidegger's supposedly neutral conception of the ontological analytic establishes conditions of possibility into which God must find some way to insert himself, Marion insists on the necessity of affirming an even more radically transcendent God, who lies beyond not only the being of metaphysics, but also beyond the ontological difference itself, and thus, as (unconditional) ἀγαπή, is not in any way at all bound by our conditions of possibility: a God who is, indeed, from our perspective impossible.[41] Marion's approach, however, appears to raise all over again the criticisms articulated by Hegel. To the extent that he *opposes* the God of love to being and reason,[42] and thus eliminates their mediating role in man's relation to God, he surrenders all "resistance," as it were, to the collapse into immediacy and the subsequent annihilation of the "distance" he precisely sought to preserve.[43] The crux of his excellent critique of Heidegger is the latter's imposition "from below" of conditions of possibility on God. This critique requires an imposing of limits on reason and a drive to get "beyond being" — in other words, an "overcoming of metaphysics" — *only if* it is the nature of reason to impose limits from below, and, correspondingly, the nature of being to submit, as it were, to the mastery of logos. But this is precisely where the most serious question lies: such an assumption follows only if one begins with Heidegger's critique of ontotheology, and allows that critique to set the terms for one's engagement with the issue. We have been suggesting, by contrast, that it is the overcoming of ontotheology that needs to be overcome.

41. Cf. *God without Being,* p. 82.

42. Cf. *God without Being,* pp. 183-84. Faith has a logic, he says, that is "*contrary to* every other logic, formal or otherwise" (emphasis added).

43. See *Idol and Distance,* esp. pp. 198-253. Marion writes that "God withdraws in the distance, unthinkable, unconditioned, and therefore infinitely closer," which raises the question: Is it possible for this infinite intimacy to be distinguished from simple identity without some mediating reality or concept?

As an alternative response to the problem of ontotheology, let us consider the resources offered by Hans Urs von Balthasar. The difference between Heidegger and Balthasar on the question of the significance of metaphysics, and in relation to this the "status" of the question of ontotheology, is palpable from the beginning and all the way through. For Heidegger — speaking, admittedly, as an "outsider" of sorts — Christianity ought fundamentally to be wary of the Western tradition of metaphysics. For Balthasar, by contrast, "the Christian is called to be the guardian of metaphysics of our time,"[44] and that guardianship, indeed, represents one of the Christian's most precious and urgent tasks. According to Heidegger, "Faith has no need of the thinking of being. If faith has recourse to it, it is already not faith. Luther understood this."[45] According to Balthasar, philosophy, which is at its heart metaphysical — and that means for him that, at its heart, it is the thinking of being — is never as such an obstacle to faith. Quite the contrary, a faith that simply dispenses with the thinking of being will turn out to be a superficial, and indeed an irrational and arbitrary faith — ultimately, not a faith in God (the God of Jesus Christ) but some form of self-contemplation.[46] Finally, while Heidegger insists that heeding the question of being, which is the most profound spiritual act, requires the overcoming of metaphysics, for Balthasar, the theological act, which in some respect does indeed transcend the metaphysical act, nevertheless occurs within the heart of the metaphysical act. In this sense, then, the glory of God, which is the final end of all things for Balthasar (who is quite Ignatian in this respect) elevates and intensifies the glory of being.[47] It is specifically because of this that Balthasar accords to the Christian the guardianship of metaphysics.

So their respective judgments on metaphysics represent a difference between the two great twentieth-century thinkers. What, then, accounts for the difference? We will sketch out what seem to be some of the basic principles of the difference in three points: (1) the notion of being in relation to God; (2) the constitution of human reason; and (3) the relation between theology and metaphysics. Obviously, these are all vast topics in themselves; here, we will limit ourselves to a fairly straightforward observation in regard to each.

44. *GL5*, p. 656.

45. Quoted in Hemming, *Heidegger's Atheism*, p. 291.

46. On this, see, e.g., "Forgetfulness of God and Christians," in *Explorations in Theology*, vol. 3: *Creator Spirit* (San Francisco: Ignatius Press, 1993), pp. 317-33.

47. For an excellent presentation of this point, see Nicholas J. Healy, *The Eschatology of Hans Urs von Balthasar: Being as Communion* (Oxford: Oxford University Press, 2005), esp. pp. 19-90.

(1) In what seems to be the only passage in which Balthasar confronts the question of ontotheology explicitly — namely, the famous footnote 10 of *Theo-Logic 2*[48] — Balthasar clarifies that his discussion of God in terms of being is not affected by Heidegger's critique insofar as that critique takes aim at the identification of God with *subsistent* being, which would imply that thinking remains within the ontological difference. For Balthasar, the Divine Being is neither simply a being, nor the Being of beings (i.e., *Seiendheit*), nor being itself thought out of the ontological difference. Rather, the Divine Being transcends worldly being altogether. While we might be tempted to interpret this affirmation in Heideggerian terms (in a manner analogous to the way Marion rereads the divine *Esse* in Aquinas as transcendent of *ens commune* in a Heideggerian spirit), Balthasar says two things in this footnote that ought to keep us from doing so. First, he points out explicitly that the Divine Being that offers itself in mystery to Christian theology manifests an "abiding difference" from being such as Heidegger conceives it in relation to his critique of ontotheology. Second, he judges in this footnote that Marion, in *L'Idole et la distance* and *Dieu sans l'être,* "seems . . . to concede too much to the critique of Heidegger." In other words, when Balthasar distinguishes his interpretation of the Divine Being from what would be called an "ontotheological conception" of God, this is not an acknowledgment of the wholesale legitimacy of that critique. It is important to keep this apparently subtle distinction in mind in order to avoid more general confusions, especially because there is so much in Heidegger's philosophy that Balthasar embraces with an astonishing warmth.

But we have at this point only insisted *that* there is a difference; it is important to specify at least in principle how that difference ought to be characterized. We saw above that a governing presupposition in the critique is that ontotheology chains God, as it were, to being, and thus identifies God with that which is the best thing reason can think. One way to elude this critique would be simply to affirm that God lies essentially *beyond* being, understood in this way. Balthasar's response is more subtle. Explicitly following Gustav Siewerth on this point, Balthasar claims that goodness, which is indeed linked to transcendence (as Marion also affirms), is at the very same time one of the transcendental attributes of being, which means that it gives expression to the intrinsic meaning of being, as we explored in chapter three. What this implies is fairly surprising: self-transcendence becomes an intrinsic property of being, so that if goodness is indeed in some sense beyond be-

48. *TL2*, pp. 134-35, n. 10.

ing, it is because *being itself is beyond being.* Opening up beyond itself is therefore not a violence that is imposed on worldly being, but is the very essence of being, as Balthasar understands it. Thinking God in terms of being, then, is not in the least "restrictive" in principle, because strictly speaking there is nothing at all restrictive about being.[49]

Now, there is a further point to make regarding the relationship between God and being, which Balthasar does not make explicit in this footnote, but which seems to be implied here and which can be inferred more directly from other places in his work (perhaps especially the presentation of metaphysics in the *Epilogue*).[50] The point is the connection between the intrinsic self-transcendence of being and the *analogia entis.* The analogy of being is, as we know, a way of affirming an intrinsic relation between the being of God and the being of the world, which does not deny God's absolute transcendence of the world (similarity within an infinite difference). While there can be a tendency to think of the analogy of being as a means of approaching God from below by means of natural reason, as if on a conceptual ladder (which is why Barth rejected it so vehemently), for Balthasar, the analogy ought to be understood *katalogically.*[51] In other words, being is analogical *because* it is most fundamentally determined from above even in its natural meaning. There is a certain paradox in this, to be sure, but it is simply another way of stating the point made above, namely, that being is intrinsically self-transcending. We will return to this at greater length in the next chapter. Being is always already "out beyond itself"; there is never an instance of being that does not have this ecstatic character. It is for this reason that Balthasar can insist on a radical discontinuity between Divine Being and worldly being (i.e., can say that the being of God cannot be deduced from what we know of creaturely being by, for example, simply affirming creaturely being and eliminating its imperfections), and at the same time never let go of the analogy that makes Divine Being an *intelligible* mystery. To think being, then, is to participate in its ecstatic movement "beyond." Which brings us to the next point:

49. Compare Marion: "The transcendence of Being does not disclose transcendence, but instead closes and limits it. . . . This ultimate transcendence . . . must be transcended if God is whom we have in mind, supposing at least that we have not buried the question beforehand in onto-theology, but are prepared to let it exercise its privilege — namely, its freedom with respect to being." "The Impossible for Man — God," in *Transcendence and Beyond: A Postmodern Inquiry,* ed. John D. Caputo and Michael J. Scanlon (Bloomington: Indiana University Press, 2007), pp. 18-19.

50. *E,* pp. 43-86.

51. See *TL2,* pp. 171-218.

(2) The second presupposition that lay behind the critique of ontotheology is what we could call an "egological" view of reason: to conceptualize is to dominate, and so in order to preserve God from human attempts at mastery, we must withhold him, as it were, from human understanding. This position, unless it is qualified, will be unable to avoid in the end a problematic faith-reason dualism. For Balthasar, reason is not essentially egological, but is rather, as we have seen in earlier chapters, essentially dramatic. As we have seen in our discussion of the "mother's smile," this means that consciousness, and therefore the "home," as it were, of all that a person will ever perceive, think, understand, or believe, is not a prestructured categorializing activity, but is first and foremost *given* to itself. It arises in and through the initiating gift of self that the mother communicates in her smiling on her child. If this is the case, the conditions of possibility that structure reason do not belong to it *prior to* its encounter with the real, but, as we saw in chapter two, are "dramatically" constituted *in* the gift of its participation in and with the reality his mother lovingly offers to him. It therefore follows that conditions of possibility are not something that reason establishes first and therefore has no choice but to impose on any encounter it might have — whether with another person, with being, or with God — but instead are simultaneously received and established. Every encounter whatsoever, from this perspective, has a certain dramatic quality; every act of reason is, at some level, the coincidence of surprise and resolution, the building up of anticipations, which are then fulfilled even as they are overturned. In other words, if consciousness grows from the beginning out of the generous gift of love, reason never simply operates "*von sich aus,*" but always, without exception, at the very same time "*vom Anderen her.*"

The moment we accept this principle as the "heart" of reason, the ontotheological problem appears in a strikingly new light. Reason does not have to impose limits on itself (to make room for faith) — which, as we saw above, it cannot do in any event without *by necessity* imposing limits at the same time on what it is to know — but receives its limits *from* its other *precisely* in its extending itself, as it were, to meet the other, and these limits therefore do not arise as a violence that frustrates reason's essential self-centeredness, as the critique of ontotheology tends to imply. Instead, these limits again and again bring to fulfillment what reason is in its most profound and original form: a generously appropriating encounter with its other. From a dramatic perspective, thinking is not an autonomous activity, but is at its core a "being moved by an other." There is, then, an ecstatic or generous dimension that forms part of the constitutive structure of reason:

to think, in this case, is to pledge oneself, to be brought out of oneself in a way that precisely allows one to give oneself. What gets criticized by the name of "ontotheology," i.e., the enlisting of God, and therefore of everything else, in reason's self-serving schemes, is therefore not an expression of reason's nature, an automatic result of every effort at conceptualization, but represents rather a failure of reason, a failure to understand — indeed, a failure to comprehend. The problem with ontotheology, in other words, is *not* that it presumptuously attempts to comprehend God, but that it does *not* attempt to comprehend God.

(3) Finally, these two points — the ecstatic character of being and the dramatic nature of reason — illuminate the reason theology has a priority over metaphysics without simply supplanting it. They also explain how it can be that man is able to be the hearer of the Word, that is, able to understand God's revelation, without reducing that revelation to what is simply humanly understandable.

As we have seen, both being and reason are determined in their innermost nature and from their earliest origins simultaneously by themselves and from above. If this is the case, then the moment of revelation, the advent of faith, will never simply be a violent intrusion that runs counter to nature, even while it remains the case that this advent will always be in a basic respect discontinuous with nature's trajectory and order. Nature is fulfilled as nature precisely by what surprises it, that is, by the gratuity of grace. It follows that, even if faith comes in some sense "later," even if the theological vision follows upon the contemplation of being that is the metaphysical act, it will nevertheless always arrive as *prior* to it, as we will explain further in the next chapter. There are two things to note about this specifically in relation to the issue we have been addressing. In the first place, it implies that there need be no anxiety about the thinking of being for a Christian. One does not have to push impatiently "past" being in order to encounter God in a nihilistic mysticism (or a mysticism of nihilism), in a delirious transcendence, in the im-possible. Notice, all of these ways of characterizing the faith-filled encounter with God imply a sort of dialectical relationship between God and being. To the contrary, being is always already God's, and we can dwell on it and in it "faith-fully." Balthasar says that the formal object of theology lies *within* the formal object of philosophy.[52] The significance of that way of conceiving the relation between the two bears long reflection.

In the second place, not only *can* we dwell on and in being as Chris-

52. *GL1*, p. 145.

tians, but in some sense *we must.* Because theology does not replace metaphysics, because God is not beyond being in a dialectical sense (perhaps we could say: yes, God is beyond being, but being, too, is beyond being), theology can never simply leave being behind; rather, to paraphrase T. S. Eliot, theology in fact brings us back to the place from which we started and allows us to see it for the first time. As Balthasar puts it, "because of that final securing of reality which the believer who encounters God in Christ experiences, the theological vision makes it possible for the first time for the philosophical act of encounter with being to occur in all its depth."[53] If God were simply beyond being, the encounter with God would entail as it were a loss of interest in the world. Faith and metaphysics would be competitors. But as Balthasar conceives it, a genuine faith always deepens one's interest in being, one's sense of responsibility for it. This, I believe, is in part what he means when he says that Christians are called to be the guardians of metaphysics.

The question *Wie kommt der Gott in die Philosophie?* ought therefore to be situated within the question *Wie kommt der Mensch in die Theologie?*, first of all because God's invitation comes before man's seeking (even if it is the case that it is only in seeking that one discovers one has already been invited),[54] and second of all because the real weight of a philosophical, a metaphysical notion of God, can be seen and appreciated only by virtue of the absolute primacy of theology. God's revelation of himself in faith becomes, for Balthasar, not only an invitation, but indeed a responsibility to understand God metaphysically.

53. *GL1*, p. 146.

54. See Balthasar, "Forgetfulness of God and Christians," pp. 319-21.

9 Discovering What Has Already Been Given: On a Recent Defense of Thomistic Natural Theology

In his first publication,[1] which launched a career devoted in significant part to philosophizing in light of and in relation to Catholic faith, Robert Spaemann pointed out a certain irony in the famous passage from the Vatican I document *Dei Filius,* in which the Church affirms that anyone who claims that the existence of God, as the "principium et finis omnium rerum," cannot be known with certainty by the natural light of reason thereby separates himself from the Church:[2] the document does not offer rational arguments for the existence of God, but simply asserts the principle that such arguments can be given. The assent that such an assertion demands is not the agreement that reason comes to at the end of a demonstration, but rather that of obedience to authority. The irony, in other words, is that this assertion of reason is not reason's self-assertion; it is instead the call for an act of faith, which goes beyond reason, though it does so in this case only to give reason an inviolable space of its own. But there is indeed a further irony in this passage: the Church does not say, here, that one who denies reason this great power excludes himself from the community of knowers (though of course the passage does not exclude this implication) but specifically from the Church, i.e., from the *community of believers.* Just as one may fairly assert that it can be reasonable to affirm something beyond reason, here we have faith insisting that faith, as it were, is not everything, but has room *inside* of itself — if we may put it thus — for something *outside* of itself.

As Spaemann goes on to explain in this essay, drawing on St. Thomas

1. Robert Spaemann, "Der Irrtum des Traditionalisten: Zur Sozialogisierung der Gottesidee im 19. Jahrhundert," *Wort und Wahrheit* 8 (1953): 493-98.

2. See *Dei Filius,* Canon II.1. Cf. chapter 2 of the same document.

Aquinas, such a safeguarding of reason by faith, though not necessary essentially and in principle, may become indispensable in certain historical circumstances. In his recent book, *Wisdom in the Face of Modernity*,[3] Fr. Thomas Joseph White suggests that the age in which we live, an age characterized largely by disillusionment regarding reason's capacity to discern a plausible meaning for human existence, presents just such circumstances (xvii). To evoke the tenor of our age, Fr. White appeals to the image of the "mid-winter spring" from T. S. Eliot's "Little Gidding": we live at present in the midst of a long and cold winter's day. And yet, though its heat may not directly be felt, the sun — the source of all light, acknowledged in the classical tradition as a privileged symbol of reason — continues to shine, with a constancy that thus may nourish the hope for a new spring.

Fr. White's book seeks to promote this renewal. By drawing on the deep resources of the classical tradition, principally Aristotle and Aquinas, he aims to provide an apology for natural theology, that is, for reason's capacity to come to know God as the transcendent cause of the cosmos. Though such an aim is by no means novel, what distinguishes his particular effort is its being made specifically in response to what he describes as the modern and postmodern critique of "ontotheology" and his accompanying critical evaluation of various recent interpretations of Aquinas, especially of three well-known twentieth-century Thomists who pursued, at least in part, a similar aim: Étienne Gilson, Jacques Maritain, and Karl Rahner.

Because his concern is closely related to the one that prompts our own book, and because his response differs from the one we offer here, it is worthwhile to explore his argument at some length. In the following chapter, we will offer a "nutshell" account of the main line of Fr. White's argument as we understand it, and point out what we take to be the importance of some of Fr. White's insights and basic interpretive positions. After this, we will argue that some of these insights threaten, on the other hand, to be undermined by the line of reasoning he develops ostensibly in support of them. We will thus try to show that the positive achievement of Fr. White's book would require a development of thinking in a somewhat different direction, indeed, ultimately in a direction that Fr. White explicitly excludes. Insofar as he does, we will argue that the basic position he defends is a problematic one. Our most basic aim here, however, is not to criticize Fr. White's book, but rather to take a dis-

3. Thomas Joseph White, O.P., *Wisdom in the Face of Modernity: A Study in Thomistic Natural Theology* (Ave Maria, FL: Sapientia Press, 2009). All unattributed parenthetical references in the text are to this work.

cussion of various claims he makes therein as an occasion to explore and reflect on fundamental questions regarding reason's relationship to God.

An Apology for Natural Knowledge of God

Fr. White develops his account of how natural reason is able to attain positive knowledge of God in some legitimate sense apart from revelation in response to two fundamental objections that he says one frequently encounters in modern thought (3-6; 282). The first comes from philosophy, and claims that it is not possible to come to knowledge of God unless one already posits the existence of God at the outset in an *a priori* way, which is ultimately without warrant. He refers to this objection as the critique of ontotheology, which was originally formulated by Kant and then reformulated in a more postmodern idiom by Heidegger.[4] Because of its aprioristic character, ontotheological thinking does not yield authentic knowledge of God. To the contrary, it reduces God, according to Fr. White's account, to the immanent structures of human thinking, turning God, in the end, into the ultimate explanatory principle of human understanding governed by a "quasi-univocal" logic.[5] This points, then, to the second, more directly theological, objection to natural knowledge of God, which we find perhaps most representatively in the work of Karl Barth, though it has clear roots in Luther's "sola fide."[6] According to this objection, the aspiration to natural knowledge arises from our concupiscence, insofar as it represents a disordered desire to *take* knowledge of God for ourselves, as it were, rather than to receive it as a gift. To insist on natural theology would be to elevate human reason in a way that compromises God's sovereignty. Both the philosophical and theological objections may be said to converge in a rejection of "conceptual idolatry," by which we divinize the products of our own thinking, however different the two objections may be in the motives they ascribe to this divinizing or the genealogy they trace for it.

4. *Wisdom*, p. 24. For Fr. White, the essential difference is that the problem of ontotheology in Kant is a necessary implication of the structure of human thinking, whereas, for Heidegger, it is due to the "*unnecessary constructions* of the thinking subject" (p. 24).

5. Although he presents ontotheology in chapter 1 of *Wisdom*, pp. 3-30, and discusses it throughout the book, Fr. White's most succinct description can be found on pp. 96-97.

6. Fr. White traces the crisis of natural theology essentially back to Luther, although he also cites Alain de Libera's suggestion that the more philosophical guise of the problem originates in Scotus's reformulation of Avicenna's metaphysics. See pp. 4-7; p. 25, n. 51.

In response to these objections, Fr. White develops a natural theology based on essentially *a posteriori* argumentation, which begins with a realist epistemology, proceeds from the things we experience in the world, drawing from that experience a genuinely metaphysical conception of being in terms of the categories of substance and accidents, act and potency, and finally moves from this conception to the ultimate cause of being, namely, God, through a disciplined application of the unique interpretation of analogy offered by Aquinas. While this progression of reason, he affirms, does indeed yield positive knowledge of the essence of God, it nevertheless brings to light at the same time, and precisely by virtue of its analogous character, the "radical incompleteness" of this knowledge (252; 273-74). In so doing, it does not in the least preempt the direct knowledge that God offers of himself to human reason in the gift of revelation. Quite to the contrary — and Fr. White's presentation is particularly compelling on this point — because a negation can occur only in relation to some affirmation, the very positivity of natural knowledge does not threaten but rather allows us to deepen the mind's openness to what lies beyond that knowledge. Thus conceived, natural knowledge of God answers both the philosophical and theological objections mentioned above. It avoids both the Scylla of "immanentism," which would eclipse God's transcendence through the restriction of theology to the limits of natural reason, and the Charybdis of "extrinsicism," which would concede a wholly secular form to human reason and make revelation and grace therefore altogether foreign to human nature. It does so through a sophisticated interpretation of analogy, which highlights in an uncommon way the importance of Aristotle.

At the heart of Fr. White's project is the development of a robust account of what he calls the "via inventionis," the path of discovery, by which reason in its specifically philosophical mode reflects on the objects of experience and moves in a methodical way to the ultimate cause of those effects. This path has as its correlate the "via judicii," which figures much less significantly in Fr. White's account (we will return to this point below), and which complements the movement of the prior via by exercising judgment on reason's starting points in the light of more ultimate discoveries.[7] Fr. White ar-

7. See *Wisdom,* p. xxix. Fr. White's description differs somewhat from Aquinas's own, as Aquinas presents it in the text cited by Fr. White, namely, *ST* 1.79.8. According to Aquinas, in the way of judgment, reason returns to the first principles in order to judge the conclusions in *their* light. Aquinas is making the point, here, that the simple apprehension of first principles — by *intellectus* — is the beginning and end of all discursive movement by *ratio.* His description of the two paths is, in this respect, a sort of *exitus* and *reditus* movement of *ratio* with respect to the intellective "rest" of the unmoving first principles.

gues that the via inventionis has a complex inner structure, which, if followed faithfully, leads to a non-ontotheological form of natural knowledge of God that does not falsely anticipate and thus compromise the novelty of revelation. The essence of his critique of the three twentieth-century Thomists he treats is that each of them short-circuited crucial aspects of this path, so to speak; each skipped over essential steps of the journey, and so ended up falling into just the sort of ontotheological dead-end the path is meant to circumvent. The great importance of Aristotle — whom Fr. White claims contemporary Thomists have tended to underestimate and who stands behind Aquinas almost as the true protagonist of this book — lies in the fact that he traced out the basic itinerary of the via inventionis, even if Aquinas provided decisive reinterpretations of that itinerary in the light of revelation.

To oversimplify to a certain extent,[8] the via inventionis prevents an over-hasty leap into the theological by requiring a patient analysis of the being that we encounter in our ordinary experiences, first in terms of its *intrinsic* causes (substance and accidents) and then in terms of its *extrinsic* causes (the categories of act and potency become crucial here). The first analysis considers being in its first act, by which it is what it is, while the second considers being in its second act, that is, in terms of its operations, by which it makes fully actual what it is and so attains its perfection. These analyses involve above all two forms of analogy that Aristotle introduced and Aquinas subsequently took over, namely, the analogy of proper proportionality, by which relations between diverse things and their properties are compared (A is to B as C is to D), and the *"pros hen"* or *ad unum* analogy (sometimes called the analogy of proportion or analogy of attribution), by which one or many things are compared to an other, which is primary. As Aristotle observed, being is not a genus, which can be understood by abstraction from all specific differences, but is distributed among all the categories differently in each case. To acquire an adequate concept of being therefore requires a comparison of the different ways in which being manifests itself. We thus compare accidents to substance, and the act-potency polarity across the different modes of being's realization. But the reflection on substance in terms of act and potency moves reason to consider the transcendent cause of substances, and so discloses the separate substance(s) as primary. Because this

8. Fr. White's account is far richer than we indicate here. The impressive sophistication of his presentation of natural reason's acquisition of analogical knowledge of God is one of the real merits of his book.

ontological primacy, however, is decidedly *not* a logical priority, in the sense that we would have to understand the cause *first* in order to understand the effects, Fr. White insists that Aristotle does not fall prey to an ontotheological conception of metaphysics.[9]

What, then, does Aquinas add to what we already have in Aristotle? According to Fr. White, Aquinas's contribution, with respect to the question of natural theology, lies not simply in *adding* something, namely, the novelty of Christian revelation, but perhaps even more significantly in preserving what is old, so to speak, within the new context that transforms it. Thus, he introduces a third kind of analogy to the two that one finds in Aristotle in order to clarify whatever ambiguity there may be regarding God's transcendence of the world, but he does so without eliminating the richly analogical sense of being founded in the ordinary experience of the world that Aristotle offers. This new kind is the "*ad alterum*" analogy, which Aquinas explicitly distinguishes from the *ad unum* analogy that would threaten to lead us to think of the difference between God and the world as encompassed by a single order of being (88-94). This form of analogy, based on a notion of God as creator, and thus of the world as entirely dependent on him in every respect, excludes the positing of a common *ratio* shared between cause and effect. God infinitely transcends the world. This means that the nature of God cannot be grasped intuitively, apprehended *per se,* or represented in any adequate sense by the knowledge we have of creatures.

Nevertheless, as we discover especially at the end of Fr. White's book, this does not mean that we are left with a radical apophaticism that would deny any positive natural knowledge whatever. To prepare for this argument, Fr. White makes the claim that, although the *ad alterum* analogy is primary for Aquinas, he does not simply reject the role played by the other two modes. In the middle chapters of his book, Fr. White attempts to show, through a discussion of three modern Thomists, what happens when one focuses in too exclusive a manner on one sort of analogy in one's philosophy, even if that happens to be the *ad alterum* analogy that Aquinas identifies as appropriate in our thinking about God, to the exclusion of the other two.

9. See *Wisdom,* pp. 64-66. Fr. White justifies Aristotle in the face of this critique, not so much on the grounds of a particular conception of God's transcendence of the world (which is certainly at the very least ambiguous in Aristotle), as in terms of his methodology: according to Fr. White, Aristotle does not *presuppose* a conception of God as the *a priori* starting point for his reflection, which is why he cannot be said to commit the fault of "ontotheological thinking." We will discuss the implications of a primarily "methodological" conception of ontotheology below.

The tendency toward ontotheology, that is, the compromise of God's transcendence through the absorption of the being of the first cause into a metaphysical horizon, might be fairly evident in the exclusive use of the analogy of proper proportionality (in which the things compared share a common ratio) and the ad unum analogy (in which many things are related to a "one" that represents their ground), which Fr. White attributes to Maritain and Rahner respectively, but somewhat more surprisingly he believes Gilson falls into ontotheology, so to speak, from the other direction because of an overemphasis on the third form. In this case, we have, more specifically, a "theo-ontology," in which the distinction between being and God is collapsed, not by reducing God to the horizon of common being, but rather by reducing common being, as it were, to the horizon of God's being (117-20). The reason this move is problematic is that if we leap over the causal analysis of created being and proceed, as it were, immediately to God, we will tend to impoverish the notions that are meant precisely to illuminate our understanding of God, so that we will require God's own self-revelation to compensate. It is not an accident, according to Fr. White, that Gilson apparently fell into crisis regarding the question how one was to demonstrate the real distinction between essence and *esse* in dialogue with Scotists, for example, or other non-Thomists, and to *explain* the meaning of *esse,* the act of being which represents the perfection of all perfections. As a result of this crisis, Gilson was eventually led to posit God's revelation of himself as "I am who am" — or rather, to highlight Aquinas's own positing of this revelation — as the origin of the notion of *esse.* By thus substituting the work of grace for that of reason, Fr. White claims, Gilson thereby abandons the possibility of a meaningful natural theology (129-32).

In the last — and perhaps most compelling — part of his book, Fr. White distinguishes his position from that of other contemporary Thomists. On the one hand, there are the Aristotelian Thomists, such as Ralph McInerny, who insist that we must begin thinking with natural philosophy as a way to the notion of an unmoved mover, and so to the concept of a "separate substance," that is necessary for metaphysics proper. Fr. White argues that these thinkers fail to see that the notions employed in physics are always already metaphysical, and also end up including God within metaphysics, rather than adhering to the proper order of the via inventionis (204-16). According to this path of discovery, God enters metaphysics, *not* as its subject (as would be the case in ontotheology), but strictly speaking *only insofar* as God is the *cause* of its subject, i.e., being. On the other hand, against contemporary Thomists such as Denys Turner who he claims "overemphasize" the apophatic element in Aquinas's thought, Fr. White argues that, even if God is not the *subject* of metaphysics, the via inventionis nevertheless opens up to *genuinely positive* knowledge of God. As a sort of counterpart to Gilson, Turner highlights the philosophical darkness, we might say, of the concept of *esse* outside of God's self-revelation, a concept to which we attain, for Turner, through a reflection on nothingness — which Fr. White points out is merely conceptual because it cannot be encountered anywhere in experience. What is missing in Turner's approach, for Fr. White, is once again the priority of a causal analysis of being, by which we gradually enrich our understanding of *esse* through *a posteriori* reflections on the beings we encounter in the world rather than through an aprioristic conception of absolute nothingness. In this latter case, we would be looking at the world too immediately, so to speak, from God's perspective, and would fail to undertake the patient labor of metaphysical reflection (265).

What this renewed emphasis on the via inventionis brings home is that, to say it again, God does not lie within the horizon of metaphysics, which is what the critique of ontotheology charges, but is nevertheless approached most truly by metaphysical reflection, and specifically *that* metaphysical reflection which faithfully follows the itinerary of the via inventionis. According to this approach, in a nutshell, reason comes to desire knowledge of the essence of causes through a contemplation of their effects. Thus, the path on which Fr. White takes thought reveals that reason *naturally* desires an end that *exceeds its nature,* and that, moreover, this incompleteness is something that reason discovers in its own operations, rigorously followed out to their proper ends, so that one cannot insist that revelation is necessary in principle to bring this incompleteness to light (287-88). Such a conception, according to Fr. White, is crucial for us to be able to say, as we must, that revelation brings a novelty to reason, i.e., that it introduces insight into God in a wholly gratuitous manner, a knowledge that reason cannot grasp on the basis of its own resources alone, and yet at the very same time it introduces this insight as something that is not simply foreign to reason, but rather fulfills its deepest aspiration.

As Fr. White sees it, natural reason leads us genuinely *to* the threshold of the order of grace and revelation, if not in fact over it. He explains that we can best formulate this complex idea by saying that philosophy ultimately posits the existence of God — i.e., it tells us simply *that* God exists — but that theology's essential role is eventually to tell us *who* or *what* God is.[10]

10. "A philosophical and Thomistic emphasis on our knowledge *that* God exists, and

Only God's gratuitous invitation into his inner life, which as subsistent intellect and will in which subject and object are identical is the wisdom itself of which our metaphysical aspirations in the face of modernity are a mere, a glorious, image, is able to bring to completion the longings of the human heart.

There are a number of things to praise about *Wisdom in the Face of Modernity.* A vigorous defense of the scope and capacity of reason is no doubt one of the greatest needs of our age, and Fr. White provides this not only in terms of the central aim of the book — namely, to demonstrate the viability of natural knowledge of God — but also through the means by which he accomplishes this aim. A sustained philosophical argument, which patiently follows each of the paths it requires and which shows a careful attention to texts, is increasingly uncommon in the contemporary American academy. At the very same time, he insists on the modesty of reason, which is paradoxically just as urgent a reminder in our age as the former. While it may seem to be precisely the opposite, in fact, as we have seen repeatedly, the genuine modesty of reason cannot be separated from its strength, and vice versa. Fr. White demonstrates this paradox in his very helpful critique of Denys Turner's negative theology, as he understands it,[11] in the book's final chapter (255-68). Turner is well known for his insistence on natural reason's ultimate inability to know anything about God's nature, and yet, as Fr. White respectfully points out, this excessive apophaticism results from a radical sense of contingency that is based on something that lies outside of any possible experience, namely, the concept of absolute nothingness, out of which God created. In this case, reason simultaneously knows both too much and too little: it begins, not with anything *given* in actual experience, but with its own projected concept, which in fact involves what Fr. White suggests is a presumptuous insight into God's intentions in creating, and it is this very presumption that eventually leads reason to an empty silence regarding the

---

our simultaneously radical ignorance of *what* God is, demonstrates the profound compatibility between Thomistic natural theology, and the claims of Christian divine revelation. Revelation is the answer of who or what God is, responding to the void in our knowledge of God that philosophy helps us to identify. This position seems comprehensive, insofar as it seeks to be a multi-sided response to the above-mentioned difficulties concerning the avoidance of both philosophical agnosticism and a rationalist presumptuousness" (*Wisdom,* pp. 253-54).

11. We make no judgment, here, on the question whether Fr. White's account of Turner is accurate or adequate. Our judgment concerns only the position he ascribes to Turner in this chapter.

nature of God. Its very "preemptive" conception of absolute nothingness makes reason improperly passive with respect to God's self-revelation once it comes.

In contrast to presumptuous passivity, Fr. White argues for the paradox of a *natural* desire for what lies *beyond nature*, which he rightly observes is the only way to avoid an extrinsicism between faith and reason that at the same time does not fall into an immanentism that would reduce faith to reason. What is certainly Fr. White's most important contribution to the discussion is his sophisticated interpretation of the three different senses of analogy in Aquinas, which balances the more apophatic aspect of the *ad alterum* analogy with the more positive aspects of the other two types. While it is true that Aquinas identifies the first as the only appropriate analogy with respect to God,[12] to isolate this analogy from the others would significantly impoverish the concept of being we analogously attribute to God, and indeed tempt us to substitute our intuitive leap to God — which Fr. White repeatedly criticizes as "aprioristic" — for the progressive development of *a posteriori* reflection. Fr. White helpfully observes that God is not revealed exclusively through the medium of existence, but also through essences, or in other words, the meaning of God comes to expression also in creatures (259-60). To find God, we might say, reason may not "leap over" or otherwise bypass the world through some aprioristic vision, but must rather patiently and attentively work its way through the world. One is reminded here of Hegel's criticism of Schelling that we mentioned in chapter one: Schelling's philosophy of religion seemed to Hegel to be "shot from a pistol."[13] In more technical language, God is indeed not in any direct manner the *subject* of metaphysics, but is rather the *cause* of its subject, which is *being qua being*. Reason's natural desire for God therefore leads it in some

12. As Fr. White observes, Aquinas explicitly states that "*only* the *ad alterum* attribution is valid for the creature/God relation" in *ST* 1.13.5 (see *Wisdom*, p. 90, nn. 67-68; pp. 90-91). Fr. White qualifies this statement shortly thereafter, however, by explaining that Aquinas speaks favorably of the analogy of proper proportionality in his more mature commentaries on Aristotle and claims, with reference to an essay by Leo Elders, that one ought not to exaggerate the discontinuities between Aquinas's early and later texts (p. 92, n. 70). It is important for Fr. White to make this point because, as we have seen, he wishes to raise a criticism of what he says is Gilson's too-exclusive use of the *ad alterum* analogy.

13. Although Hegel did not mention Schelling by name, it is clear that he has his old seminary roommate in mind when he criticizes the "rapturous enthusiasm which, like a shot from a pistol, begins straight away with absolute knowledge, and makes short work of other standpoints by declaring that it takes no notice of them" (preface, *Phenomenology of Spirit*, trans. A. V. Miller [Oxford: Oxford University Press, 1977], p. 16).

sense first into the being of the world, and only then into its transcendent principle. This is a principle that we cannot forget without far-reaching deleterious consequences for both reason and faith. Fr. White's emphasis on the causal analysis of being as an indispensable moment of natural theology is crucial in this regard.

Restricting God and Reason

On the other hand, however, there are a number of philosophical decisions that Fr. White makes that, we hope to show, are not necessary to his essential positions and, moreover, in certain important respects weaken or even work against the very contributions his book offers. As we will see, these tend to concern not so much his positive claims as it does what he believes these claims have to exclude. It is not, of course, possible to comment on every argument constructed in the book, though his claims are so interesting and provocative that one is quite tempted to do so. Nor is there space here to pass judgment on the accuracy of his interpretations in every particular case. It would become too complex too quickly to try to sort out, for example, Fr. White's interpretation of Gilson's interpretation of Aquinas's interpretation of Aristotle's interpretation of reality, and in any event such an endeavor can only be of secondary importance in the end.[14] Instead, we will focus on certain basic positions that Fr. White adopts and judgments he makes, which we will evaluate, so to speak, on their own merits and above all in terms of their logical implications, leaving open in the present context the question to what extent his account of Maritain, for example, or Aquinas is an adequate one. As far as those questions go, the best hermeneutical approach is no doubt the one Eric Voegelin offers in another context (and incidentally reflects the Catholic spirit of St. Ignatius): when one is faced with textual ambiguities in the writings of a great thinker that allow several possible readings, the best interpretation is always the most profound one.

Fr. White, for his part, follows this principle with respect to Aristotle, when he rightly claims it is problematic to make him a simple foil against which to demonstrate the novelty of Christianity, as certain Thomists have a tendency to do (33). His book is a testimony to the way one's thinking can be

14. This is not to say that questions of the accuracy of interpretations are without significance even with respect to what we are proposing as being of primary importance, namely, the judgment of the truth and goodness of philosophical claims.

enriched if one avoids such a temptation. On the other hand, however, Fr. White himself falls to this temptation in his reading of other thinkers, and his own reflections are all the worse for it. We will begin our assessment by focusing on just two examples, which prove to be decisive for Fr. White's book. On the one hand, there is Fr. White's reading of Plato, whom he presents, so to speak, as a simple foil against which to demonstrate the novelty of Aristotle. On the other hand, there is his reading of Heidegger, in particular the philosopher's notion of "ontotheology," which is pivotal for Fr. White's general argument since it sets the terms of the problem to which he intends to respond. To say it again, our point in discussing his interpretations of these two thinkers is not in the first case to quibble over the right reading of their work — indeed, to do so would require a lengthy presentation and comparison of texts, along with discussions of different scholarly judgments on them, for which there is no space in the present context — but rather to show the implications Fr. White's rather narrow interpretations have for the content of his own thinking.

Fr. White's interpretation of Plato boils down to two basic judgments: that Plato failed to come to any satisfactory articulation of the nature of wisdom, insofar as he offers a "progressively evolving" attempt (35), through his early, middle, and late dialogues, to reach a goal that remained elusive; and, second, that he conceived the ultimate cause of the cosmos, namely, the good, in a strictly univocal fashion (38). One of the implications of this univocity is that Plato is led to identify what is first in the order of logic with what is first in the order of being — which, as we will see in a moment, is a primitive incidence of what Fr. White will call ontotheology. We will pass over Fr. White's first judgment, which presents a strangely flat-footed reading of Plato that demonstrates little sensitivity to the interpretive demands of the dialogue genre, not to mention the fact that the best recent scholarship on Plato, for good philosophical, historical, and philological reasons, no longer follows a simple "developmental" ordering of the dialogues.[15] More directly relevant to the discussion to follow is the second judgment. Fr. White's suggestion that Plato reduced the good to what Aristotle calls the

15. Although nondevelopmental interpretations of Plato have never been lacking, we may fairly say that such interpretations have become mainstream in recent scholarship on Plato, at least among those outside of the analytic school. In 1991, Jacob Howland published an essay that demonstrated incontrovertibly that all of the attempts to establish a chronology of the dialogues are question-begging, resting on a set of prior assumptions about the content of that philosophy. See Howland, "Re-Reading Plato: The Problem of Platonic Chronology," *Phoenix* 45, no. 3 (1991): 189-214.

formal cause[16] overlooks a host of claims Plato makes about the good in the main place in his corpus it arises, i.e., books 6 and 7 of the *Republic.* There, Plato not only refers to the good as a "form," or more precisely, an "idea" (*Rep.*, 505a) (which does not have the technical meaning that "formal cause" has, though it is clearly related in some sense), but he also identifies it as the *source* of all being, truth, and knowledge (*Rep.*, 509b) (that is, as what one might call the supreme "efficient" cause) and defines it as that which everyone desires in everything he does (*Rep.*, 505d-e) (i.e., as a "final cause"). Moreover, it is just this "comprehensively causal" character, as it were, which is due to its ultimacy, that complicates our attempts to know it: the soul, he says, is "unable to get a sufficient grasp of just what it is" (505e). The good, for Plato, can never be a simple object for the mind, as is the univocal concept to which Fr. White reduces it, because it is the cause of the mind's objects and indeed of the very light by which the mind comes to know them. As I have tried to show at length elsewhere,[17] Plato articulates a very sophisticated analogy by which the mind progressively ascends toward the good, but at the same time finds its path reversed to the extent that the good, which the mind discovers only at the *end* of its thinking,[18] is never *merely* the end but reveals itself at the same time and for the same reason as *prior* to everything that the mind has thought.

Plato calls the good the "unhypothetical first principle" (*Rep.*, 510b), which is a paradox. Normally, because one can never achieve an absolute perspective from which to start (*pace* transcendental idealism), the starting points of one's thinking are relative and so conditional, requiring confirmation by other discoveries. This is what makes them "hypothetical," meaning both what undergirds and thus supports one's thinking, and also what depends on something other than itself for its own truth. But the good, which is for Plato *absolutely first,* is a governing principle of thought without being

16. According to Fr. White, in Plato, "as a universal form, the good is conceived in a strictly univocal fashion" (*Wisdom*, p. 38). He goes on to say that "Plato's quest for wisdom implies an identification of this wisdom with the form of the good, and entails a corresponding problem of how all things participate in this universal (univocal) form. . . . Aristotle, however, demonstrates that God (or the divine) cannot be the formal cause of the goodness of things" (*Wisdom,* p. 41).

17. D. C. Schindler, *Plato's Critique of Impure Reason: On Goodness and Truth in the Republic* (Washington, DC: Catholic University Press of America, 2008), pp. 139-75.

18. "At all events, this is the way the phenomena look to me: in the knowable the last thing to be seen, and that with considerable effort, is the *idea* of the good; but once seen, it must be concluded that this is in fact the cause of all that is right and fair in everything." *Republic* 517b-c.

conditional: its truth does not depend on something else, i.e., it cannot be demonstrated in terms of something more fundamental and thereby confirmed, but for this very reason it cannot be a simple starting point for thinking. The good is therefore not an "aprioristic" concept from which one starts as a secure possession and which therefore "grounds" all of one's subsequent thinking; instead, it is as he famously says, "beyond being" (*Rep.*, 509b), which means in this context that, because being is the proper object of reason (*Rep.*, 477c-d; 478a), the good *is prior to the beginning*, just as it is *posterior to the end.* The a priority of the *a posteriori*, if we may put the paradox thus, is arguably the hallmark of the Platonic tradition in matters of natural theology; we will return to its significance with respect to Fr. White's general argument in a moment.

Fr. White's treatment of Plato is not unrelated to the account he offers of Heidegger's critique of ontotheology. The issue in this case is not so much a facile dismissal as an oversimplification, which has an even more direct bearing since Fr. White constructs his interpretation of Aquinas (and various Thomists) precisely in response to and in the terms set by what he identifies as ontotheology. According to Fr. White, the core problem that Heidegger refers to as the "onto-theo-logical constitution of metaphysics" that defines Western thinking is that it

> attempts to study the conditions of existence for any possible being. To do so it must have recourse to a consideration of the immanent laws of human systematic thinking (i.e., principles of causality and sufficient reason) that are employed when metaphysicians attempt to explain sensible reality. The use of these principles eventually requires (or invites) the invocation of an aprioristic concept of God in order to explain the sum total of all possible knowledge and experience. This structure of thinking places God at the summit of the science of metaphysics and simultaneously makes him the ultimate explanatory principle of human understanding. God is thereby assimilated by natural theology into its own systematic representation of "being," and in this process the divine is inevitably conceived as the "supreme being" who alone is self-caused *(causa sui).* (96-97)

The oversimplification that occurs in Fr. White's interpretation of the critique of ontotheology becomes apparent in the fact that he takes it ultimately to concern *methodology.* The next sentence after the text just cited runs: "By these standards of measure, however, Aquinas's methodological procedure cannot be characterized as ontotheological" (97). Whenever Fr. White mentions ontotheology, which represents as we have seen a central theme of his book, he essentially reduces it to a critique of "aprioristic" thinking about God.[19] This is thinking that does not so to speak work its way gradually up to God (in a manner that leaves thinking open for revelation), but rather takes a concept of God for granted in one way or another as the basis of its interpretation of everything else: philosophical thinking *starts* with God, in other words, when it should rather *end* with him. *Because* this is the essence of the problem, as Fr. White sees it, a satisfying response requires little else, in the end, than developing a natural theology "that does not presuppose implicitly that which it seeks to attain by rational argument" (xxx), which means that, for a natural theology to be adequate, arguments for God must be "*uniquely* a posteriori" (97), based on experience of real beings rather than on concepts of possibility.

An even cursory consideration of what is no doubt Heidegger's most succinct explicit statement of the problem of ontotheology, a passage from the essay "The Onto-theo-logical Constitution of Metaphysics" that Fr. White himself cites (23-24, n. 49), suffices to show that the issue is not primarily one of methodology but of substance (and *therefore* also of methodology):

> Because Being appears as ground, beings are what is grounded; the highest being, however, is what accounts in the sense of giving the first cause. When metaphysics thinks of being with respect to the ground that is common to all beings as such, then it is logic as onto-logic. When metaphysics thinks of beings as such as a whole, that is, with respect to the highest being which accounts for everything, then it is logic as theo-logic. . . . The onto-theological constitution of metaphysics stems from the prevalence of that difference which keeps Being as the ground, and beings as what is grounded and what gives account, apart from and related to each other; and by this keeping, perdurance is achieved. . . . The deity enters into philosophy through the perdurance . . . the perdurance results in and gives Being as the generative ground. This ground itself needs to be properly accounted for by that for which it accounts, that is, by the causation through the supremely original matter — and that is

19. See, e.g., *Wisdom*, pp. xxx, xxii, 26, 29, 34, 64, 65, 97, 174, 191, 201, 204, 206, and so forth. Perhaps the clearest example of this association, which connects the problematic directly with the question of the philosophy-theology relationship, can be found on pp. 249-50.

> the cause as *causa sui.* This is the right name for the god of philosophy. Man can neither pray nor sacrifice to this god.[20]

As the text makes evident, the problem is not, in the first place, that one presupposes what one ought to prove — i.e., it is not simply "aprioristic" thinking — but rather concerns most fundamentally our understanding of the nature of being, of the relationship that holds sway between Being and beings, of cause, and of reason generally. As we saw in the previous chapter, Heidegger suggests that classical metaphysics tends to enclose reality, we might say, at its most basic level inside a relationship of ground to the grounded, so that even God himself is presented in essentially the same terms. In metaphysics, God appears as the "causa sui." The upshot of such a conception is that nothing in the world stands outside of this essentially transitive relationship of one thing *acting on* another. One of the implications of ontotheology, in other words, is a world vulnerable to, and in fact positively inviting of, the tyranny of technology. This is why Heidegger responds to the problem, not, like Fr. White, by insisting on exclusively *a posteriori* reasoning, but rather by thinking of Being in a way he takes to be radically different from the main current of the Western tradition: namely, most ultimately in ungrounded or noncausal terms. The strange language he uses — the "lighting" or "clearing," the "Er-eignis," the "Es gibt" — serves to evoke an attentiveness to the event of the "thereness" of Being, which gives itself to our grateful thinking *(denken als danken),* without invoking a discrete cause that produces an effect. The disorientation that this alien idiom brings about is meant in part to make us fall poetically silent before the mystery of Being so that we may be alert to its own creative silence. The West has "forgotten" Being because it has become incapable of meditative silence.

This is of course just a thumbnail sketch of one aspect of Heidegger's critique, which we elaborated more substantially in chapters seven and eight. The point in raising this as a contrast to Fr. White's understanding of the matter, to say it again, is not in the first place to make an argument about proper readings of Heidegger, nor is it to defend him or his critique of ontotheology. In fact, we argued in the last chapter that Catholics have generally been too quick to concede the terms of the problem Heidegger sets, and have typically responded only by showing why one figure or another ought to be excepted from his critique. This is essentially what Fr. White

20. Martin Heidegger, "The Onto-theo-logical Constitution of Metaphysics," in *Identity and Difference,* trans. J. Staumbaugh (New York: Harper & Row, 1969), pp. 42-74; here, 70-72. Cited in *Wisdom,* pp. 23-24, n. 49.

does in the present book, specifically with respect to Aristotle and an Aristotelian reading of Aquinas. A more fundamental response would require challenging the basic presuppositions regarding the nature of God, cause, being, thinking, and philosophy that lie behind Heidegger's critique.[21]

In the present context, there is of course no room to present such a challenge, aspects of which we undertook in the previous two chapters. We wish only to suggest here that a narrow interpretation of Heidegger's critique will provoke a narrow response. An engagement with Heidegger ought to provide the occasion, not simply for the articulation of a "general order of metaphysical inquiry,"[22] but more fundamentally for a reflection on the very nature of reason in its relation to being and to God. Indeed, a prioritizing of methodology is arguably an expression of the very technologizing of thinking that Heidegger had in mind in his critique, so that an argument for exclusively *a posteriori* reasoning offends the spirit precisely in (and because of) its attempt to obey the letter of that critique. In what follows we will try to show that Fr. White's reductive interpretation of Heidegger, along with his facile dismissal of Plato, lead to problematically restrictive notions of both God and reason, and therefore to an inadequate conception of the relationship between philosophy and theology. More specifically, we will argue: (1) that the mode of reasoning that Fr. White champions finitizes God for the mind; (2) that the argument he advances for natural theology unreflectively presupposes the modern impoverished conception of reason that neglects the primacy of *intellectus* over *ratio;* and (3) that he leaves philosophy and theology ultimately too extrinsic to one another. We will also try to show that these three shortcomings are all logically connected.

1. Let us begin with the first charge. To put it in a nutshell, our claim is that an *exclusively "a posteriori"* approach to knowledge of God renders God a finite object to the extent that he is intelligible at all — a reduction that cannot be remedied by an insistence on the ultimate apophaticism of natural theology, as we shall see in a moment. There are two aspects to this problem. The first is that exclusively *a posteriori* reasoning makes the intelligibility of God unilaterally dependent on the intelligibility of the things we experience and reflect on

21. In a footnote, Fr. White does cite positively one of the rare examples of a genuine "turning of the tables" on Heidegger, namely, David Bentley Hart's essay, "The Offering of Names: Metaphysics, Nihilism, and Analogy," in *Reason and the Reasons of Faith,* ed. Paul Griffiths and Reinhard Hütter (New York: T. & T. Clark, 2005), pp. 255-94, but he does not weigh the implications for his own discussion.

22. See chapter 7 of *Wisdom,* pp. 201-50.

in the world. Fr. White affirms that our knowledge of "the existence of God . . . is derived from creatures" (271). How strictly does he mean that what we know of God is *derivative?* Is God's intelligibility less than and subordinate to the intelligibility of creatures? An appeal to the *quoad nos–in se* distinction does not suffice to avoid the disorder that this implication represents. Fr. White anticipates this potential problem by insisting on the *analogical* character of our knowledge of God, which comes about through the classical threefold method of naming God that Fr. White elaborates in the book's final chapter: one posits a (finite) notion, negates whatever imperfection lies within it, and then attributes the thus purified notion in a "super-eminent" sense to God (268-74). The point of this method is precisely to avoid attributing something to God in a merely finite sense; the negation in the second moment allows the notion to stand for *more* in relation to God than it does when ascribed to creatures. But the danger is that, if the difference between God and the world is conceived in an exclusively negative manner, which is to say that if one moves from the finite to the infinite only by *removing* something, as it were (namely, what is taken to be an imperfection), then anything positive in one's resultant knowledge of God remains altogether finite.[23] In this case, the "super-eminent" name of God would essentially be a "super-sized" finite intelligibility, alongside of which one would append an indeterminate openness to the infinity of God, which is void of content precisely because it is based simply on a negation. The "more" of God's intelligibility in this approach lies therefore precisely *outside* of our thinking, rather than also in some (yet to be determined) sense "inside" of it. The significance of this crucial point will become more evident as we proceed.

The only way to avoid simply juxtaposing the excess to the determinate concept is to acknowledge that the infinity of God bears in some sense positively on our understanding in the finite order. What could this mean? Here we come to the second aspect. To think of God as something we attain only at the end of our reasoning, i.e., in an exclusively *a posteriori* manner, assumes that God lies, so to speak, "out *there*," and *not* in any sense "in *here*"

23. Along similar lines, but in a different context, Balthasar signals the danger in the philosophy of religion of "constructing" an idea of God by combining finite notions, in this case simply identifying the nonsubsistence of *esse* with essence as we understand it to achieve a concept of *Ipsum Esse subsistens:* "Thinking about the two finitudes together (even the nonsubsistence of the real points to such a finitude) does not result in the absolute" (*E,* p. 49). If we acknowledge that the notion of the infinite achieved by simply negating the finite is a finite notion of the infinite, we ought to heed the same warning in applying the divine names according to the method Fr. White elaborates.

and always already present in our thinking, or to put it in more technical language, that it is possible to affirm God's transcendence without necessarily and as a function thereof also affirming God's immanence. It is precisely in this respect that Fr. White's facile dismissal of Plato, and by extension the broad Christian tradition inspired by him, comes back as it were to haunt him. Fr. White insists on the priority of a causal analysis of being in the development of a natural theology, and claims that a proper (natural) understanding of God emerges in our consideration of the extrinsic causes of being. Perhaps as a result of the importance Fr. White gives to Aristotle, he describes God almost exclusively in terms of final causality, and so in terms, not of being's first act (its internal cause, namely, its substance), but of being's second act, the operation by which being achieves its perfection. There is virtually no discussion, here, of God as creator, specifically as the *first* cause of the creative act that is in some respect prior even to substance. The danger here, of course, is that God thereby threatens to become a being that does not concern things in any sense as they are in themselves, but only that to which they subsequently relate. But, as the Platonic tradition strives always to recollect, as it were, if God is the transcendent cause of reality, then the meaning of God does not simply emerge *after* we get clear about the meaning of the world and so wholly on the basis of that meaning, but rather precisely because it is the meaning *of God* we must come to see that this meaning was always already operating in a manner that we can only ever be insufficiently aware of at any point over the course of our thinking. In other words, reason cannot attain to God exclusively in an *a posteriori* manner, but God must always also be "*a priori*" in some respect precisely insofar as he is the transcendent cause of all reality. This means that we cannot move, as it were, from A to B to C and then to God, but the attainment of God in our thinking necessarily requires us to go back to A, B, and C all over again and rethink their thus-transformed significance. This is what it would mean to say that the infinity of God bears *positively* on our notions, and is not something simply negatively derived therefrom. We will return to this point in a moment when we consider Fr. White's conception of reason.

One of the reasons Fr. White insists on excluding any "aprioristic" approaches to God is the very good one that it compromises God's transcendence. If Aquinas acknowledges some "presentiment of God," he explains, it has nothing to do with any "innate ideas" but is rather a desire for our perfection that is by implication a desire for God.[24] The rejection of Cartesian

24. *Wisdom*, p. 247. Although speaking of a "presentiment of God," Fr. White indi-

"innate ideas," however, and the compromise of God's transcendence that they certainly do represent, need not lead to a rejection of any and all traces of the *"a priori,"* beyond a very general desire for perfection, in reason's relation to God. One might say that the false dilemma that Fr. White presents himself — either *a priori* or *a posteriori* — is the price he pays for his facile dismissal of Plato. For a further alternative, beyond the two Fr. White allows, we might consider St. Augustine's reflections on the mind's relationship to God in the *Confessions,* above all in book X. Here, St. Augustine asks "where" and "when" it is he first encounters God, and passes from the "external" world of the senses to the "internal" world of the soul,[25] getting closer as it were with each step, until he reaches the innermost region of the mind from which all of its powers spring, the region he calls *memory.* While one expects him to come upon God once this final door, so to speak, is opened, Augustine instead encounters a difficulty: to have a memory presupposes that one already has knowledge, that the encounter has already at some point taken place, which would mean that he had not yet in fact found the origin of that encounter. Affirming God as already part of one's memory — as an "innate idea," one might say — would compromise God's transcendence, and ultimately eliminate the gratuity of the encounter with grace. On the other hand, however, Augustine points out that one could not *seek* God, and indeed could not recognize God if one in fact were to find him, unless one *did* already have a memory of God.[26] This is, of course, a variation of "Meno's paradox," which Plato discusses in the dialogue of that name, and it repre-

---

cates only one aspect of what Aquinas says regarding the appetitive order, and does not consider what he says regarding the understanding specifically. Aquinas insists in fact that God is implicit in our will, not only as final cause but also as efficient cause, and in our intellect as exemplar cause: "All things naturally tend to God, but not explicitly. . . . Accordingly, because God is the last end, He is sought in every end, just as, because He is the first efficient cause, He acts in every agent" (*De ver.* 22.2); "All cognitive beings also know God implicitly in any object of knowledge. Just as nothing has the note of appetibility except by a likeness to the first goodness, so nothing is knowable except by a likeness to the first truth" (*De ver.* 22.2ad1). The word "likeness" indicates the order of form.

25. Augustine, *Confessions,* trans. R. S. Pine-Coffin (New York: Penguin Books, 1961), X.6-8.

26. "So I must go beyond memory too, if I am to reach the God who made me different from the beasts that walk on the earth and wiser than the birds that fly in the air. I must pass beyond memory to find you, my true Good, my sure Sweetness. But where will the search lead me? Where am I to find you? If I find you beyond my memory, it means that I have no memory of you. How, then, am I to find you, if I have no memory of you?" (*Confessions* X.17).

sents a variation of the Kantian concession to idolatry that we discussed in chapter two.[27]

Augustine solves the problem without short-circuiting the complexity through some reduction, and ends up describing the reality of the mind's relation to God in extremely paradoxical terms: to put it succinctly, God lies indeed beyond the mind, and so beyond the memory, but not in the sense that God comes simply after the mind, as something it subsequently discovers simply outside of itself. Instead, God also comes before the mind; he is, so to speak, *earlier than the mind's memory.* Thus, after noting God's presence in his memory,[28] Augustine reflects: "Where, then, did I find you so that I could learn of you? For you were not in my memory before I learned of you. Where else, then, did I find you, to learn of you, *unless it was in yourself, above me?*"[29] So, Augustine, here, reverses the perspective, as it were, and so discovers his mind in God rather than discovering God "in" his mind as an innate idea.[30] This leads to the temporal paradox we have indicated, which he ascribes to God specifically as Beauty — "I have learnt to love you late, Beauty, at once so ancient and so new! I have learnt to love you late" — and provokes the realization: "You were with me, but I was not with you."[31] This, one could say, is the epistemological implication of the ontological truth Augustine affirms, namely, that God is "interior intimo meo et superior summo meo."[32] It serves to show that the issue of ontotheology cannot be decided by methodology alone, since the *nature* of the object reason discovers has, we might say, retroactive implications for reason's approach.

Our understanding of God is, for Augustine, neither merely *a posteriori* nor merely *a priori,* but is in fact both at once, because God could not genuinely transcend the mind without also being at the same time already present within it. We genuinely discover God as a truth that we did not know before, but we discover him precisely *as* preceding and enabling our search,

27. Plato, *Meno* 80e. Plato solves the paradox through what he presents as a *myth* of recollection, according to which the soul already knows what it "learns" in time. The fact that it is presented as a myth, and has obvious logistical problems, indicates that Plato does not mean it in the "literalistic" sense it is often presumed to have. In any event, Augustine's problem is even more difficult since it involves a truth *above* the soul rather than one that is ultimately identical to it, as Plato appears to believe that the truth of the forms is.

28. *Confessions* X.24-25.

29. *Confessions* X.26. Emphasis added.

30. I owe this formulation to Michael Hanby.

31. *Confessions* X.27.

32. *Confessions* III.6.

as already having been present in and guiding it all along the way. To reject this "*a priori*" dimension and insist that our knowledge of God is not presupposed in any sense by our inquiry but results simply from the purely natural efforts of reason is what we might call "epistemological semipelagianism."[33] The affirmation that our knowledge of God is *a priori because* it is *a posteriori,* to say it again, is nothing more than the epistemological expression of the ontological truth that God is immanent in all things precisely *because* he transcends them all, so that to deny his immanence is to deny his transcendence.[34] This paradox is summed up perhaps most succinctly in Nicholas of Cusa's famous formulation: God is so other, he is the *not other,* the "*non aliud.*"[35] The Christian tradition took over and deepened this originally Platonic insight into the mind's relation to the first cause for what is no doubt the best possible reason: because it is undeniably true.

Now, to be sure, it was not Augustine's aim, in book X of the *Confessions,* to present an argument for the existence of God. Instead, he was simply reflecting in these passages on the mind's relation to God within the context of an already-established faith. It would be important to explore in detail what the truth of the paradox would imply for such arguments, which we cannot do in the present context except to make a very general observation.[36] At the very least, one would have to say that the simple *a priori* (so to speak) rejection in principle of all *a priori* arguments for the existence of God is suspicious — as would be any claim that only *a priori* arguments are legitimate. There would have to be room for both, with a priority given to *a posteriori* arguments insofar as God's immanence is a function of his transcendence rather than the reverse. In this respect, we would have to reflect on why Fr. White, who otherwise champions Aquinas's natural theology, would believe it necessary to reject Aquinas's "fourth way" to God, which he deems to be itself "aprioristic" as Aquinas presents it, and which he therefore

33. While Pelagianism concerned a particular interpretation of Adam and the effects of original sin, "semipelagianism," which was defined as a heresy at the Second Council of Orange in 529, consists of the claim that affirming the *freedom* of the act of faith requires that we conceive the act as initiated by an act of the natural will alone, without the aid of grace, even if one allows grace to give subsequent aid and bring the act of will to its fruition.

34. More specifically, to reject God's immanence is to put God's being in competition, as it were, with the world's being (where the world is, God is not, and vice versa), which is to reduce God and the world to beings of the same order, and thus to deny God's transcendence of that order.

35. Nicholas of Cusa, *De li non aliud.*

36. This is essentially what de Lubac does in *The Discovery of God,* esp. chapter 3 (Grand Rapids: Eerdmans, 1996), pp. 57-86.

insists must be reread as founded on one of the other, more evidently *"a posteriori,"* arguments (168).

2. The paradox of the mind's approach to God, in which it discovers *"a posteriori"* that God has preceded it, leads us to examine, not just reason's initial principles, but more fundamentally the nature and operation of reason itself. If Augustine's description of the mind's relation to God is a good one, it is clearly insufficient to think of reason as following a simple progressive path from its self-evidential starting points, through an analysis of its experience, all the way up to God. The point is not to reject this path, but to refuse to isolate it as the whole of reason's journey. Although it is certainly true that reason moves in a progressive way, if we absolutize this aspect, we will end up with what we might call an essentially "centrifugal" notion of reason, a view of reason as "fleeing its origins." If, by contrast, it is indeed the case that the ultimate cause that reason seeks, adequately conceived, lies just as much at the origin as at the end, then on the one hand we will have to elevate the significance of reason's "downward" or "reverse" path, by which it judges and so reconsiders its starting premises in the light of its later insights, and, on the other hand, we will have to enrich our sense of the intelligibility of the *given,* of what therefore precedes and enables the subsequent work that reason carries out in its achievement of knowledge. We will see how both of these dimensions come into play in aspects of Fr. White's criticisms of Maritain and Gilson.

Let us recall, first of all, that Fr. White's case for natural theology centers on what he calls the "via inventionis," the "path of discovery," which he follows St. Thomas in distinguishing from the "via judicii," the "path of judgment": "Aquinas himself distinguishes between a philosophical *via inventionis,* or way of inquiry, by which the intellect proceeds from initial, self-evident principles to scientific conclusions, and the *via judicii,* by which the intellect judges in the light of its more ultimate discoveries the initial principles from which it began" (xxix). Although he mentions at one point that both dimensions are part of philosophical reflection in Aquinas's conception of the matter,[37] he also admits that he focuses almost exclusively on

37. See *Wisdom,* p. 250. Although he refers to "philosophical thought" here, Fr. White clarifies elsewhere that Aquinas himself did not seek to distill a philosophical discourse about God for believers that is relatively autonomous with respect to a specifically theological discourse. Nevertheless, Fr. White's argument is that such a distillation can be carried out on principles that Aquinas articulates — which means that the distinction between philosophy and theology is not foreign to his thought, even if it is one that he does not himself make explicitly.

the via inventionis. In fact, he tends to identify the path of discovery with philosophy simply.[38] It ought to be clear how the identification of philosophy with this path fits in with Fr. White's interpretation of the problem of ontotheology: Fr. White wishes to show that reason does not ("aprioristically") *assume* God at the outset, but must make its own way on the basis of ordinary experience to come to an (always analogical) understanding of God. It is precisely *because* the insights acquired, the discoveries made, are due to reason's own efforts, for Fr. White, that we can call them genuinely philosophical. What was already disclosed to reason, before its labors, is therefore precisely not philosophical.

This assumption regarding the nature and operation of reason becomes apparent in Fr. White's criticism of Maritain: the French Thomist, he explains, misunderstands the place of the transcendentals in Aquinas's thought, and is thereby led to a form of ontotheology in his natural theology. As we discussed in our first chapter, Maritain believes that metaphysics begins with what he calls an "intuition of being," an intuition that includes the fundamental properties of being — unity, truth, goodness, and beauty.[39] Given the "quasi-immediate" intuition of being,[40] and the "resolutio" of this intuition into the transcendental properties, one is able to move directly to a demonstration of the existence of God by way of the analogy of proper proportionality. For Maritain, the transcendentals thus form part of the *subject* of metaphysics, and it is essentially on their basis that we proceed to natural knowledge of God (147). According to Fr. White, because Maritain bypasses a causal analysis of the beings in ordinary experience, he thinks of the mind's journey to God as consisting of an unpacking, so to speak, of the original intuition of being in which God is implicitly contained, and so overlooks the role of the *ad alterum* analogy, which Aquinas thinks is necessary for protecting God's transcendence.

Setting aside the question of the accuracy of Fr. White's characteriza-

38. See, e.g., *Wisdom*, pp. 68 and 73.

39. See *Wisdom*, p. 139. Jacques Maritain considered beauty a transcendental property, whereas Fr. White does not. In this, he appears to follow Jan Aertsen, according to whom beauty does not add anything that is not already present in goodness precisely as following upon truth in the proper order of the transcendentals. This position is consistent with the "linear" interpretation of reason that we are suggesting Fr. White is advocating in the present book.

40. The reason it is not simply immediate is that Maritain affirms that this intuition is not innate but is achieved through the judgment of existence, and so preceded by that judgment (see *Wisdom*, p. 139).

tion of Maritain, let us consider his assessment from the perspective of what it reveals about his own suppositions regarding the operation of reason. Fr. White affirms, with Maritain, that "resolutio" is an essential part of metaphysics, but he argues that Maritain misunderstands what this term designates in Aquinas. Fr. White makes two judgments in this regard that are decisive with respect to the question of the nature of reason. First, Fr. White explains that "resolutio" is not principally an intuitive act for Aquinas, but is instead essentially reflexive — i.e., we are not simply given the simple notions that lie at the foundation of metaphysics, but instead we arrive at them through a process of *reasoning* (143-44). This process, moreover, takes two forms in Aquinas, namely, a "forward-moving" or "scientific" form, by which reason proceeds from experience to first principles, which allows demonstration, and a "backward-moving" form in which reason analyzes the various definitions it assumes of things, reducing them to their most basic notions (144). According to Fr. White, the transcendentals do not arise through the former of these forms of *resolutio,* as Maritain seems to think, but through the latter. This leads to the second judgment Fr. White makes: this latter form of resolutio is *epistemological,* he says, *rather than ontological;* it concerns our most basic *notions* rather than causes of being. In fact, he goes on to identify the transcendental properties as in this respect similar to the principles of identity and noncontradiction, laws that regulate our thinking rather than aspects of being (144-45) — an astonishingly Kantian position for one who claims to be responding to modern thought with a classical wisdom. This interpretation entails Fr. White's judgment that the transcendentals do not represent the subject of metaphysics for Aquinas, a role reserved for the basic parts of causal analysis, namely, substance and accidents, act and potency. The study of these causes, according to Fr. White, involves, indeed, the *resolutio* that founds genuine metaphysical inquiry, but in this case it is specifically the "forward-moving" (i.e., *a posteriori*) form of *resolutio,* which Fr. White connects with the *via inventionis.*[41] In a word,

41. See *Wisdom,* p. 144: "[T]he first form of *resolutio,* meanwhile, 'goes backward' from basic experience to see what were the initial starting-points of human knowledge. It is an epistemological study, meant to discern the underlying archeology of all rational reflection, the most basic concepts from which all laws of thought are derived. The discovery of the transcendentals as the genetically primary notions common to all acts of understanding comes about, for Aquinas, through this latter form of study. We can deduce, upon rational reflection, that there are certain starting-points to our thinking, that were always, already there, even if we were not reflexively aware of them. Here we discover the primary notions that are the basis for such axioms as the law of non-contradiction and the principle of identity."

metaphysics is identified with the path of discovery, which is in turn identified with the particular work, the reflexive activity, of reasoning as opposed to the intuitive act of understanding or insight.

The classical tradition generally draws a distinction, in our knowing, between the intuitive moment *(intellectus),* by which the mind directly apprehends its object or perceives its self-evident first principles, and the discursive moment *(ratio),* by which the mind makes inferences, reasoning from principles to conclusions. According to Aquinas, these are not two separate acts, but rather two distinct aspects of the same act, just as the principle of movement and rest are one and the same. *Ratio* relates to *intellectus,* then, as movement to rest.[42] Fr. White's assessment of Maritain, as we have sketched it here, reveals that he tends to reduce philosophy to *ratio.* That he generally *excludes intellectus* from what counts as reason in the proper philosophical sense is revealed in the fact that he regularly refers to the "intellective" moment of thought as "fore-theoretical."[43] His distance from the classical tradition becomes unmistakable here: the word "theoretical" comes from θεωρία, meaning, above all, "contemplation," which is principally an act of νόησις or intellection rather than διάνοια or ratiocination. For Aquinas, as for the classical tradition more broadly, intellection is the more perfect act; ratiocination exists as subordinate to and for the sake of intellection, just as movement is for the sake of rest. *Intellectus* is not simply a springboard for reason, but governs reasoning as both its origin and end. Thus, in calling the *intellectus* dimension of reason "pre-theoretical," Fr. White has it exactly backwards: the via inventionis he elevates and in a certain sense isolates as the essence of reason is in fact "post-theoretical," or perhaps in another respect it is itself "pre-theoretical" insofar as it aims to make genuine insight possible. It is in either case an *instrument* of the more fundamentally receptive act that characterizes genuine "theory." If Josef Pieper is right that the eclipse of *intellectus* by *ratio* is one of the defining marks of the modern form of thought,[44] then in this respect Fr. White's conception of reason bears a strong resemblance to that of the very modernity in the face of which he intends to throw ancient wisdom.

What are the implications of reducing the operation of the intellect to *ratio,* that is, reducing reason to the work of reasoning? We get an overshad-

42. Aquinas, *ST* 1.79.8.

43. E.g., *Wisdom,* pp. 134, 205, 210-11, 246, and so forth.

44. Josef Pieper, *Leisure: The Basis of Culture,* trans. Gerald Malsbary (South Bend, IN: Saint Augustine's Press, 1998), pp. 9-14.

owing of the two dimensions that we noted above are essential for reason in relation to God. On the one hand, one would be inclined to minimize the significance of the *given* that precedes one's reasoning, and on the other hand one would tend to neglect the "downward path" of reason, the "via judicii," by which reason judges its starting points (that which is first *quoad nos*) in the light of its ultimate discoveries (that which is first *per se*). We will consider Fr. White's minimizing of the "given" in just a moment. As for the second point, we have already observed that Fr. White admits it does not play a significant role in his argument (250). Why would it not? There is a curious similarity between reason's path of judgment, as Fr. White describes it, and the role that Aquinas ascribes to faith in its distinction from what he calls the philosopher's use of natural reason in the *Summa Contra Gentiles:* in natural reason, we begin with creatures and end with God, while for faith God comes first and we consider creatures in the light of God, who represents their first principle.[45] Now, an interesting dilemma arises here for one who thinks of reason primarily in terms of its discursive work of demonstration. If it is the case that what we know of the first principle is simply what we have inferentially derived from creatures (as we described above according to Fr. White's "path of discovery"), then there is nothing to be gained by this "return trip" from God to creatures, and there is everything to be lost: for I am either simply acknowledging what it was I took for granted at the outset, or, if I purport to offer a *demonstration* of some aspect of the creatures on the basis of the conclusions I reached regarding the first principle for which they functioned as premises, then I am trapping myself in a vicious circle that would seem to undermine the philosophical legitimacy of what I thought I had initially demonstrated.

Things appear differently from the perspective of a more ample notion of reason that we are advocating. If one grasps the superabundant intelligibility of what precedes our reasoning, one can see that the work of *ratio* would bring to light more than one explicitly understood at the outset of the very principle that enables one's work. In this case, judging one's starting points in the light of one's discoveries would represent a genuine gain. At the same time, and for the same reason, however, it also introduces another paradox, because the development of our insight into our starting points implies, in turn, that we need to rethink our discoveries. And then of course this leads us to the necessity of a new judgment of our starting points. Instead of a simple linear progression, then, by which thought establishes "A"

45. *SCG* II.4.

in a definitive way, then proceeds on its basis to an equally definitive "B," and so on up the line — an itinerary Fr. White traces out in distinct stages in the penultimate chapter of his book — what we have here is rather a never-ending circle, whereby our most ultimate discoveries and our most basic starting assumptions reciprocally illuminate each other, and through this simultaneous ascent and descent reason penetrates ever more profoundly into its object. We will return to this "circle" when we address the relationship between philosophy and theology in the following chapter.

With this paradoxically progressing circling in mind, let us return to Fr. White's judgment of Maritain. Fr. White contends that the mind "resolves" its matter in two different directions: the first is epistemological; it is a movement ever more deeply into the mind, as it were, by which reason comes to see what was always already intuitively grasped *(intellectus)* and thereby presupposed in its thinking. It is here that the transcendentals reveal themselves. The second movement is ontological; it is a movement ever more deeply into being, as it were, by which reason comes to grasp the essential causes of things through analysis *(ratio)*. This is metaphysics proper. According to Fr. White, Maritain confuses these two movements by making the transcendentals the subject of metaphysics. Note that Fr. White is taking for granted, here, the very modern assumption that because the transcendentals are presupposed *a priori in* all of our thinking, therefore they are epistemological — i.e., just "notions" or "definitions" — rather than ontological. An alternative approach would be to take them as presupposed in all of our causal analyses, but not simply as a springboard necessary to get our thinking started, a nonontological tool that subsequently enables our inquiry into the being that lies "out there" beyond the mind. Rather, in line with Aquinas's description of the relation between *intellectus* and *ratio,* as the most basic features of the being that is the first notion to enter the mind, they stand among the first principles that form the bases of our discoveries, but then in turn they cast a light for the judgment of what we have discovered. More specifically, we presuppose a grasp of the good, the one, and the true, but flesh out their intelligible content through a causal analysis of substance, accidents, act, and potency, and then in turn judge the meaning of these on the basis of the transcendentals. We need to understand actuality in order to know what goodness is, but we also need to know what goodness is to understand actuality properly. Once again, what comes to light *a posteriori* illuminates what was already present *a priori.*

We noted above that a reduction of reason to *ratio* leads one to minimize the significance of the *given* in one's view of reason. We can see how this occurs by considering Fr. White's assessment of Gilson, which will lead us then to the final theme regarding the implications of all of this for the relationship between philosophy and theology. As Fr. White explains it, Gilson's great insight into the uniqueness, the perfection, of *esse,* which Gilson takes to be Aquinas's principal contribution to philosophy, was at the same time the cause of an intellectual crisis: the notion is so fundamental it seems to be indemonstrable, and so faced with the question of whence reason obtains such a notion, Gilson was forced by his presuppositions ultimately to appeal to revelation (104). But this, Fr. White judges, is fideism, insofar as it makes revelation the foundation of philosophical reflection, and substitutes grace for the work of natural reason. Against Gilson's reading of Aquinas, Fr. White argues that the real distinction between *esse* and essence can be developed organically through an analysis of the internal and external causes of being, which means that, even if Aristotle did not affirm the real distinction in Aquinas's sense, we can nevertheless draw it out of notions he *does* affirm (104). If we succeed in doing so, it shows that there is no need to turn to revelation to come to an understanding of God as transcendent cause of the world in order to understand the being that forms the subject of metaphysics.

Now, the key text that Fr. White cites from Gilson as the basis for his charge of fideism is a passage from *Elements of Christian Philosophy* in which Gilson asks whence Aquinas obtained his "new notion" of *esse,* and replies: "[He] may well have first conceived the notion of an act of being [*esse*] in conversation with God and then starting from God, made use of it in his analysis of the metaphysical structure of composite substances."[46] After pointing out that Aquinas himself explains that Moses himself learned "the sublime truth" that God is his own existence, Gilson observes: "This invites us to admit that, according to Aquinas himself, the notion of esse can be learned from the very words of God."[47] Fr. White infers, then, from these very words of Gilson: "The intelligence, instructed by revelation, achieves a correct *philosophical* outlook upon reality. The nature of the intelligence is thus restored by grace to its original metaphysical capacities," and then offers what he takes to be a summary statement of Gilson's position: "henceforth, it must be admitted that a realistic metaphysical knowledge of being and of God is possible for the human person only in cooperation with revelation. True philosophy must be conducted under the illuminating influence of

46. Étienne Gilson, *Elements of Christian Philosophy* (Garden City, NY: Doubleday, 1960), pp. 131-32; cited in *Wisdom,* p. 117.

47. Gilson, cited in *Wisdom,* p. 118.

Christian faith" (118). What a remarkable inference! Gilson states that *it is possible* for reason to achieve a philosophical insight in the light of faith, and Fr. White hears him saying that metaphysics has no beginning other than the Nicene Creed.

The point in drawing attention to this straw man is, once again, not primarily to dispute Fr. White's interpretation of Gilson, but to think through the implications more generally of the position he takes with respect to Gilson. Gilson does not think that the possibility that reason may achieve a philosophical insight within the mind's illumination by faith entails a compromise of reason's integrity. It is interesting to note that, as Fr. White admits in a footnote, Gilson does not in fact deny that one can discern the real distinction "through general philosophical analysis of beings we experience."[48] Fr. White takes Gilson's later statement here to be a kind of confusion regarding the origin of this notion, but the more evident interpretation is that Gilson does not see faith and reason as opposed, in the sense that, if faith is at all operative in one's thinking, then reason precisely to that extent is not. It is worth noting that this is the very same opposition that semipelagianism takes for granted with respect to the order of the will. For Gilson, the possibility that faith might enable philosophical reason to attain *its own* insight does not exclude the possibility that reason may come to this insight by other means (e.g., through demonstration). Fr. White's assessment of Gilson reveals, by contrast, that he takes these to be necessarily exclusive, which means that, for him, faith and reason are opposed to each other in principle — though this does not mean that they will be opposed *de facto.* As we will see in a moment, Fr. White avoids opposing faith and reason simply by separating their spheres of sovereignty, so to speak, and believes that an insistence on the necessity of each in their separate spheres suffices as an affirmation of their integration.

48. See *Wisdom,* p. 119, n. 31. Fr. White cites what he calls, with Ralph McInerny, a "logical contradiction" in Gilson, who seems, on the one hand, to make the real distinction something established only at the end of metaphysical reflection and, on the other hand, to posit it at the same time as the "initial proper object" of Aquinas's metaphysics. In fact, however, Gilson interprets Aquinas as affirming "being qua being" as the initial proper object of metaphysics, the *"first sense"* of which is substance. See Gilson, *Being and Some Philosophers,* 2nd ed. (Toronto: Pontifical Institute of Medieval Studies, 1952), p. 157 (emphasis added), even if this does not remain its *only* sense. Rather, Aquinas deepens this notion in part in the light of creation and revelation. In this, we have an example of that which is first being "retroactively" transformed by what follows. There is contradiction here only if one reduces reason to a unilateral linear discursus.

The key to the difference between Gilson and Fr. White has to do with the rational significance of the *given.* As we suggested above, reason, for Fr. White, can claim for itself *only* those notions it has worked out on its own. This is what we have referred to as "epistemological semipelagianism." For Gilson, by contrast, what is given to reason — and to that extent from "outside" of reason's deliberate acts — may nevertheless belong to reason as its own. We can thus speak of a reciprocal illumination between the *a priori* and *a posteriori:* while it is true, as Fr. White argues, that a causal analysis of being can make the notion of *esse* (and its real distinction from essence) intelligible, giving it a certain concrete content through the interplay of different sorts of analogies, it is also true that the perfection of *esse* can never simply be derived from such an analysis; the meaning of *ipsum esse* has a wholeness, a "once-and-for-all-ness," that cannot be pieced together from any number of conceptual parts — substance, accidents, act, and potency. Indeed, it reveals the proper meaning of the very parts from which it would be derived, which means that they depend on it even more than it depends on them. This is behind Gilson's insistence that Aquinas takes over intact Aristotle's notion of being, and at the same time radically transforms its meaning in the light of the notion of creation.[49] Reason moves simultaneously from above and from below, but no matter which way reason initially proceeds, the former has an absolute priority over the latter. To affirm this is simply to unfold the implications of affirming the primacy of *intellectus* over *ratio.*

3. Finally, a reductive concept of reason, such as we have been describing it, leads of necessity to an extrinsicist understanding of the relationship between faith and reason, theology and philosophy, no matter how much one insists on their close cooperation. Let us recall the indispensable point Fr.

49. Gilson, *Being and Some Philosophers,* p. 160: "The Aristotelian substance remains intact in the doctrine of Thomas Aquinas. Yet, the Aristotelian substance cannot enter the world of St. Thomas Aquinas without at the same time entering a Christian world; and this means that it will have to undergo many inner transformations in order to become a created substance." Fr. White also admits that Aquinas transforms Aristotle, but gives little indication of what this means other than adding new notions such as the *ad alterum* analogy or extending Aristotle's concepts into new areas; see *Wisdom,* p. 67. He is explicit that the light of faith cannot effect the sort of "inner transformations" that Gilson describes; see, for example, *Wisdom,* p. xxv, n. 9, in which he says that faith can purify one's capacity to exercise natural knowledge but that it does not bear in any way on the "structure," i.e., on the inner content, of that knowledge.

White insists on in this book, namely, that unless reason is capable of attaining knowledge of God, the revelation of faith will remain a foreign imposition, reason will not be *intrinsically* open to faith. These affirmations imply a unity coincident with an irreducible difference, and moreover indicate an internal connection rather than an external one. As we put it at the very outset of this chapter, faith has room for natural reason *inside* of itself, and we may add now that the movement toward faith must originate from within reason rather than arise after reason has, so to speak, come to a stop.

Given these parameters, let us consider Fr. White's formulation of the relationship that he offers at the end of his book. As we noted at the outset, Fr. White explains the mutual cooperation without interference between faith and reason by saying that philosophy proves *that* God exists, while theology interprets the revelation of *who and what* God is. This would seem to harmonize faith and reason by ascribing to each a distinct responsibility in our coming to understand God. But in fact the moment we press below the surface of this formulation, the matter becomes much more complex: Does natural reason tell us *nothing at all* about the essence of God? In his criticism of Denys Turner, Fr. White argues that metaphysics does offer positive, substantial (though of course analogical) knowledge of God's nature.[50] In this case, philosophy does not simply prove that God exists but reveals in its own way something of what God is.

To the extent that this is true, we next have to ask: What is the relationship between this natural knowledge, which reason works out on its own, and the knowledge that is given in faith? Does revelation simply *add* something to what reason already knows of God in philosophy, so that this natural knowledge remains unchanged in the light of faith? There is a dilemma here. If we say that philosophy yields *some truth* about the nature of God in complete independence of faith, a truth that remains in every respect the

50. There is a curious shift in emphasis in the book: in the early chapters, Fr. White insists that philosophy yields no knowledge at all of God's essence (see, e.g., p. 97: "The discovery of God's causality of existence in creatures permits an analogical attribution of perfections to God *ad alterum,* which implies no apprehension of God's essence or nature"), but argues in the final chapter that there *is* some positive knowledge ("our naming of God signifies truly *what God* is *substantially in himself,*" p. 272). These two statements do not necessarily contradict each other; indeed, in the latter text Fr. White explicitly states that this does not entail any "quidditative knowledge." But it would seem to be more in line with the text that he cites from Aquinas (*ST* 1.13.2) to say that the knowledge gained "falls short of full representation" rather than to deny that it is quidditative. What, after all, could absolutely non-quidditative knowledge be?

same even once it is affirmed again by a believer, it means that what is revealed in faith has no bearing whatsoever on that particular philosophical truth. Now, Fr. White made the important point that we cannot construct a natural theology independently of faith as a standard by which the contents of faith are subsequently measured (xxiv). But it seems that he cannot avoid doing just this given his construal of the nature of philosophical reason. Faced with this problem, Fr. White follows what would seem to be the obvious "escape hatch": one says that natural theology, properly understood, not only obtains certain insights into the nature of God, but at the very same time recognizes its inadequacy, and this, then, opens reason up in a positive way to revelation (274). But this is no escape hatch! In fact, it only leads one deeper into the hole. For if one continues to maintain that what reason, even in its "radical imperfection" (254), comes to know of God is carried over into faith without any transformation, then one is in fact saying not only that faith is measured unilaterally with respect to these particular truths by reason, but now in addition that it is measured by a reason that is self-professedly inadequate! Here we have a prime example of the problem of reason simultaneously claiming both too much and too little.

It does not do, at this point, to surrender all "positive" yield in philosophy, that is, to become excessively apophatic in one's philosophizing and say that natural theology tells us only the sheer fact that God *is,* which is separate from all of the theological insight into what or who God is, for at least two reasons: this formulation would compromise divine simplicity, and it would leave reason and faith altogether external to one another, so that reason is structurally indifferent to God's essence, and faith has no bearing on what it means to say that God exists. Nor can we content ourselves by saying philosophy tells us only what God *is not,* for, unless we revisit the basic presupposition we have been discussing, this denial trumps any positive disclosure of faith *precisely insofar as reason is concerned.* The whole content of theological dogma would in this case become sheer fideistic positivism. We cannot simply separate into two packages our natural theology and our sacred theology, even if we subsequently tie the two together. As Fr. White correctly affirms, there is "significant overlap" in fact between the two realms (255). But in this case, which has ultimate jurisdiction, so to speak, over this common area? We must be able to articulate the relationship between the two in such a way that we compromise neither the integrity of reason nor the ultimate authority of faith.

Our proposal here is that this can be done only by affirming the paradox of the a priority of the *a posteriori,* which we described earlier in the workings of reason. Let us take an example. Following the itinerary Fr. White describes in chapter 7, through an analysis of the internal and external causes of being, reason discerns the real distinction between *esse* and essence in creatures and thereby comes to affirm the noncomposition of God's being. In other words, reason, through its own reflections, achieves an insight into divine simplicity: God is absolutely one. As it turns out (!), this is also what theology says about God, only theology says at the same time that God is a Trinity of Persons, each of whom is really (not merely conceptually) distinct from the others.[51] In other words, theology reveals that the affirmation of divine simplicity does not entail the denial of all *real distinction* in principle. Note, this revelation is not a rejection of natural theology, insofar as the dogmatic formulation of this mystery continues to affirm absolute simplicity, but at the same time the revelation implies a genuine transformation of the natural knowledge at issue here. We come to see that the affirmation of simplicity does not require the rejection of real distinction altogether, even if we would almost inevitably have assumed it did if we had never been enabled to rise above the insight into simplicity, so to speak, and consider it from a higher perspective. Once we do "rise above" it, however, we see that the notion acquires a new content, but that it does so without changing into some other notion. If one were, by contrast, to reject any transformation in principle, and insist that in all cases of an "overlap" between philosophy and theology, philosophy measures theology precisely as far as reason is concerned, one would have to say that the revelation of the Trinitarian nature of God is a pure datum of faith, that the real distinction among the Persons is strictly speaking irrelevant for how we interpret the meaning of divine simplicity, and, in short, that the Trinity is meaningless for us precisely as rational animals, i.e., as human beings.[52] The data of faith can be *meaningful* only if faith speaks *to* reason, rather than shouting over its head, as it were, and it

51. *ST* 1.28.3.

52. It is well known that Aquinas affirms the doctrine of the Trinity as lying above all reason, but the argument that he gives against Richard of St. Victor on this question is surely not his best. According to Aquinas, Richard of St. Victor's argument that God is perfect charity, and that perfect charity requires plurality, does not work because sharing — i.e., relation to an other — is not necessary if one has perfect goodness already in oneself (!). See *ST* 1.32.1ad2. It would seem that one could protect what Aquinas wants to protect without being forced to make such a problematic argument by saying that the doctrine of the Trinity does indeed lie beyond reason, but it nevertheless speaks to reason in some respect, along the lines we have been tracing. If Aquinas argues against a rational proof for the doctrine of the Trinity, he also insists that reasons can be given for its "fittingness" after the doctrine is known. In this case, the revelation does indeed speak to reason.

can speak to reason only if it has something to say about the concepts reason rightfully takes to be its own. In other words, faith has to have rational implications, which means that it must have philosophical implications.

Following out this example further, we can see how the transformation we are describing gives more substance to reason's desire for what lies beyond itself. Although Fr. White affirms this crucial principle, he is led by his presuppositions to interpret it primarily in formal terms: "Because revelation is not derivable from metaphysical knowledge of God, it remains extrinsic to and transcendent of human nature. However, because it responds to the deepest human inclination toward truth, authentic revelation also fulfills gratuitously the deepest intrinsic teleological dimension of the human person" (255). Without further qualification, this may be interpreted as saying that the mind desires truth; the Christian God happens to be true; and so revelation fulfills this desire. It is similar, incidentally, to Fr. White's interpretation of Aquinas's affirmation that man implicitly knows God in all that he knows: we desire happiness; God turns out to be what ultimately makes us happy; and so we can in this way, and only in this way, say that we have some "presentiment of God." But notice how question-begging both of these arguments are. How is it specifically God that satisfies our natural desire if it is not in fact a desire *for God?* How, with respect to the first argument, can the mind recognize the *truth* of God as the truth that it has been seeking? We face, here, the Meno problem once again, and the problem that Augustine wrestled with in book X of the *Confessions,* namely, that if we did not already have a memory of God, we would be unable to recognize him once we encountered him. Given a rationalistic reduction of reason, there is no answer to this problem; there is no way we could say that the revelation of the Trinity satisfies the mind's desire for truth. Indeed, revelation as such would be extraneous — just as it is, in the end, for Kant, as we saw in chapter two. The only intelligible content that could speak to the mind's desire would be the "monotheistic natural theology" that Fr. White repeatedly refers to in the book; in other words, if the essence of reason is *a posteriori* demonstration, as Fr. White suggests, it can be satisfied qua reason only by what it can demonstrate itself, and therefore by definition *without any need for revelation.* In this case, if it happens to accept revelation, it can be of necessity only for extrinsic reasons — that is, for "reasons" that are strictly extrarational.[53]

53. This is not to say that we ought to accept faith only because of its rationality. Rather, faith is extrarational, but not *only* extrarational: properly understood, it also speaks *to* reason.

The example we presented above offers an alternative approach to this problem. In determining the truth of divine simplicity, reason desires the *truth* of that truth, which means it desires the most complete disclosure of that truth. If the Trinity of Persons is irrelevant to the meaning of divine simplicity, reason has no intrinsic interest in it. But if this revelation *recasts* the meaning of simplicity by revealing a more profound content to it than was initially evident, reason will rejoice in the discovery precisely *as* reason: it will experience the disclosure as an unanticipated fulfillment, that is, as a genuine novelty *(a posteriori)* that is what it always wanted *(a priori)* without knowing it. But this has a further unexpected implication: by virtue of this ultimate discovery, reason now sees that plurality of a certain sort is not inimical to perfection as it may initially have thought to the extent that it was led to posit an identity of essence and existence in the first cause, and so reason discovers that it is true but inadequate to say that natural theology is essentially "monotheistic," at least in the sense that would exclude in principle a plurality of divine Persons. But this means that its search for the first cause is not a search only for absolute simplicity, i.e., the perfection of unity, but is also in some sense a search for the perfection of difference.[54] The question of what such a search would look like cannot be pursued here, but we may at least see that this complex path would represent a concrete example of the point we made above, namely, that reason is brought by its later insights to reconsider its original assumptions. We will return to this in the following chapter.

In his exposition of Aquinas's natural theology in chapter 3, Fr. White explains that, for Aquinas, following Avicenna and contra Averroes, the proper subject of metaphysics is not separate substance (i.e., God), but rather *common being* (78-79). God is not included within common being. But this does not mean that God is simply irrelevant to metaphysics; rather, according to Fr. White, God enters into this field of study precisely insofar as he is the cause of its subject. *Because* reason in its metaphysical dimension desires to understand being as being, it will seek knowledge of whatever bears on this understanding, preeminent among which is the *cause* of being. If we extend this line of reflection, we would have to say that reason, moreover, seeks to understand whatever bears on the nature of the cause of being, again, precisely insofar as it has being qua being as its subject. This leads to a question that cannot be dismissed: granted that revelation discloses to us

54. We might consider here, for example, Richard of St. Victor's reflection on the nature of God, as "that than which nothing greater can be thought," in the light of the notions of goodness, glory, and charity.

something of the inner essence of God, which would otherwise be unavailable to reason in its own speculative reflections, does revelation bear on the meaning of God *precisely* qua the cause of being? Although it is customary to respond to this question that the Persons act as one *ad extra,* which then is typically taken to mean that such action can be understood simply "monotheistically" and therefore independently of any revelation,[55] Aquinas himself affirms that the revelation of the Trinity allows a proper understanding of creation insofar as it is precisely the processions of the Persons in God that present the "*ratio creationis*"[56] — which cannot mean anything other than that the content of revelation illuminates the cause of being. To the extent that this is indeed the case, metaphysics cannot be said simply to exclude the revealed God from its purview.

The tricky question, of course, is the precise extent to which and the precise manner in which this is the case. A full discussion of the Trinity and creation, which a proper response to this question would require, is not possible here. But we may at least articulate a few general principles about the relationship between reason and revelation, before we return to a fuller consideration of that relationship in the next chapter. First, if God as cause of being enters metaphysics only indirectly, we might say that revelation in turn bears only indirectly on God's causing of being (which, we hasten to emphasize, does not in either case imply that God is only *accidentally* related to the subject matter). In other words, there would seem to be required here a further analogy, beyond even the *ad alterum* analogy that opens reason to God as transcendent cause, namely, something like an "analogy of faith," which would reflect on the specifically metaphysical significance of the revealed God.[57] This analogy would not operate primarily in an ascent, from creatures to God, as would the analogy *ad alterum,* but rather primarily in the

55. In other words, the truth of the statement that God acts as one *ad extra* begs the further question whether faith transforms the content of the notion of oneness at issue.

56. *ST* 1.32.1ad3. Fr. White insists that Aquinas "understands the reason for creation *philosophically*" in the *SCG,* but then deepens this reason *theologically* in the *Summa Theologiae.* The question of course is what sense "deepen" has here: Is it the addition of something simply new (which raises the question in turn of what significance this has with respect to what precedes it) or is it a fuller disclosure of philosophy's own object? In this case, then, one could speak of faith deepening the specifically *philosophical* reflection in a way that remains distinct from theology in the strict sense.

57. Here would be a point at which we could affirm Karl Barth's notion of the "analogia fidei," but we would do so in a certain sense against Barth: rather than posit it precisely *in the stead of* the metaphysical *analogia entis,* as Barth does, we are proposing it as inclusive of natural theology: not an "either-or" but a "both-and."

manner of a descent, from God to creatures, because such a movement would preserve the quality of revelation by beginning specifically with God as *given*.[58] Second, for this very reason, we would be led to affirm both against ontotheology that metaphysics is *not necessarily theological*, i.e., informed by revelation, but also against the *critique* of ontotheology that metaphysics is *not necessarily not theological* in this sense. In other words, while we avoid making God a logically necessary dimension of metaphysical thinking (by for example including him within the field of common being through an improper use of the *ad unum* analogy or the analogy of proper proportionality), we are not permitted positively to exclude the illumination of faith or to define metaphysics as nontheological (or more specifically: nonilluminated by faith) in principle and by definition.

This leads to two general principles regarding the relation between reason and revelation, the second more forceful than the first, which we will consider in closing with reference to concrete examples. We will also see how both have been embraced by the Church in the encyclical *Fides et ratio*. The first is that theology may *gratuitously* inform philosophical thinking, which means that it offers something that is not strictly necessary for reason without being for all that irrelevant.[59] We saw this in Gilson's observation that Aquinas, who cites Moses as his authority with respect to his description of God as *ipsum esse*, "may very well" have come to see the significance of *esse* as a result of the illumination of revelation. Gilson insists that this nevertheless remains a philosophical insight — it is philosophical, we might observe, since it is after all an insight into the meaning of being qua being, which is the proper subject of metaphysics. Because Gilson makes a positive reference to revelation in philosophy, Fr. White accuses him of substituting grace for nature. But this would be the case only given the assumptions of what we have been calling "epistemological semipelagianism," which can affirm a natural act of reason only by denying that faith is operating in any intrinsic way in reason, but at best merely clears the ground, so to speak, so that reason can act on its own.[60]

58. As Aquinas puts it in *SCG* II.4, faith begins with the truth as God himself knows it (at least insofar as this is knowable to creatures), which is the truth *of God*, but also the truth of creatures *in God*.

59. This formulation does not exclude the affirmation that it is necessary in a gratuitous sense, i.e., that reason *needs* precisely something *gratuitous*, which is simply another way of saying, as Fr. White does, that reason naturally desires something that lies beyond its natural capacity.

60. Consider, again, Fr. White's explanation at *Wisdom*, p. xxv, n. 9.

As Aquinas affirms, however, grace does not destroy, but rather elevates and purifies nature: it opens to nature vistas that *may* not otherwise have been accessible to it, without for all that being any less natural. According to Gilson, considered historically, the encounter with Christian revelation broadened the scope of philosophy. This point, which Fr. White objects to in Gilson, has been very clearly affirmed by the magisterium:

> Revelation clearly proposes certain truths which might never have been discovered by reason unaided, although they are not of themselves inaccessible to reason. Among these truths is the notion of a free and personal God who is the Creator of the world, a truth which has been so crucial for the development of philosophical thinking, especially the philosophy of being. There is also the reality of sin, as it appears in the light of faith, which helps to shape an adequate philosophical formulation of the problem of evil. The notion of the person as a spiritual being is another of faith's specific contributions: the Christian proclamation of human dignity, equality and freedom has undoubtedly influenced modern philosophical thought. In more recent times, there has been the discovery that history as event — so central to Christian Revelation — is important for philosophy as well. It is no accident that this has become pivotal for a philosophy of history which stakes its claim as a new chapter in the human search for truth.[61]

The more one reduces reason to its discursive operations, the more difficult it becomes to accommodate this point, for in that case the data of revelation could be included as having significance for reason only as an essential part of rational demonstration, and this would compromise both the gratuity of faith and the integrity of reason.

But we can draw out an even more provocative implication. The reason that metaphysics cannot positively define itself as excluding revelation is that philosophy would thereby make itself *essentially* theological in an improper way: the possibility that revelation will be irrelevant to the meaning of God as the cause of being cannot be determined prior to revelation. To make that determination, then, presupposes revelation, which means that, if one *defines* metaphysics as studying being as being in a manner that excludes the illumination of faith, one is, as it were, building a theological judgment into the essential structure of one's metaphysics. But acknowledging this

61. *Fides et ratio,* 76.

point pushes us a step further. It is not enough for us, given this point, simply to insist on reserving judgment regarding the relevance of revelation (which is what Heidegger means by defending an *essentially* atheistic philosophy as a means of respecting theology). While such a reservation is possible in principle, a possibility that could no doubt be realized in certain circumstances, the fact of the matter is that revelation has been given. If it is possible for faith to illuminate reason (without compromising its rational character), then, granted that, as part of the Western tradition, we do our thinking *de facto,* and whether or not we are believers, within a horizon that has been definitively stamped by Christian revelation, we cannot in principle exclude the possibility that our most basic philosophical concepts have been colored in profound and subtle ways by revelation.

Here is the claim, then: to the extent that this is so, as Ferdinand Ulrich has pointed out, it follows that *it is in fact only a person philosophizing in faith who is able to philosophize purely naturally,* because only such a one is able positively to acknowledge the gratuity of the light that comes "from above" and so avoid appropriating it as a light generated by its own labors.[62] According to Ulrich, the most significant philosophies in the modern — i.e., post-Christian — era tend to be pseudo-philosophies because they are hiddenly theological, by which he means that they are systems of thought that have co-opted profound elements of Christian revelation, which they have falsified in this case precisely by so doing.[63] To the extent that this is true, faith is no obstacle to engagement with modern philosophy, as those who insist on "natural reason" as a means of dialogue might fear, but in fact presents a privileged entry into the heart of these philosophies, as well as a clarifying light that enables the liberation of reason in its naturalness. If we accept the principle that grace does not destroy nature, but elevates and perfects it, we must allow that faith can elevate reason without annulling its nat-

62. Ferdinand Ulrich, *Homo Abyssus: Das Wagnis der Seinsfrage,* 2nd ed. (Freiburg: Johannes Verlag, 1998), p. 2.

63. *Homo Abyssus,* p. 56. This judgment is not unique to Ulrich, of course. He himself cites Erich Przywara in making the claim. Indeed, it is, from a different perspective, the point of Heidegger's critique of ontotheology, which would mean that the light of faith would put one in a privileged position to engage with the whole tradition that Heidegger intends by this critique. Heidegger himself is simply an echo of Nietzsche's judgment that the German philosophers were all secret theologians. More recently, Jean-Luc Marion has pointed to the specifically Christian notions that lie in the philosophy of Descartes, Malebranche, Leibniz, and others. See "Christian Philosophy: Hermeneutic or Heuristic?" in *The Visible and the Revealed* (New York: Fordham University Press, 2008), pp. 66-79; here, 67.

ural character. Indeed, we would have to affirm that reason therefore becomes more fully reasonable, more truly and authentically natural, under the generous activity of grace. In this case, just as we affirm that the divine Personhood of Christ does not eliminate the natural operations of his human nature, and just as we affirm that there are "infused" natural virtues that are distinct both from acquired natural virtues and specifically theological virtues, so too must we say that there is a distinction between philosophy carried out in some explicit manner in faith, and theology in the strict sense. We will develop this suggestion further in the next chapter.

The work of Ferdinand Ulrich, in fact, provides a striking example of the possibilities of such a philosophy. Hans Urs von Balthasar described his thought as a metaphysics that "stands in intimate contact with the mysteries of revelation, offers an access to them, and yet never abandons the strictly philosophical domain. In this sense it overcomes the baneful dualism between philosophy and theology, and it does so perhaps more successfully than ever before."[64] Although there is no room in the present context to give an account of his philosophy,[65] it is worth mentioning a basic feature of his thought, which exemplifies what we have been discussing in this last section. Ulrich seeks to understand being as being, and in this sense his thinking is a work of metaphysics from first to last. Moreover, he works out his understanding in the context of a profound engagement with a host of modern thinkers, Christians and atheists alike: Schelling, Hegel, Nietzsche, Marx, Kierkegaard, Heidegger, and so forth. And yet, following Aquinas's principle that "omnis agens agit sibi simili," Ulrich interprets being as the "similitudo divinae bonitatis."[66] But the Trinitarian perichoresis and the incarnation of the Son reveal the depths of God's goodness, of which being is the likeness. Thus, one of Ulrich's basic aims is to think through the nonsubsistence of *esse* by analogy to the Father's self-donation in the generation of the Son, and the Son's kenosis in the incarnation. This leads to an extraordinarily rich understanding of the ontological difference between being and beings *(Sein* and *das Seiende),* and of the meaning of man who allows being to come to fruition in his reason and love. In short, it is an interpretation of being as

64. This is a quotation from a letter that Balthasar wrote to Ulrich, a passage from which appears as a "blurb" on the cover of *Homo Abyssus.*

65. For an excellent account of Ulrich's approach to philosophy and the central themes of his thought, see Stefan Oster, "Thinking Love at the Heart of Things: The Metaphysics of Being as Love in the Work of Ferdinand Ulrich," *Communio* 37 (Fall 2010): 660-700. See also Martin Bieler's introduction to *Homo Abyssus,* pp. xii-liv.

66. *De ver.* 22.2.2.

love, an ontology that Ulrich describes as transcending itself toward anthropology, which in turn transcends itself toward Christology.[67]

But the explicit acknowledgment of the data of faith does not mean his philosophy overreaches the natural realm of reason. To the contrary, the very generosity of the goodness revealed in the Christian mysteries liberates nature and natural reason, so that in principle, the closer one gets to the center of those mysteries, the firmer is the foundation of the autonomy of philosophy.[68] Thinking inside the Western tradition, one does not best protect the integrity of philosophy by establishing an *a priori* "no" to faith, but by saying "yes," like Mary, who represents for Ulrich the authentic meaning of "natura pura." Though the phrase is used here in a sense completely opposed to the typical connotation, like all things transformed by grace it both surprises and fulfills its initial meaning. John Paul II, in conjunction with the Church Fathers, likewise points to Mary as a sort of *Realsymbol* of philosophy in *Fides et ratio:*

> And just as in giving her assent to Gabriel's word, Mary lost nothing of her true humanity and freedom, so too *when philosophy heeds the summons of the Gospel's truth its autonomy is in no way impaired. Indeed, it is then that philosophy sees all its enquiries rise to their highest expression.* This was a truth which the holy monks of Christian antiquity understood well when they called Mary "the table at which faith sits in thought." In her they saw a lucid image of true philosophy and they were convinced of the need to *philosophari in Maria.*[69]

In the end, we can affirm, with Fr. White, the indispensable character of natural knowledge of God. And we must affirm everything necessary to preserve its genuinely natural character. One of those necessary things is an intrinsic and positive openness to revelation, an openness that will in fact require the explicit acknowledgment of faith the more this knowledge comes

67. *Homo Abyssus,* p. 1: "Im Zug der Sache habe ich daher die Ontologie in die Anthropologie und diese in die Christologie überstiegen." Note, he does not "impose" the higher perspective, but rather follows the natural "pull" of the matter itself: "im *Zug* der Sache. . . ."

68. This of course does not mean that any given philosopher who acknowledges faith will necessarily have a purer philosophy than any given non-Christian philosopher. Rather, the principle leaves open the possibility that an ostensibly atheistic philosopher may nevertheless betray an even greater openness, however hidden, to the invitation of grace in his thinking than even the one who explicitly affirms faith.

69. *Fides et ratio,* 108. Emphasis added.

to be within the historical situation of an intellectual tradition informed by Christianity, and the closer this knowledge comes to matters directly implicated in the faith. What we must therefore reject is epistemological semi-pelagianism, which insists that reason remains natural only to the extent that it remains uninformed by faith. But this means we must also and therefore reject any approach to natural theology that forces us into a false dichotomy: *either* the data of faith function as a premise within philosophical reasoning, in which case both the integrity of reason and the gratuity of faith are compromised, *or* faith has no bearing on the meaning of philosophical concepts. We cannot avoid this dilemma if we reduce reason to its discursive operation. To respond to the philosophical problems of modernity requires, indeed, that we recover the ancient σοφία, which Aristotle defined as an ordered unity of νοῦς and ἐπιστήμη. In other words, it requires an embrace of the classical notion of reason, one that affirms the priority of *intellectus* over *ratio,* and so one that gives a central place to the *given* in our thinking and the *descent* in our reasoning, by which we open our eyes more and more widely in wonder to the mystery of being and the even more luminous mystery of its first cause. This wonder, which is the heart of philosophical reason, is not dulled but is rather doubled when we come to realize that that which we could never have anticipated has always already been present to us all along the path of discovery.

10 Philosophy and Theology

An affirmation of the catholicity of reason in the twenty-first century cannot avoid confronting the relationship, on the one hand, between faith and reason, and, on the other hand, between philosophy and theology.

As for the first: If reason aspires to the whole, what is it to make of the revelation of a principle that lies in an irreducible way beyond it, and so introduces a more encompassing order than it can grasp by itself? Can reason still, in the context of faith, understand itself as *catholic,* i.e., as concerned with reality in its most comprehensive sense, or must it now yield that claim to faith, and resign itself, instead, to a more modest aspiration? In this case, philosophy cannot be said to be concerned with ultimacy, but henceforward only with "penultimacy." Or must reason, by contrast, necessarily and precisely on its own terms accept what is given in revelation, in which case faith would be nothing more than an occasion for reason's self-extension? This is clearly an extraordinarily difficult aporia, and, on the face of it, the question presents fundamental problems however one responds.

As for the second: the historically inevitable "encounter" between faith and reason raises the question of the precise nature of the relationship between theology and philosophy, and whether that relationship coincides with the relationship between faith and reason. Is it possible for some sort of integration between faith and reason, not only within theology, but also within philosophy? We can formulate this by saying an affirmation of the catholicity of reason will at some point raise the question of the Catholicity of reason. To put the question in concrete terms: Is it meaningful to speak of a "Christian" or a "Catholic" philosophy that would be ultimately distinct from theology?

These two questions are vast — far too vast to be definitively resolved in the present context, and perhaps in any particular context — and could be fruitfully engaged in any number of ways. Rather than approach the issue from a historical perspective, which may be the most obvious starting point insofar as a variety of substantial and substantially different claims have been made regarding faith and reason, theology and philosophy, in intellectual history, this chapter will proceed in a more general and systematic fashion. Our aim here is to sketch a model against the background of the notion of reason we have been developing over the course of this book. We intend only to present a proposal for a way to think about philosophy in relation to theology, without claiming to provide a complete argument in its favor or to address all possible objections. We take for granted at the outset that there *is* such a thing as faith and reason, which means we take as given that the Christian God, who perfectly transcends the world, has revealed himself in history, that a new meaning, which could not have been anticipated by reason and remains in some essential way beyond its grasp, has in fact been given, and that, even if it lies beyond reason, this meaning still concerns reason.

This assumption entails three things: that faith and reason are irreducibly distinct from one another; that they are nevertheless *intrinsically,* rather than merely extrinsically, related to each other; and, finally, that the reciprocal relationship between faith and reason is an *asymmetrical* one in the sense that faith retains a superiority to reason even within an intrinsic relation to it. How and why these claims follow from the givenness of God's self-revelation in history would be in itself a matter worthy of exploration and justification, but in the present context we will simply take the unity and distinctness of faith and reason as an ideal, a standard by which our model will be measured, and we will attempt to work out a concept of the relationship between philosophy and theology that best preserves both the unity and the difference between the two. Indeed, the ideal pursued is a relationship in which the unity liberates the difference and the difference deepens the unity. At the same time, a proper model must do justice to the intrinsic demands of faith and reason, each considered in itself, and to the proper self-understanding of both philosophy and theology.

Determining the relationship between philosophy and theology is notoriously difficult, a fact evinced not only by the great variety of positions taken by serious Christian thinkers, but also by what I take to be a common experience, an experience that has certainly been my own: the moment one draws a settled line between the two, one thinks of problems and exceptions that continually bring one "back to the drawing board," in order to rethink everything again from the beginning. There is a sense in which this problem presents an essentially moving target, and that the boundaries between the two are, concretely speaking, in flux without ever being for all that nonexistent or insignificant. Part of the goal in the present proposal is to make room for the concrete fluidity while at the same time holding on to an "absolute" difference between faith and reason (and by implication theology and philosophy). Here is in part wherein the complexity lies: as many thinkers have observed, the difference between philosophy and theology can and ought to be drawn formally, but the difference between the two becomes increasingly difficult to determine the closer one gets to the concrete. To what extent do I owe any particular insight to reason, and to what extent to faith? For example, is the view that the world was created by God *ex nihilo* a philosophical or a theological doctrine?

At the same time, precisely because faith comes to be properly speaking only with God's self-revelation in history, there is another sense in which the difference between faith and reason cannot be defined merely formally, i.e., in essential terms and so in abstraction from history, but requires reference to the *de facto* content of revelation (including, for example, conciliar formulations of dogma), and moreover to the historical circumstances of any particular act of philosophizing (or theologizing). Indeed, as we will see below, once we affirm the intrinsic relation between theology and philosophy, we must acknowledge that philosophy, too, is not an abstraction, but is a reality that has unfolded in a concrete tradition and is carried out by an individual who stands in some relationship to the advent of revelation. There is therefore a sense in which the relationship between philosophy and theology can only be determined formally, in abstraction, and there is a sense in which the relationship between the two cannot be determined formally and in abstraction. This is a problem that can grow imposingly complex in an instant.

We begin our approach to this problem quite generally, by taking our bearings from the Catholic magisterium. We affirm a fundamental and irreducible difference between philosophy and theology:

> The Catholic Church, with one consent, has also ever held and does hold that there is a twofold order of knowledge, distinct both in principle and also in object; in principle, because our knowledge in the one is by natural reason, and in the other by divine faith; in object, because, besides those things to which natural reason can attain, there are proposed to our belief mysteries hidden in God, which, unless divinely revealed, cannot be known.[1]

1. *Dei Filius,* chapter IV.

This is an indispensable claim that must belong to any genuinely Catholic position, and implies that the two are in some decisive way *beyond* each other, i.e., "external" to each other, and thus that they represent an "extra" in relation to each other: philosophy is not merely a branch of theology and theology is not merely a branch of philosophy. But how are we to affirm this without falling into an extrinsicist view of their relationship, i.e., a view that would hold the two to be *merely* external to each other? If they are merely extrinsic, they are alien (from *aliud,* "other") to each other, which means that each would enter into the other only as a foreign presence, a threat that compromises the integrity of each in itself. To bring them together at all could mean in this case only to juxtapose them as altogether separate parts of a whole. So uniting them would raise in turn the question whether the whole that is thus composed belongs to philosophy or to theology. Because it cannot belong to either one simply without collapsing the irreducible difference between them, we would have to posit a new science of the whole, of which philosophy and theology are individual branches. Not only is this conception problematic *prima facie,* and not only does this conception fail to do justice to the self-understanding of *both* theology and philosophy, but it also simply recasts the same problem without resolving it: What is the nature of the relationship between philosophy and theology such that they can function as parts of a whole science? To avoid this problem, we have to say that, not only can an affirmation of the reciprocally excessive character of philosophy and theology *allow* for an intrinsic connection between the two, but it necessarily requires it.

Now, there is scarcely a soul in contemporary discussions who would explicitly defend a purely "extrinsicist" view of the relationship between theology and philosophy. But this does not mean the problem has been solved: extrinsicism can show up in a much more subtle form, and when one considers the implied features of extrinsicism, one realizes that, in spite of explicit denials, such a view is actually quite common. An essentially extrinsicist conception of a relationship is one in which the relata have their defining essence *apart* from one another, so that if they relate at all, they begin from *within themselves* interpreted as from *outside of the other,* and connect, then, with the other *only subsequent to* their standing within themselves. The most basic distinguishing feature of a conception that is extrinsicist in its logic if not also in name, in other words, is that the relata are connected only, so to speak, at the outer edges. This implies two things: first, it implies that each has merely a negative, regulatory role in the other, that is, each determines the limits of the other from the outside, rather than playing a positive role of *in-forming* the content that belongs properly to the other. In this case, theology would, so to speak, correct the judgments that philosophy makes if philosophy overreaches its own "jurisdiction," however unwittingly. From the other side, philosophy would "purify" theology by determining the proper meaning of the rational concepts it cannot help but use, overstepping its limits by imposing a meaning on concepts "from above," and therefore essentially arbitrarily, i.e., in a way that cannot be justified rationally. Second, a merely extrinsicist conception would imply that each approaches the other *precisely to the extent that* it moves away from its center, from its most proper sense. In this case, philosophy becomes less genuinely philosophical the more it acquires "theological" features — specifically, the more it depends on authority, the more it proceeds from a "given" that it cannot account for on its own terms, the more it receives and relies on the data of revelation, and so forth.

Now, it is not that any of these notions about the relationship between philosophy and theology are *simply* false. In fact, they are true to the extent that philosophy and theology are to some degree "external" to one another just by virtue of remaining abidingly different. But if one takes the position sketched above to represent the essence of the relationship as one understands it, then one is holding an extrinsicist notion, which will entail all of the attendant problems. As an example of what we mean here, let us consider a few views, hardly rare, that give some evidence of extrinsicism. One may think of theology as requiring philosophy to provide the definition of the terms it uses, which implies that theology is not, itself, concerned with the intrinsic meaning of things, but only with the use that can be made of those things with respect to revelation. Or one may think that, because of the special status of faith, theology has a need for philosophy in order to universalize its scope, in order, that is, to speak to *human beings* rather than simply to Christians or Catholics. On the other side, we encounter a nearly universal interpretation of philosophy in relation to faith, according to which one opens philosophy to theology precisely by showing how philosophical concepts, reason's pretensions, ultimately break down as they approach what is ultimate. The suggestion is made, for example, that philosophy in the end falls into self-contradiction if it does not transcend itself into theology. Or from a different direction, one is thus led to affirm the reality and significance of faith by cutting reason short: to put it in more familiar language, one endeavors to set limits to reason in order to make room for faith. However noble the motivation, such a maneuver kills the vital principle of reason, and, indeed, if faith and reason are intrinsically connected, eventually undermines the very thing for which one sought to make room. To say that philosophy opens up to theology only when — at its outer edges, its extremities — it collapses, and to say that theology is forced to turn to philosophy in order to define its terms, or achieve a universality in scope, is to say that the relationship is *founded* on their respective weaknesses or incapacities. In psychology, such a relationship is called "co-dependency," which is a kind of disorder: the more each is truly himself in a co-dependent relationship, the more indifferent he becomes to the other; he opens to the other *when* he is weak and *because* he is weak, and this opening up therefore invariably turns the other into an instrument that serves to return the one to strength and therefore to indifferent independence. Such a relationship is an endless dialectic of (false) power and (false) submission, a reciprocal manipulation.

Our contention is that the most common understanding of philosophy and theology relates them in a manner that exhibits the symptoms of co-dependency: it argues in favor of the connection between the two by showing the inadequacy of each alone and at the same time it takes each to be most fully itself when most distant from, most cheerfully independent of, the other.

By contrast, a healthy relationship is one in which each person opens most profoundly to the other precisely when he is at his best, when he is most fully himself. We propose, along these lines, that a proper relationship between philosophy and theology is one in which each opens up to the other in the first place when it is most perfect, a relationship in which philosophy is understood to lie at the heart of theology, and theology to lie in the center of philosophy. What could this mean? It must mean that each in its own way is "ordered" to the other, not in the sense that the other adds the "missing piece" that brings the disciplines to completion, but, first and most fundamentally, that the movement "beyond" itself coincides with its own internal completion; second, it must mean that because it coincides with the completion, the transition toward the other discipline exhibits, not exclusively a *need,* but more basically an essential *gratuity,* though in a different sense in each case: the movement from philosophy to theology is due primarily to a gratuity "from above," whereas theology's opening to philosophy occurs primarily by virtue of its internal gratuity; and, third, again because the transcendence coincides with the completion, it means that the movement beyond turns out to be, not an arbitrary move, but a free necessity, which thereby reinforces and enhances the internal completion of each discipline in itself.

It may seem especially strange to speak of theology opening up at its center to philosophy, which is in some sense "beyond" it — indeed, in what possible sense, one might be inclined to ask, could philosophy be said to *transcend* theology? Indeed, it is traditional to think of philosophy needing to pass over, for a believer, ultimately to theology insofar as theology is the higher, in fact, the highest discourse. But while this is true in a certain respect, we will argue that there cannot be a relationship that is not *in some sense* reciprocal (though this does *not* mean symmetrical). As we will show below, without this reciprocity, there can be no unity that respects difference in an abiding way.[2]

Essential Features of Each Discipline

To speak of each discipline arising at the center of the other requires pushing beyond a merely formal account of the relationship between philosophy and theology, and taking into consideration the substantial character of each; in other words, determining the relationship entails characterizing the proper nature of each in itself, even if we can do so here only in terms of sketching basic principles and setting general parameters. We will simply enumerate four basic principles for each in turn, which do not pretend to be exhaustive in either case.[3]

A philosophy that exists in a sound relationship to theology, or that is apt for such a relationship in principle, will have the following characteristics, which have been elaborated in one respect or another over the course of this book. Our claim is that these are necessary elements in a description of the *essence* of philosophy, its perfection, considered even in itself without any reference to theology. It is significant that each of these was first embodied in a definitive way by Plato, arguably the founder of the "perennial philosophy."

1. Philosophy will have the whole of the real as its scope; in technical terms, it will be the science of being qua being. Being qua being is the most *unlimited* horizon there can be for reflection; it is clearly broader than logi-

2. Without reciprocity, A is ultimately subordinated to B, which means that A simply gets entirely included "under" B, and no longer in any significant way *exceeds* it. This makes A, then, not different from B but only a lesser version of the same thing.

3. For another list of essential characteristics of philosophy, see *Fides et ratio,* nos. 81-83. Cf. also Kenneth Schmitz, "Metaphysics: Radical, Comprehensive, Determinate Discourse," in *The Texture of Being* (Washington, DC: Catholic University of America Press, 2007), pp. 3-20. Our list is not meant to replace but to complement these descriptions.

cal possibility, material evidence, subjectivity, language, and so forth, even if it includes all of these. In principle, properly understood, there is no object more resistant to philosophy's tendency, at least in the modern era, toward a self-sealed system, what Levinas called "totalité."[4] It is well known that Heidegger has called into question the adequacy of metaphysics understood in these terms to the extent that, in his view, it necessarily interprets being only insofar as it comes to expression as it were in the beingness of beings *(die Seiendheit des Seienden)*. Heidegger thus calls instead for a more primordial thinking of the truth of being. Part of this thinking is an experience of "the nothing" beyond beings in their totality. We have discussed Heidegger in earlier chapters; we note here only that, whatever other judgment one might make in its regard, this is not in fact a call for something other than being, but simply a radically different understanding of being than what is normally — but by no means indissolubly — associated with the notion of metaphysics as the study of being qua being. Jean-Luc Marion, noting this association, proposes *givenness* as more primordial even than being,[5] but one has to insist that it can be more primordial only than a limited conception of being. Givenness after all "is." According to Aquinas, being is "extra-mental" *(extra animam)*;[6] in phenomenological language, being necessarily exceeds all intentionality, all phenomena. The point here is that philosophy is philosophy only if it desires the most comprehensive whole, and it is *therefore* in its essence ordered to being qua being. As Plato explains, a lover loves the whole of what he loves;[7] the object of the philosopher's desire is "the sight of truth";[8] and to love the *whole* of the sight of truth means to desire things specifically in their being: "Won't it be reasonable for us to plead in [the philosopher's] defense that it is the nature of the real lover of learning to struggle toward *what is,* not to remain with any of the many things that are believed to be, that, as he moves on, he neither loses nor lessens his erotic love until he grasps the being of each nature itself?"[9]

4. Levinas himself, of course, sought an object "otherwise than being" because he connected being and immanence, but the terms become quite different if one affirms at the outset a specifically analogical notion of being, as we proposed in chapter one.

5. Jean-Luc Marion, *Being Given: Toward a Phenomenology of Givenness,* trans. Jeffrey Kossky (Stanford, CA: Stanford University Press, 2002), pp. 7-70.

6. See, e.g., Aquinas, *ST* 1.85.2.

7. Plato, *Republic* 474c.

8. Plato, *Republic* 475c.

9. Plato, *Republic* 490a-b. Emphasis added.

But if being is *analogical,* it does not have a single essence, a meaning that can be grasped once and for all in a univocal concept, in such a way that this basic task of philosophy would come to an astonishingly quick end. Instead, the meaning of being reveals itself anew in every being, and indeed always reveals that there is ever more to be revealed. That on which philosophy sets its heart is always itself "underway" to the *semper maior.* Moreover, because it aspires to comprehensiveness, and because religion is part of the reality on which it reflects, philosophy will have to include the religious dimension of existence, and indeed ultimately on religion's own terms, because it would otherwise be guilty of the reductiveness that is a betrayal of its own essence. In this respect, as we suggested in chapter two, the encounter with theology, for all its surprise, will be "natural" to philosophy.

2. A philosophy understood as apt for union with theology would have to be radically inquisitive, in the sense that it would set its desire to know on nothing less than the highest causes, the most profound and originary principles. This characteristic is clearly connected with the one preceding. Being set on the highest cause entails a twofold attitude: both a radical openness that never excludes the possibility of a more profound grasp and a confidence in what one has come to understand. Socrates' disposition as Plato describes it in the *Phaedo* is paradigmatic on this score. On the one hand, Socrates criticizes the misology, the contempt for reason, that feeds on despair of ever knowing truth,[10] while on the other hand he presents his philosophy as a "second sailing," referring approvingly to Simmias' characterization of the search for the sturdiest raft possible on the sea of inquiry in expectant waiting for "some divine logos" (λόγου θείου τινός) (*Phaedo,* 85d). Thus understood, philosophy precisely qua philosophy (and not merely as relative to theology) would have to remain open even when it comes to final conclusions. Because, as we argued in chapter seven, it appears to be the nature of fundamental realities to disclose themselves otherwise than as simple ideas that can be grasped "clearly and distinctly," once and for all, without further reflection, true philosophy will always exhibit both the abundance and the poverty of eros;[11] it will always be "beginning again" rather than contentedly filling its stores. In its ideal sense — which is the sense with which we are occupied here — the love of wisdom requires the kind of total gift of self that is possible only when one experiences the object to which one gives oneself as supreme. This love implies the positive affirmation of, and desire for, a truth

10. Plato, *Phaedo* 89d-90e.

11. See Plato, *Symposium* 203e.

that lies beyond any relative grasp. To affirm this does not mean to surrender to a total restlessness or an absolute dynamism; as we have argued above, it does not mean that one absolutizes philosophy's questions rather than its answers or that one makes aporia ultimate in the manner of a Strauss or a Heidegger. Instead, as we have been arguing in different ways over the course of this book, philosophy's deepest disposition is a hungry satisfaction, a happy restlessness, the simultaneity of openness and closure.

3. A proper philosophy would recognize that reason, even outside of the encounter with faith, is inevitably, and in every instance of its exercise, dependent on what lies outside of itself. In the first place, reason never makes its judgments as the absolute sovereign, but always as subordinate to the judgment of reality itself. As we proposed in chapter three, the grasp of truth always occurs inside the self-transcendence implied in beauty and goodness. Reason's most spontaneous judgment inevitably possesses a receptive structure; it takes its bearings from within a context, even though it transcends that context. The Enlightenment pursuit of an *ultimately* self-grounding reason has turned out to be necessarily vain: ironically, the very basis that Descartes sought to be able to distinguish dream from reality turns out itself to be a figment of the imagination. Nietzsche associated this pursuit with the mythical Baron von Münchhausen, who, having fallen into quicksand, pulled himself up to safety by his own hair.

As we have been arguing in this book, reason is inherently ec-static. It is not merely that reason cannot help but operate with some "given," which provides the substance to which to apply, so to speak, its digestive juices. Rather, this receptive relation to what lies beyond it remains its essential form. While it is true, as the classical tradition has held, that the act of *intellectus* is more fundamental than the discursive act of *ratio,* it is also the case that *intellectus* is not merely a direct appropriation of reality into itself, as implied in the modern notion of intuition, but, as we suggested in chapter one, most basically an insertion of itself into reality, an expropriative "standing out" and only thereby a taking hold of the real. The real thus becomes intelligible always as at the same time "supra-rational." The realm of truth, according to Plato, can be attained only by a "winged mind," a mind drawn outside of itself by beauty.[12] Plato, once again, presents a paradigm here in the regular acknowledgment he makes of myth and tradition as extending in some sense beyond the sphere of logos and yet making it possible, even while logos retains a responsibility for judging myth in turn. It is remarkable that

12. Plato, *Phaedrus* 249c.

the founder of Western philosophy himself expressed a deferential piety toward the ancients, and so acknowledged that thinking occurs always inside of a tradition.[13]

4. Finally, perhaps most importantly and inseparably from what has been stated thus far, philosophy in its most proper sense regards wonder, and its objective correlate mystery, as altogether positive. According to Plato, wonder is the most proper πάθος of philosophy and its sole source (ἀρχή).[14] Interestingly, Plato also refers approvingly to the etymology that makes Thaumus, Wonder, the father of Iris, the messenger from heaven. We argued in chapter seven for a positive conception of wonder as convertible with the perfection of philosophical knowledge. If wonder and knowledge are opposed, then one would either have to interpret philosophy as having its perfection in the absence of wonder, in which case it would undergo a crisis, it would "break down," if it faced an object — such as the transcendent cause and end of the world — that it could not intellectually master. This would be a philosophy *opposed* to theology in principle, however much it might possess a dialectical need for it. Or one would have to define philosophy in terms of wonder *rather than* knowledge, and one would end up promoting a philosophy indistinguishable from mythology, and therefore from theology.[15] In this case, theology would lose any priority over philosophy; they would both represent a kind of endless play that never permitted anything to be disclosed in a definitive way. A proper philosophy, by contrast, would understand being itself as wonderfull by nature, so that an increase in awe would be itself a *direct* sign of deeper understanding, and the two — wonder and knowledge — would be experienced as flipsides, so to speak, of the same coin. In this view, the silent gaze of amazement would represent the paradigm of philosophical achievement, its completion or closure, which is approximated in every single philosophical act, every instance of true knowing, without excep-

13. On this, see Josef Pieper, *The Platonic Myths* (South Bend, IN: St. Augustine's Press, 2011); *Tradition: Concept and Claim,* trans. E. Christian Kopf (South Bend, IN: St. Augustine's Press, 2010).

14. Plato, *Theaetetus* 155d.

15. For an example of this less-common alternative, see Mary-Jane Rubenstein, *Strange Wonder: The Closure of Metaphysics and the Opening of Awe* (New York: Columbia University Press, 2008). Rubenstein intends to argue for a *positive* sense of wonder as the very element of philosophy, but as the title of her book already betrays, she leaves the opposition between wonder and knowledge in place (even as she insists at various points that both are necessary): metaphysics has to close in order to open space for awe.

tion. We might consider, here, the culminating insight into beauty that the philosopher achieves in the *Symposium.*[16]

The constellation of these four aspects describes a philosophy that, given the context of faith, opens up to theology precisely at its center, at the moment it perfects itself as philosophy, which is to say, the moment it is most truly philosophical. Because philosophy seeks the most comprehensive interpretation of reality, and inquires into its most ultimate principle, theology speaks *directly* to its central aims; because it is by nature ec-static and so always in some respect dependent on a supra-rational authority, the language of theology is not simply foreign to it; and, because wonder represents not only its beginning but, as abiding source, also its end, the mystery of faith is not simply an intrusion — however unexpected it may be — on its own most proper activity.

There are likewise four basic aspects of theology we may indicate that bring to light its generous capacity to open up to its other, philosophy. Each of these points would of course in another context require elaboration and theological justification in terms of conciliar dogma, magisterial pronunciations, and theological traditions. Here, we simply enumerate the points to show their interconnection. It is worth observing that these points are affirmed precisely as *given* in revelation and in theological reflection on the data; they are not an imposition of rational speculation on theology, which would be the height of presumption.

1. Most obviously, we have to understand God's "fundamental option," as it were, for the world, as revealed in the doctrines of creation and redemption, and the Trinity and incarnation. As Aquinas made definitively evident, God did not need to create the world to accomplish any purpose;[17] even "for the sake of his glory" is not an extrinsic end in a relationship to which the world is a means. The world has no purpose other than *to be,* and *thus* to give glory to God. The doctrine of creation implies that the world's goodness has an "absolute" character, and the doctrine of redemption reveals in a surprising way that the absoluteness is, as it were, so absolute that even God subordinates himself to it without any coercive need whatsoever: the Cross is — with all appropriate qualifications — God's giving preference to the world over himself, God's freely subordinating himself to the world. That God can thus give himself so radically is possible without loss only because, as Trinity, God is already perfect self-gift *in* himself and so prior to any rela-

16. Plato, *Symposium* 211d-212a.

17. Aquinas, *ST* 1.44.4.

tion to the world (i.e., God's relativizing himself to an other is not something that the *world* introduces into God). Ultimately, this means that the world's otherness to God is "inside" God's otherness to himself.

Now, theology is not a merely abstract intellectual exercise. It is a μαθήσις θέου: simultaneously a study of God and a discipleship, a *following,* of God. The theologian goes where God goes, and, in loving God, loves what God loves. In this respect, a theologian must take an interest in the world not simply in relation to God, but in itself, for its own sake (which is not opposed to, but coincides with, taking an interest in it for God's sake). Note that, thus understood, the interest in philosophy — a study of the intrinsic meaning of the world — is not something that *intrudes* into theology from the outside, but springs from the deepest springs of its own heart, and does so gratuitously, but not arbitrarily.

2. God does not merely act "on behalf of" the world in creation and redemption, but *reveals* himself in it, and revelation of course intends understanding. Christ calls the disciples friends rather than slaves precisely because slaves do not know what their master is doing (John 15:15): they are friends, he says, "because everything I learned from my Father I have made known (ἐγνώρισα)" to them. Revelation, whatever else one would say about it, is a communication *of meaning.* As such, if it is not addressed uniquely to human reason, God's self-revelation is certainly addressed *also* to reason. In this respect, insofar as faith seeks understanding *(fides quaerens intellectum),* it is simply following its natural path. We saw the importance of this point to Hegel in chapter eight; we can affirm it, however, in a non-Hegelian sense, that is, by insisting on the intrinsic significance of reason's appropriation without saying, as Hegel eventually does, that faith has significance *only to the extent* that it is appropriated by reason. We addressed this problem in our discussion of Hegel and ontotheology. The point, here, is to make clear that, contrary to those who take for granted that the desire to understand is always a sinful self-assertion that needs to be chastened by faith, this desire can be a profound act of obedience, so much so that the refusal to penetrate the mysteries of revelation conceptually, to appropriate them, make them one's own, in a rational way, and even to "speculate" in an ongoingly fruitful way on their significance, can be an act of disobedience, itself a kind of self-assertion, even if it claims to be, and in fact sincerely wants to be, an expression of modesty and respect. We may think, in this context, of the sinful servant who took the talent given to him and buried it, to protect it, presumably out of respect for the authority of the master, as opposed to the servant who appropriated what was given, "speculated," one may say, with it, as if it were

his own, and thus, through his own spontaneous agency, multiplied the original gift in a manner pleasing to his master. According to the parable, he was given even more as a reward, the gift of which included what was taken away from the ostensibly modest servant.

3. The doctrine of creation has an obviously universal scope: it concerns the world precisely in its *natural* structure, which, as such, is something accessible in principle, as Vatican I taught, to reason simply, unaided by faith. In this sense, the notion belongs in some evident sense to philosophy, even if the doctrine acquires a transformed significance in theological reflection, when creation is seen, that is, not merely as the transcendent cause of the being of the world, but as a gift of love within the exchange of the Trinitarian Persons. Given this characterization of creation, the temptation is to think that, because the strictly theological doctrine of redemption depends, by contrast, quite directly on faith, and because, therefore, it is accessible ultimately only to believers, it does *not* have universal significance. This temptation acquires almost insurmountable power in the context of a culture defined by liberal ideology, according to which matters of faith are essentially private. Succumbing to this temptation would lead one to think of theology as inherently sectarian, and thus as needing to translate itself, as it were, into philosophical language in order to speak publicly, in order to address the world. The confusion of this assumption can lead to tragic-comic situations, such as the one described by Tracey Rowland in relation to ethics: modern Catholics, she suggests, contrived the philosophical language of natural law precisely in order to speak to the world, but in fact the only ones who listened were other Catholics — presumably because they could hear echoes of the original language in the translation.[18] There is no doubt that prudence is necessary when speaking of matters of faith to those who do not share it, and that in doing so one will necessarily make use of analogies drawn from nature and reason, notions drawn from philosophy, and so forth, in one's attempt to communicate. What is being disputed, here, is the assumption that revelation has only a limited scope. It if did, it would *need* philosophy in a disordered way, and for this very reason it would simply *use* philosophy for its own ends. The relationship would resemble the "co-dependence" we spoke of earlier. The move to philosophy will be a generous

18. Tracey Rowland, "Natural Law: From Neo-Thomism to Nuptial Mysticism," *Communio* 35 (Fall 2008): 374-96; here, 375. This is not at all to deny the importance of natural law in ethics, or indeed its specifically philosophical dimension. What is being disputed is a primarily *strategic* understanding of its importance.

one, by contrast, if we recognize that revelation, while certainly particular, is nevertheless radically universal already considered in itself and in relative abstraction from its relationship to philosophy. This is a dimension that Benedict XVI has masterfully demonstrated in his interpretation of Scripture, and, in particular, the relationship of the new covenant to the old, which itself simply recapitulates in a surprisingly novel way a movement that can already be traced in the Old Testament itself.[19] In this case, the opening to philosophy is the novel, gratuitous, expression of something perfectly natural to theology in itself.

4. The last point will certainly be the most controversial, but it bears a direct relationship to the first point made: the Paschal Mystery is the foundation — *within theology* — for the radical autonomy of philosophy. One of the meanings of the "autonomy" of reason (and whether this is the best or most adequate meaning is irrelevant here) is that reason operates according to its own laws, which means that it does its thinking *in a certain respect* in the "absence" of God. Rather than viewing this autonomy in the customary negative terms of philosophy asserting its rights over against theology, we may see it as a gift of love, in which, to use Ferdinand Ulrich's expression, the lover "separates" himself from the gift. At the Last Supper, just before the beginning of the Passion, Jesus warns his disciples that he would soon no longer be with them (John 13:33). This is, of course, not meant as a cause of joy (cf. Matt. 9:15). But Jesus also explains the necessity of his disappearance, in order that, post-Easter, the Spirit may come, who will guide them "into all truth" (John 16:13). Theologically considered, the withdrawal of God on Holy Saturday, ultimately into the depths of Hades and beyond the horizon of human experience and the world more generally, is a decisive moment of Christ's redemptive mission. Just as the deepest heart of the doctrine of creation lies within the intimacy of the inner Trinitarian conversation, so too does the act of redemption come to completion in the secret of God. It is a silent drama that takes place, not on the stage, but in the wings beyond view. And yet, this drama is the literal crux of the matter.

Moreover, far from being a "marginal" moment, mentioned in the Gospel but forgotten by the Church, the disappearance of God is "celebrated" every year as the crowning of Lent, or, perhaps better as the moment beyond the crowning of Lent: there is one day every year when Christ is removed from the altar of every Catholic church, a single day in which not a

19. Benedict XVI (Joseph Ratzinger), *Truth and Tolerance: Christian Belief and World Religions* (San Francisco: Ignatius Press, 2004), pp. 149-56.

Mass is said on the planet. It has often been pointed out that the "death of God" that Nietzsche proclaimed as the true kairos of the free spirit required for genuine philosophical thinking was not his own invention, but was *given* to him already by Christianity. The point, here, is not to affirm a Christian atheism, in the manner, for example, of a Gianni Vattimo, who absolutizes the death of the *Logos* as the ultimate eclipse of truth by love.[20] Instead, we mean to indicate only that the movement of love that theology follows reaches a point wherein the object of faith "disappears" from view (which is not to say it is destroyed or undermined). Indeed, this point comes at the extreme of love (John 13:1: εἰς τέλος ἠγάπησεν αὐτούς). If philosophy is characterized in a certain respect as a reflection on reality that is not carried out in immediate reference to the revelation given in faith, this disappearance at the "end" of love, the end to which the theologian must follow Christ in discipleship,[21] means that theology opens up to philosophy precisely at the moment that it reaches its own perfection. Despite the *prima facie* impression, this is not a "Hegelian" subordination of religion to philosophy for two reasons: first, the claim is that philosophy remains in fact ultimately subordinate to theology; and, second, it does so in part because the movement we are describing is not a logical necessity that we deduce from speculative thought, but a generous movement of love. The absence of God is not *required,* but it is given; it thus opens up a space for the autonomy of reason without limiting the all-encompassing scope of faith. The point in other words is that, however paradoxical it may seem, even the nonexplicit reference to the data of faith that one associates with philosophy is not simply foreign to theology.

What becomes clear is that the unity in difference and the difference in unity of philosophy and theology cannot be affirmed as a general principle but presupposes a "catholic" Christianity and what we may call a classical notion of philosophy (as opposed, for example, to what is called today analytic philosophy or continental philosophy), for in these traditions, the world is essentially "God-centered," and God is, in a certain respect, "world-centered." If the points enumerated above do indeed capture something essential in both philosophy and theology, it follows that any theologian who does not in principle have an intrinsic interest in philosophy qua philosophy

20. See Gianni Vattimo, *Nihilism and Emancipation: Ethics, Politics, and Law* (New York: Columbia University Press, 2004). Cf. "Toward a Nonreligious Christianity," in *After the Death of God* (New York: Columbia University Press, 2007), pp. 27-46.

21. Cf. Matthew 10:22.

will be a second-rate theologian, and any philosopher not interested in principle in theology betrays something essential to philosophy.

A Possible Model

Philosophy and theology have *distinct* principles: the principle of theology is faith and the principle of philosophy is reason. Having affirmed this, we must recognize that these principles are not simply separate from each other, and certainly not opposed. To say that the principle of theology is faith does not mean that theology excludes the use of reason. This may be regrettably true of certain theologians (!), but it is certainly not true of theology itself, which is after all a *logos* of God. And, *a fortiori,* it would be foolish to say that theology is less theological the more use it makes of reason. What distinguishes it as theology is that reason is placed immediately at the service of faith, and carries out that service according to the measure of faith. Granted that there is no simple symmetry in the relationship between faith and reason, can we nevertheless affirm, conversely, some involvement of faith — genuine, explicit Christian faith — in reason in a manner that remains altogether philosophical? We will explore this question as we address the relationship of the respective objects of the two disciplines.

In the most general terms, the objects of philosophy and theology are quite distinct: philosophy is a "worldly" science, occupied with being qua being, while theology is a "divine science"; it is rational discourse concerning God, i.e., a theo-logos. But, as we have seen already, the two disciplines open up to each other from their center because of the nature of their objects — being is analogical and God "so loved the world" — and of the intrinsic relation between faith and reason. This means that an awareness of the "dynamism" inherent in each ought to belong to our characterization of their respective objects: philosophy is a study of being that continually opens up to its "principium et finis," its deepest source and therefore ultimate end, while theology studies, not just God, but the Trinitarian God revealed in the incarnate Christ who entered into the world in assuming flesh. If, as Plato once described it, philosophy is an ascent (ἀνάβασις),[22] then theology is a descent (κατάβασις). Thomas Aquinas captures something of this movement when he distinguishes the teaching of philosophy from the teaching of faith in terms of a reverse order: "[I]n the teaching of philosophy, which considers

22. Plato, *Republic* 519c.

creatures in themselves and leads us from them to the knowledge of God, the first consideration is about creatures; the last of God. But in the teaching of faith, which considers creatures only in their relation to God, the consideration of God comes first, that of creatures afterwards."[23] And so we may think of philosophy and theology, not just as ordered to a distinct object, but in fact ordered to a distinct object that is itself, in a certain sense, in motion, so that the two objects in fact cover a similar range — both God and creatures — but from a different perspective: philosophy thus conceived is a movement "from below," and theology is a movement "from above."

But this formulation can only be a starting point. If it is true that the disciplines open up to each other from their centers, and that faith and reason are *intrinsically* related in their abiding difference, then it follows that the movement that belongs most properly to each cannot be simply foreign to the other but must be shared, though in a manner appropriate to the essence of each. We saw something similar in our discussion of the relation between the intellect and will in chapters three and four. In the present case, the movement from below will be "inserted within" theology's native movement from above, and philosophy will include a movement "from above" inside of its ascent. What results, then, is a more complex pair of movements: philosophy "takes its stand" in the world, it is defined by its interest in the world, and yet by virtue of the analogical nature of being, this very interest implies a movement beyond the world to its source. And then, again because an insight into the source introduces a new meaning of being, the defining interest of philosophy returns it to the world, which it sees, now, with so to speak "new eyes" in the light of what it has come to grasp of the nature of its first principle. We saw an example of this in the last chapter. Philosophy, in short, is a movement from the world to God to the world. On the other hand, theology "takes its stand" in God, but follows God's own movement into the world. And this movement into the world, in fact, reveals one might say ever-greater depths of the mystery of God, insofar as it is a manifestation of the love that God *is* in his innermost life: love does not only proclaim itself; most profoundly it *shows* its truth in *deed*.[24] Reflection on God's acts *ad extra*, on the doctrine of creation, and even more the incarnation and the Son's soteriological mission in history, reveals far more of the nature of God than could be gained simply through a con-

23. Aquinas, *SCG* 2.4.

24. See St. Ignatius, *Spiritual Exercises*, the Contemplation to Attain the Love of God, note.

templation of God "in himself." The interest in God that defines theology brings it into the place wherein God manifests himself, and then returns it to, so to speak, the reality itself. Theology is a movement from God to the world to God.

The difference between philosophy and theology, it ought to be evident, does not isolate them into two separate fields of work, as it were, but rather opens up many of the same areas to be explored from abidingly different perspectives. So, for example, while it lies closer to the central tasks of philosophy to engage with those thinkers who have opened up the basic meaning of reality and taken some decisive position with respect to it — whether in the ancient world (Plato, the Stoics, and so forth) or the modern (Descartes, Kant, Hegel, Nietzsche, and so forth) — such engagement would not be foreign to theology. But one would generally expect that the theologian would engage them above all with the intent of passing a judgment in the light of faith in order to make more evident the significance of faith, the perhaps unexpected scope of its content: the Christian philosopher, by contrast, would tend to read them "from below," to think with them toward the ultimate questions, and to open them up thus from within as far as one is able. In reading Plato, for instance, the theologian would want to show above all what novelty Christianity brings to Platonic metaphysics; the Catholic philosopher would want above all to show his anonymous "*anima Christiana*" as far as it is indeed there — that is, not to show first of all where Plato falls short, but how his thought anticipates revelation and is thus open for a transformative recapitulation in the light of faith. These two modes, of course, are not contradictory, but complementary, and both of them, properly understood, would want to do full justice to Plato himself.

Because both of these movements are circular, rather than linear, it becomes clear that neither represents a task that can be finished once and for all, but each allows for a constant deepening: the mystery of God and the mystery of being are inexhaustible, particularly when each is seen in the light of the other. At the same time, however, the movements are not ceaseless in a mechanical way, but they are expressions of a *principle,* which means that each has an origin and destination, and so a place of genuine rest, that distinguishes it from the other. Let us note, in this regard, a point that will be developed below: because philosophy thus conceived contains within itself in principle a "from above" moment, a descending movement from God to the world, without this moment *defining* it, we can accept the possibility that philosophy, in its circulation from the world to God and back, can receive the light of revelation into its proper object, "being qua being," without losing its philosophical character. As we saw in the previous chapter, the analogy that opens philosophy to the *principium et finis mundi* does *not* "measure" God by the being of the world, but vice versa; reason is thereby led, according to its own natural movement, to receive a "new" meaning of the world in the light of this principle, which is why the descent is not simply a retracing of the same steps up in reverse order, but a genuine discovery, a movement forward. In this case, philosophical reflection within the concrete, historical circumstances of Christian reflection may receive a new meaning of being by virtue of God's self-revelation without betraying the movement that constitutes its nature in distinction from theology. We will unfold this possibility in more detail below.

Now, it just so happens that Hans Urs von Balthasar presented this description of two overlapping circular movements as a way of characterizing the unity in difference of the two "states of life," marriage and consecration.[25] This coincidence suggest an analogy, which turns out to be quite fruitful. There are in fact several reasons to draw the analogy: first, the vows that constitute the states of life are total and definitive, just as the disciplines lay claim to the whole of a person — an eros for the ultimate in philosophy, and a discipleship of God *(mathēsis theou)* in theology — as we saw above; second, according to the Church's understanding of the states of life, they are abidingly distinct within a unity and indeed, just like theology and philosophy, they are asymmetrically related within that unified difference; and, third, their spheres of activity overlap in principle considerably almost to the point of coinciding — both states carry out their work in some respect in the world and do their work for the glory of God — and yet the way they engage this activity is radically different in the two cases because of the abiding difference between the two states. While both states of life are a living out of the definitive "sealing" of one's being in baptism, one state is constituted in the consecration to the following of Christ in an immediate way, while the other is a consecration to Christ in and through the mediation of one's total belonging, as spouse, to another human being and to the family that grows from that union.

Let us consider some of the ways in which this analogy illuminates the relationship between theology and philosophy. First of all, because the distinction between religious consecration and sacramental marriage reveals two irreducibly different ways of belonging to Christ, it makes evident a way

25. Balthasar's essay "A Theology of the Evangelical Counsels," *Cross Currents* (Spring 1966): 214-36 and (Summer 1966): 325-37, was the original inspiration for the model of the relationship between philosophy and theology being proposed here.

of drawing a distinction that is not always made, and the absence of which will force unnecessary and indeed problematic inferences: namely, the distinction between the relationship of faith and reason, on the one hand, and the relationship of theology and philosophy, on the other. Simply identifying faith with theology and reason with philosophy is a problematic oversimplification. Without the distinction, one would be without any solid ground for thinking of the philosopher as anything but a "theologian *manqué*." If it is the case that the ultimate meaning of reality is revealed in faith, there would be no intrinsic reason for contemplating the world "merely" philosophically, which would in this case mean by "bracketing out" the data of revelation, but one would do so, if at all, for extrinsic reasons or strategic purposes (e.g., in order to communicate with nonbelievers). Lacking a positive ground for its difference from theology, philosophy has historically been led to the ultimately suicidal decision to protect its autonomy by carving out a smaller niche, and defining itself in less than ultimate terms. It thus ceased to be about the world in God, but simply about the world *tout court* in contrast to God, and eventually — because being is in fact analogical, one cannot bracket out God without finally bracketing out being — only about what we mean when we speak about the world.

The problem of justifying philosophy in light of the higher meaning of the world given in faith is similar to the existential conundrum that often faces serious believers in vocational discernment: How can one justify anything but consecration if one loves God with all one's heart, strength, and soul? This question has received some further clarity, objectively if not necessarily existentially, in the Church's recognition of marriage as a *state of perfection,* which is similar to consecration in precisely that respect, even though, in the Church's teaching, it remains subordinate to consecration. Both states are an expression of the one definitive belonging to Christ effected at baptism, but each expresses that belonging in an irreducibly different way, and both ways of belonging are necessary to express the whole compass of Christian life. It is ultimately "sterilizing" to distinguish the two by separating the spheres of sovereignty, as it were: the religious are experts in Church matters while the married lay are experts in worldly matters, for this juxtaposes a clericalistic world-less Church and an ontologically God-less world. As the model we mentioned above suggests, properly understood, *both* involve both God and the world, but differently, according to different orders.[26] By anal-

26. The key difference seems to be immediacy of relation to God compared to mediation, or in John Paul II's terminology, original solitude and original unity.

ogy, we may say that, for a Christian, both philosophy and theology are best understood as an expression of a total assent of reason to faith, but they express that assent according to irreducibly distinct principles. The difference in principles does not sort them into two separate spheres but in fact relates them differently to what is essentially one and the same sphere, namely, the whole as illuminated by revelation and understood by reason.

An obvious objection can be raised here. As just formulated, it appears that we are defining philosophy as the study of God and the world in the light of revelation, and are thus simply conflating what *Dei Filius* referred to as the distinct principles of philosophy and theology. We would thus appear to contradict the clear teaching of the document, which insists, as we have seen, that there are *two orders* (a *"duplex ordo"*) of knowledge, one defined by faith, and the other defined by reason. Moreover, the Council unequivocally affirms the ability of *unaided* reason to carry out the essential task of philosophy, namely, to think the world in relation to its transcendent cause. This is a weighty objection, and responding to it gives us an opportunity to clarify further the nature of the distinctness of philosophy. Let us address first the question of principles and second the question of objects that distinguish the two sciences without compromising their unity. The analogy of the states of life proves to illuminate both aspects. At the end of this chapter we will respond to the question of the role of unaided reason in the light of the model we have developed.

The problem in terms of principle appears to be the following. On the one hand, we distinguish philosophy from theology by saying that philosophy judges principally by *reason*, but then, on the other hand, we say that a believer who philosophizes welcomes the light of faith, which by its very nature is superior to reason. To include faith at all would seem to require making faith the judge, in which case faith could not but appropriate to itself, as it were, reason's role as principle, and what we are calling philosophy would be indistinguishable from theology. The dilemma would seem inescapable: if faith enters into the picture, it can only be as the proper principle, and so philosophy can remain philosophy only by excluding faith and therefore by limiting itself and so surrendering its original aspiration to totality. But so formulated the objection misconceives the nature of reason, and the dilemma follows necessarily only from this misconception. We indicated above a point argued for over the course of this book, namely, that reason is essentially ecstatic. This essence bears on its mode of judgment. To appeal to a classic distinction, in making its judgments, reason has *authority*, we might say, rather than *power;* in other words, it always exercises its judgment in deference to, and representative of, what is greater than it, even when it is operating "unaided." In the most evident sense, this greater reality is being itself. And if being is analogical, it is always "more greater," so to speak. In discussing the nature of philosophy in distinction from theology, Gilson describes philosophy as ruled by a "common judge," namely, "reason, *as judged itself by reality*."[27] The principle of philosophy is always and everywhere subordinate to something that exceeds it, and this subordination does not compromise its normative character. If this is always the case, then the subordination of reason to the specific higher principle of reality illumined even explicitly by the data of revelation need not be excluded. Reason judges being: but as *given* to it, as a reality that exceeds it and so that presents itself for judgment without compromise of its superiority. So, too, reason judges faith, or more adequately, reason is illumined in its own operation by faith: but again, as *given,* and in this case, as given wholly gratuitously by God in Christ. We may think of faith as offering itself to the judgment of reason out of the gratuity that belongs essentially to it, according to the description sketched above. A faith in the God who subjects himself to the judgment of the Cross without in any way compromising his sovereignty can subordinate itself to the (always relative!) judgment of reason without betraying its ultimacy.

With regard to its object, philosophy is the science of being qua being. But, as we have been arguing, to say this does *not* mean that philosophy has no interest in God. This much is not so controversial, since philosophy perennially has included God as the transcendent cause of its proper object. But, perhaps more controversially, philosophy cannot be defined as having no interest in God *specifically as he has revealed himself in history,* unless God's self-revelation has nothing to do with the meaning of its proper object, i.e., with the meaning of being qua being, as we suggested in the previous chapter. But faith tells us that it does, and in fact quite radically. If this is true, one cannot "bracket out" the contribution of faith without denying the integrity of the object of philosophy. It therefore follows that the philosopher, in faith, takes a fundamental interest in God's self-revelation precisely as a function of his proper inquiry. But this interest remains abidingly different from a specifically theological interest, because — by analogy — the theological interest is a direct and immediate one, while philosophy's interest is always indirect and mediated through the more direct interest in the meaning of being qua being. Note, we are not saying that philosophy in the

27. Étienne Gilson, *Unity of Philosophical Experience* (San Francisco: Ignatius Press, 1999), p. 36. Emphasis added.

post-Christian period is *essentially* defined by God's self-revelation in history; to say this would indeed be to conflate philosophy and theology. We are saying that philosophy is defined by its own distinct and proper principle and object, but that these, of themselves, may open up *de facto* according to the particular case of the person philosophizing at their center to the light of faith in the historical context in which God has revealed himself in Christ.

To formulate the unity and difference between philosophy and theology in general and somewhat oversimplified terms: for the Christian, in faith, the world speaks everywhere of God both in the order of creation and in the order of redemption. Given this context, which is common to all Christians by virtue of faith, the theologian is interested in the world primarily (though not exclusively) because it discloses more and more who God is, whereas the philosopher celebrates the world as a manifestation of God primarily (though not exclusively) because this so radically "charges" the meaning of being in itself. The qualifier "not exclusively" is crucial in both cases because each includes within itself an interest in the interest of the other, even if it is contextualized by its own principles. In any event, these two interests are irreducible to one another, insofar as they bring out a dimension that is not directly present in the other, even if it is certainly not excluded; thus understood, they clearly deepen and enhance one another precisely in their difference; and, finally, they are not, for all that, simply symmetrically related: the world is an expression of God, while God is never an expression of the world, and, no matter how deeply and wholeheartedly one can be "in" the world, one cannot in fact *belong* to it. Both the philosopher and the theologian belong to God.

Let us return to the analogy of the states of life to see what light it sheds on what it might mean to think in a specifically *philosophical,* rather than theological, manner in the light of faith. On the one hand, a sacramental marriage is a marriage definitively and explicitly placed under the sign of Christ; it is in this sense consecrated, i.e., committed to the living out of the Christian life. Indeed, it is not only some part of the relationship that is so committed, or some portion of its free time or surplus savings that are sacrificed to some religious purpose, but the *whole* of it that is handed over. This explicit commitment to the Christian faith, however, does not make it "religious"; it does not transform it into the other state of life. The reason it does not is that the individuals do not vow themselves individually in an "exclusive" manner to God as they do in religious life, but, rather, they vow themselves *to* each other *in* Christ. Henceforward, their relationship to Christ is mediated by their relationship to their spouse: they still belong wholly to

Christ, but they do so precisely *as* a whole, in the integrity of the new community of the "one flesh" union. The individuals are now members of a larger whole, and this membership entails its own responsibilities and distinct content even in its belonging to Christ. By analogy, the "making explicit" of faith does not necessarily transform philosophy into theology; there remains the question of the differentiation of the precise manner of the relationship between faith and the understanding. As we have described the two, thinking in faith is theological when faith is the principle of the understanding; it is philosophical, by contrast, if relative priority is given to reason: in this case, reason, we might say, does not vow itself in an exclusive manner to revelation, but is instead "wedded" to being qua being, and this relationship as a whole — reason as ordered to the comprehensive scope of being — in its full integrity, according to the responsibilities and distinctive content that belongs to it, places itself at the service of faith.

On the other hand, a sacramental marriage is still a marriage; it is generally recognized as such, it "functions" as such in the public order, and it can be counted unproblematically alongside other, nonsacramental marriages. The fact of its being consecrated does not, at least at one level, present the least stumbling block for the general understanding. Those in sacramental marriages can have unstrained conversations with those in nonsacramental marriages about the trials and joys of married life. But this does not mean that the sacrament makes no difference. Indeed, it makes a radical difference, ontologically, according to its self-understanding, and even in the day-to-day experience of the marriage. It is just that this radical difference is not a foreign intrusion that somehow compromises its natural reality as marriage. Quite to the contrary, properly understood, sacramental marriage is more truly natural insofar as it gives the specific realities of marriage an infinite density, the weight of a vocation. What ought to be most immediately striking about those in a sacramental marriage is not that they continually "foreground" the explicitly ecclesial aspect of their state of life, but that they take the reality of marriage itself so seriously, though one would expect that the reason they do so would be or become manifest to others as appropriate — i.e., in a "natural" way. Because of the "enhanced" attention to its reality, we could say that sacramental marriage, in principle, represents not something "other" than marriage, but a paradigm that reveals its meaning in general. It is not accidental that marriage at large almost always has a religious dimension even if it is not sacramental: love necessarily implies transcendence, in some analogous form. It is also, therefore, not accidental that those who reject the religious dimension of marriage altogether tend not to acknowledge much significance in its natural reality.

Of course, these assertions would require more elaboration and qualification if we intended to develop an account here of the nature of marriage, the sacrament, the states of life, and so forth.[28] The point here is simply to indicate the principle of the analogy to the philosophy-theology relationship: reason has an "ecstatic" dimension, without which it loses its integrity as reason; philosophy, as the fullness of reason, does not cease to be philosophy in the context of faith, and Catholic philosophy, which is irreducibly different from theology even if it shares a commitment to faith, can be counted among philosophies generally, and can enter into unstrained dialogue with them. When thinking through some problem with others, a Catholic philosopher could leave his faith implicit and reflect on experience as it is simply given, introducing his faith at a particular point (if at all) because the matter under consideration has unfolded to such a depth that the question of faith becomes directly relevant: insofar as the world is created, our inquiry into the ultimate meaning of things will ultimately have to open to the meaning of God. Or, on the other hand, he could make his faith explicit from the outset as a background to a point he is arguing, not as the logical justification for his conclusion, but, more organically, as the source, so to speak, of the light by which a matter illuminates itself. For example, one might propose to a Neoplatonist philosopher — who claims that beauty, as "unity-in-diversity," is caused by unity — that difference is an essential co-cause of beauty. Doing so, it would not be inappropriate in particular circumstances to explain that one is led to this proposal because of a notion of God, not as absolute simplicity, but as *triune*, a notion that implies the equiprimordiality of unity and difference. One would nevertheless have to point to the evidence in experience that there is a reciprocal dependence, however asymmetrical, between unity and difference in beauty. To what extent, whether in the case wherein faith is left implicit or the case wherein it is made explicit, the other with whom one dialogues would have to hypothesize a triune God or even in fact to *assent* to such a notion — i.e., to have the theological virtue of faith — in order to see even the natural evidence as the believer does is impossible finally to deter-

28. A fuller treatment, for example, would reflect on the further distinction the magisterium makes in the consecrated state between the religious orders and secular institutes: these latter would seem to represent more directly the moment of theology's movement into the world while the former would represent more directly theology's abiding in God. There is thus an analogy between this distinction and that between non-sacramental and sacramental marriage.

mine. But to the extent that faith does bear on the evidence of experience given in the example, indeed in an *intrinsic* way, the invitation to faith is, as it were, given objectively *in* the example itself. Properly understood, the light of faith does not make a philosopher less attentive to concrete experience or concerned with the integrity and demands of reason, but always more. Thus, Catholic philosophy, so conceived, would represent at least in principle a paradigm of philosophy generally.[29] It is perhaps not an accident that some of the strongest cases made on behalf of *reason* and philosophy are today being made by the Catholic magisterium;[30] Balthasar called specifically on the Christian to be the "guardian of metaphysics."[31]

Let us return to the final aspect of the objection raised above concerning unaided reason. To speak of Catholic philosophy as a paradigm would seem to run afoul of Vatican I's description of reason's capacities outside of the influence of faith. But it is essential to note that the Council does not present the unaided exercise of reason as a description of reason in its *essence* or indeed as the paradigm of philosophy; it is affirmed, rather, as a possibility that cannot be denied without compromising the integrity of reason (and ultimately of the natural order generally). The proposal we are making here affirms this possibility unequivocally, but it affirms this possibility as a moment of a larger whole. Thus, reason's ascent from the world to its source, carried by the analogical character of being itself and so not immediately dependent on the aid of faith, is indispensable; but to say this does not require the exclusion of the distinct moment in which reason returns (katalogically) to reflect on being anew in light of its first principle, and indeed eventually in light of this first principle insofar as it freely reveals itself and so opens the novel insights of faith. Nor does it exclude, in fact, a renewed movement "from below," an ascending inquiry into the nature of God as originating source of being within the space opened up and by virtue of the desire enkindled explicitly by faith. All of these belong to the ceaseless task of phi-

29. It is important to say "in principle" because it is not necessarily the case that Catholic philosophers are more genuinely philosophical *in fact* than their non-Catholic counterparts.

30. In addition to the insistence in *Dei Filius* on the intrinsic capacity of reason to attain God unaided, we have powerful recent apologies for reason, for example, in John Paul II, *Fides et ratio*, and Benedict XVI, "Address to Young University Professors," 19 August 2011; "Identity and Mission of the Catholic University," 17 April 2008; "Lecture at Sapienza," 17 January 2008; and "Faith, Reason, and the University: Memories and Reflections" ("The Regensburg Address"), 12 September 2006.

31. Balthasar, *GL5*, p. 656.

losophy when we consider it, not reductively according to its perennial essence alone or in its historical reality alone, but comprehensively according to both.

The encyclical *Fides et ratio* offers a list of thinkers in the modern era who may be taken as paradigms of the integration of faith and reason, and so models to be followed by philosophers who are also believers (no. 74). Alasdair MacIntyre has recently pointed out the curious fact that the philosophers mentioned represent not only a significant diversity of perspectives but in some cases represent opposing positions on some question or another of genuine importance.[32] MacIntyre interprets this as a sign that the magisterium acknowledges the *conflictual* nature of tradition, namely, the fact that a tradition is not a monolithic set of ideas but includes contention within a unity of the particular questions at the root of the various disputes: "It is, so the list of names makes clear, a history not only of past, but of continuing disagreements."[33] The model of the relationship between philosophy and theology that we are considering here allows a different interpretation: once we affirm an intrinsic, *generous* relation between faith and reason that both broadens and deepens the scope of each, we see that there is room for relatively opposed philosophies without sacrificing the substantial unity of truth by reducing it to what threatens to collapse into a mere formalistic commitment to particular questions, particular approaches, or particular propositions.[34] There is, indeed, a kind of "opposition" between the ascent of reason to God and its descent from God, between reason's inquiry unaided by faith and reason's discoveries inside of faith, but these oppositions would become outright contradictions only if we absolutized one aspect in a way that in principle precluded the complementary one. In other words, we face contradiction if we abandon the essential catholicity of reason. More concretely, to

32. Alasdair MacIntyre, *God, Philosophy, Universities: A Selective History of the Catholic Philosophical Tradition* (Lanham, MD: Rowman & Littlefield, 2009), p. 169.

33. MacIntyre, *God, Philosophy, Universities,* p. 169.

34. The difference may appear to be above all a matter of emphasis: MacIntyre affirms that the disagreements in the tradition are made possible because of deeper commitments (principally concerning either the starting point or the ending point of the philosophical enterprise; p. 170). But rather than claim an underlying unity by virtue of particular agreements that are common, which are then juxtaposed, as it were, to the disagreements that remain opposed to each other, we are claiming that the unity is a whole that is able in principle to embrace both sides of the disagreements in different respects. In this way, one is not forced either to take a side in an absolute sense in the disagreements, or to think that the matter about which there is disagreement is not important (i.e., at least not as important as the agreement).

take two figures not mentioned in *Fides et ratio,* a proper understanding of the relation between faith and reason has room to include *both* Maurice Blondel, who in his early work insisted on the radical autonomy of reason with respect to faith, which nevertheless could be shown to open up inexorably of itself to the supernatural, *and* Ferdinand Ulrich, who, as we saw in the previous chapter, claimed that philosophy in the modern world can be "purely" natural only when enacted explicitly within faith. Though these represent relatively opposed approaches to philosophy, it is not necessary to eliminate one in order to affirm the other. We would have to exclude any such perspectives only to the extent that the particular perspective *excluded itself* from the greater whole by excluding any other approach relatively opposed to itself. The greater whole is ultimately the endless task of philosophy itself, which can thrive as a whole only if it vigilantly refuses to allow any reduction to a single aspect of its aim. In the end, we return to the beginning: the fate of philosophy hangs on fidelity to the catholicity of reason.

It may be proposed in fact that this fidelity depends in turn — at least at this point in history — on an affirmation of the Catholicity of reason, or at least the Christian roots of reason's catholicity. The Neoplatonic tradition that forms the core of the "perennial" philosophy, we ought to recall, refused to make reason ultimate, but bound it to *being,* the second hypostasis, eternally subordinate to the sole absolute, the One. In this case, philosophical reason, to the extent that it remains true to itself, ultimately falls as it were to its knees in the end and yields its place to supra-rational "contemplation," which is in reality not a contemplation but a mystical flight of the "alone to the Alone" (φυγὴ μόνου πρὸς μόνον).[35] The Church Fathers appropriated a great deal of Neoplatonic thought in their encounter with the wisdom of the Greeks — perhaps more and better than is generally acknowledged — but this is one element that was definitively rejected. The Logos, for Christians, is not subordinate to God, but was "in the beginning with God," and indeed "was God." The way the Trinitarian dogma was formulated requires us to think of "intellect" as indeed "second," but without for all that being subordinate to the "first." Instead, in this case the "first" and "second" remain equally ultimate in the eternal unity of the Spirit. We may see here a radical justification for making philosophy co-ultimate with theology in their abiding difference. Faith, far from humiliating reason, and so philosophy, has elevated it beyond the aspirations of even the boldest thinkers, ancient and modern alike.

35. Plotinus, *Ennead* V.9.11.

Bibliography

Aertsen, Jan. "Beauty in the Middle Ages: A Forgotten Transcendental?" *Medieval Philosophy and Theology* 1 (1991): 68-97.

———. *Medieval Philosophy and the Transcendentals: The Case of Thomas Aquinas.* Leiden: Brill, 1996.

———. "The Philosophical Importance of the Doctrine of the Transcendentals in Thomas Aquinas." *Revue internationale de philosophie* 52 (1998): 249-68.

Albert the Great. *De pulchro et bono.* In Thomas Aquinas, *Opera Omnia.* Volume VII. Edited by Roberto Busa. Stuttgart: Frommann-Holzboog, 1980.

Alexander of Hales. *Summa fratris Alexandri.* Edited by Bernardini Klumper and the Quarracchi Fathers. 4 volumes. Rome: Collegii S. Bonaventurae, 1924-1948.

Aquinas, Thomas. *Collationes super Credo in Deum.* Paris: Nouvelles Éditions Latines, 1969.

———. *Commentary on the Book of Causes.* Translated by V. Guagliardo, C. Hess, and R. Taylor. Washington, DC: Catholic University of America Press, 1996.

———. *De potentia dei.* Edited by P. M. Pession. In *Questiones disputatae,* edited by Raymundus Spiazzi, volume 2. Turin and Rome: Marietti, 1965.

———. *De principiis naturae.* Edited by J. J. Pauson, translated by V. J. Bourke. Fribourg: Société Philosophique, 1950.

———. *De veritate.* Volume 22, parts 1-3, of *Sancti Thomae de Aquino opera omnia.* Leonine Edition. Rome: Editori di San Tommaso, 1975-1976.

———. *In duodecim libros Metaphysicorum Aristotelis expositio.* Edited by M. R. Cathala and R. M. Spiazzi. Turin and Rome: Marietti, 1964.

———. *In librum de causis expositio.* In *Opuscula Omnia,* volume 1, edited by P. Mandonnet. Paris: P. Lethielleux, 1927.

———. *On the Eternity of the World.* Translated by Robert T. Miller. http://www.fordham.edu/halsall/basis/aquinas-eternity.asp (accessed 1/10/2012).

———. *Scriptum super libros Sententiarum magistri Petri Lombardi episcopi Parisiensis.*

Volumes 1-2, edited by P. Mandonnet. Paris: P. Lethielleux, 1929. Volumes 3-4, edited by M. Moos. Paris: P. Lethielleux, 1933-1947.

———. *Summa Contra Gentiles I-III.* Translated by A. Pegis, J. Anderson, and V. J. Burke. Garden City, NY: Doubleday, 1952, 1955, 1956.

———. *Summa Theologiae.* Volumes 4-12 of *Sancti Thomae Aquinatis opera omnia.* Leonine Edition. Rome, 1888-1906.

———. *The Summa Theologica of St. Thomas Aquinas.* Volumes 1-5. Translated by Fathers of the English Dominican Province. New York: Benziger, 1948.

Arendt, Hannah. *The Life of the Mind.* Volume 2: *Willing.* New York: Harcourt Brace Jovanovich, 1978.

Aristotle. *Aristotle's Physics: A Guided Study.* Translated by Joe Sachs. New Brunswick, NJ: Rutgers University Press, 1995.

———. *The Basic Works.* Edited by Richard McKeon. New York: Random House, 1941.

Augustine. *Confessions.* Translated by R. S. Pine-Coffin. New York: Penguin Books, 1961.

Bacon, Francis. *Novum Organum.* In *The English Philosophers from Bacon to Mill.* Edited by Edwin A. Burtt. New York: Random House, 1939.

Balthasar, Hans Urs von. *Die Entwicklung der musikalischen Idee,* 2nd ed. Freiburg: Johannes Verlag, 1999.

———. *Epilogue.* Translated by Edward T. Oakes, S.J. San Francisco: Ignatius Press, 2004.

———. "Forgetfulness of God and Christians." In *Explorations in Theology.* Volume 3: *Creator Spirit.* San Francisco: Ignatius Press, 1993.

———. *Glaubhaft ist nur Liebe,* 6th ed. Freiburg: Johannes Verlag, 2000.

———. *The Glory of the Lord: A Theological Aesthetics.* Volumes 1-7. Translated by Erasmo Leiva-Merikakis, Andrew Louth, Brian McNeil, Oliver Davies, Francis McDonagh, John Saward, Martin Simon, and Rowan Williams. San Francisco: Ignatius Press, 1982-1991.

———. *The Grain of Wheat: Aphorisms.* San Francisco: Ignatius Press, 1995.

———. *Love Alone Is Credible.* San Francisco: Ignatius Press, 2004.

———. "Movement Toward God." In *Explorations in Theology.* Volume 3: *Creator Spirit.* San Francisco: Ignatius Press, 1993.

———. *My Work in Retrospect.* San Francisco: Ignatius Press, 1993.

———. "Philosophy, Christianity, Monasticism." In *Explorations in Theology.* Volume 2: *Spouse of the Word.* San Francisco: Ignatius Press, 1991.

———. *Theo-Drama: Theological Dramatic Theory.* Volumes 1-5. Translated by Graham Harrison. San Francisco: Ignatius Press, 1988-1998.

———. *Theo-Logic.* Volumes 1-3. Translated by Adrian Walker and Graham Harrison. San Francisco: Ignatius Press, 2000-2005.

———. "Theology and Sanctity." In *Explorations in Theology.* Volume 1: *The Word Made Flesh.* San Francisco: Ignatius Press, 1989.

———. *The Theology of Karl Barth.* San Francisco: Ignatius Press, 1992.

———. "A Theology of the Evangelical Counsels." *Cross Currents* (Spring 1966): 214-36 and (Summer 1966): 325-37.

Balthasar, Hans Urs von, ed. *Anthologien: Vom vornehmen Menschen, Vergeblichkeit* and *Von Gut und Böse.* Freiburg: Johannes Verlag, 2000.

Barth, Karl. *Church Dogmatics.* New York: Continuum, 2009.

Baumgarten, Alexander. *Theoretische Ästhetik: Die grundlegenden Abschnitte aus der "Aesthetica" (1750/58).* Translated and edited by H. R. Schweizer. Hamburg: F. Meiner, 1983.

Benedict XVI (Joseph Ratzinger). "Address to Young University Professors." 19 August 2011.

———. "Identity and Mission of the Catholic University." 17 April 2008.

———. "Lecture at Sapienza." 17 January 2008; and "Faith, Reason, and the University: Memories and Reflections" ("The Regensburg Address"), 12 September 2006.

———. *Truth and Tolerance: Christian Belief and World Religions.* San Francisco: Ignatius Press, 2004.

Bersanelli, Marco. "Wonder and Knowledge: Scientific Investigation and the Breadth of Human Reason." Unpublished manuscript.

Bieler, Martin. "Meta-anthropology and Christology: On the Philosophy of Hans Urs von Balthasar." *Communio* 20 (1993): 129-46.

Blankenhorn, Bernhard, O.P. "Balthasar's Method of Divine Naming." *Nova et Vetera* 1, no. 2 (2003): 245-68.

Blondel, Maurice. *The Letter on Apologetics & History and Dogma.* Translated by Alexander Dru and Illtyd Trethowan. Grand Rapids: Eerdmans, 1994.

Bonaventure. *The Mind's Road to God.* Translated by George Boas. New York: Macmillan, 1985.

Boutot, Alain. *Heidegger et Platon: Le problème du nihilisme.* Paris: Presses Universitaires de France, 1987.

Brugnoli, Andrea. "Rifondazione del 'verum' a partire dal 'bonum' nella filosofia di Balthasar." *Sensus communis* 3 (2002): 267-86.

Burtt, E. A. *The Metaphysical Foundations of Modern Physical Science: A Historical and Critical Essay.* London: Routledge, 1932.

Caputo, John. *Heidegger and Aquinas.* New York: Fordham University Press, 1987.

Carlyle, Thomas. *Sartor Resartus.* Oxford: Oxford University Press, 2008.

Carraud, Vincent. *Causa sive ratio: La Raison de la cause de Suarez à Leibniz.* Paris: Presses Universitaires de France, 2002.

Chesterton, G. K. *Orthodoxy.* In *The Everyman Chesterton.* New York: Knopf, 2011.

Claudel, Paul. "Introduction à un poème sur Dante." In *Positions et propositions.* Paris: Gallimard, 1928.

———. "Religion and the Artist: Introduction to a Poem on Dante." *Communio* 22, no. 2 (Summer 1995): 357-67.

Cooper, John. "Introduction" to Plato's *Complete Works.* Indianapolis: Hackett, 1997.

Czapiewski, Winfried. *Das Schöne bei Thomas von Aquin.* Freiburg: Herder, 1964.

Dawkins, Richard. *The Selfish Gene.* 30th anniversary ed. Oxford: Oxford University Press, 2006.

Descartes, René. *Passions of the Soul.* Indianapolis: Hackett, 1989.

———. *The Philosophical Works of Descartes.* Volume 1. Translated by Elizabeth Haldane and G. R. T. Ross. Cambridge: Cambridge University Press, 1973.

Dewan, Laurence, O.P. "Is Truth a Transcendental in Aquinas?" *Nova et Vetera* 2, no. 1 (2004): 1-21.

Diels, Hermann, and Walter Kranz. *Die Fragmente der Vorsokratiker.* Zürich: Weidmann, 1985.

Dihle, Albrecht. *The Theory of Will in Classical Antiquity.* Berkeley: University of California Press, 1982.

Dionysius the Areopagite. *De divinis nominibus.* Edited by Beate Regina Suchla. New York: De Gruyter, 1990.

Disse, Jörg. "Liebe und Erkenntnis: Zur Geistesmetaphysik Hans Urs von Balthasars." *Münchner Theologische Zeitschrift* 54, no. 3 (1999): 215-27.

Dupré, Louis. *Religion and the Rise of Modern Culture.* South Bend, IN: University of Notre Dame Press, 2008.

Eckermann, J. P. *Gespräche mit Goethe.* Volume 2. 6th edition. Leipzig: F. A. Brockhaus, 1885.

Eco, Umberto. *Art and Beauty in the Middle Ages.* New Haven: Yale University Press, 1986.

Fichte, J. G. *Attempt at a Critique of All Revelation.* Translated by Garrett Green. Cambridge: Cambridge University Press, 2010.

Figal, Günther. "Introduction." In *The Heidegger Reader,* ed. G. Figal. Bloomington: Indiana University Press, 2009.

Finance, Joseph de. *Être et agir dans la philosophie de saint Thomas.* Rome: Gregorian University Press, 1965.

Fisichella, R. "Oportet philosophari in theologia (I)." *Gregorianum* 76, no. 2 (1995): 221-62.

———. "Oportet philosophari in theologia (II)." *Gregorianum* 76, no. 3 (1995): 503-34.

———. "Oportet philosophari in theologia (III)." *Gregorianum* 76, no. 4 (1995): 701-28.

Frede, Michael. "The Original Notion of Cause." In *Essays in Ancient Philosophy.* Minneapolis: University of Minnesota Press, 1987.

Friedländer, Paul. *Plato.* Volume 1. 3rd edition. Berlin: De Gruyter, 1964.

Gallagher, David. "Person and Ethics in Thomas Aquinas." *Acta Philosophica* 4 (1995): 51-71.

———. "Thomas Aquinas on Will as Rational Appetite." *Journal of the History of Philosophy* (1991): 559-84.

Gilbert, Paul. "L'articulation des transcendentaux selon Hans Urs von Balthasar." *Revue Thomiste* 86 (1986): 616-29.

Gilson, Étienne. *Being and Some Philosophers.* Toronto: Pontifical Institute of Medieval Studies, 1952.

———. *Elements of Christian Philosophy.* Garden City, NY: Doubleday, 1960.

———. "Notes pour l'histoire de la cause efficiente." *Archives d'histoire doctrinale et littéraire du Moyen Age* 29 (1962): 7-31.

———. *The Philosophy of St. Thomas Aquinas.* New York: Dorset Press, 1948.

———. *The Spirit of Medieval Philosophy.* New York: Charles Scribner's Sons, 1940.

———. *Unity of Philosophical Experience.* San Francisco: Ignatius Press, 1999.

Godzieba, Anthony. "Prolegomena to a Catholic Theology of God Between Heidegger and Postmodernity." *Heythrop Journal* 40 (1999): 319-39.

Goethe, Johann Wolfgang von. "On Interpreting Aristotle's *Poetics* (1827)." In *The Collected Works.* Volume 3: *Essays on Art and Literature.* Translated by Ellen and Ernest von Nardroff. Princeton: Princeton University Press, 1986.

Guagliardo, Vincent A. "Introduction" to Aquinas, *Commentary on the Book of Causes.* Washington, DC: Catholic University of America Press, 1996.

Guindon, André. "L'émerveillement: Étude du vocabulaire de l'admiratio chez Thomas d'Aquin." *Église et Théologie* 1 (1976): 61-97.

Hanby, Michael. *Augustine and Modernity.* London: Routledge, 2003.

———. "Creation without Creationism: Toward a Theological Critique of Darwinism." *Communio* (Winter 2003): 654-94.

Hart, David Bentley. *The Beauty of the Infinite: The Aesthetics of Christian Truth.* Grand Rapids: Eerdmans, 2003.

———. "The Offering of Names: Metaphysics, Nihilism, and Analogy." In *Reason and the Reasons of Faith,* edited by Paul Griffiths and Reinhard Hütter. New York: T. & T. Clark, 2005.

Hayens, André. "Le lien de la connaissance et du vouloir dans l'acte d'exister selon saint Thomas d'Aquin." *Doctor communis* 3 (1950): 54-72.

———. *L'Intentionnel selon saint Thomas.* Paris: Desclée de Brouwer, 1954.

Healy, Nicholas J. *The Eschatology of Hans Urs von Balthasar: Being as Communion.* Oxford: Oxford University Press, 2005.

Hegel, Georg Wilhelm Friedrich. *Early Theological Writings.* Chicago: University of Chicago Press, 1948.

———. *Gesammelte Werke.* Edited by the Rheinisch-Westfälische Akademie der Wissenschaften. Hamburg: Felix Meiner Verlag, 1968.

———. *Lectures on the Philosophy of Religion.* Volume 1: *Introduction and the Concept of Religion.* Edited by Peter Hodgson. Berkeley: University of California Press, 1984.

———. *The Phenomenology of Spirit.* Translated by A. V. Miller. Oxford: Oxford University Press, 1977.

———. *Philosopy of Mind.* Translated by A. V. Miller. Oxford: Clarendon, 1971.

———. *Science of Logic.* Translated by A. V. Miller. Atlantic Highlands, NJ: Humanities Press International, 1969.

Heidegger, Martin. *Basic Questions of Philosophy: Selected "Problems" of "Logic."* Trans-

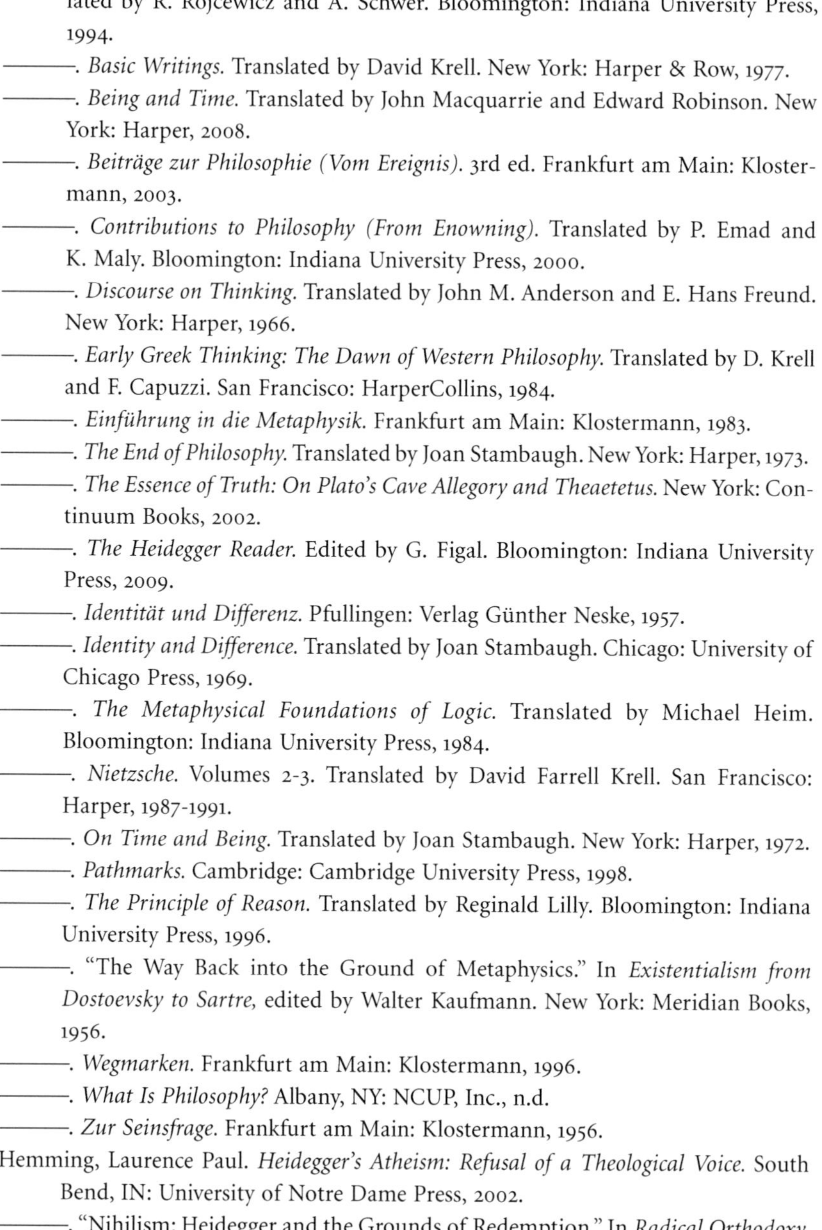

lated by R. Rojcewicz and A. Schwer. Bloomington: Indiana University Press, 1994.

———. *Basic Writings.* Translated by David Krell. New York: Harper & Row, 1977.

———. *Being and Time.* Translated by John Macquarrie and Edward Robinson. New York: Harper, 2008.

———. *Beiträge zur Philosophie (Vom Ereignis).* 3rd ed. Frankfurt am Main: Klostermann, 2003.

———. *Contributions to Philosophy (From Enowning).* Translated by P. Emad and K. Maly. Bloomington: Indiana University Press, 2000.

———. *Discourse on Thinking.* Translated by John M. Anderson and E. Hans Freund. New York: Harper, 1966.

———. *Early Greek Thinking: The Dawn of Western Philosophy.* Translated by D. Krell and F. Capuzzi. San Francisco: HarperCollins, 1984.

———. *Einführung in die Metaphysik.* Frankfurt am Main: Klostermann, 1983.

———. *The End of Philosophy.* Translated by Joan Stambaugh. New York: Harper, 1973.

———. *The Essence of Truth: On Plato's Cave Allegory and Theaetetus.* New York: Continuum Books, 2002.

———. *The Heidegger Reader.* Edited by G. Figal. Bloomington: Indiana University Press, 2009.

———. *Identität und Differenz.* Pfullingen: Verlag Günther Neske, 1957.

———. *Identity and Difference.* Translated by Joan Stambaugh. Chicago: University of Chicago Press, 1969.

———. *The Metaphysical Foundations of Logic.* Translated by Michael Heim. Bloomington: Indiana University Press, 1984.

———. *Nietzsche.* Volumes 2-3. Translated by David Farrell Krell. San Francisco: Harper, 1987-1991.

———. *On Time and Being.* Translated by Joan Stambaugh. New York: Harper, 1972.

———. *Pathmarks.* Cambridge: Cambridge University Press, 1998.

———. *The Principle of Reason.* Translated by Reginald Lilly. Bloomington: Indiana University Press, 1996.

———. "The Way Back into the Ground of Metaphysics." In *Existentialism from Dostoevsky to Sartre,* edited by Walter Kaufmann. New York: Meridian Books, 1956.

———. *Wegmarken.* Frankfurt am Main: Klostermann, 1996.

———. *What Is Philosophy?* Albany, NY: NCUP, Inc., n.d.

———. *Zur Seinsfrage.* Frankfurt am Main: Klostermann, 1956.

Hemming, Laurence Paul. *Heidegger's Atheism: Refusal of a Theological Voice.* South Bend, IN: University of Notre Dame Press, 2002.

———. "Nihilism: Heidegger and the Grounds of Redemption." In *Radical Orthodoxy.* New York: Routledge, 1999.

Hemming, Laurence Paul, ed., with Susan Frank Parsons. *Restoring Faith in Reason.* London: SCM Press, 2002.

Henrici, Peter. "La dramatique entre l'esthétique et la logique." In *Pour une philosophie chrétienne.* Namur, Belgium: Culture et Vérité, 1983.

Hittinger, F. Russell. "When It Is More Excellent to Love Than to Know: The Other Side of Thomistic 'Realism.'" *Proceedings of the American Catholic Philosophical Association* 57 (1983): 171-79.

Hölderlin, Friedrich. *Hyperion.* In *Sämtliche Werke und Briefe.* Volume 1. Darmstadt: Wissenschaftliche Buchgesellschaft, 1998.

Hooff, Anton E. van. "Facticité et argumentation: Réflexions sur la méthode en théologie fondamentale." *Recherches de science religieuse* 86, no. 4 (1998): 549-58.

Howland, Jacob. "Re-Reading Plato: The Problem of Platonic Chronology." *Phoenix* 45 (1991): 189-214.

Hughes, Kevin. "Remember Bonaventure? (Onto) Theology and Ecstasy." *Modern Theology* 19, no. 4 (2003): 529-45.

Hume, David. *An Enquiry Concerning Human Understanding.* 2nd ed. Indianapolis: Hackett, 1993.

Hütter, Reinhard. "The Directedness of Reasoning and the Metaphysics of Creation." In *Reason and the Reasons of Faith,* edited by Paul J. Griffiths and Reinhard Hütter. New York: T. & T. Clark, 2005.

Hütter, Reinhard, ed., with Paul J. Griffiths. *Reason and the Reasons of Faith.* New York: T. & T. Clark, 2005.

Ide, Pascal. *Être et mystère: La philosophie de Hans Urs von Balthasar.* Brussels: Culture et Vérité, 1995.

Ignatius of Loyola. *Spiritual Exercises.* Translated by George Ganss. Chicago: Loyola Press, 1992.

Jackson, Henry. "On Plato's *Republic* VI 509d sqq." *The Journal of Philology* 10 (1882): 132-50.

John Paul II. *Fides et ratio.*

Jonas, Hans. *The Phenomenon of Life: Toward a Philosophical Biology.* Evanston, IL: Northwestern University Press, 2001.

Jordan, Mark. "The Grammar of *Esse:* Re-reading Thomas on the Transcendentals." *The Thomist* 44 (1980): 1-26.

———. "The Transcendentality of Goodness and the Human Will." In *Being and Goodness: The Concept of the Good in Metaphysics and Philosophical Theology.* Ithaca, NY: Cornell University Press, 1991.

Kant, Immanuel. *Critique of Judgment.* Translated by Werner Pluhar. Indianapolis: Hackett, 1987.

———. *The Critique of Pure Reason.* Translated by Howard Caygill and Norman Kemp Smith. New York: Palgrave Macmillan, 2003.

———. *Prolegomena to Any Future Metaphysics.* Translated by Gary Hatfield. Cambridge: Cambridge University Press, 1997.

———. *Religion within the Limits of Reason Alone.* Translated by Theodore M. Greene and Hoyt H. Hudson. New York: Harper & Row, 1960.

Kierkegaard, Søren. "Of the Difference Between a Genius and an Apostle." In *The Present Age.* New York: Harper & Row, 1962.

Kovach, Francis. *Die Ästethik des Thomas von Aquin: Eine genetische und systematische Analyse.* Berlin: De Gruyter, 1961.

———. "The Transcendentality of Beauty in Thomas Aquinas." In *Miscellanea Mediaevalia.* Volume 2: *Die Metaphysik in Mittelalter,* edited by P. Wilpert. Berlin: De Gruyter, 1963.

Latourelle, R., and R. Fisichella, eds. *Dictionary of Fundamental Theology.* New York: Crossroad, 1994.

Lear, Jonathan. *Aristotle: The Desire to Understand.* Cambridge: Cambridge University Press, 1988.

Levering, Matthew. *Scripture and Metaphysics: Aquinas and the Renewal of Trinitarian Theology.* Oxford: Blackwell, 2004.

Levinas, Emmanuel. "Philosophy and the Idea of the Infinite." In *To the Other: An Introduction to the Philosophy of Emmanuel Levinas,* by Adriaan Peperzak. West LaFayette, IN: Purdue University Press, 1993.

———. *Totality and Infinity.* Translated by Alphonso Lingis. Pittsburgh: Duquesne University Press, 1969.

Lubac, Henri de. *The Discovery of God.* Grand Rapids: Eerdmans, 1996.

———. *The Mystery of the Supernatural.* New York: Crossroad, 1998.

MacIntyre, Alasdair. *God, Philosophy, Universities: A Selective History of the Catholic Philosophical Tradition.* Lanham, MD: Rowman & Littlefield, 2009.

Manent, Pierre. *The City of Man.* Translated by Marc A. LePain. Princeton: Princeton University Press, 1998.

———. *An Intellectual History of Liberalism.* Princeton: Princeton University Press, 1995.

Mansini, Guy. "Balthasar and the Theodramatic Enrichment of the Trinity." *The Thomist* 54 (2000): 499-519.

Marcel, Gabriel. "Author's Preface to the English Edition." In *Metaphysical Journal,* translated by Bernard Wall. Chicago: Regnery, 1952.

———. *Position et Approches du mystère ontologique.* Paris: Desclée de Brouwer, 1933.

Marion, Jean-Luc. *Being Given: Toward a Phenomenology of Givenness.* Translated by Jeffrey Kossky. Stanford, CA: Stanford University Press, 2002.

———. *God without Being.* Chicago: University of Chicago Press, 1991.

———. *The Idol and Distance: Five Studies.* Translated by Thomas Carlson. New York: Fordham University Press, 2001.

———. "The Impossible for Man — God." In *Transcendence and Beyond: A Postmodern Inquiry,* edited by John D. Caputo and Michael J. Scanlon. Bloomington: Indiana University Press, 2007.

———. *Reduction and Givenness: Investigations of Husserl, Heidegger, and Phenomenology.* Translated by Thomas A. Carlson. Evanston, IL: Northwestern University Press, 1998.

———. "Saint Thomas d'Aquin et l'onto-théo-logie." *Revue Thomiste* 1 (1995): 31-66.

———. *The Visible and the Revealed.* New York: Fordham University Press, 2008.

Maritain, Jacques. *Art et scholastique.* Paris: Librairie de l'Art Catholique, 1947.

———. *Preface to Metaphysics: Seven Lectures on Being.* New York: Sheed & Ward, 1939.

McAleer, Graham. *Ecstatic Morality and Sexual Politics: A Catholic and Nontotalitarian Theory of the Body.* New York: Fordham University Press, 2005.

McGinley, John. "The Doctrine of the Good in the *Philebus.*" *Apeiron* 11 (1977): 27-57.

McGrath, Sean. *The Early Heidegger and Medieval Philosophy: Phenomenology for the Godforsaken.* Washington, DC: Catholic University of America Press, 2006.

Metz, J.-B. *Christliche Anthropozentrik. Über die Denkform des Thomas von Aquin.* München: Kösel-Verlag, 1962.

Nicholas of Cusa. *On God as Not Other (De li non aliud).* Translated by Jasper Hopkins. Minneapolis: Arthur J. Banning Press, 1987.

Nietzsche, Friedrich. *Die fröhliche Wissenschaft.* Volume 3 of the *Kritische Studienausgabe,* edited by G. Colli and M. Montinari. Berlin: De Gruyter, 1988.

———. *The Gay Science.* Translated by W. Kaufmann. New York: Vintage Books, 1974.

———. *Nachlaß 1869-1874.* Volume 7 of the *Kritische Studienausgabe,* edited by Giorgio Colli and Mazzino Montinari. Berlin: De Gruyter, 1999.

———. *Twilight of the Idols.* In *The Portable Nietzsche.* Translated by Walter Kaufmann. New York: Penguin Books, 1976.

O'Collins, Gerald, S.J. *Retrieving Fundamental Theology: The Three Styles of Contemporary Theology.* New York: Paulist, 1993.

Oliver, Simon. *Philosophy, God and Motion.* London: Routledge, 2005.

Oster, Stefan. "Thinking Love at the Heart of Things: The Metaphysics of Being as Love in the Work of Ferdinand Ulrich." *Communio* 37 (Fall 2010): 660-700.

Peperzak, Adriaan. "Heidegger and Plato's Idea of the Good." In *Reading Heidegger,* edited by John Sallis. Bloomington: Indiana University Press, 1993.

———. *To the Other: An Introduction to the Philosophy of Emmanuel Levinas.* West Lafayette, IN: Purdue University Press, 1993.

Perl, Eric. "The Demiurge and the Forms: A Return to the Ancient Interpretation of Plato's *Timaeus.*" *Ancient Philosophy* 18 (1998): 81-92.

———. *Theophany: The Neoplatonic Philosophy of Dionysius the Areopagite.* Albany: State University of New York Press, 2007.

Pickstock, Catherine. *After Writing: On the Liturgical Consummation of Philosophy.* Oxford: Blackwell, 1998.

———. "The Soul in Plato." In *Explorations in Contemporary Continental Philosophy of Religion,* edited by D. Baker and P. Maxwell. New York: Radopi, 2003.

Pieper, Josef. *Faith — Hope — Love.* San Francisco: Ignatius Press, 1997.

———. *Leisure: The Basis of Culture.* South Bend, IN: St. Augustine's Press, 1998.

———. *The Platonic Myths.* South Bend, IN: St. Augustine's Press, 2011.

———. *Tradition: Concept and Claim.* Translated by E. Christian Kopf. South Bend, IN: St. Augustine's Press, 2010.

———. *Unaustrinkbares Licht.* München: Kösel-Verlag, 1963.

———. *Wahrheit der Dinge.* München: Kösel-Verlag, 1947.

Plato. *Complete Works.* Edited by John M. Cooper. Indianapolis: Hackett, 1997.

———. *Works in Twelve Volumes.* Loeb Classical Library. Cambridge, MA: Harvard University Press, 1914-1927.

Plotinus. *Enneads.* 7 volumes. Loeb Classical Library. Translated by A. H. Armstrong. Cambridge, MA: Harvard University Press, 1966-1988.

Polanyi, Michael. "Faith and Reason." *Journal of Religion* 41, no. 4 (1961): 237-47.

———. *Personal Knowledge: Towards a Post-Critical Philosophy.* Chicago: University of Chicago Press, 1962.

———. *The Tacit Dimension.* London: Routledge, 1966.

Pöltner, Günther. *Schönheit: Eine Untersuchung zum Ursprung des Denkens bei Thomas von Aquin.* Freiburg: Herder, 1978.

Przywara, Erich. *Analogia Entis. Metaphysik: Ur-Struktur und All-Rhythmus.* Einsiedeln: Johannes Verlag, 1962.

Richard of St. Victor. *On the Trinity (De Trinitate).* Translated by Ruben Angelici. Eugene, OR: Cascade Books, 2011.

Rojcewicz, Richard. *The Gods and Technology: A Reading of Heidegger.* Albany: State University of New York Press, 2006.

Rougement, Denis de. *L'Amour et l'Occident.* Paris: Librairie Plon, 1992.

Rousselot, Pierre. *The Eyes of Faith.* Translated by Joseph Donceel and Avery Dulles. New York: Fordham University Press, 1990.

———. *Intelligence: Sense of Being, Faculty of God.* Translated by Andrew Tallon. Milwaukee: Marquette University Press, 1999.

———. *The Problem of Love in the Middle Ages: A Historical Contribution.* Translated by Alan Vincelette. Milwaukee: Marquette University Press, 2001.

Rowland, Tracey. "Natural Law: From Neo-Thomism to Nuptial Mysticism." *Communio* 35 (Fall 2008): 374-96.

Rubenstein, Mary-Jane. *Strange Wonder: The Closure of Metaphysics and the Opening of Awe.* New York: Columbia University Press, 2008.

Sachs, Joe. *Aristotle's Physics: A Guided Study.* New Brunswick, NJ: Rutgers University Press, 1995.

Saint-Pierre, Mario. *Beauté, Bonté, Vérité chez Hans Urs von Balthasar.* Paris: Éditions du Cerf, 1998.

Sara, Juan. "Knowledge, the Transcendentals, and Community." *Communio* 28 (2001): 505-32.

Schenk, Richard. "Ist die Rede vom leidenden Gott theologisch zu vermeiden? Reflexion über den Streit von K. Rahner und H. U. von Balthasar." In *Der Leidende Gott: Eine philosophische und theologische Kritik,* edited by Peter Koslowski and Friedrich Hermanni. München: Wilhelm Fink Verlag, 2001.

Schiller, Friedrich. "Kallias or Concerning Beauty: Letters to Gottfried Körner." In *Clas-*

sic and Romantic German Aesthetics, edited by J. M. Bernstein. Cambridge: Cambridge University Press, 2003.

———. *Letters on the Aesthetic Education of Man.* Translated by Elizabeth Wilkinson and L. A. Willoughby. In *Essays,* edited by Walter Hinderer and Daniel Dahlstrom. New York: Continuum, 2001.

Schindler, David L. "The Given as Gift: Creation and Disciplinary Abstraction in Science." *Communio* 38 (Spring 2011): 52-102.

———. "God and the End of Intelligence: Knowledge as Relationship." *Communio* 26 (1999): 510-40.

———. "History, Objectivity, and Moral Conversion." *The Thomist* 37 (July 1973): 569-88.

Schindler, D. C. *Hans Urs von Balthasar and the Dramatic Structure of Truth: A Philosophical Investigation.* New York: Fordham University Press, 2004.

———. *Plato's Critique of Impure Reason.* Washington, DC: Catholic University of America Press, 2008.

———. "The Redemption of Eros: Philosophical Reflections on Benedict XVI's First Encyclical." *Communio* 33 (Fall 2008): 375-99.

———. "What's the Difference? On the Metaphysics of Participation in Plato, Plotinus, and Aquinas." *Nova et Vetera* 5, no. 3 (2007): 583-618.

Schmitz, Kenneth. "Enriching the Copula." *Review of Metaphysics* 27 (1974): 492-512.

———. *The Gift: Creation.* Milwaukee: Marquette University Press, 1982.

———. *The Texture of Being.* Washington, DC: Catholic University of America Press, 2007.

Schürmann, Reiner. *Heidegger on Being and Acting: From Principles to Anarchy.* Bloomington: Indiana University Press, 1987.

Sheehan, Thomas. "Geschichtlichkeit/Ereignis/Kehre." *Existentia* 11, nos. 3-4 (2001): 241-51.

Siewerth, Gustav. *Metaphysik der Kindheit.* Einsiedeln: Johannes Verlag, 1957.

Simmel, Georg. *Fragmente und Aufsätze.* München: Drei Masken, 1923.

Simonin, H.-D. "La notion d'intentio dans l'oeuvre de saint Thomas." *Revue des Sciences Philosophiques et Théologiques* 19 (1930): 445-63.

———. "La Primauté de l'Amour dans la Doctrine de saint Thomas d'Aquin." *La Vie spirituelle* 53 (1937): 129-43.

Smith, James K. A. *Introducing Radical Orthodoxy: Mapping a Post-secular Theology.* Grand Rapids: Baker Academic, 2004.

Sokolowski, Robert. *Introduction to Phenomenology.* Cambridge: Cambridge University Press, 2000.

Soskice, Janet Martin. "Naming God: A Study in Faith and Reason." In *Reason and the Reasons of Faith,* edited by Paul J. Griffiths and Reinhard Hütter. New York: T. & T. Clark, 2005.

Spaemann, Robert. "Der Irrtum des Traditionalisten: Zur Sozialogisierung der Gottesidee im 19. Jahrhundert." *Wort und Wahrheit* 8 (1953): 493-98.

———. *Die Frage Wozu?* München: Piper-Verlag, 1981.

———. "Wirklichkeit als Anthropomorphismus." In *Grundvollzüge der Person,* edited by H.-G. Nissing. München: Institut zur Förderung der Glaubenslehre, 2008.

Stambaugh, Joan. "Introduction" to *On Time and Being.* New York: Harper, 1972.

Strauss, Leo. *Natural Right and History.* Chicago: University of Chicago Press, 1965.

Tourpe, Emmanuel. "La logique de l'amour: Propos de quelques volumes récemment traduits de H. U. von Balthasar." *Revue Théologique de Louvain* 29 (1998): 202-28.

Ulrich, Ferdinand. *Gegenwart der Freiheit.* Einsiedeln: Johannes Verlag, 1974.

———. *Homo Abyssus: Das Wagnis der Seinsfrage.* 2nd ed. Freiburg: Johannes Verlag, 1998.

Vattimo, Gianni. *Nihilism and Emancipation: Ethics, Politics, and Law.* New York: Columbia University Press, 2004.

———. "Toward a Nonreligious Christianity." In *After the Death of God.* New York: Columbia University Press, 2007.

Veatch, Henry. *Two Logics: The Conflict Between Classical and Neo-Analytical Philosophy.* Evanston, IL: Northwestern University Press, 1969.

Vetö, Miklos. *La naissance de la volonté.* Paris: L'Harmattan, 2002.

Waddell, Michael. "Aquinas on the Light of Glory." *Tópicos: Rivista de Filosofia* 40 (2011): 105-32.

———. "Truth or Transcendentals: What *Was* St. Thomas's Intention at *De Veritate* 1.1?" *The Thomist* 67 (2003): 197-219.

Walker, Adrian. "Personal Simplicity and the *Communio Personarum:* A Creative Development of Thomas Aquinas's Doctrine of *Esse Commune.*" *Communio* 31 (Fall 2004): 457-79.

Weber, Max. *The Protestant Ethic and the Spirit of Capitalism.* New York: Charles Scribner's Sons, 1958.

Westphal, Merold. *Overcoming Ontotheology: Toward a Postmodern Christian Faith.* New York: Fordham University Press, 2001.

———. *Transcendence and Self-Transcendence: On God and the Soul.* Bloomington: Indiana University Press, 2004.

White, Thomas Joseph, O.P. *Wisdom in the Face of Modernity: A Study in Thomistic Natural Theology.* Ave Maria, FL: Sapientia Press, 2009.

Wilhelmsen, Frederick. *The Paradoxical Structure of Existence.* Irving, TX: University of Dallas Press, 1970.

Wilken, Robert Louis. *The Spirit of Early Christian Thought.* New Haven: Yale University Press, 2003.

Wippel, John. "Essence and Existence in Later Medieval Philosophy." In *Cambridge History of Medieval Philosophy.* Cambridge: Cambridge University Press, 1982.

Yates, Frances. *The Art of Memory.* Chicago: University of Chicago Press, 1966.

Index